**The
Crossword Completion
Dictionary**

R. J. Edwards

The
Crossword Completion
Dictionary

Stanley Paul
London Melbourne Sydney Auckland Johannesburg

Stanley Paul & Co. Ltd

An imprint of the Hutchinson Publishing Group

17–21 Conway Street, London W1P 6JD

Hutchinson Group (Australia) Pty Ltd
30–32 Cremorne Street, Richmond South, Victoria 3121
PO Box 151, Broadway, New South Wales 2007

Hutchinson Group (NZ) Ltd
32–34 View Road, PO Box 40–086, Glenfield, Auckland 10

Hutchinson Group (SA) (Pty) Ltd
PO Box 337, Bergvlei 2012, South Africa

First published 1983
© Rik Edwards 1983

Printed in Great Britain by The Anchor Press Ltd
and bound by Wm Brendon & Son Ltd,
both of Tiptree, Essex

British Library Cataloguing in Publication Data
Edwards, R. J.
    The crossword completion dictionary.
    1. Crossword puzzles – Glossaries, vocabularies, etc.
    I. Title
    793.73′2   GV1507.C7

ISBN 0 09 153350 3

How to use the dictionary

This book may appear unusual, but after a little practice it is very simple and quick to use.

Words are grouped according to length, and arranged in alphabetical order from the end of each word. So words ending in –AA are first, followed by –BA, –CA, –DA and so on, through to words ending in –Z.

Suppose you come across the clue, 'Frustrate Diana's show (10)' and you know from other solutions that the word has the letters ––––––––E–T. Simply look up words ending in 'T' in the ten-letter section. Now look through the eighth column for the letter 'E', and you will find 'DISCONCERT'.

Or suppose the clue reads, 'Drab Roast right out at sea (9)' with the letters –––––––A–D. Look up words ending in 'D' in the nine-letter section. Now look through the seventh letter column for the letter 'A', and you will find 'STARBOARD'.

To save space, most plurals and regular endings have been omitted. Thus when a nine-letter solution is obviously a plural, it must be sought under the eight-letter section. For example, 'Condemns organisations for writers (9)' with the letters –––––––CE–. The plural 'organisations' tells us that the solution is a plural. So look up words ending in –CE in the eight-letter section, and you will find 'sentence' – giving the solution 'SENTENCES'.

Similarly, when the solution is obviously a participle, remove the ending and look up only the basic word. For example, 'Slightly injured, so taken out of the race (9)' with the letters ––––T–H–D. The past form 'injured' tells us the solution ends in –ED. So look up words ending in 'H' in the seven-letter section, and look for words with 'T' in the fifth column. You will find 'scratch' – giving 'SCRATCHED'.

'Assembling for the colour ceremony (8)' with the letters –––OP–––. The present form 'assembling' tells us the solution ends in –ING. So look up words ending –OP in the five-letter section, where you will find 'troop' – giving 'TROOPING'.

By making adjustments in this way, you can significantly extend the scope of the dictionary. It will be an invaluable piece in the armoury of every crossword enthusiast.

--A	HOB	KED	NEE	LYE	ERG
	JOB	LED	PEE	PYE	BUG
BAA	KOB	PED	REE	RYE	DUG
OCA	LOB	RED	SEE	WYE	FUG
KEA	MOB	TED	TEE		HUG
LEA	NOB	WED	VEE		JUG
PEA	ROB	ZED	WEE	**--F**	LUG
SEA	SOB	AID	ZEE		MUG
TEA	YOB	BID	AGE	OAF	PUG
YEA	ORB	DID	CHE	KEF	RUG
AGA	BUB	FID	SHE	OFF	TUG
AHA	CUB	GID	THE	ELF	VUG
CHA	DUB	HID	DIE	OOF	
RIA	HUB	KID	FIE	ERF	
VIA	NUB	LID	GIE		**--H**
ALA	PUB	MID	HIE		
ANA	RUB	RID	LIE	**--G**	BAH
BOA	SUB	YID	PIE		FAH
GOA	TUB	ELD	TIE	BAG	HAH
KOA		OLD	VIE	DAG	LAH
MOA		AND	EKE	FAG	PAH
ZOA	**--C**	END	OKE	GAG	RAH
SPA		IND	ALE	HAG	YAH
BRA	LAC	BOD	ULE	JAG	OCH
ERA	MAC	COD	ANE	LAG	EDH
ETA	SAC	GOD	ONE	MAG	UGH
ITA	TAC	HOD	DOE	NAG	DOH
QUA	VAC	MOD	FOE	RAG	NOH
OVA	ABC	NOD	HOE	SAG	SOH
TWA	SEC	POD	JOE	TAG	ASH
	TEC	ROD	MOE	WAG	ETH
	HIC	SOD	ROE	BEG	
--B	SIC	TOD	TOE	KEG	
	TIC	YOD	VOE	LEG	**--I**
CAB	ROC	BUD	WOE	PEG	
DAB	SOC	CUD	APE	TEG	KAI
FAB	ARC	DUD	OPE	EGG	SAI
GAB	ORC	FUD	ARE	BIG	TAI
JAB		LUD	ERE	CIG	OBI
LAB		MUD	IRE	DIG	LEI
NAB	**--D**	PUD	ORE	FIG	CHI
TAB		SUD	URE	GIG	GHI
EBB	BAD		USE	JIG	PHI
DEB	CAD		ATE	LIG	SKI
NEB	DAD	**--E**	CUE	PIG	POI
WEB	FAD		DUE	RIG	SRI
BIB	GAD	HAE	GUE	TIG	PSI
DIB	HAD	NAE	HUE	WIG	TUI
FIB	LAD	TAE	RUE	BOG	TWI
GIB	MAD	WAE	SUE	COG	
JIB	PAD	ACE	AVE	DOG	
LIB	RAD	ICE	EVE	FOG	**--J**
NIB	SAD	IDE	AWE	HOG	
RIB	TAD	ODE	EWE	JOG	RAJ
SIB	WAD	BEE	OWE	LOG	TAJ
ALB	ADD	CEE	AXE	MOG	
BOB	ODD	DEE	AYE	NOG	
COB	BED	FEE	BYE	SOG	
FOB	FED	GEE	DYE	TOG	
GOB	GED	LEE	EYE	WOG	

--K	HEM	DIN	PRO	GUP	ASS
	REM	FIN	DUO	HUP	ESS
DAK	OHM	GIN	QUO	PUP	ITS
OAK	AIM	HIN	TWO	SUP	BUS
YAK	DIM	KIN	DZO	TUP	PUS
ELK	HIM	PIN		GYP	
ILK	MIM	SIN		HYP	
INK	NIM	TIN	--P		--T
BOK	RIM	WIN			
ARK	VIM	YIN	BAP	--R	BAT
ERK	ELM	ANN	CAP		CAT
IRK	POM	INN	DAP	BAR	EAT
ASK	ROM	CON	GAP	CAR	FAT
AUK	TOM	DON	HAP	EAR	GAT
YUK	ARM	EON	JAP	FAR	HAT
	ISM	ION	LAP	GAR	JAT
	BUM	NON	MAP	JAR	KAT
--L	CUM	PON	NAP	LAR	LAT
	GUM	SON	PAP	MAR	MAT
DAL	HUM	TON	RAP	OAR	OAT
GAL	LUM	WON	SAP	PAR	PAT
PAL	MUM	YON	TAP	TAR	RAT
SAL	RUM	URN	WAP	WAR	SAT
BEL	SUM	BUN	YAP	EER	TAT
EEL	TUM	DUN	ZAP	HER	VAT
GEL	VUM	FUN	HEP	OER	WAT
SEL	GYM	GUN	NEP	PER	ACT
ZEL		HUN	PEP	AIR	BET
AIL		NUN	REP	FIR	GET
MIL	--N	PUN	YEP	MIR	HET
NIL		RUN	DIP	SIR	JET
OIL	BAN	SUN	HIP	COR	LET
TIL	CAN	TUN	KIP	DOR	MET
ALL	DAN	AWN	LIP	FOR	NET
ELL	FAN	OWN	NIP	LOR	PET
ILL	GAN		PIP	MOR	RET
COL	HAN		RIP	NOR	SET
MOL	MAN	--O	SIP	TOR	VET
POL	PAN		TIP	ERR	WET
SOL	RAN	ADO	YIP	BUR	YET
VOL	SAN	LEO	ZIP	CUR	AFT
AWL	TAN	NEO	ALP	FUR	EFT
OWL	VAN	AGO	AMP	LUR	OFT
	WAN	EGO	IMP	OUR	AIT
	BEN	MHO	BOP	PUR	BIT
--M	DEN	OHO	COP		DIT
	EEN	RHO	DOP		FIT
BAM	FEN	THO	FOP	--S	HIT
CAM	GEN	WHO	HOP		KIT
DAM	HEN	ZHO	KOP	GAS	NIT
GAM	KEN	BOO	LOP	HAS	PIT
HAM	MEN	COO	MOP	RAS	SIT
JAM	PEN	GOO	OOP	VAS	TIT
LAM	SEN	HOO	POP	WAS	WIT
PAM	TEN	LOO	SOP	YES	ALT
RAM	WEN	MOO	TOP	BIS	ANT
SAM	YEN	TOO	WOP	HIS	COT
TAM	ZEN	WOO	ASP	LIS	DOT
YAM	AIN	ZOO	CUP	SIS	GOT
GEM	BIN	FRO	DUP	COS	HOT

3

---A		WOMB	GOAD	GILD	PARD
	PROA	DUMB	LOAD	MILD	SARD
ABBA	STOA	NUMB	ROAD	WILD	WARD
TUBA	PAPA	BLOB	TOAD	BOLD	YARD
PACA	PUPA	SLOB	WOAD	COLD	HERD
MICA	PARA	KNOB	BRAD	FOLD	BIRD
PICA	RARA	SNOB	TRAD	GOLD	GIRD
INCA	LIRA	BOOB	QUAD	HOLD	CORD
COCA	DORA	BARB	DYAD	SOLD	FORD
DADA	AURA	GARB	WADD	TOLD	LORD
EDDA	MESA	HERB	RUDD	WOLD	WORD
VEDA	VISA	KERB	ABED	BAND	CURD
SODA	ROSA	SERB	DEED	HAND	KURD
IDEA	URSA	VERB	FEED	LAND	SURD
RHEA	DATA	SORB	HEED	RAND	TURD
SHEA	RATA	CURB	MEED	SAND	FYRD
FLEA	TATA	DAUB	NEED	WAND	GAUD
PLEA	BETA	CHUB	REED	BEND	LAUD
ZOEA	SETA	CLUB	SEED	FEND	MAUD
AREA	VITA	FLUB	TEED	LEND	SCUD
UREA	IOTA	SLUB	WEED	MEND	FEUD
UVEA	ROTA	KNUB	AGED	PEND	THUD
ALFA	SKUA	SNUB	SHED	REND	LOUD
SOFA	JAVA	DRUB	DIED	SEND	SPUD
TUFA	KAVA	GRUB	LIED	TEND	CRUD
GAGA	LAVA	STUB	PIED	VEND	STUD
RAGA	DEVA		TIED	WEND	BAWD
SAGA	DIVA		BLED	ZEND	GAWD
VEGA	RIVA	---C	FLED	BIND	LEWD
TOGA	SIVA		SLED	FIND	DOWD
YOGA	VIVA	ALEC	COED	HIND	
HAHA	NOVA	SPEC	TOED	KIND	
EPHA	SOYA	LAIC	SPED	MIND	---E
ARIA		ODIC	BRED	RIND	
KAKA	---B	CHIC	USED	WIND	BLAE
EOKA		EPIC	HUED	BOND	BRAE
GALA	SCAB	SPIC	AWED	FOND	FRAE
VELA	BLAB	ERIC	OWED	POND	BABE
OLLA	SLAB	URIC	EYED	BUND	ABBE
COLA	DOAB	TALC	LAID	FUND	GIBE
KOLA	ARAB	ZINC	MAID	TYND	JIBE
HULA	CRAB	BLOC	PAID	FEOD	KIBE
LAMA	DRAB	DISC	RAID	SHOD	VIBE
MAMA	GRAB	FISC	SAID	CLOD	LOBE
BEMA	STAB		ACID	PLOD	ROBE
LIMA	SWAB	---D	CHID	SNOD	TOBE
ALMA	BEEB		SKID	FOOD	CUBE
EMMA	PLEB	SCAD	SLID	GOOD	JUBE
COMA	ABIB	BEAD	AMID	HOOD	RUBE
SOMA	GLIB	DEAD	VOID	MOOD	TUBE
PUMA	CRIB	HEAD	ARID	ROOD	GYBE
CYMA	DRIB	LEAD	GRID	WOOD	DACE
VENA	BULB	MEAD	QUID	PROD	FACE
MINA	IAMB	READ	AVID	TROD	LACE
ULNA	JAMB	EGAD	BALD	QUOD	MACE
ANNA	LAMB	CHAD	WALD	BARD	PACE
MONA	LIMB	SHAD	GELD	CARD	RACE
ETNA	BOMB	CLAD	HELD	HARD	TACE
TUNA	COMB	GLAD	VELD	LARD	BICE
WHOA	TOMB		WELD	NARD	DICE

LICE	MAGE	BILE	VANE	HYPE	ELSE
MICE	PAGE	FILE	WANE	TYPE	COSE
NICE	RAGE	MILE	ACNE	BARE	DOSE
PICE	SAGE	PILE	DENE	CARE	HOSE
RICE	WAGE	RILE	GENE	DARE	LOSE
VICE	EDGE	TILE	TENE	FARE	NOSE
ONCE	DOGE	VILE	BINE	HARE	POSE
VOCE	LOGE	WILE	DINE	MARE	ROSE
DUCE	URGE	BOLE	FINE	PARE	APSE
LUCE	HUGE	COLE	KINE	RARE	ARSE
PUCE	ACHE	DOLE	LINE	TARE	ERSE
BADE	BRIE	HOLE	MINE	WARE	FUSE
CADE	BAKE	JOLE	NINE	YARE	MUSE
FADE	CAKE	MOLE	PINE	ACRE	RUSE
GADE	FAKE	POLE	SINE	BERE	BATE
HADE	HAKE	ROLE	TINE	CERE	CATE
JADE	LAKE	SOLE	VINE	HERE	DATE
LADE	MAKE	VOLE	WINE	MERE	FATE
MADE	RAKE	ISLE	BONE	SERE	GATE
WADE	SAKE	MULE	CONE	WERE	HATE
CEDE	TAKE	PULE	DONE	OGRE	LATE
MEDE	WAKE	RULE	GONE	DIRE	MATE
BIDE	PEKE	TULE	HONE	FIRE	PATE
HIDE	BIKE	YULE	LONE	HIRE	RATE
RIDE	DIKE	AXLE	NONE	LIRE	SATE
SIDE	HIKE	CAME	PONE	MIRE	TATE
TIDE	KIKE	DAME	TONE	SIRE	FETE
VIDE	LIKE	FAME	ZONE	TIRE	METE
WIDE	MIKE	GAME	ERNE	WIRE	TETE
BODE	PIKE	HAME	DUNE	BORE	BITE
CODE	TIKE	LAME	JUNE	CORE	CITE
LODE	COKE	NAME	LUNE	FORE	KITE
MODE	JOKE	SAME	RUNE	GORE	LITE
NODE	POKE	TAME	TUNE	LORE	MITE
RODE	TOKE	ACME	DYNE	MORE	RITE
DUDE	YOKE	DEME	TYNE	PORE	SITE
NUDE	DUKE	DIME	OBOE	SORE	TITE
RUDE	JUKE	LIME	SHOE	TORE	VITE
OGEE	LUKE	MIME	ALOE	WORE	ANTE
GHEE	NUKE	RIME	FLOE	YORE	COTE
THEE	PUKE	TIME	SLOE	CURE	DOTE
AKEE	YUKE	COME	CAPE	LURE	HOTE
ALEE	DYKE	DOME	GAPE	PURE	LOTE
FLEE	TYKE	HOME	JAPE	SURE	MOTE
GLEE	BALE	NOME	NAPE	BYRE	NOTE
SMEE	DALE	ROME	RAPE	EYRE	ROTE
KNEE	GALE	SOME	TAPE	GYRE	TOTE
EPEE	HALE	TOME	PIPE	LYRE	VOTE
FREE	KALE	FUME	RIPE	PYRE	CUTE
TREE	MALE	CYME	WIPE	TYRE	JUTE
TWEE	PALE	ZYME	COPE	BASE	LUTE
CAFE	RALE	BANE	DOPE	CASE	MUTE
SAFE	SALE	CANE	HOPE	EASE	BYTE
FIFE	TALE	DANE	LOPE	RASE	AGUE
LIFE	VALE	FANE	MOPE	VASE	BLUE
RIFE	WALE	JANE	NOPE	BISE	CLUE
WIFE	ABLE	LANE	POPE	PISE	FLUE
ORFE	IDLE	MANE	ROPE	RISE	GLUE
CAGE	PELE	PANE	TOPE	VISE	SLUE
GAGE	OGLE	SANE	DUPE	WISE	MOUE

DUCK	HUNK	GOWK	CEIL	HULL	SEAM
FUCK	JUNK		TEIL	LULL	TEAM
LUCK	PUNK		VEIL	MULL	CHAM
MUCK	SUNK	---L	BOIL	NULL	SHAM
PUCK	AMOK		COIL	PULL	CLAM
RUCK	BOOK	BAAL	FOIL	GAOL	FLAM
SUCK	COOK	DEAL	MOIL	IDOL	SLAM
TUCK	GOOK	HEAL	ROIL	VIOL	IMAM
YUCK	HOOK	LEAL	SOIL	COOL	FOAM
KEEK	KOOK	MEAL	TOIL	DOOL	LOAM
LEEK	LOOK	PEAL	ARIL	FOOL	ROAM
MEEK	NOOK	REAL	EVIL	POOL	CRAM
PEEK	ROOK	SEAL	AXIL	TOOL	DRAM
REEK	SOOK	TEAL	BALL	WOOL	GRAM
SEEK	TOOK	VEAL	CALL	AWOL	PRAM
WEEK	BARK	WEAL	FALL	CARL	TRAM
TREK	CARK	ZEAL	GALL	EARL	SWAM
BALK	DARK	DHAL	HALL	FARL	EXAM
CALK	HARK	DIAL	MALL	JARL	DEEM
TALK	LARK	RIAL	PALL	MARL	SEEM
WALK	MARK	VIAL	TALL	GIRL	TEEM
WELK	NARK	ANAL	WALL	BURL	AHEM
YELK	PARK	COAL	BELL	CURL	THEM
BILK	SARK	FOAL	CELL	FURL	CLEM
MILK	WARK	GOAL	DELL	GURL	POEM
SILK	JERK	OPAL	FELL	HURL	ITEM
FOLK	MERK	ORAL	HELL	PURL	STEM
POLK	PERK	URAL	JELL	CAUL	MAIM
YOLK	BIRK	DUAL	PELL	GAUL	SHIM
BULK	DIRK	OVAL	SELL	HAUL	WHIM
HULK	KIRK	GYAL	TELL	MAUL	SKIM
SULK	MIRK	RYAL	WELL	PAUL	GLIM
BANK	CORK	GAEL	YELL	SAUL	PLIM
DANK	FORK	TAEL	BILL	WAUL	SLIM
FANK	PORK	FEEL	DILL	ELUL	BRIM
HANK	WORK	HEEL	FILL	FOUL	GRIM
LANK	YORK	KEEL	GILL	SOUL	PRIM
RANK	LURK	PEEL	HILL	BAWL	TRIM
SANK	MURK	REEL	KILL	PAWL	URIM
TANK	TURK	SEEL	MILL	YAWL	SWIM
YANK	BASK	TEEL	PILL	MEWL	BALM
FINK	CASK	NOEL	RILL	BOWL	CALM
GINK	MASK	DUEL	SILL	COWL	HALM
JINK	TASK	FUEL	TILL	DOWL	MALM
KINK	DESK	KOHL	VILL	FOWL	PALM
LINK	BISK	BUHL	WILL	HOWL	HELM
MINK	DISK	BAIL	BOLL	JOWL	FILM
PINK	FISK	DAIL	DOLL	YOWL	HOLM
RINK	RISK	FAIL	JOLL	IDYL	CULM
SINK	BOSK	HAIL	LOLL	AMYL	WHOM
TINK	BUSK	JAIL	MOLL		BOOM
WINK	DUSK	KAIL	NOLL		DOOM
CONK	HUSK	MAIL	POLL	---M	LOOM
HONK	MUSK	NAIL	ROLL		ROOM
MONK	RUSK	PAIL	TOLL	MAAM	ZOOM
ZONK	TUSK	RAIL	BULL	SCAM	FROM
BUNK	CAUK	SAIL	CULL	ADAM	PROM
DUNK	DAWK	TAIL	DULL	EDAM	ATOM
FUNK	GAWK	VAIL	FULL	BEAM	BARM
GUNK	HAWK	WAIL	GULL	REAM	FARM

8

HARM	KEEN	ICON	TOWN	TIRO	PALP
MARM	PEEN	AEON		EURO	HELP
WARM	SEEN	NEON		PYRO	KELP
BERM	TEEN	PEON	---O	PESO	YELP
DERM	WEEN	LION		ALSO	HOLP
GERM	THEN	ZION	AMBO	SOSO	GULP
HERM	WHEN	IKON	UMBO	NATO	PULP
PERM	LIEN	ANON	HOBO	VETO	CAMP
TERM	MIEN	BOON	BUBO	ALTO	DAMP
FIRM	GLEN	COON	PACO	INTO	GAMP
CORM	AMEN	GOON	TACO	ONTO	LAMP
FORM	OMEN	LOON	FICO	UNTO	RAMP
GORM	OPEN	MOON	COCO	LOTO	SAMP
NORM	BREN	NOON	LOCO	OTTO	TAMP
WORM	WREN	SOON	DADO	AUTO	VAMP
SCUM	STEN	TOON	REDO	VIVO	HEMP
CHUM	EVEN	ZOON	DIDO	KAYO	KEMP
ALUM	OVEN	UPON	LIDO	YOYO	GIMP
GLUM	OXEN	IRON	UNDO		LIMP
PLUM	SIGN	ETON	DODO		PIMP
SLUM	JOHN	EXON	TODO	---P	WIMP
ARUM	CAIN	BARN	JUDO		POMP
BRUM	FAIN	DARN	LUDO	HEAP	ROMP
DRUM	GAIN	EARN	OLEO	LEAP	YOMP
GRUM	LAIN	TARN	INFO	NEAP	BUMP
STUM	MAIN	WARN	DAGO	REAP	DUMP
OVUM	NAIN	YARN	SAGO	CHAP	HUMP
SWUM	PAIN	FERN	GOGO	CLAP	JUMP
AZYM	RAIN	HERN	LOGO	FLAP	LUMP
	VAIN	KERN	ERGO	SLAP	MUMP
	WAIN	TERN	ECHO	KNAP	PUMP
---N	ODIN	BORN	YOHO	SNAP	RUMP
	REIN	CORN	AGIO	SOAP	SUMP
SCAN	VEIN	HORN	OLIO	CRAP	CHOP
BEAN	AGIN	LORN	BRIO	TRAP	SHOP
DEAN	CHIN	MORN	TRIO	WRAP	WHOP
GEAN	SHIN	PORN	HALO	SWAP	CLOP
JEAN	THIN	SORN	KILO	DEEP	FLOP
LEAN	WHIN	TORN	SILO	JEEP	PLOP
MEAN	AKIN	WORN	POLO	KEEP	SLOP
SEAN	SKIN	BURN	SOLO	PEEP	KNOP
WEAN	COIN	OURN	DEMO	SEEP	COOP
YEAN	FOIN	TURN	MEMO	VEEP	HOOP
KHAN	JOIN	FAUN	HOMO	WEEP	LOOP
THAN	LOIN	SHUN	SUMO	PREP	POOP
CLAN	SPIN	NOUN	LENO	STEP	ROOP
ELAN	GRIN	SPUN	FINO	CHIP	CROP
FLAN	QUIN	STUN	KINO	SHIP	DROP
PLAN	RUIN	DAWN	LINO	WHIP	PROP
LOAN	TWIN	FAWN	WINO	SKIP	ATOP
MOAN	KILN	LAWN	MONO	BLIP	STOP
ROAN	DAMN	PAWN	JUNO	CLIP	SWOP
SPAN	LIMN	SAWN	SHOO	FLIP	LAPP
BRAN	HYMN	YAWN	EXPO	SLIP	REPP
CRAN	FINN	HEWN	FARO	SNIP	CARP
DUAN	GINN	SEWN	TARO	DRIP	HARP
YUAN	JINN	DOWN	HERO	GRIP	WARP
SWAN	LINN	GOWN	ZERO	TRIP	DORP
EDEN	SUNN	MOWN	AFRO	QUIP	BURP
BEEN	EBON	SOWN	THRO	CALP	GASP

HASP	BRER	FOES	PUSS	ABET	CELT
RASP	USER	AXES	RUSS	BEET	FELT
WASP	AVER	EYES	SUSS	FEET	KELT
LISP	EVER	OYES	OATS	MEET	MELT
WISP	OVER	BAGS	RATS	WHET	PELT
CUSP	EWER	DIGS	HOTS	DIET	TELT
COUP	DYER	DAIS	LOTS	POET	WELT
ROUP	OYER	IBIS	NUTS	FRET	GILT
SOUP	FAIR	EGIS	ZEUS	TRET	HILT
GAWP	HAIR	THIS	THUS	STET	JILT
	LAIR	IRIS	PLUS	DUET	KILT
	PAIR	KRIS	ANUS	SUET	LILT
---R	VAIR	ISIS	ONUS	DAFT	MILT
	HEIR	YWIS	URUS	HAFT	SILT
	WEIR	AXIS	NOUS	RAFT	TILT
SCAR	WHIR	HOLS	OPUS	WAFT	WILT
ADAR	AMIR	TEMS	YAWS	DEFT	BOLT
BEAR	EMIR	ALMS	MEWS	HEFT	COLT
DEAR	SMIR	ARMS	NEWS	LEFT	DOLT
FEAR	COIR	SANS	KEYS	REFT	HOLT
GEAR	STIR	GENS		WEFT	JOLT
HEAR	THOR	LENS		GIFT	VOLT
LEAR	BOOR	PONS	---T	LIFT	CULT
NEAR	DOOR	EPOS		RIFT	BANT
PEAR	MOOR	EROS	SCAT	SIFT	CANT
REAR	POOR	REPS	BEAT	LOFT	KANT
SEAR	PARR	ALPS	FEAT	SOFT	PANT
TEAR	HERR	MARS	GEAT	TOFT	RANT
WEAR	DORR	HERS	HEAT	TUFT	WANT
YEAR	BURR	OURS	MEAT	BAIT	BENT
AFAR	PURR	BASS	NEAT	GAIT	CENT
CHAR	GAUR	LASS	PEAT	WAIT	DENT
LIAR	BLUR	MASS	SEAT	OBIT	FENT
AJAR	SLUR	PASS	TEAT	ADIT	GENT
ALAR	SMUR	SASS	CHAT	EDIT	KENT
KNAR	DOUR	TASS	GHAT	CHIT	LENT
BOAR	FOUR	CESS	THAT	SHIT	PENT
HOAR	HOUR	JESS	WHAT	WHIT	RENT
ROAR	POUR	LESS	FIAT	SKIT	SENT
SOAR	SOUR	MESS	FLAT	FLIT	TENT
SPAR	TOUR	NESS	PLAT	SLIT	VENT
TSAR	YOUR	DISS	SLAT	EMIT	WENT
STAR	SPUR	HISS	GNAT	OMIT	AINT
CZAR		KISS	BOAT	SMIT	DINT
TZAR		MISS	COAT	KNIT	HINT
ICER	---S	PISS	GOAT	UNIT	LINT
BEER		SISS	MOAT	DOIT	MINT
DEER		BOSS	SPAT	SPIT	PINT
JEER	BIAS	DOSS	BRAT	BRIT	TINT
LEER	LIAS	FOSS	DRAT	FRIT	VINT
NEER	ALAS	HOSS	PRAT	GRIT	DONT
PEER	UPAS	JOSS	SWAT	WRIT	FONT
SEER	TWAS	LOSS	TWAT	QUIT	WONT
VEER	EYAS	MOSS	DEBT	SUIT	AUNT
BIER	DIBS	POSS	FACT	TWIT	BUNT
PIER	ODDS	TOSS	PACT	EXIT	CUNT
TIER	MODS	BUSS	TACT	HALT	HUNT
ONER	SUDS	CUSS	SECT	MALT	PUNT
BOER	IDES	FUSS	PICT	SALT	RUNT
DOER	LEES	MUSS	DUCT	BELT	SCOT
GOER	DOES				

10

SHOT	OAST	DOUT	PHEW	STYX	LAKY
RIOT	PAST	GOUT	SHEW		OAKY
BLOT	VAST	LOUT	THEW		INKY
CLOT	WAST	NOUT	WHEW	---Y	POKY
PLOT	BEST	POUT	VIEW		PALY
SLOT	GEST	ROUT	SKEW	DDAY	ABLY
KNOT	HEST	TOUT	BLEW	VDAY	IDLY
SNOT	JEST	NEWT	CLEW	OFAY	RELY
BOOT	LEST	NOWT	FLEW	CHAY	UGLY
COOT	NEST	NEXT	SLEW	SHAY	LILY
FOOT	PEST	TEXT	SMEW	OKAY	OILY
HOOT	REST		ANEW	CLAY	WILY
LOOT	TEST		ENEW	FLAY	ALLY
MOOT	VEST	---U	KNEW	PLAY	INLY
ROOT	WEST		SPEW	SLAY	ONLY
SOOT	ZEST	BEAU	BREW	BRAY	HOLY
TOOT	CIST	FRAU	CREW	DRAY	MOLY
SPOT	FIST	LUAU	DREW	FRAY	DULY
GROT	GIST	BABU	GREW	GRAY	JULY
TROT	HIST	ZEBU	STEW	PRAY	RULY
SWOT	LIST	URDU	SCOW	TRAY	GAMY
EYOT	MIST	LIEU	CHOW	XRAY	DEMY
RYOT	SIST	EMEU	DHOW	STAY	LIMY
RAPT	WIST	RAHU	SHOW	QUAY	RIMY
KEPT	COST	JEHU	ALOW	AWAY	ELMY
SEPT	DOST	JUJU	BLOW	SWAY	AMMY
WEPT	HOST	TOLU	FLOW	BABY	ARMY
RIPT	LOST	LULU	GLOW	GABY	FUMY
COPT	MOST	ZULU	SLOW	GOBY	MANY
CART	POST	MUMU	ENOW	TOBY	ZANY
DART	TOST	MENU	KNOW	ORBY	DENY
FART	ERST	NONU	SNOW	RUBY	MINY
HART	BUST	CHOU	BROW	LACY	PINY
KART	DUST	THOU	CROW	RACY	TINY
MART	FUST	OGPU	GROW	LADY	VINY
PART	GUST	ECRU	PROW	WADY	WINY
TART	JUST	PERU	TROW	EDDY	BONY
WART	LUST	GURU	STOW	TIDY	CONY
CERT	MUST	JESU	AVOW	BODY	PONY
PERT	OUST			TODY	PUNY
VERT	RUST	---V	---X	JUDY	AWNY
WERT	CYST			OBEY	AHOY
DIRT	XYST	SLAV	AJAX	THEY	CLOY
GIRT	MATT	CHIV	FLAX	WHEY	PLOY
BORT	TATT	SPIV	COAX	SLEY	TROY
FORT	WATT	DERV	HOAX	JOEY	BUOY
PORT	NETT		IBEX	GREY	PIPY
SORT	BITT		FLEX	PREY	COPY
TORT	MITT	---W	ILEX	QUEY	DOPY
WORT	BUTT		APEX	DEFY	ROPY
CURT	MUTT	CHAW	CALX	AFFY	ESPY
HURT	PUTT	SHAW	MANX	IFFY	ISPY
BAST	TAUT	THAW	JINX	CAGY	NARY
CAST	ABUT	CLAW	MINX	EDGY	OARY
EAST	SCUT	FLAW	LYNX	BOGY	VARY
FAST	SHUT	GNAW	FLUX	FOGY	WARY
GAST	GLUT	CRAW	CRUX	ORGY	ADRY
HAST	SLUT	DRAW	ONYX	ACHY	AERY
LAST	SMUT	CHEW	ORYX	ASHY	EERY
MAST	BOUT				

SAVED	YIELD	IZARD	PENCE	LYCEE	TINGE
WAVED	CHILD	SHERD	MINCE	MELEE	WINGE
JAWED	BUILD	LAIRD	SINCE	RAMEE	CONGE
UNWED	GUILD	WEIRD	WINCE	DONEE	LUNGE
TAXED	SCOLD	THIRD	BONCE	COOEE	ELOGE
VEXED	WORLD	ABORD	NONCE	TEPEE	BARGE
MIXED	COULD	CHORD	PONCE	TOPEE	LARGE
RAYED	MOULD	FIORD	DUNCE	RUPEE	MARGE
KEYED	WOULD	FJORD	OUNCE	SCREE	SARGE
SIZED	SHAND	SWORD	FARCE	AGREE	TARGE
PLAID	VIAND	GOURD	TERCE	SPREE	MERGE
BRAID	BLAND	FRAUD	SAUCE	PUREE	SERGE
TRAID	ELAND	ALOUD	EDUCE	FUSEE	VERGE
STAID	GLAND	CLOUD	DEUCE	ETWEE	DIRGE
RABID	BRAND	PROUD	TRUCE	PAYEE	FORGE
TABID	GRAND	CROWD	SHADE	FUZEE	GORGE
REBID	STAND	SLOYD	BLADE	CHAFE	PURGE
UNBID	FIEND		GLADE	GAFFE	SURGE
LUCID	PIEND		SLADE	KNIFE	GAUGE
UNDID	BLEND	----E	SPADE	ADAGE	GOUGE
BIFID	AMEND		GRADE	PLAGE	ROUGE
RIGID	EMEND	ALGAE	IRADE	IMAGE	CACHE
ALGID	SPEND	PUPAE	TRADE	OSAGE	NICHE
APHID	UPEND	SETAE	STADE	USAGE	RUCHE
UNKID	TREND	NOVAE	EVADE	STAGE	RAPHE
CALID	BYEND	GLEBE	GLEDE	BADGE	BATHE
VALID	TEIND	GREBE	PLEDE	CADGE	LATHE
GELID	BLIND	BRIBE	SUEDE	FADGE	RATHE
SOLID	GRIND	TRIBE	SWEDE	HEDGE	LETHE
TIMID	BLOND	ADOBE	ABIDE	KEDGE	LITHE
HUMID	FROND	NIOBE	CHIDE	LEDGE	TITHE
TUMID	MAUND	GLOBE	ELIDE	SEDGE	WITHE
SLOID	BOUND	PROBE	GLIDE	WEDGE	LYTHE
ZOOID	FOUND	UTUBE	SLIDE	KIDGE	SYTHE
AVOID	HOUND	MAYBE	AMIDE	MIDGE	BOGIE
OVOID	MOUND	PEACE	SNIDE	RIDGE	DOGIE
HYOID	POUND	GLACE	BRIDE	BODGE	BELIE
RAPID	ROUND	PLACE	GRIDE	DODGE	RAMIE
SAPID	SOUND	APACE	PRIDE	HODGE	GENIE
VAPID	WOUND	SPACE	ASIDE	LODGE	ERNIE
TEPID	UNGOD	BRACE	GUIDE	PODGE	AERIE
LIPID	EPHOD	GRACE	OXIDE	BUDGE	EERIE
CUPID	SYNOD	TRACE	LANDE	FUDGE	CURIE
ACRID	BLOOD	NIECE	RONDE	JUDGE	EYRIE
JERID	FLOOD	PIECE	ABODE	NUDGE	UNTIE
LURID	SNOOD	DEICE	CHODE	PUDGE	CUTIE
FETID	BROOD	SLICE	DIODE	LIEGE	MOVIE
PUTID	STOOD	AMICE	ANODE	SIEGE	BOWIE
FLUID	BIPOD	VOICE	EPODE	GREGE	ZOWIE
SQUID	SCROD	SPICE	SPODE	BEIGE	DIXIE
DRUID	BEARD	GRICE	ERODE	BILGE	PIXIE
PAVID	HEARD	PRICE	EXODE	BULGE	MOXIE
LIVID	YEARD	TRICE	HORDE	MANGE	SHAKE
VIVID	CHARD	JUICE	ELUDE	RANGE	FLAKE
SCALD	SHARD	TWICE	CRUDE	VENGE	SLAKE
HEALD	BOARD	DOLCE	PRUDE	BINGE	SNAKE
WEALD	HOARD	DANCE	ETUDE	HINGE	SPAKE
SKALD	GUARD	LANCE	EXUDE	MINGE	BRAKE
FIELD	AWARD	FENCE	ALBEE	SINGE	CRAKE
WIELD	SWARD	HENCE	EMCEE		DRAKE

STAKE	STILE	CTENE	TROPE	ENURE	VERSE
QUAKE	GUILE	SEINE	STOPE	INURE	CORSE
AWAKE	AXILE	CHINE	MYOPE	USURE	DORSE
WACKE	EXILE	RHINE	COUPE	AZURE	GORSE
ALIKE	ANKLE	SHINE	DRUPE	LIVRE	HORSE
SPIKE	INKLE	THINE	STUPE	ABASE	MORSE
TRIKE	BELLE	WHINE	SCARE	CEASE	NORSE
CHOKE	TULLE	CLINE	CHARE	LEASE	TORSE
BLOKE	DHOLE	OPINE	PHARE	MEASE	WORSE
SMOKE	THOLE	SPINE	SHARE	PEASE	BURSE
SPOKE	WHOLE	BRINE	BLARE	TEASE	CURSE
BROKE	PROLE	TRINE	CLARE	CHASE	NURSE
PROKE	STOLE	URINE	FLARE	PHASE	PURSE
WROKE	MAPLE	QUINE	GLARE	UKASE	BASSE
STOKE	AMPLE	OVINE	SNARE	BLASE	PASSE
EVOKE	APPLE	SWINE	SPARE	ERASE	TASSE
AWOKE	DUPLE	TWINE	STARE	PRASE	FESSE
BURKE	MERLE	BONNE	AWARE	OBESE	FOSSE
FLUKE	AISLE	TONNE	SWARE	GEESE	POSSE
SCALE	LISLE	SCONE	SABRE	NEESE	CAUSE
SHALE	TITLE	PHONE	FIBRE	THESE	PAUSE
WHALE	IXTLE	RHONE	OMBRE	RAISE	ABUSE
STALE	THULE	SHONE	NACRE	ANISE	SCUSE
DWALE	BOULE	ALONE	LUCRE	NOISE	REUSE
SWALE	JOULE	CLONE	SUCRE	POISE	AMUSE
CABLE	OVULE	NOONE	CADRE	TOISE	BOUSE
FABLE	DOWLE	CRONE	PADRE	ARISE	DOUSE
GABLE	CHYLE	DRONE	THERE	PRISE	HOUSE
SABLE	HOYLE	KRONE	WHERE	GUISE	LOUSE
TABLE	STYLE	PRONE	TWERE	FALSE	MOUSE
BIBLE	SHAME	TRONE	EAGRE	SALSE	ROUSE
AMBLE	BLAME	ATONE	OCHRE	BULSE	SOUSE
COBLE	FLAME	STONE	AFIRE	DULSE	TOUSE
NOBLE	FRAME	OZONE	SHIRE	PULSE	CRUSE
RUBLE	THEME	KERNE	MOIRE	TEMSE	DRUSE
MACLE	CREME	TERNE	SPIRE	MANSE	HAWSE
UNCLE	CHIME	BORNE	QUIRE	CENSE	TAWSE
SOCLE	CLIME	MESNE	SWIRE	DENSE	DOWSE
CYCLE	SLIME	PRUNE	GENRE	SENSE	TOWSE
LADLE	ANIME	PEKOE	SCORE	TENSE	ABATE
ADDLE	CRIME	CANOE	ADORE	RINSE	AGATE
SIDLE	GRIME	SCAPE	AFORE	CHOSE	SKATE
BODLE	PRIME	AGAPE	CHORE	THOSE	ALATE
YODLE	LUMME	CHAPE	SHORE	WHOSE	BLATE
ABELE	GNOME	SHAPE	WHORE	CLOSE	ELATE
ANELE	FORME	CRAPE	SNORE	BOOSE	PLATE
STELE	FLUME	DRAPE	SPORE	GOOSE	SLATE
RIFLE	GLUME	GRAPE	CRORE	LOOSE	AMATE
EAGLE	PLUME	TRAPE	FRORE	MOOSE	SPATE
ANGLE	SPUME	CLEPE	STORE	NOOSE	CRATE
INGLE	GRUME	CREPE	SWORE	AROSE	GRATE
BOGLE	CHYME	SNIPE	METRE	BROSE	IRATE
BUGLE	RHYME	GRIPE	PETRE	EROSE	ORATE
EDILE	THYME	TRIPE	LITRE	PROSE	PRATE
AGILE	AZYME	STIPE	MITRE	LAPSE	URATE
CHILE	THANE	SWIPE	NITRE	COPSE	STATE
WHILE	PLANE	SCOPE	TITRE	CARSE	OVATE
SMILE	INANE	ELOPE	ANTRE	PARSE	ARETE
ANILE	CRANE	SLOPE	OUTRE	HERSE	SHITE
SPILE	SCENE	GROPE	EMURE	TERSE	WHITE

NASAL	RAVEL	SPILL	VINYL	STORM	ASIAN
VASAL	BEVEL	BRILL	BERYL	CHASM	PEKAN
SISAL	LEVEL	DRILL	BUTYL	PLASM	UHLAN
FATAL	REVEL	FRILL		SPASM	SOLAN
NATAL	RIVEL	GRILL	----M	DEISM	DAMAN
OCTAL	HOVEL	KRILL		SEISM	ADMAN
FETAL	NOVEL	TRILL		APISM	HEMAN
METAL	JEWEL	STILL	MADAM	PRISM	LEMAN
PETAL	NEWEL	QUILL	UNDAM	ABYSM	UNMAN
VITAL	BOWEL	SWILL	ABEAM	IMAUM	NOMAN
DOTAL	DOWEL	TWILL	FLEAM	ALBUM	ROMAN
TOTAL	ROWEL	KNOLL	GLEAM	ODEUM	TOMAN
EQUAL	TOWEL	DROLL	BREAM	RHEUM	WOMAN
USUAL	VOWEL	TROLL	CREAM	ILEUM	HUMAN
NAVAL	PIXEL	ATOLL	DREAM	BEGUM	SLOAN
NIVAL	GAZEL	SCULL	STEAM	ALGUM	GROAN
RIVAL	HAZEL	SKULL	OGHAM	ODIUM	JAPAN
GAYAL	BEZEL	TRULL	ISLAM	ILIUM	SAPAN
LOYAL	OUZEL	IDYLL	SCRAM	OPIUM	KORAN
ROYAL	FLAIL	CIBOL	NIZAM	OAKUM	QORAN
BABEL	SNAIL	COBOL	MODEM	HOKUM	QURAN
LABEL	BRAIL	ALGOL	XYLEM	VELUM	NISAN
REBEL	FRAIL	ARGOL	PROEM	HILUM	SATAN
GIBEL	GRAIL	XYLOL	HAREM	LARUM	TITAN
LIBEL	TRAIL	SPOOL	TOTEM	SCRUM	WITAN
UMBEL	QUAIL	DROOL	CLAIM	SERUM	DIVAN
EXCEL	AVAIL	STOOL	BEDIM	FORUM	SIVAN
BEDEL	VIGIL	CAROL	HAKIM	JORUM	ELVAN
MODEL	ARGIL	ENROL	DENIM	STRUM	GOWAN
YODEL	TAMIL	EXTOL	MINIM	DATUM	ROWAN
WHEEL	SPOIL	PEARL	ASWIM	NOTUM	ARYAN
KNEEL	BROIL	GNARL	MAXIM	SHAWM	LADEN
SPEEL	PUPIL	KNARL	REALM		WIDEN
CREEL	PERIL	SNARL	SHALM		OLDEN
STEEL	ZORIL	WHIRL	PSALM	----N	SHEEN
ANGEL	APRIL	SWIRL	QUALM		GREEN
SPIEL	BASIL	TWIRL	WHELM	URBAN	PREEN
ARIEL	FUSIL	CEORL	HAULM	CUBAN	QUEEN
ORIEL	UNTIL	WHORL	SODOM	PECAN	TWEEN
YOKEL	CAVIL	CHURL	IDIOM	OSCAN	ASHEN
CAMEL	DEVIL	KNURL	AXIOM	REDAN	ALIEN
PANEL	CIVIL	MIAUL	VENOM	SEDAN	BAKEN
LAPEL	ANVIL	PICUL	BLOOM	SUDAN	OAKEN
REPEL	SCALL	WOFUL	GLOOM	PAEAN	TAKEN
IMPEL	BEALL	AWFUL	BROOM	OCEAN	WAKEN
CUPEL	SHALL	MOGUL	GROOM	SKEAN	LIKEN
EXPEL	SMALL	ANNUL	CAROM	CLEAN	SOKEN
MOREL	STALL	GHOUL	BESOM	GLEAN	TOKEN
SOREL	SHELL	SHAWL	BOSOM	SPEAN	YAMEN
EASEL	SMELL	SPAWL	BUXOM	QUEAN	SEMEN
EISEL	KNELL	BRAWL	REARM	PAGAN	ELMEN
OUSEL	SNELL	CRAWL	CHARM	BEGAN	WOMEN
RATEL	SPELL	DRAWL	ALARM	VEGAN	LUMEN
BETEL	QUELL	TRAWL	SMARM	LIGAN	RUMEN
HOTEL	DWELL	SCOWL	ENARM	WIGAN	HYMEN
MOTEL	SWELL	THOWL	UNARM	LOGAN	LINEN
CRUEL	CHILL	GROWL	SWARM	ORGAN	RIPEN
GRUEL	SHILL	PROWL	THERM	CHIAN	ASPEN
GAVEL	THILL	SIBYL	SPERM	APIAN	OATEN
NAVEL	SKILL	ETHYL	CHIRM	ARIAN	PATEN

CLASP	OTTAR	EGGER	GONER	PAVER	KAFIR
GRASP	SOWAR	NIGER	LONER	RAVER	FAKIR
CRISP	BOYAR	TIGER	TUNER	SAVER	CHOIR
SCAUP	IYYAR	ALGER	AWNER	WAVER	TAPIR
TIEUP	BAZAR	ANGER	OWNER	FEVER	ASTIR
ALLUP	LAZAR	ROGER	SHOER	LEVER	LABOR
PINUP	SIZAR	URGER	WOOER	NEVER	TABOR
TONUP	CABER	AUGER	CAPER	SEVER	ARBOR
SUNUP	SABER	USHER	GAPER	DIVER	DECOR
CROUP	FIBER	ETHER	PAPER	FIVER	NIDOR
GROUP	GIBER	OTHER	RAPER	GIVER	TUDOR
STOUP	LIBER	SKIER	TAPER	HIVER	RIGOR
TWOUP	AMBER	FLIER	LEPER	LIVER	VIGOR
TIPUP	EMBER	PLIER	PIPER	RIVER	ABHOR
SIRUP	UMBER	BRIER	VIPER	VIVER	ICHOR
SYRUP	SOBER	CRIER	WIPER	COVER	EPHOR
GETUP	TUBER	DRIER	ROPER	HOVER	PRIOR
LETUP	FACER	PRIER	TOPER	LOVER	MAJOR
SETUP	MACER	TRIER	UPPER	MOVER	COLOR
FITUP	PACER	OSIER	DUPER	ROVER	ARMOR
PUTUP	RACER	BAKER	SUPER	SAWER	HUMOR
MIXUP	DICER	FAKER	PARER	TAWER	TUMOR
POLYP	ULCER	LAKER	AIRER	HEWER	MANOR
	ONCER	MAKER	HIRER	SEWER	SENOR
	WADER	RAKER	WIRER	BOWER	TENOR
----R	ADDER	SAKER	BORER	COWER	MINOR
	UDDER	TAKER	PORER	DOWER	DONOR
DEBAR	AIDER	WAKER	CURER	LOWER	HONOR
UNBAR	CIDER	HIKER	LASER	MOWER	FLOOR
LOBAR	EIDER	LIKER	MASER	POWER	SPOOR
VICAR	RIDER	PIKER	MISER	ROWER	SAPOR
OSCAR	SIDER	ANKER	RISER	SOWER	VAPOR
RADAR	ALDER	JOKER	LOSER	TOWER	SOPOR
CEDAR	ELDER	POKER	POSER	TAXER	ERROR
SHEAR	UNDER	ASKER	MUSER	VEXER	FUROR
BLEAR	ORDER	ESKER	CATER	FIXER	JUROR
CLEAR	CYDER	BALER	DATER	MIXER	VISOR
SMEAR	CHEER	IDLER	HATER	SIXER	ACTOR
ANEAR	SHEER	OGLER	LATER	BOXER	FETOR
SPEAR	FLEER	FILER	MATER	LAYER	MOTOR
DREAR	AMEER	MILER	PATER	PAYER	ROTOR
SWEAR	EMEER	OILER	RATER	SAYER	TUTOR
CIGAR	SNEER	TILER	TATER	FLYER	FLUOR
SUGAR	FREER	SOLER	WATER	PLYER	FAVOR
BRIAR	STEER	RULER	DETER	FOYER	SAVOR
FRIAR	QUEER	NAMER	METER	DRYER	MAYOR
MALAR	WAFER	TAMER	PETER	FRYER	RAZOR
VELAR	DEFER	KHMER	AFTER	PRYER	VIZOR
HILAR	REFER	TIMER	BITER	TRYER	CHARR
MOLAR	OFFER	COMER	LITER	BUYER	GNARR
POLAR	FIFER	HOMER	ALTER	GAZER	STARR
SOLAR	LIFER	VOMER	ENTER	MAZER	WHIRR
VOLAR	INFER	ORMER	INTER	SIZER	SMIRR
ULNAR	GOFER	DINER	DOTER	DOZER	SCAUR
SONAR	EAGER	FINER	VOTER	CHAIR	OCCUR
LUNAR	JAGER	LINER	ASTER	FLAIR	RECUR
TATAR	LAGER	MINER	OTTER	GLAIR	INCUR
SITAR	WAGER	VINER	UTTER	STAIR	AUGUR
ALTAR	YAGER	INNER	OUTER	NADIR	MOHUR
ATTAR	LEGER	BONER	LAVER	THEIR	DEMUR

20

KNELT	SHUNT	APART	EXIST	BAYOU	UNSEX
SPELT	BLUNT	SPART	CANST	COYPU	LATEX
DWELT	COUNT	START	GHOST	UHURU	RADIX
SPILT	FOUNT	QUART	BOOST	BUSSU	AFFIX
ATILT	MOUNT	SWART	ROOST	BANTU	INFIX
STILT	BRUNT	CHERT	FROST	VERTU	UNFIX
BUILT	GRUNT	ALERT	YTOST	VIRTU	SALIX
GUILT	STUNT	INERT	VERST		HELIX
QUILT	JABOT	APERT	FIRST		ADMIX
UBOLT	SABOT	AVERT	WORST	----W	VARIX
SMOLT	ABBOT	OVERT	BURST		BRONX
FAULT	ROBOT	EXERT	CURST	MACAW	PHLOX
GAULT	ASCOT	SHIRT	DURST	PSHAW	XEROX
VAULT	ESCOT	SKIRT	HURST	PILAW	BEAUX
ADULT	FAGOT	FLIRT	ADUST	INLAW	SIOUX
MOULT	BEGOT	SPIRT	JOUST	UNLAW	CALYX
POULT	BIGOT	QUIRT	ROUST	BYLAW	
EXULT	GIGOT	ABORT	CRUST	PAPAW	
SCANT	JIGOT	SHORT	FRUST	STRAW	----Y
LEANT	INGOT	WHORT	TRUST	SQUAW	
MEANT	ARGOT	AMORT	TRYST	BEDEW	EMBAY
CHANT	ERGOT	SNORT	SCATT	ASKEW	DECAY
SHANT	IDIOT	APORT	BEAUT	UNMEW	TODAY
GIANT	HELOT	SPORT	GHAUT	RENEW	TOKAY
RIANT	PILOT	BLURT	KRAUT	SINEW	MALAY
PLANT	ALLOT	COURT	DEBUT	SCREW	BELAY
SLANT	SCOOT	SPURT	REBUT	SHREW	DELAY
GRANT	AFOOT	BEAST	UNCUT	STREW	RELAY
QUANT	SHOOT	FEAST	GAMUT	UNSEW	ALLAY
SCENT	SNOOT	LEAST	DONUT	NAVEW	INLAY
AGENT	CAPOT	REAST	ABOUT	MIAOW	SPLAY
AMENT	DEPOT	YEAST	SCOUT	ELBOW	UPLAY
ANENT	REPOT	GHAST	SHOUT	EMBOW	REPAY
SPENT	IMPOT	BLAST	CLOUT	OXBOW	UNPAY
BRENT	TAROT	BOAST	FLOUT	WIDOW	FORAY
YRENT	BESOT	COAST	KNOUT	ENDOW	MORAY
EVENT	ASSOT	HOAST	SNOUT	NOHOW	SPRAY
FAINT	DIVOT	ROAST	SPOUT	BELOW	ARRAY
PAINT	PIVOT	TOAST	CROUT	AGLOW	STRAY
SAINT	ADAPT	AVAST	GROUT	ALLOW	UNSAY
TAINT	LEAPT	DREST	TROUT	SCROW	ASSAY
FEINT	INAPT	PREST	STOUT	THROW	ESSAY
SKINT	UNAPT	WREST	CAPUT	ARROW	ALWAY
FLINT	WRAPT	GUEST	INPUT	STROW	NOWAY
GLINT	ADEPT	QUEST	STRUT		BYWAY
JOINT	SLEPT	ANGST	TWIXT		ARABY
POINT	INEPT	WAIST		----X	CABBY
PRINT	CREPT	ODIST			GABBY
STINT	SWEPT	DEIST	----U	ADDAX	TABBY
QUINT	KEMPT	HEIST		RELAX	DEBBY
SUINT	TEMPT	WHIST	PILAU	BORAX	WEBBY
FRONT	ADOPT	FOIST	NOYAU	HYRAX	BOBBY
BURNT	COOPT	HOIST	NANDU	UNTAX	HOBBY
TISNT	ERUPT	JOIST	HINDU	INDEX	LOBBY
DAUNT	EGYPT	MOIST	PERDU	CODEX	NOBBY
GAUNT	CRYPT	ROIST	ADIEU	TELEX	CUBBY
HAUNT	SCART	GRIST	SNAFU	SILEX	HUBBY
JAUNT	HEART	TRIST	FICHU	ANNEX	TUBBY
TAUNT	CHART	WRIST	SAJOU	CAREX	GLEBY
VAUNT	SMART	TWIST	BIJOU	MUREX	RUGBY

BOOBY	CURDY	PEGGY	HANKY	DILLY	STIMY
LOOBY	GURDY	PIGGY	LANKY	FILLY	BALMY
DERBY	HURDY	BOGGY	DINKY	HILLY	PALMY
HERBY	GAUDY	DOGGY	KINKY	SILLY	FILMY
BUSBY	STUDY	FOGGY	PINKY	WILLY	GAMMY
DAUBY	BAWDY	MOGGY	ZINKY	COLLY	JAMMY
LAYBY	DOWDY	SOGGY	HONKY	DOLLY	LAMMY
BACCY	HOWDY	BUGGY	WONKY	FOLLY	MAMMY
SPICY	ROWDY	MUGGY	FUNKY	GOLLY	SAMMY
JUICY	ABBEY	BULGY	HUNKY	HOLLY	TAMMY
FANCY	LACEY	MANGY	CHOKY	JOLLY	GEMMY
NANCY	DICEY	RANGY	SMOKY	LOLLY	JEMMY
ZINCY	CAGEY	DINGY	HOOKY	POLLY	JIMMY
FARCY	BOGEY	MINGY	KOOKY	BULLY	POMMY
MERCY	FOGEY	ELOGY	NOOKY	CULLY	TOMMY
SAUCY	ALLEY	PORGY	ROOKY	DULLY	DUMMY
BEADY	MULEY	SURGY	BARKY	FULLY	GUMMY
HEADY	LIMEY	TECHY	DARKY	GULLY	LUMMY
LEADY	PINEY	VICHY	NARKY	HULLY	MUMMY
READY	CONEY	ITCHY	PARKY	SULLY	RUMMY
SHADY	HONEY	DUCHY	SARKY	DIMLY	TUMMY
GLADY	MONEY	WASHY	JERKY	MANLY	ROOMY
TOADY	GOOEY	MESHY	PERKY	WANLY	BARMY
BADDY	JASEY	DISHY	MIRKY	COOLY	DORMY
CADDY	MOSEY	FISHY	CORKY	HAPLY	WORMY
DADDY	NOSEY	BUSHY	FORKY	REPLY	PLUMY
FADDY	MATEY	CUSHY	PORKY	AMPLY	SPUMY
PADDY	CUTEY	MUSHY	MURKY	IMPLY	THYMY
NEDDY	GLUEY	RUSHY	PESKY	APPLY	MEANY
TEDDY	COVEY	LATHY	RISKY	DUPLY	TEENY
BIDDY	SKYEY	PITHY	ENSKY	EARLY	RAINY
GIDDY	LEAFY	WITHY	BOSKY	BURLY	SHINY
NODDY	BEEFY	BOTHY	SHALY	CURLY	SPINY
SODDY	AREFY	MOTHY	NOBLY	HURLY	BRINY
TODDY	DAFFY	LEAKY	BADLY	SURLY	CANNY
BUDDY	TAFFY	PEAKY	MADLY	FATLY	FANNY
CUDDY	JIFFY	SHAKY	SADLY	FITLY	NANNY
DUDDY	TOFFY	FLAKY	ODDLY	HOTLY	FENNY
MUDDY	HUFFY	SNAKY	REDLY	APTLY	JENNY
RUDDY	PUFFY	BRAKY	GODLY	TRULY	PENNY
NEEDY	EDIFY	QUAKY	DAILY	RAWLY	FINNY
REEDY	DEIFY	TACKY	GAILY	NEWLY	HINNY
SEEDY	UNIFY	WACKY	HAILY	LOWLY	NINNY
WEEDY	COMFY	DICKY	SHILY	LAXLY	PINNY
BANDY	GOOFY	MICKY	SLILY	SHYLY	TINNY
CANDY	WOOFY	COCKY	DOILY	SLYLY	BONNY
DANDY	SURFY	POCKY	DRILY	COYLY	NONNY
HANDY	TURFY	ROCKY	DALLY	DRYLY	SONNY
RANDY	STAGY	DUCKY	PALLY	WRYLY	BUNNY
SANDY	LEDGY	LUCKY	RALLY	BEAMY	DUNNY
BENDY	SEDGY	MUCKY	SALLY	SEAMY	FUNNY
WINDY	RIDGY	YUCKY	TALLY	FLAMY	GUNNY
GOODY	DODGY	REEKY	WALLY	FOAMY	RUNNY
MOODY	PODGY	SPIKY	BELLY	LOAMY	SUNNY
WOODY	PUDGY	YUKKY	FELLY	ENEMY	TUNNY
HARDY	ELEGY	MILKY	JELLY	PIGMY	EBONY
LARDY	BAGGY	SILKY	NELLY	PYGMY	PEONY
PARDY	JAGGY	BULKY	TELLY	BLIMY	AGONY
TARDY	RAGGY	HULKY	WELLY	SLIMY	PHONY
WORDY	LEGGY	SULKY	BILLY	GRIMY	PIONY

ACETIC	BEADED	MASKED	GIFTED	TORPID
EMETIC	HEADED	HUSKED	TUFTED	HISPID
NOETIC	LEADED	TUSKED	GAITED	STUPID
POETIC	BLADED	SCALED	UNITED	HYBRID
CRITIC	LOADED	FABLED	BELTED	MADRID
CELTIC	WEDDED	KEELED	KILTED	FLORID
KELTIC	LIDDED	ANGLED	TENTED	HORRID
BIOTIC	CODDED	TAILED	WONTED	TORRID
EROTIC	PODDED	ANKLED	BOOTED	PUTRID
EXOTIC	REEDED	CELLED	FOOTED	LIQUID
MYOTIC	SEEDED	BILLED	ROOTED	GRAVID
AZOTIC	BANDED	MILLED	FORTED	FERVID
PEPTIC	HANDED	POLLED	MASTED	RIBALD
SEPTIC	LANDED	CURLED	VESTED	HERALD
COPTIC	MINDED	AISLED	LISTED	AFIELD
AORTIC	BONDED	MISLED	HATTED	SHIELD
MASTIC	HOODED	TITLED	MATTED	KOBOLD
GESTIC	WOODED	SOULED	NETTED	BIFOLD
FISTIC	CORDED	COWLED	PITTED	ENFOLD
FUSTIC	EXCEED	PALMED	WITTED	INFOLD
RUSTIC	INDEED	HELMED	LEAVED	UNFOLD
CYSTIC	SCREED	DOOMED	VALVED	BEHOLD
MYSTIC	JEREED	WORMED	GLOVED	UPHOLD
SLAVIC	LEAFED	PLUMED	NERVED	UNSOLD
PELVIC	HOOFED	OMENED	CURVED	UNTOLD
MANIOC	HAGGED	VEINED	CLAWED	SHOULD
	JAGGED	SPINED	THEWED	RIBAND
	RAGGED	DAMNED	OXEYED	UNHAND
-----D	LEGGED	FINNED	CRAZED	INLAND
	PEGGED	DARNED	INLAID	POLAND
BEHEAD	WIGGED	CORNED	REPAID	UPLAND
THREAD	DOGGED	HORNED	UNPAID	ISLAND
UNREAD	RUGGED	NEAPED	AFRAID	DEMAND
SPREAD	FANGED	UNIPED	UNSAID	REMAND
PLEIAD	RINGED	HUMPED	FORBID	REPAND
MYRIAD	WINGED	CAPPED	MORBID	EXPAND
BALLAD	LUNGED	HIPPED	TURBID	ERRAND
MAENAD	NICHED	LIPPED	OUTBID	STRAND
OGDOAD	ARCHED	WARPED	PLACID	UNBEND
UNLOAD	UNSHED	SCARED	RANCID	ASCEND
ABROAD	RUBIED	SEARED	VISCID	DEFEND
INROAD	BODIED	FLARED	CANDID	OFFEND
BYROAD	ALLIED	INBRED	SORDID	FAGEND
TETRAD	MONIED	SACRED	NEREID	LEGEND
HEPTAD	ESPIED	SPIRED	TRIFID	FRIEND
WEBBED	VARIED	FURRED	FRIGID	ONLEND
RIBBED	BURIED	HATRED	FULGID	DEPEND
BULBED	BEAKED	BIASED	TURGID	IMPEND
LIMBED	PEAKED	IRISED	ORCHID	APPEND
COMBED	SOAKED	LAPSED	EYELID	EXPEND
TANBED	NECKED	VERSED	PALLID	INTEND
BARBED	PICKED	CURSED	STOLID	ATTEND
AIRBED	WICKED	JESSED	CUBOID	EXTEND
HOTBED	COCKED	UNUSED	FUCOID	WAXEND
DAYBED	PINKED	ABATED	GADOID	UNBIND
VOICED	ZONKED	TEATED	XYLOID	UPBIND
PRICED	HOOKED	ELATED	GANOID	BEHIND
FENCED	MARKED	SLATED	CONOID	UNKIND
FORCED	CORKED	COATED	DEVOID	REMIND
DEUCED	FORKED	STATED	LIMPID	UNWIND

STOGIE	BABBLE	FUDDLE	DEBILE	PURPLE
PORGIE	DABBLE	HUDDLE	MOBILE	COUPLE
BOTHIE	GABBLE	MUDDLE	NUBILE	HASSLE
PINKIE	RABBLE	PUDDLE	FACILE	TUSSLE
HUNKIE	WABBLE	RUDDLE	DOCILE	TOUSLE
BOOKIE	PEBBLE	NEEDLE	AEDILE	SUBTLE
COOKIE	DIBBLE	BRIDLE	DEFILE	BEETLE
ROOKIE	KIBBLE	CANDLE	AWHILE	CANTLE
BAILIE	NIBBLE	DANDLE	SIMILE	MANTLE
GILLIE	COBBLE	HANDLE	SENILE	GENTLE
COLLIE	GOBBLE	KINDLE	VIRILE	PINTLE
COOLIE	HOBBLE	FONDLE	RESILE	KIRTLE
STYMIE	WOBBLE	BUNDLE	ENSILE	HURTLE
BEANIE	BUBBLE	BOODLE	FUSILE	TURTLE
WEENIE	RUBBLE	DOODLE	MOTILE	MYRTLE
MAGPIE	FEEBLE	NOODLE	FUTILE	CASTLE
KELPIE	TREBLE	POODLE	SUTILE	NESTLE
YOPPIE	EDIBLE	GIRDLE	REVILE	PESTLE
KEWPIE	FOIBLE	CURDLE	GRAKLE	JOSTLE
CORRIE	GAMBLE	HURDLE	CACKLE	BUSTLE
AUNTIE	RAMBLE	CAUDLE	HACKLE	HUSTLE
SORTIE	NIMBLE	DAWDLE	TACKLE	JUSTLE
PASTIE	WIMBLE	BAFFLE	HECKLE	RUSTLE
OUTVIE	FUMBLE	RAFFLE	FICKLE	BATTLE
REMAKE	HUMBLE	WAFFLE	MICKLE	CATTLE
UNMAKE	JUMBLE	MUFFLE	PICKLE	RATTLE
STRAKE	MUMBLE	RUFFLE	SICKLE	TATTLE
BETAKE	RUMBLE	TRIFLE	TICKLE	WATTLE
RETAKE	TUMBLE	STIFLE	COCKLE	FETTLE
INTAKE	GARBLE	PURFLE	BUCKLE	KETTLE
BELIKE	MARBLE	BEAGLE	HUCKLE	METTLE
UNLIKE	WARBLE	DAGGLE	SUCKLE	NETTLE
SHRIKE	BAUBLE	GAGGLE	RANKLE	SETTLE
STRIKE	DOUBLE	HAGGLE	TINKLE	LITTLE
STROKE	ROUBLE	WAGGLE	WINKLE	TITTLE
REVOKE	BAWBLE	GIGGLE	DARKLE	BOTTLE
INVOKE	ORACLE	HIGGLE	VIELLE	MOTTLE
UNYOKE	ICICLE	JIGGLE	FAILLE	POTTLE
REBUKE	CIRCLE	BOGGLE	GRILLE	CUTTLE
PERUKE	MASCLE	GOGGLE	CREOLE	GUTTLE
LOCALE	MUSCLE	JOGGLE	ORIOLE	EPAULE
REGALE	BEADLE	TOGGLE	CAJOLE	LOBULE
INHALE	CRADLE	GUGGLE	PAROLE	TUBULE
EXHALE	PADDLE	JUGGLE	STAPLE	MODULE
TAMALE	RADDLE	PAIGLE	TRIPLE	NODULE
FEMALE	SADDLE	BANGLE	SAMPLE	LIGULE
FINALE	WADDLE	DANGLE	TEMPLE	PILULE
EMPALE	HEDDLE	JANGLE	DIMPLE	ZONULE
IMPALE	MEDDLE	MANGLE	PIMPLE	LUNULE
MORALE	PEDDLE	TANGLE	SIMPLE	CUPULE
RESALE	REDDLE	DINGLE	WIMPLE	FERULE
POTALE	DIDDLE	JINGLE	RUMPLE	CURULE
LIABLE	FIDDLE	MINGLE	PEOPLE	COTYLE
VIABLE	MIDDLE	SINGLE	DAPPLE	DAZZLE
ENABLE	PIDDLE	TINGLE	NIPPLE	FIZZLE
UNABLE	RIDDLE	BUNGLE	RIPPLE	MIZZLE
ARABLE	CODDLE	JUNGLE	TIPPLE	SIZZLE
USABLE	NODDLE	GARGLE	HOPPLE	NOZZLE
STABLE	TODDLE	BURGLE	TOPPLE	GUZZLE
SUABLE	CUDDLE	GURGLE	SUPPLE	MUZZLE

NUZZLE	FERINE	SEVERE	DEBASE	CUISSE
PUZZLE	SHRINE	TUYERE	INCASE	TSETSE
BECAME	SASINE	CAFFRE	UNCASE	CLAUSE
MADAME	COSINE	ZAFFRE	PLEASE	ACCUSE
DEFAME	URSINE	MEAGRE	CREASE	INCUSE
ASHAME	EQUINE	MAIGRE	GREASE	EXCUSE
AFLAME	RAVINE	CHIGRE	PHRASE	REFUSE
RENAME	SAVINE	EMIGRE	CHEESE	EFFUSE
BYNAME	DIVINE	MAUGRE	CREESE	INFUSE
SESAME	ALVINE	EUCHRE	CHAISE	BEMUSE
RACEME	BOVINE	ADMIRE	BRAISE	CHOUSE
SCHEME	UNDONE	BEMIRE	FRAISE	BLOUSE
REGIME	BEGONE	VENIRE	PRAISE	SPOUSE
GRAMME	BYGONE	EMPIRE	INCISE	AROUSE
BECOME	DEPONE	UMPIRE	EXCISE	GROUSE
INCOME	THRONE	ASPIRE	VALISE	CERUSE
CHROME	TYRONE	EXPIRE	DEMISE	PERUSE
LEGUME	DITONE	DESIRE	CERISE	DISUSE
INHUME	INTONE	SATIRE	UPRISE	MISUSE
EXHUME	BOURNE	RETIRE	BRUISE	OBTUSE
RELUME	PUISNE	ENTIRE	CRUISE	RETUSE
ILLUME	LAGUNE	ATTIRE	PAVISE	BROWSE
VOLUME	TRIUNE	SQUIRE	ADVISE	DROWSE
RESUME	JEJUNE	ENCORE	DEVISE	DEBATE
ASSUME	IMMUNE	BEFORE	REVISE	REBATE
ENZYME	UNTUNE	ENGORE	UNWISE	LOBATE
URBANE	ATTUNE	ASHORE	NOWISE	JUBATE
ARCANE	GROYNE	GALORE	GRILSE	VACATE
BYLANE	CHIGOE	IGNORE	FLENSE	LOCATE
HUMANE	FELLOE	FURORE	JOCOSE	PEDATE
INSANE	DIPLOE	GOITRE	NODOSE	SEDATE
BUTANE	HOOPOE	CENTRE	RUGOSE	CREATE
NICENE	TIPTOE	DARTRE	OTIOSE	LEGATE
EOCENE	ESCAPE	BISTRE	FILOSE	DOGATE
ACHENE	SCRAPE	LUSTRE	HAMOSE	JUGATE
SERENE	RECIPE	SECURE	RAMOSE	RUGATE
THRENE	UNRIPE	ENDURE	OSMOSE	OPIATE
ESSENE	STRIPE	ORDURE	CYMOSE	PALATE
ADVENE	ASLOPE	FIGURE	VENOSE	OBLATE
RUBINE	EUROPE	LIGURE	CHOOSE	BELATE
ALDINE	METOPE	ABJURE	DEPOSE	DELATE
UNDINE	STEPPE	ADJURE	REPOSE	RELATE
IODINE	GRIPPE	INJURE	IMPOSE	DILATE
THEINE	THORPE	ALLURE	OPPOSE	HAMATE
DEFINE	TROUPE	COLURE	EXPOSE	INMATE
REFINE	POLYPE	DEMURE	VIROSE	LANATE
ENGINE	ECTYPE	IMMURE	MOROSE	SENATE
SALINE	CURARE	MANURE	GYROSE	AGNATE
FELINE	SQUARE	TENURE	SETOSE	BINATE
UPLINE	BEWARE	IMPURE	FAVOSE	INNATE
FAMINE	GUEBRE	RASURE	ELAPSE	DONATE
TAMINE	TIMBRE	ENSURE	CORPSE	ZONATE
ERMINE	SOMBRE	INSURE	HEARSE	ORNATE
CANINE	FIACRE	UNSURE	COARSE	LUNATE
RAPINE	ADHERE	ASSURE	HOARSE	KARATE
REPINE	INHERE	MATURE	SPARSE	AERATE
ALPINE	COHERE	NATURE	AVERSE	BERATE
LUPINE	SPHERE	FUTURE	BOURSE	CERATE
SUPINE	AMPERE	SUTURE	COURSE	PIRATE
MARINE	REVERE	LOUVRE	THYRSE	BORATE

CEREAL	NOUNAL	CUDGEL	AGNAIL	IREFUL
UNREAL	CARPAL	BUSHEL	ASSAIL	USEFUL
BOREAL	SACRAL	NICKEL	DETAIL	RUEFUL
UNSEAL	SPIRAL	SHEKEL	RETAIL	EYEFUL
SQUEAL	CHORAL	ENAMEL	ENTAIL	WILFUL
REVEAL	FLORAL	POMMEL	BEWAIL	ARMFUL
JINGAL	AMORAL	KUMMEL	PENCIL	MANFUL
FUNGAL	CORRAL	PUMMEL	UNVEIL	SINFUL
TERGAL	MITRAL	OXYMEL	FULFIL	CAPFUL
FRUGAL	ASTRAL	SPINEL	RECOIL	CUPFUL
NUCHAL	NEURAL	FENNEL	UNCOIL	EARFUL
LETHAL	PLURAL	KENNEL	UPCOIL	VATFUL
WITHAL	CRURAL	FUNNEL	ASSOIL	FITFUL
LABIAL	TARSAL	GUNNEL	FIBRIL	ARTFUL
TIBIAL	DORSAL	RUNNEL	TONSIL	LAWFUL
FACIAL	VASSAL	TUNNEL	DOSSIL	JOYFUL
RACIAL	MISSAL	LIONEL	FOSSIL	BEFOUL
UNCIAL	CAUSAL	DARNEL	DENTIL	CONSUL
SOCIAL	FOETAL	KERNEL	LENTIL	SCRAWL
RADIAL	HYETAL	CORNEL	PASTIL	SPRAWL
MEDIAL	CENTAL	CHAPEL	DISTIL	METHYL
BELIAL	DENTAL	COMPEL	PISTIL	DACTYL
FILIAL	MENTAL	PROPEL	INSTIL	
DENIAL	RENTAL	CARPEL	WEEVIL	
GENIAL	FONTAL	DISPEL	BRAZIL	-----M
MENIAL	AORTAL	GOSPEL	RECALL	
VENIAL	MORTAL	BARREL	BEFALL	SALAAM
FINIAL	PORTAL	SORREL	APPALL	BELDAM
ESPIAL	CURTAL	PETREL	THRALL	SCREAM
NARIAL	FESTAL	LAUREL	SQUALL	STREAM
AERIAL	VESTAL	TEASEL	INWALL	LINGAM
FERIAL	DISTAL	WEASEL	BEDELL	GRAHAM
SERIAL	COSTAL	DIESEL	BEFELL	DURHAM
ATRIAL	POSTAL	CHISEL	UNWELL	GOTHAM
BURIAL	BRUTAL	DAMSEL	REFILL	LOGJAM
MESIAL	UNGUAL	TINSEL	UPHILL	BEDLAM
JOVIAL	MANUAL	MORSEL	SHRILL	BALSAM
JACKAL	ANNUAL	TASSEL	THRILL	JETSAM
WADMAL	CASUAL	VESSEL	SQUILL	TAMTAM
HAEMAL	VISUAL	MUSSEL	SCROLL	BANTAM
HIEMAL	ACTUAL	HOUSEL	ENROLL	WIGWAM
ANIMAL	RITUAL	MANTEL	UNROLL	DIADEM
PRIMAL	MUTUAL	LINTEL	STROLL	TANDEM
MAMMAL	SEXUAL	CARTEL	GAMBOL	REDEEM
DERMAL	COEVAL	PASTEL	SYMBOL	BESEEM
FORMAL	LARVAL	HOSTEL	MONGOL	ESTEEM
NORMAL	SERVAL	CAUTEL	THYMOL	SACHEM
DISMAL	AVOWAL	SEQUEL	BEFOOL	ANTHEM
BRUMAL	BIAXAL	GRAVEL	KAGOOL	MAYHEM
REGNAL	ISRAEL	TRAVEL	SCHOOL	EMBLEM
SIGNAL	ISABEL	SNIVEL	JAROOL	MOSLEM
RHINAL	BARBEL	DRIVEL	PATROL	PHLOEM
SPINAL	CORBEL	SWIVEL	PETROL	SYSTEM
CRINAL	CANCEL	SHOVEL	PISTOL	PHLEGM
TRINAL	PARCEL	GROVEL	UNCURL	DRACHM
URINAL	TERCEL	CARVEL	UPCURL	MEGOHM
HYMNAL	RONDEL	MARVEL	UNFURL	RHYTHM
CARNAL	FARDEL	CREWEL	BULBUL	ELOHIM
VERNAL	SEAEEL	THOWEL	TUBFUL	MUSLIM
FAUNAL	DUFFEL	TROWEL	WOEFUL	PAYNIM

MEGRIM	OIDIUM	SAMIAN	DEADEN	CARMEN
ANTRIM	INDIUM	SIMIAN	LEADEN	GERMEN
PASSIM	PODIUM	BANIAN	MADDEN	ACUMEN
VICTIM	SODIUM	FENIAN	SADDEN	DEEPEN
EMBALM	KALIUM	IONIAN	REDDEN	HOLPEN
BECALM	OSMIUM	PARIAN	HIDDEN	DAMPEN
NAPALM	MINIUM	DORIAN	MIDDEN	HEMPEN
SITCOM	BARIUM	DURIAN	SODDEN	REOPEN
SELDOM	CERIUM	SYRIAN	SUDDEN	HAPPEN
RANDOM	CORIUM	TYRIAN	SWEDEN	BARREN
WISDOM	ATRIUM	TROJAN	MAIDEN	WARREN
FATHOM	BUNKUM	POLLAN	HOIDEN	BUNSEN
SLALOM	VELLUM	SEAMAN	MILDEN	CHOSEN
WHILOM	PHYLUM	CABMAN	GOLDEN	LOOSEN
ABLOOM	ASYLUM	MADMAN	GULDEN	WORSEN
SIMOOM	PLENUM	HODMAN	LINDEN	LESSEN
HANSOM	MAGNUM	FOEMAN	WOODEN	PLATEN
RANSOM	LIGNUM	BAGMAN	GARDEN	PECTEN
LISSOM	WAMPUM	RAGMAN	HARDEN	SOFTEN
DIATOM	ALARUM	CAIMAN	WARDEN	WHITEN
TOMTOM	LABRUM	DOLMAN	BURDEN	MOLTEN
FANTOM	SACRUM	PENMAN	HOYDEN	LENTEN
CUSTOM	QUORUM	TINMAN	BALEEN	MARTEN
BOTTOM	BAYRUM	YEOMAN	SPLEEN	FASTEN
DISARM	OMASUM	BARMAN	CAREEN	HASTEN
ASWARM	GYPSUM	CARMAN	SCREEN	LISTEN
AFFIRM	POSSUM	GERMAN	MOREEN	BATTEN
INFIRM	RECTUM	HERMAN	TUREEN	FATTEN
SQUIRM	DICTUM	MERMAN	UNSEEN	LATTEN
DEFORM	SEPTUM	AIRMAN	LATEEN	PATTEN
REFORM	SCUTUM	FIRMAN	SATEEN	RATTEN
BIFORM	SPUTUM	NORMAN	POTEEN	KITTEN
INFORM	ADYTUM	DESMAN	DEAFEN	MITTEN
ORGASM	VACUUM	BATMAN	TURFEN	GOTTEN
CUBISM	EPONYM	HITMAN	EXOGEN	ROTTEN
RACISM		PITMAN	OXYGEN	GLUTEN
SADISM		BOWMAN	LICHEN	HEAVEN
IODISM	-----N	CAYMAN	HYPHEN	LEAVEN
NUDISM		LAYMAN	LATHEN	CRAVEN
THEISM	TURBAN	TOYMAN	WEAKEN	ELEVEN
SCHISM	VULCAN	FINNAN	SHAKEN	UNEVEN
MONISM	CANCAN	BEMOAN	KRAKEN	DRIVEN
EGOISM	TINCAN	TRAPAN	AWAKEN	CLOVEN
CHRISM	TUSCAN	TREPAN	SICKEN	SLOVEN
PORISM	TOUCAN	SAMPAN	SILKEN	PROVEN
PURISM	LURDAN	TYMPAN	SUNKEN	FLAXEN
TRUISM	ANDEAN	TARPAN	SPOKEN	WEAZEN
CIVISM	AUGEAN	INSPAN	BROKEN	BRAZEN
SEXISM	DEMEAN	TEHRAN	DARKEN	FROZEN
CAECUM	SLOGAN	SOVRAN	HARKEN	MIZZEN
TALCUM	AFGHAN	PLATAN	FALLEN	MALIGN
VISCUM	ORPHAN	KAFTAN	POLLEN	BENIGN
LYCEUM	FABIAN	SULTAN	SULLEN	DESIGN
MUSEUM	MEDIAN	TARTAN	STOLEN	RESIGN
TARGUM	INDIAN	RATTAN	FLAMEN	ENSIGN
LABIUM	LYDIAN	BHUTAN	STAMEN	ASSIGN
ERBIUM	MAGIAN	SILVAN	FOEMEN	IMPUGN
RADIUM	DELIAN	SYLVAN	DOLMEN	OPPUGN
MEDIUM	EOLIAN	LIBYAN	CULMEN	EXPUGN
TEDIUM	JULIAN	BANYAN	YEOMEN	ORDAIN

ZINGER	BACKER	WHALER	WARMER	BUMPER
CONGER	LACKER	AMBLER	DORMER	JUMPER
MONGER	PACKER	FEELER	FORMER	LUMPER
HUNGER	RACKER	PEELER	RHYMER	MUMPER
MERGER	DECKER	RIFLER	OPENER	PUMPER
VERGER	PECKER	EGGLER	SIGNER	COOPER
FORGER	BICKER	ANGLER	GAINER	HOOPER
PURGER	DICKER	BUGLER	SEINER	PROPER
GAUGER	KICKER	JAILER	SHINER	DAPPER
LECHER	PICKER	NAILER	WHINER	LAPPER
ARCHER	WICKER	RAILER	COINER	RAPPER
ETCHER	COCKER	SAILER	JOINER	SAPPER
HIGHER	DOCKER	SMILER	RUINER	PEPPER
CIPHER	LOCKER	BOILER	LIMNER	DIPPER
GOPHER	MOCKER	TOILER	BANNER	KIPPER
CYPHER	ROCKER	CALLER	FANNER	NIPPER
DASHER	BUCKER	WALLER	LANNER	COPPER
LASHER	DUCKER	FELLER	MANNER	HOPPER
MASHER	PUCKER	SELLER	TANNER	LOPPER
RASHER	SUCKER	TELLER	PENNER	TOPPER
WASHER	TUCKER	FILLER	DINNER	SUPPER
FISHER	SEEKER	KILLER	FINNER	HARPER
WISHER	CALKER	MILLER	SINNER	WARPER
COSHER	TALKER	TILLER	TINNER	JASPER
GUSHER	WALKER	ROLLER	WINNER	RASPER
BATHER	MILKER	TOLLER	GUNNER	VESPER
FATHER	BANKER	CULLER	RUNNER	LISPER
GATHER	CANKER	FULLER	IRONER	PAUPER
LATHER	HANKER	GAOLER	KRONER	BEARER
RATHER	SINKER	CHOLER	STONER	HEARER
NETHER	TINKER	COOLER	DARNER	TEARER
TETHER	WINKER	CURLER	EARNER	WEARER
WETHER	CONKER	HURLER	GARNER	SHARER
CITHER	BUNKER	HITLER	WARNER	SNARER
DITHER	HUNKER	ANTLER	CORNER	ROARER
EITHER	JUNKER	OSTLER	HORNER	STARER
HITHER	CHOKER	BUTLER	BURNER	JEERER
TITHER	SMOKER	CUTLER	TURNER	SCORER
WITHER	COOKER	SUTLER	PRUNER	ADORER
ZITHER	HOOKER	HAULER	FAWNER	SNORER
ANTHER	LOOKER	BOWLER	PAWNER	STORER
BOTHER	BROKER	FOWLER	UNDOER	USURER
FOTHER	STOKER	HOWLER	LEAPER	TEASER
MOTHER	MARKER	SEAMER	REAPER	CHASER
POTHER	CORKER	ROAMER	SHAPER	ERASER
TOTHER	PORKER	FRAMER	DIAPER	KAISER
DEFIER	WORKER	SEEMER	DRAPER	RAISER
RELIER	LURKER	PRIMER	KEEPER	POISER
DENIER	MASKER	PALMER	PEEPER	GUISER
RAPIER	TASKER	GAMMER	WEEPER	CENSER
COPIER	RISKER	HAMMER	SNIPER	RINSER
VISIER	BUSKER	RAMMER	HELPER	CLOSER
HOSIER	TUSKER	DIMMER	CAMPER	PROSER
PITIER	CAUKER	SIMMER	DAMPER	WORSER
ENVIER	HAWKER	HUMMER	HAMPER	CURSER
VIZIER	SCALER	MUMMER	PAMPER	PURSER
BEAKER	DEALER	RUMMER	TAMPER	GASSER
SHAKER	HEALER	SUMMER	VAMPER	PASSER
SOAKER	SEALER	ROOMER	TEMPER	LESSER
QUAKER	THALER	FARMER	SIMPER	TOSSER

36

ZOUNDS	ORCHIS	MORASS	ODIOUS	MUSCAT
THEBES	CULLIS	STRASS	FAMOUS	KITCAT
FAECES	CAULIS	CAVASS	RAMOUS	DEFEAT
APICES	DERMIS	KAVASS	LIMOUS	ORGEAT
CALCES	TENNIS	ABBESS	TIMOUS	REPEAT
FASCES	ADONIS	ACCESS	HUMOUS	HEREAT
PISCES	PATOIS	RECESS	CYMOUS	THREAT
FAUCES	DEBRIS	EXCESS	VENOUS	RESEAT
SHADES	MAORIS	UNLESS	VINOUS	UNSEAT
HYADES	FERRIS	CARESS	SEROUS	CAVEAT
LACHES	MORRIS	EGRESS	POROUS	LOGGAT
RICHES	PHASIS	OGRESS	JOYOUS	NOUGAT
FISHES	CRASIS	STRESS	SCAPUS	TOPHAT
RUSHES	THESIS	DURESS	PALPUS	CUSHAT
RABIES	TMESIS	OBSESS	CAMPUS	LARIAT
LADIES	CRISIS	ASSESS	RUMPUS	FORMAT
ORGIES	GNOSIS	JEWESS	PAPPUS	AFLOAT
ALLIES	MYOSIS	GNEISS	CIPPUS	THROAT
SANIES	GRATIS	REMISS	CARPUS	CRAVAT
SERIES	IRITIS	KUMISS	CORPUS	TANVAT
MOVIES	OTITIS	EMBOSS	ACARUS	REDACT
UMBLES	MANTIS	ACROSS	UTERUS	IMPACT
THAMES	TRAVIS	GROATS	WALRUS	INTACT
KERMES	PELVIS	ASSETS	CHORUS	DEFECT
ECHOES	PARVIS	LIGHTS	CYPRUS	AFFECT
HEROES	PRAXIS	TIGHTS	CIRRUS	EFFECT
TRAPES	YOICKS	EREBUS	CITRUS	INFECT
STAPES	STOCKS	IAMBUS	TAURUS	ABJECT
STIPES	BREEKS	NIMBUS	RHESUS	OBJECT
SWIPES	THANKS	ABACUS	CENSUS	DEJECT
HERPES	BRANKS	SULCUS	TARSUS	REJECT
AZORES	VITALS	CROCUS	VERSUS	INJECT
SEVRES	SOWANS	CIRCUS	MISSUS	SELECT
THESES	ATHENS	DISCUS	BYSSUS	ASPECT
CRISES	SOWENS	CUSCUS	MEATUS	EXPECT
IRISES	BRAINS	CAUCUS	HIATUS	DIRECT
LENSES	BATHOS	EXODUS	STATUS	ARRECT
MENSES	PATHOS	ADIEUS	CACTUS	RESECT
WHITES	CURIOS	PILEUS	FOETUS	BISECT
GENTES	COSMOS	SOLEUS	CULTUS	INSECT
BOOTES	KOSMOS	CEREUS	CESTUS	DETECT
CERTES	LLANOS	FUNGUS	CISTUS	ADDICT
CORTES	TRIPOS	TYPHUS	XYSTUS	INDICT
LEAVES	PHAROS	RADIUS	NAEVUS	RELICT
LOAVES	CANTOS	REGIUS	PLEXUS	DEPICT
GRAVES	CENTOS	GENIUS	ALWAYS	STRICT
STAVES	CUSTOS	SIRIUS	NOWAYS	DECOCT
KNIVES	BRAVOS	OBELUS	MONEYS	ABDUCT
CALVES	BICEPS	CALLUS		DEDUCT
SELVES	THRIPS	OBOLUS		INDUCT
WOLVES	TRUMPS	STYLUS	-----T	RABBET
HOOVES	WHOOPS	LACMUS		GIBBET
TURVES	TROOPS	ANIMUS	COMBAT	GOBBET
CALXES	SHEARS	PRIMUS	WOMBAT	BARBET
CALAIS	SHEERS	LITMUS	FOXBAT	DULCET
GLACIS	PLIERS	THYMUS	SEACAT	LANCET
PRECIS	DIVERS	URANUS	GIBCAT	AVOCET
CADDIS	REPASS	MUCOUS	BOBCAT	FAUCET
HAGGIS	BYPASS	RUFOUS	TOMCAT	UNMEET
RACHIS	HARASS	RUGOUS	TIPCAT	AFREET

STREET	BULLET	CLOSET	MISFIT	OCTANT
BUFFET	CULLET	AVOSET	OUTFIT	NUTANT
FIDGET	GULLET	CORSET	SUNLIT	EXTANT
BUDGET	MULLET	BASSET	SUBMIT	TRUANT
NUGGET	PULLET	COSSET	COMMIT	SAVANT
PARGET	CAMLET	POSSET	SUMMIT	LEVANT
TARGET	HAMLET	GUSSET	HERMIT	BEZANT
FORGET	SAMLET	RUSSET	PERMIT	ACCENT
GORGET	GIMLET	OUTSET	UNKNIT	DECENT
CACHET	ARMLET	CRUSET	SENNIT	RECENT
SACHET	RUNLET	SEPTET	DACOIT	ASCENT
ROCHET	VIOLET	SESTET	DAKOIT	LUCENT
SOVIET	VARLET	FUSTET	ADROIT	CADENT
GASJET	CUTLET	SEXTET	ARMPIT	INDENT
JACKET	OUTLET	MINUET	TANPIT	RODENT
PACKET	AMULET	PIQUET	RATPIT	ARDENT
RACKET	HOWLET	COQUET	SAWPIT	REGENT
PICKET	STYLET	BREVET	SPIRIT	COGENT
TICKET	HELMET	PRIVET	ESPRIT	ARGENT
WICKET	KISMET	TRIVET	WORRIT	URGENT
COCKET	PLANET	VELVET	OUTSIT	CLIENT
DOCKET	MAGNET	CURVET	TIMTIT	ORIENT
LOCKET	SIGNET	BEREFT	ACQUIT	TALENT
POCKET	CYGNET	UPLIFT	JESUIT	RELENT
ROCKET	SPINET	ADRIFT	INTUIT	SILENT
SOCKET	GANNET	SHRIFT	GODWIT	DOLENT
BUCKET	JENNET	THRIFT	PEEWIT	LAMENT
TUCKET	RENNET	HEIGHT	OUTWIT	CEMENT
JUNKET	LINNET	WEIGHT	COBALT	DEMENT
MARKET	BONNET	ALIGHT	BASALT	FOMENT
BASKET	SONNET	BLIGHT	INFELT	LOMENT
CASKET	RUNNET	FLIGHT	UNFELT	MOMENT
GASKET	LIONET	PLIGHT	SPOILT	REPENT
MUSKET	GARNET	SLIGHT	UNBOLT	PARENT
CHALET	CORNET	ANIGHT	REVOLT	ABSENT
GABLET	HORNET	KNIGHT	OCCULT	RESENT
TABLET	BURNET	ARIGHT	INCULT	UNSENT
GIBLET	GURNET	BRIGHT	TUMULT	ASSENT
GOBLET	LIMPET	FRIGHT	PENULT	LATENT
SUBLET	LAPPET	WRIGHT	RESULT	PATENT
OMELET	TAPPET	CAUGHT	INSULT	DETENT
EYELET	SIPPET	NAUGHT	DREAMT	INTENT
EAGLET	TIPPET	BOUGHT	VACANT	POTENT
REGLET	POPPET	FOUGHT	DECANT	EXTENT
AIGLET	PUPPET	NOUGHT	RECANT	FLUENT
GIGLET	CARPET	STRAIT	SECANT	ADVENT
PIGLET	TOUPET	RABBIT	PEDANT	INVENT
TOILET	CLARET	TIDBIT	INFANT	PLAINT
ANKLET	LABRET	GAMBIT	PLIANT	QUAINT
BALLET	TABRET	TITBIT	SEJANT	SPLINT
CALLET	SECRET	ELICIT	ASKANT	ANOINT
MALLET	REGRET	CREDIT	VOLANT	AROINT
PALLET	FLORET	BANDIT	ASLANT	SPRINT
WALLET	AMORET	PANDIT	TENANT	SQUINT
PELLET	GARRET	PUNDIT	SONANT	FLAUNT
BILLET	FERRET	ALBEIT	ARRANT	AVAUNT
FILLET	TURRET	DECEIT	ERRANT	AMOUNT
MILLET	TEASET	SOFFIT	TYRANT	AROYNT
RILLET	OFFSET	COMFIT	NATANT	PURBOT
COLLET	SUNSET	PROFIT	NATANT	TURBOT

MASCOT	RETORT	WHILST	BOWSAW	SYNTAX
FLYFOT	EXTORT	ACCOST	MILDEW	SURTAX
FAGGOT	CAVORT	ALMOST	SUNDEW	EARWAX
MAGGOT	UNHURT	INMOST	MAYDEW	PAXWAX
SPIGOT	RECAST	UPMOST	CURFEW	CAUDEX
FORGOT	DICAST	UTMOST	ESCHEW	REFLEX
REDHOT	UPCAST	IMPOST	NEPHEW	POLLEX
UPSHOT	BREAST	THIRST	CASHEW	DIPLEX
GALIOT	AGHAST	ROBUST	REVIEW	IMPLEX
HERIOT	DYNAST	LOCUST	CURLEW	DUPLEX
ZEALOT	REPAST	AUGUST	SEAMEW	UNISEX
OCELOT	AMIDST	ADJUST	HEBREW	SUSSEX
GIGLOT	INCEST	UNJUST	SUNBOW	VERTEX
BALLOT	ELDEST	THRUST	SEACOW	CORTEX
HARLOT	MODEST	ENCYST	MOSCOW	VORTEX
MARMOT	INFEST	MOTETT	MEADOW	CONVEX
CANNOT	DIGEST	UMLAUT	SHADOW	SPADIX
UNROOT	INGEST	HAGBUT	WINDOW	PREFIX
UPROOT	BEHEST	CATGUT	ANYHOW	SUFFIX
TEAPOT	PRIEST	LOGHUT	BYBLOW	BOLLIX
INKPOT	MOLEST	PEANUT	INFLOW	PROLIX
BESPOT	HONEST	PIGNUT	CALLOW	COMMIX
DESPOT	UNREST	WALNUT	FALLOW	MATRIX
CARROT	FOREST	ECONUT	HALLOW	SPHINX
GARROT	ARREST	RAGOUT	MALLOW	SYRINX
PARROT	OBTEST	MAHOUT	SALLOW	LARYNX
DRYROT	DETEST	SPROUT	TALLOW	ICEBOX
ACCEPT	ATTEST	DEVOUT	WALLOW	SEAFOX
EXCEPT	DEVEST	OUTPUT	BELLOW	MUSKOX
YCLEPT	DIVEST	BEIRUT	FELLOW	COWPOX
UNWEPT	INVEST		MELLOW	ADIEUX
SCRIPT	LOWEST		YELLOW	REFLUX
EXEMPT	CUBIST	-----U	BILLOW	EFFLUX
PROMPT	RACIST		PILLOW	INFLUX
ABRUPT	SADIST	LANDAU	WILLOW	HALLUX
GOCART	NUDIST	BUREAU	FOLLOW	BIJOUX
DEPART	THEIST	BATEAU	HOLLOW	COCCYX
IMPART	LEGIST	NILGAU	ERENOW	
THWART	SCHIST	PILLAU	MINNOW	
EXPERT	ENLIST	APERCU	WINNOW	-----Y
DESERT	TIMIST	MANCHU	BARROW	
INSERT	TANIST	ORMOLU	FARROW	BOMBAY
ASSERT	MONIST	AMADOU	HARROW	MIDDAY
ADVERT	OBOIST	CONGOU	MARROW	OFFDAY
REVERT	EGOIST	CACHOU	NARROW	DOGDAY
DIVERT	PAPIST		YARROW	FRIDAY
INVERT	RAPIST		BORROW	MONDAY
COVERT	TYPIST	-----W	MORROW	SUNDAY
SQUIRT	CHRIST		SORROW	MAYDAY
ESCORT	AURIST	GUFFAW	BURROW	PAYDAY
EFFORT	JURIST	GEWGAW	FURROW	HEYDAY
DEHORT	PURIST	BASHAW	BESTOW	LINHAY
COHORT	LYRIST	HAWHAW		SASHAY
EXHORT	DESIST	MOBLAW		MELLAY
DEPORT	RESIST	OUTLAW	-----X	REPLAY
REPORT	INSIST	REDRAW		BYPLAY
IMPORT	ASSIST	SEESAW	CEEFAX	PARLAY
EXPORT	ARTIST	JIGSAW	CLIMAX	MISLAY
RESORT	LUTIST	WARSAW	THORAX	OUTLAY
ASSORT	SEXIST	PITSAW	STORAX	WAYLAY

TIDILY	SIMPLY	BRAINY	AWEARY	PRIORY
BODILY	COMPLY	GRAINY	VAGARY	MEMORY
UGLILY	TWOPLY	HOMINY	SUGARY	ARMORY
WILILY	SUPPLY	ROSINY	APIARY	MOTORY
HOLILY	DEARLY	SATINY	AVIARY	SAVORY
FANILY	NEARLY	MUTINY	SALARY	SCARRY
HOMILY	PEARLY	SHANNY	CANARY	CHARRY
ROPILY	YEARLY	CRANNY	PANARY	SPARRY
WARILY	GNARLY	GRANNY	DENARY	STARRY
VERILY	FAIRLY	BLENNY	SENARY	QUARRY
AIRILY	POORLY	JOHNNY	BINARY	CHERRY
EASILY	HOURLY	SHINNY	ZONARY	SHERRY
COSILY	SOURLY	WHINNY	HORARY	WHERRY
BUSILY	MEASLY	SKINNY	ROSARY	SKERRY
LAZILY	GRISLY	SPINNY	NOTARY	SCURRY
MAZILY	NEATLY	FELONY	ROTARY	SKURRY
COZILY	FLATLY	COLONY	VOTARY	FLURRY
WEAKLY	SUBTLY	POLONY	UNWARY	POETRY
SICKLY	MEETLY	SIMONY	WARCRY	PALTRY
MEEKLY	DEFTLY	SPOONY	DESCRY	PELTRY
WEEKLY	SOFTLY	BARONY	OUTCRY	SULTRY
LANKLY	SALTLY	BETONY	SUNDRY	PANTRY
RANKLY	GENTLY	BRYONY	BAWDRY	GENTRY
DARKLY	PARTLY	THORNY	TAWDRY	SENTRY
REALLY	TARTLY	BRAWNY	CHEERY	WINTRY
ORALLY	PERTLY	TOMBOY	EGGERY	PASTRY
OVALLY	PORTLY	CARBOY	SPHERY	VESTRY
SHELLY	CURTLY	POTBOY	BRIERY	AUGURY
CHILLY	FASTLY	COWBOY	OSIERY	INJURY
FRILLY	LASTLY	LOWBOY	BAKERY	PENURY
STILLY	VASTLY	DEPLOY	CELERY	FLOURY
WHOLLY	COSTLY	EMPLOY	OILERY	DYSURY
COOLLY	MOSTLY	SHAMOY	TILERY	LUXURY
WOOLLY	JUSTLY	TEAPOY	OWLERY	CHOWRY
BROLLY	UNDULY	CONVOY	VENERY	UNEASY
TROLLY	UNRULY	SLEEPY	FINERY	CREASY
FOULLY	SLOWLY	CREEPY	PINERY	GREASY
SEEMLY	GLEAMY	STEEPY	VINERY	QUEASY
GRIMLY	CREAMY	SWEEPY	ORNERY	EXTASY
PRIMLY	DREAMY	SWAMPY	NAPERY	CHEESY
TRIMLY	STEAMY	CLUMPY	PAPERY	HERESY
CALMLY	INFAMY	PLUMPY	EMPERY	CUTESY
WARMLY	BIGAMY	GRUMPY	POPERY	KECKSY
TERMLY	BULIMY	STUMPY	ROPERY	BALLSY
FIRMLY	SHAMMY	CANOPY	DUPERY	WHIMSY
GLUMLY	WHAMMY	CHAPPY	ORRERY	FLIMSY
LEANLY	CLAMMY	PREPPY	MISERY	CLUMSY
MEANLY	SCUMMY	CHIPPY	ROSERY	QUINSY
KEENLY	CHUMMY	CHOPPY	WATERY	ARGOSY
OPENLY	CRUMMY	SHOPPY	ARTERY	CHOOSY
EVENLY	SODOMY	FLOPPY	LIVERY	APEPSY
GAINLY	BLOOMY	SLOPPY	RIVERY	DROPSY
MAINLY	GLOOMY	CROPPY	TAWERY	CLASSY
VAINLY	BROOMY	CHIRPY	BOWERY	GLASSY
THINLY	STORMY	CRISPY	LOWERY	BRASSY
UNHOLY	RHEUMY	OCCUPY	TOWERY	GRASSY
DEEPLY	LITANY	GROUPY	BELFRY	CRESSY
TRIPLY	BOTANY	SYRUPY	HUNGRY	DRESSY
DIMPLY	SHEENY	BLEARY	EXPIRY	TRESSY
PIMPLY	GREENY	DREARY	THEORY	FLOSSY

------A	CUMBRIA	FURCULA	TESSERA	ARCHAIC
	NIGERIA	VASCULA	PODAGRA	ARAMAIC
COPAIBA	ALGERIA	LINGULA	URETHRA	HEBRAIC
CALUMBA	ASTERIA	FORMULA	HETAIRA	PROSAIC
COLUMBA	PELORIA	CANNULA	MADEIRA	DELTAIC
CATAWBA	AUSTRIA	PINNULA	PAREIRA	VOLTAIC
POLACCA	DYSURIA	SCAPULA	AMPHORA	ALEMBIC
FELUCCA	ARGYRIA	SPATULA	SIGNORA	RHOMBIC
JAMAICA	APHASIA	FISTULA	SPECTRA	PLUMBIC
REPLICA	XERASIA	ALABAMA	SHASTRA	SEBACIC
AMERICA	AMNESIA	DIORAMA	PURPURA	BORACIC
TAPIOCA	FUCHSIA	GRANDMA	CAESURA	SILICIC
FLORIDA	APEPSIA	EMPYEMA	BRAVURA	TRIADIC
VERANDA	QUASSIA	DRACHMA	FORMOSA	NOMADIC
PUDENDA	INDUSIA	DIGAMMA	POTASSA	MONADIC
ROTUNDA	MILITIA	DILEMMA	STOMATA	FARADIC
SPIRAEA	COMITIA	SARCOMA	CANTATA	DRUIDIC
PANACEA	AMENTIA	LEUCOMA	TAFFETA	SCALDIC
CETACEA	OPUNTIA	DIPLOMA	EXCRETA	MELODIC
TRACHEA	INERTIA	CHIASMA	INFANTA	MONODIC
COCHLEA	BOLIVIA	MAHATMA	MAGENTA	SYNODIC
DEEPSEA	SYNOVIA	BANDANA	POLENTA	PARODIC
OVERSEA	PYREXIA	INDIANA	MOMENTA	MALEFIC
BEEFTEA	PALOOKA	TYMPANA	JAKARTA	TRAFFIC
ALFALFA	BAZOOKA	SULTANA	ALBERTA	PACIFIC
GALANGA	MAZURKA	MONTANA	CANASTA	MIRIFIC
SYRINGA	CABBALA	ECHIDNA	INGESTA	OSSIFIC
NAPHTHA	MARSALA	MURAENA	REGATTA	VIVIFIC
ACANTHA	URODELA	VERBENA	ARIETTA	PELAGIC
BRECCIA	SEQUELA	PISCINA	BIRETTA	ELLAGIC
GONIDIA	RUBELLA	GLUCINA	DECIDUA	ENERGIC
RATAFIA	PADELLA	STAMINA	PIRAGUA	GEORGIC
OTALGIA	LAMELLA	TORMINA	SILIQUA	BACCHIC
MYALGIA	CANELLA	ALUMINA	CASSAVA	STICHIC
GEORGIA	PATELLA	OCARINA	BONANZA	PSYCHIC
MORPHIA	CEDILLA	CZARINA	CADENZA	GRAPHIC
REGALIA	CODILLA	TZARINA		DELPHIC
LOBELIA	ARMILLA	PLATINA		SAPPHIC
MYCELIA	MANILLA	FLUTINA	------B	GLYPHIC
AURELIA	VANILLA	HOSANNA		MYRRHIC
SEDILIA	PAPILLA	SAVANNA	TAXICAB	PYRRHIC
SCHOLIA	BARILLA	GEHENNA	COXCOMB	GNATHIC
ANAEMIA	GORILLA	ANTENNA	COULOMB	SPATHIC
URAEMIA	MAXILLA	MADONNA	SUCCUMB	XANTHIC
PYAEMIA	VEXILLA	CREMONA	CORNCOB	VOCALIC
BULIMIA	COROLLA	PERSONA	RHUBARB	ANGELIC
ANOSMIA	MEDULLA	ARIZONA	PROVERB	PHALLIC
RUMANIA	AMPULLA	ECTOZOA	PERTURB	IDYLLIC
SIRENIA	TOMBOLA	BRYOZOA	DISTURB	ECBOLIC
ACTINIA	GONDOLA	POLYZOA		BUCOLIC
BEGONIA	RUBEOLA	GRANDPA		DYNAMIC
APHONIA	AUREOLA	MASCARA	------C	CERAMIC
VALONIA	ROSEOLA	CITHARA		KERAMIC
AMMONIA	BOFFOLA	CHIKARA	CARDIAC	ANAEMIC
PETUNIA	VARIOLA	ALGEBRA	ELEGIAC	PYAEMIC
SEQUOIA	PIANOLA	HETAERA	COELIAC	ENDEMIC
ECTOPIA	HEXAPLA	VISCERA	SHELLAC	POLEMIC
MALARIA	SPECULA	RIVIERA	ALMANAC	TOTEMIC
VELARIA	SPICULA	CHOLERA	CHAMPAC	CHROMIC
VIVARIA	VINCULA	TEMPERA	BIVOUAC	ENTOMIC

PTARMIC	LUNATIC	CATHEAD	TOOTHED	GRAINED
THERMIC	HEPATIC	IMPLEAD	MOUTHED	TRAINED
PLASMIC	PIRATIC	MISLEAD	SCYTHED	DEFINED
SEISMIC	ERRATIC	LIPREAD	FANCIED	REFINED
OCEANIC	ASTATIC	BESTEAD	CANDIED	ERMINED
ORGANIC	EXTATIC	INSTEAD	STUDIED	GROINED
MELANIC	AQUATIC	CHILIAD	BELLIED	CHINNED
ROMANIC	DEICTIC	FOOTPAD	POPPIED	TWINNED
SATANIC	ASCETIC	GWYNEDD	STORIED	LEARNED
TETANIC	APHETIC	TIARAED	MARRIED	STERNED
TITANIC	MIMETIC	SCABBED	BERRIED	ACORNED
BOTANIC	GENETIC	CRABBED	SERRIED	CORSNED
EUGENIC	KINETIC	KNOBBED	HURRIED	UNOWNED
STHENIC	ALOETIC	STUBBED	UNTRIED	CROWNED
GALENIC	PARETIC	BONEBED	DAISIED	UNWOOED
SELENIC	HERETIC	SICKBED	HOGTIED	YCLEPED
SPLENIC	PYRETIC	BARKBED	CRACKED	LOBIPED
PHRENIC	ZETETIC	COALBED	FROCKED	SOLIPED
ARSENIC	AUGITIC	THUMBED	STALKED	STRIPED
TECHNIC	OOLITIC	CAMPBED	SHANKED	CRAMPED
ACTINIC	POLITIC	DIRTBED	TRUNKED	UNHOPED
STANNIC	HAMITIC	FLEECED	CROOKED	CHAPPED
BUBONIC	SEMITIC	POUNCED	UNASKED	SCARPED
LACONIC	PYRITIC	ARCADED	PEBBLED	KINDRED
OBCONIC	LEVITIC	STUDDED	CIRCLED	HUNDRED
MECONIC	FRANTIC	PLAIDED	MUSCLED	ULCERED
HEDONIC	IDENTIC	UNAIDED	WHEELED	OSIERED
DEMONIC	CHAOTIC	BRAIDED	MUFFLED	WATERED
AARONIC	IDIOTIC	DECIDED	RUFFLED	LIVERED
CHRONIC	NILOTIC	BRANDED	DEFILED	TOWERED
MORONIC	DEMOTIC	BLINDED	PICKLED	RETIRED
MASONIC	OSMOTIC	BRINDED	SCALLED	VISORED
OLYMPIC	ZYMOTIC	BOUNDED	SHELLED	KNARRED
STEARIC	HENOTIC	BEARDED	SKILLED	STARRED
CAMBRIC	SCEPTIC	SHARDED	QUILLED	SPURRED
SUBERIC	SKEPTIC	GUARDED	DIMPLED	GOITRED
SPHERIC	GLYPTIC	CLOUDED	PIMPLED	FIGURED
HOMERIC	CRYPTIC	CROWDED	DAPPLED	ASSURED
GENERIC	STYPTIC	SUCCEED	PEARLED	SUTURED
ENTERIC	ELASTIC	PROCEED	GNARLED	DEBASED
EMPIRIC	PLASTIC	MISDEED	WHORLED	ADVISED
SATIRIC	SPASTIC	INBREED	MEASLED	OPPOSED
CALORIC	DRASTIC	ANISEED	BOBSLED	EXPOSED
PELORIC	DEISTIC	LINSEED	KIRTLED	BLESSED
CHLORIC	ERISTIC	HAYSEED	CASTLED	TRESSED
PYLORIC	GNOSTIC	SEAWEED	WATTLED	CROSSED
ARMORIC	CAUSTIC	CUDWEED	METTLED	TRUSSED
FLUORIC	GLOTTIC	SCARFED	SETTLED	ACCUSED
CENTRIC	BARYTIC	ENGAGED	MOTTLED	BEMUSED
GASTRIC	MOLLUSC	VISAGED	ASHAMED	UNDATED
DYSURIC		CRAGGED	UNNAMED	NODATED
SATYRIC		FROGGED	UNTAMED	TOGATED
BUTYRIC	------D	OBLIGED	CHARMED	JUGATED
LIASSIC		FRINGED	UNARMED	RELATED
CLASSIC	BAGHDAD	PRONGED	CHASMED	LUNATED
GLOSSIC	GRANDAD	BEACHED	VOLUMED	BLOATED
SCIATIC	GODHEAD	POUCHED	ASSUMED	AURATED
ASIATIC	EGGHEAD	SLASHED	WIZENED	LYRATED
SOMATIC	BIGHEAD	FLESHED	FEIGNED	UNACTED
FANATIC	WARHEAD	SPATHED	BRAINED	RIVETED

SHAFTED	PYRAMID	MIDLAND	DYEWOOD	HALBERD
SIGHTED	PLACOID	ICELAND	DOGWOOD	COWHERD
PLAITED	CRICOID	IRELAND	LOGWOOD	EGGBIRD
LIMITED	ZINCOID	ELFLAND	CAMWOOD	CATBIRD
STILTED	SARCOID	ENGLAND	BARWOOD	CONCORD
VAULTED	DISCOID	HOLLAND	BOXWOOD	DISCORD
SLANTED	MUSCOID	FINLAND	PLYWOOD	APPLAUD
SAINTED	FUNGOID	GARLAND	DECAPOD	DEFRAUD
JOINTED	XIPHOID	ZETLAND	HEXAPOD	ROSEBUD
POINTED	TYPHOID	LOWLAND	LYCOPOD	BECLOUD
FRONTED	LITHOID	COMMAND	OCTOPOD	
HAUNTED	TENIOID	GORMAND	BOMBARD	
MOUNTED	HYALOID	WEASAND	LOMBARD	------E
STUNTED	TABLOID	WEAZAND	PLACARD	
BIGOTED	CYCLOID	PREBEND	BROCARD	APHTHAE
UNNOTED	MYELOID	DESCEND	DISCARD	SCORIAE
DEVOTED	COLLOID	FORFEND	UNHEARD	EXUVIAE
PIVOTED	AMYLOID	WEEKEND	HAGGARD	TABULAE
HEARTED	STYLOID	COMMEND	LAGGARD	NEBULAE
CHESTED	SIGMOID	STIPEND	NIGGARD	MACULAE
CRESTED	ETHMOID	COMPEND	POCHARD	INFULAE
WORSTED	ADENOID	PERPEND	ORCHARD	PAPULAE
FRETTED	CTENOID	SUSPEND	DIEHARD	SQUAMAE
KNOTTED	CRINOID	GODSEND	BEGHARD	THERMAE
SPOTTED	FIBROID	SUBTEND	PONIARD	STRUMAE
VOLUTED	ANDROID	PRETEND	TANKARD	VAGINAE
CLOUTED	ANEROID	CONTEND	MALLARD	LAMINAE
SNOUTED	STEROID	PROTEND	BOLLARD	LACUNAE
SUBDUED	NEGROID	PORTEND	LOLLARD	PATERAE
TONGUED	CHOROID	DISTEND	POLLARD	PLEURAE
STATUED	SAUROID	MINUEND	DULLARD	MEDUSAE
UNPAVED	THYROID	ABSCIND	FOULARD	ASCRIBE
SLEEVED	CISSOID	RESCIND	GURNARD	MICROBE
BELOVED	DELTOID	EXSCIND	REYNARD	DISROBE
REMOVED	LENTOID	MANKIND	INBOARD	VENDACE
UNMOVED	MASTOID	ABSCOND	JEOPARD	PREFACE
SINEWED	CESTOID	DIAMOND	LEOPARD	SURFACE
UNTAXED	RHIZOID	DROMOND	BASTARD	OUTFACE
UNMIXED	INSIPID	DESPOND	DASTARD	BULLACE
MONEYED	SCABRID	RESPOND	COSTARD	REPLACE
FRIEZED	HYDATID	REBOUND	BUSTARD	GRIMACE
UNSIZED	CAROTID	UNBOUND	CUSTARD	PINNACE
BRONZED	PAROTID	REDOUND	MUSTARD	FURNACE
BLOWZED	LANGUID	REFOUND	HARVARD	EMBRACE
DEAFAID	PIEBALD	IMPOUND	SEAWARD	UNBRACE
BARMAID	EMERALD	EXPOUND	GODWARD	TERRACE
MERMAID	WERGILD	AGROUND	LEEWARD	RETRACE
PREPAID	REBUILD	RESOUND	STEWARD	CADDICE
UPBRAID	PENFOLD	UNSOUND	AWKWARD	SUFFICE
OVERBID	TENFOLD	ASTOUND	SUNWARD	EDIFICE
SUBACID	PINFOLD	OROTUND	FROWARD	ORIFICE
ANTACID	SIXFOLD	PEASCOD	FORWARD	CHALICE
FLACCID	CUCKOLD	DEMIGOD	OUTWARD	TITMICE
KATYDID	REMOULD	DRYSHOD	WAYWARD	CORNICE
ARANEID	DISBAND	SEAFOOD	SKYWARD	REJOICE
PROTEID	HUSBAND	CUBHOOD	HALYARD	INVOICE
SYLPHID	DEODAND	MANHOOD	LANYARD	COPPICE
SQUALID	BRIGAND	CATHOOD	MAZZARD	HOSPICE
INVALID	OFFHAND	BOYHOOD	GIZZARD	AUSPICE
ANNELID	BOWHAND	REDWOOD	BUZZARD	AVARICE

CAPRICE	CARBIDE	MATINEE	APANAGE	PROTEGE
MORRICE	DEICIDE	CALIPEE	CRANAGE	CORTEGE
MORTICE	SUICIDE	REFEREE	TEENAGE	NEGLIGE
JUSTICE	ECOCIDE	COWTREE	COINAGE	VESTIGE
LATTICE	CONFIDE	BOXTREE	SPINAGE	INDULGE
CREVICE	COWHIDE	FORESEE	TANNAGE	EFFULGE
SERVICE	COLLIDE	DEVISEE	TONNAGE	DIVULGE
ENHANCE	BROMIDE	OVERSEE	DUNNAGE	MELANGE
ASKANCE	CYANIDE	LEGATEE	TUNNAGE	DERANGE
BALANCE	HYDRIDE	MANATEE	PEONAGE	ARRANGE
VALANCE	ASTRIDE	GRANTEE	CARNAGE	STRANGE
ROMANCE	OUTRIDE	PICOTEE	RAMPAGE	REVENGE
PENANCE	HAYRIDE	DEVOTEE	UMBRAGE	LOZENGE
FINANCE	SEASIDE	TRUSTEE	PEERAGE	UNHINGE
SONANCE	SUBSIDE	MARQUEE	PIERAGE	IMPINGE
DURANCE	PRESIDE	AGRAFFE	AVERAGE	SPRINGE
ADVANCE	OUTSIDE	GIRAFFE	MOORAGE	SYRINGE
LICENCE	WAYSIDE	MIDWIFE	STORAGE	EXPUNGE
CADENCE	EBBTIDE	ALEWIFE	BARRAGE	GAMBOGE
DEFENCE	PROVIDE	HUSWIFE	OUTRAGE	ANAGOGE
OFFENCE	DIOXIDE	CABBAGE	COURAGE	ENLARGE
FAIENCE	ZINCODE	GARBAGE	PRESAGE	IMMERGE
SCIENCE	SARCODE	HERBAGE	CORSAGE	DETERGE
VALENCE	CATHODE	SOCCAGE	MASSAGE	DIVERGE
SILENCE	IMPLODE	BROCAGE	PASSAGE	REGORGE
ABSENCE	EXPLODE	DISCAGE	MESSAGE	ENGORGE
ESSENCE	ALAMODE	BOSCAGE	SAUSAGE	SCOURGE
FLOUNCE	COMMODE	BANDAGE	WAFTAGE	PANACHE
ENOUNCE	CORRODE	WINDAGE	VOLTAGE	EARACHE
FROUNCE	EPISODE	BONDAGE	VANTAGE	ATTACHE
TROUNCE	OCCLUDE	FARDAGE	CENTAGE	GOUACHE
DEFORCE	ECLUDE	CORDAGE	VENTAGE	CAROCHE
ENFORCE	INCLUDE	MILEAGE	MINTAGE	STROPHE
DIVORCE	EXCLUDE	LINEAGE	VINTAGE	BREATHE
DEHISCE	PRELUDE	ACREAGE	PONTAGE	WREATHE
TRADUCE	COLLUDE	LEAFAGE	CARTAGE	SMOOTHE
SUBDUCE	OBTRUDE	BAGGAGE	PORTAGE	CHARLIE
CONDUCE	DETRUDE	FOGGAGE	WASTAGE	OVERLIE
PRODUCE	INTRUDE	LUGGAGE	HOSTAGE	DOMINIE
PREPUCE	EXTRUDE	BURGAGE	POSTAGE	GRANNIE
LETTUCE	FREEBEE	COWHAGE	UPSTAGE	TRANNIE
FORBADE	FRISBEE	FOLIAGE	WATTAGE	BROWNIE
BROCADE	FIANCEE	LEAKAGE	COTTAGE	CHARPIE
CASCADE	CHALDEE	SOAKAGE	POTTAGE	DIRTPIE
COCKADE	GRANDEE	PACKAGE	SCUTAGE	GROUPIE
BALLADE	SPONDEE	SACKAGE	AJUTAGE	COTERIE
ROULADE	FEOFFEE	DOCKAGE	ESCUAGE	REVERIE
CHAMADE	PLEDGEE	LOCKAGE	ASSUAGE	PRAIRIE
MANMADE	THUGGEE	BROKAGE	SALVAGE	SMYTRIE
GRENADE	OBLIGEE	TALLAGE	SELVAGE	CRUISIE
CHARADE	PERIGEE	PILLAGE	BREWAGE	BRASSIE
DEGRADE	REFUGEE	TILLAGE	FLOWAGE	NECKTIE
UPGRADE	TROCHEE	VILLAGE	STOWAGE	PANCAKE
COMRADE	COUCHEE	COLLAGE	DRAYAGE	FORSAKE
ESTRADE	BANSHEE	TOLLAGE	QUAYAGE	PARTAKE
CRUSADE	PRITHEE	HAULAGE	BUOYAGE	MISTAKE
PERVADE	JUBILEE	PRIMAGE	ABRIDGE	GODLIKE
COUVADE	GALILEE	RUMMAGE	ADJUDGE	MANLIKE
PRECEDE	SHEENEE	PLUMAGE	BESIEGE	WARLIKE
CONCEDE	NOMINEE	THANAGE	COLLEGE	DISLIKE

MISLIKE	THIMBLE	SNUGGLE	ARMHOLE	PINNULE
RAMPIKE	SCUMBLE	SPANGLE	MANHOLE	CAGOULE
CONVOKE	CRUMBLE	BRANGLE	PINHOLE	STIPULE
PROVOKE	GRUMBLE	WRANGLE	EARHOLE	SPORULE
DISYOKE	STUMBLE	TWANGLE	RATHOLE	FERRULE
VANDYKE	IGNOBLE	SHINGLE	POTHOLE	MISRULE
CHORALE	ENNOBLE	CRINGLE	FOXHOLE	CAPSULE
GUNWALE	SOLUBLE	TRINGLE	KEYHOLE	PUSTULE
PACABLE	VOLUBLE	SWINGLE	FOLIOLE	VALVULE
VOCABLE	TROUBLE	GRACILE	CARIOLE	CONDYLE
AFFABLE	DEBACLE	PROFILE	PETIOLE	DRIZZLE
EFFABLE	TREACLE	FRAGILE	OSTIOLE	FRIZZLE
PLIABLE	MANACLE	COMPILE	TADPOLE	GRIZZLE
AMIABLE	MIRACLE	FEBRILE	CONSOLE	INFLAME
FRIABLE	CORACLE	STERILE	RISSOLE	PENNAME
TRIABLE	CUBICLE	PUERILE	PISTOLE	SIRNAME
SALABLE	RADICLE	PENSILE	SYSTOLE	SURNAME
RULABLE	VEHICLE	TENSILE	VACUOLE	MISNAME
NAMABLE	SILICLE	SESSILE	STEEPLE	TRIREME
TAMABLE	PANICLE	FISSILE	MANIPLE	SUPREME
TENABLE	SANICLE	MISSILE	TRAMPLE	EXTREME
FINABLE	FUNICLE	SUBTILE	EXAMPLE	SUBLIME
TUNABLE	UTRICLE	TACTILE	CRIMPLE	RAGTIME
CAPABLE	AURICLE	SECTILE	CRUMPLE	CENTIME
DUPABLE	VESICLE	FICTILE	GRAPPLE	PASTIME
PARABLE	OSSICLE	COCTILE	CRIPPLE	MISTIME
CURABLE	ARTICLE	DUCTILE	STIPPLE	DAYTIME
DURABLE	CUTICLE	PANTILE	STOPPLE	WELCOME
DISABLE	BINOCLE	GENTILE	DECUPLE	OUTCOME
EATABLE	MONOCLE	REPTILE	SCRUPLE	AWESOME
HATABLE	OPUSCLE	FERTILE	OCTUPLE	NOISOME
RATABLE	RECYCLE	TORTILE	ENTITLE	IRKSOME
CITABLE	BICYCLE	HOSTILE	STARTLE	FULSOME
NOTABLE	CALYCLE	TEXTILE	CHORTLE	WINSOME
POTABLE	TREADLE	BEGUILE	TRESTLE	TWOSOME
MUTABLE	STADDLE	SERVILE	WRESTLE	LISSOME
EQUABLE	SWADDLE	FLEXILE	THISTLE	EPITOME
SAVABLE	TWADDLE	SHACKLE	WHISTLE	RHIZOME
LOVABLE	TREDDLE	CRACKLE	EPISTLE	PERFUME
MOVABLE	GRIDDLE	GRACKLE	BRISTLE	DEPLUME
TAXABLE	TWIDDLE	SPECKLE	GRISTLE	SUBSUME
FIXABLE	WHEEDLE	FRECKLE	APOSTLE	PRESUME
MIXABLE	SPINDLE	PRICKLE	BRATTLE	CONSUME
PAYABLE	BRINDLE	TRICKLE	PRATTLE	COSTUME
TRYABLE	DWINDLE	STICKLE	TWATTLE	HENBANE
SIZABLE	SWINDLE	CHUCKLE	WHITTLE	COWBANE
BRABBLE	TRUNDLE	KNUCKLE	SKITTLE	CHICANE
CRIBBLE	URODELE	TRUCKLE	SPITTLE	MUNDANE
DRIBBLE	UKELELE	CRANKLE	BRITTLE	LURDANE
FRIBBLE	SNAFFLE	CRINKLE	SCUTTLE	PROFANE
QUIBBLE	WHIFFLE	WRINKLE	SHUTTLE	METHANE
STUBBLE	SKIFFLE	TWINKLE	GLOBULE	BIPLANE
AUDIBLE	SCUFFLE	SPARKLE	BARBULE	GERMANE
LEGIBLE	SHUFFLE	GABELLE	SACCULE	PLATANE
RISIBLE	SNUFFLE	MOSELLE	SPICULE	BELTANE
VISIBLE	SOUFFLE	GAZELLE	BASCULE	SOUTANE
FUSIBLE	TRUFFLE	BRAILLE	CELLULE	EPICENE
SHAMBLE	DRAGGLE	BRICOLE	GEMMULE	MIOCENE
BRAMBLE	WRIGGLE	CONDOLE	PLUMULE	OBSCENE
TREMBLE	SMUGGLE	DOGHOLE	GRANULE	EPIGENE

HYGIENE	TONTINE	BONFIRE	TORTURE	EXPANSE
SCALENE	DESTINE	GUNFIRE	NURTURE	RECENSE
AMYLENE	BOTTINE	GASFIRE	PASTURE	LICENSE
TERRENE	ROUTINE	JAGHIRE	GESTURE	INCENSE
CONVENE	BEGUINE	PISMIRE	VESTURE	DEFENSE
BENZENE	GENUINE	VAMPIRE	POSTURE	OFFENSE
EPERGNE	OLIVINE	RESPIRE	TEXTURE	IMMENSE
COCAINE	CERVINE	INSPIRE	FIXTURE	EXPENSE
DELAINE	CORVINE	SALTIRE	MIXTURE	INTENSE
ROMAINE	ENTWINE	ACQUIRE	NERVURE	GIBBOSE
MORAINE	INTWINE	REQUIRE	FLEXURE	GLOBOSE
COMBINE	UNTWINE	ENQUIRE	DASYURE	HERBOSE
CARBINE	CAYENNE	INQUIRE	SEIZURE	VERBOSE
TURBINE	JAWBONE	ESQUIRE	DIABASE	TALCOSE
VACCINE	CONDONE	FORBORE	SURBASE	GLUCOSE
CALCINE	SOMEONE	MOIDORE	PINCASE	ENCLOSE
HIRCINE	FORGONE	BANDORE	NUTCASE	INCLOSE
PORCINE	ABALONE	PANDORE	DECEASE	UNCLOSE
FASCINE	CYCLONE	INSHORE	RELEASE	VILLOSE
PISCINE	ANEMONE	DEPLORE	APPEASE	PLUMOSE
SARDINE	DISPONE	IMPLORE	DISEASE	SPINOSE
CONFINE	ACETONE	EXPLORE	ENCHASE	CABOOSE
IMAGINE	OXYTONE	EYESORE	DIOCESE	UNLOOSE
MACHINE	CANZONE	RESTORE	SIAMESE	VAMOOSE
ERRHINE	LUCARNE	BIZARRE	BURMESE	ADIPOSE
OPALINE	LUCERNE	THEATRE	CHINESE	COMPOSE
HYALINE	DEMESNE	SPECTRE	MALTESE	PROPOSE
DECLINE	TRIBUNE	PHILTRE	MALAISE	SUPPOSE
RECLINE	COMMUNE	SCEPTRE	UPRAISE	PURPOSE
INCLINE	NEPTUNE	EPICURE	PRECISE	DISPOSE
BEELINE	FORTUNE	PROCURE	CONCISE	SUCROSE
ANILINE	ANODYNE	OBSCURE	OXIDISE	OPEROSE
CARLINE	GUMSHOE	PERDURE	ELEGISE	DOGROSE
MARLINE	BAGPIPE	VERDURE	REALISE	LEPROSE
OUTLINE	SYNCOPE	HACHURE	UTILISE	CIRROSE
CAULINE	APOCOPE	CONJURE	IDOLISE	LACTOSE
PAULINE	OUTDARE	PERJURE	CHEMISE	PECTOSE
BOWLINE	WELFARE	FAILURE	PREMISE	RELAPSE
EXAMINE	FANFARE	GUIPURE	PROMISE	ILLAPSE
FULMINE	CARFARE	COUPURE	SURMISE	TRAIPSE
BROMINE	WARFARE	MEASURE	AGONISE	ECLIPSE
CARMINE	CAVIARE	ERASURE	LIONISE	ELLIPSE
JASMINE	DECLARE	LEISURE	DESPISE	GLIMPSE
ASININE	ENSNARE	CENSURE	SUNRISE	IMMERSE
QUININE	INSNARE	TONSURE	REPRISE	ASPERSE
LEONINE	PREPARE	CLOSURE	EMPRISE	OBVERSE
HEROINE	COMPARE	FISSURE	APPRISE	ADVERSE
VULPINE	HECTARE	FEATURE	LOWRISE	REVERSE
CHOPINE	UNAWARE	STATURE	POETISE	DIVERSE
ZEBRINE	TINWARE	LECTURE	AZOTISE	INVERSE
UTERINE	MACABRE	PICTURE	BAPTISE	ENDORSE
TIGRINE	CALIBRE	CULTURE	MORTISE	INDORSE
CHORINE	CONACRE	MULTURE	PREVISE	UNHORSE
CAPAPIE	CHANCRE	VULTURE	PARVISE	REMORSE
LATRINE	SINCERE	DENTURE	ENDWISE	ACCURSE
PETRINE	NOWHERE	VENTURE	ANYWISE	BAGASSE
CITRINE	CHIMERE	CLOTURE	REPULSE	FINESSE
TAURINE	COMPERE	CAPTURE	IMPULSE	PELISSE
CUISINE	AUSTERE	RAPTURE	APPULSE	BECAUSE
DENTINE	GRUYERE	RUPTURE	CLEANSE	DIFFUSE

SUFFUSE	ULULATE	DEPLETE	GAVOTTE	EROSIVE
CONFUSE	EMULATE	REPLETE	TRIBUTE	CURSIVE
PROFUSE	CREMATE	COMPETE	EXECUTE	MASSIVE
RECLUSE	CLIMATE	SECRETE	CONFUTE	PASSIVE
UNHOUSE	ANIMATE	EXCRETE	POLLUTE	MISSIVE
ESPOUSE	PRIMATE	NAIVETE	COMMUTE	JUSSIVE
CAROUSE	PALMATE	CALCITE	PERMUTE	ABUSIVE
UPROUSE	GEMMATE	CORDITE	COMPUTE	ELUSIVE
CONTUSE	BROMATE	ERUDITE	DISPUTE	AMUSIVE
PERTUSE	KHANATE	BAALITE	HIRSUTE	AMATIVE
DIALYSE	EMANATE	HYALITE	STATUTE	FICTIVE
ANALYSE	CRENATE	ZEOLITE	ACOLYTE	UNITIVE
GLOBATE	MAGNATE	ZOOLITE	RESIDUE	CAPTIVE
PROBATE	COGNATE	HOPLITE	OVERDUE	TORTIVE
PLACATE	URINATE	STYLITE	FATIGUE	FURTIVE
BACCATE	RUINATE	ADAMITE	ECLOGUE	FESTIVE
PLICATE	PINNATE	EREMITE	EXERGUE	RESTIVE
SPICATE	CONNATE	TERMITE	DEVALUE	COSTIVE
FALCATE	TERNATE	GRANITE	REVALUE	SURVIVE
SULCATE	LIBRATE	SYENITE	REVENUE	BIVALVE
FURCATE	VIBRATE	LIGNITE	RETINUE	ABSOLVE
EDUCATE	CEDRATE	KAINITE	CACIQUE	RESOLVE
GRADATE	HYDRATE	CRINITE	SALIQUE	DEVOLVE
PREDATE	OPERATE	MANNITE	OBLIQUE	REVOLVE
OXIDATE	ITERATE	EBONITE	SILIQUE	INVOLVE
MANDATE	REGRATE	ACONITE	COMIQUE	UNGLOVE
CORDATE	MIGRATE	REUNITE	ANTIQUE	COMMOVE
MISDATE	INGRATE	DESPITE	CAZIQUE	REPROVE
CAUDATE	NARRATE	RESPITE	BEZIQUE	IMPROVE
GALEATE	SERRATE	DIORITE	BAROQUE	APPROVE
PILEATE	NITRATE	CUPRITE	BRUSQUE	INNERVE
LINEATE	TITRATE	AZURITE	REISSUE	UNNERVE
CUNEATE	PULSATE	REWRITE	HABITUE	OBSERVE
OCREATE	DICTATE	FELSITE	CONCAVE	DESERVE
ROSEATE	NICTATE	HUSSITE	UPHEAVE	RESERVE
FOVEATE	ACETATE	APATITE	BEREAVE	RECURVE
FRIGATE	AGITATE	REQUITE	INWEAVE	INCURVE
VULGATE	IMITATE	ANDANTE	UNWEAVE	OVERAWE
VIRGATE	PELTATE	INFANTE	FORGAVE	PICKAXE
LABIATE	DENTATE	ENTENTE	ENCLAVE	GOODBYE
RADIATE	HASTATE	EPIDOTE	EXCLAVE	DEADEYE
MEDIATE	TESTATE	PROMOTE	ENSLAVE	BUCKEYE
FILIATE	INSTATE	CONNOTE	ENGRAVE	WALLEYE
FOLIATE	COSTATE	OUTVOTE	DEPRAVE	CATSEYE
MINIATE	GUTTATE	IMPASTE	ACHIEVE	EMBLAZE
EXPIATE	SCUTATE	MODISTE	BELIEVE	SQUEEZE
SERIATE	ARCUATE	ARTISTE	RELIEVE	TRAPEZE
STRIATE	SINUATE	RIPOSTE	KHEDIVE	LAICIZE
MURIATE	LIQUATE	VEDETTE	DECEIVE	OXIDIZE
SATIATE	ACTUATE	VIDETTE	RECEIVE	RESEIZE
VITIATE	SITUATE	PALETTE	FORGIVE	REALIZE
OBVIATE	CLAVATE	FUMETTE	MISGIVE	UTILIZE
DEVIATE	ELEVATE	GENETTE	ARCHIVE	ATOMIZE
PRELATE	PRIVATE	DINETTE	BEEHIVE	EBONIZE
INFLATE	VALVATE	LUNETTE	OUTLIVE	AGONIZE
COLLATE	OBOVATE	PIPETTE	CONNIVE	LIONIZE
BULLATE	EXEGETE	ROSETTE	DEPRIVE	OZONIZE
ISOLATE	MACHETE	GAZETTE	SUASIVE	HEROIZE
OCULATE	ESTHETE	CALOTTE	EVASIVE	CAPSIZE
ADULATE	ATHLETE	GAROTTE	PENSIVE	POETIZE

BAPTIZE	SHADING	PICKING	PRIMING	TEASING
ANALYZE	LOADING	TICKING	LEMMING	CLOSING
	TRADING	SUCKING	GUMMING	CURSING
	MADDING	TALKING	WYOMING	PASSING
------F	PADDING	WALKING	FARMING	MISSING
	WADDING	HULKING	MEANING	BUSSING
TEALEAF	BEDDING	BANKING	OPENING	AMUSING
DISTAFF	WEDDING	SINKING	EVENING	HOUSING
BAILIFF	BIDDING	SMOKING	VEINING	MOUSING
MIDRIFF	NODDING	BROKING	SHINING	ROUSING
SHERIFF	BUDDING	WORKING	JOINING	BEATING
CAITIFF	PUDDING	HAWKING	TWINING	HEATING
PONTIFF	FEEDING	DEALING	DAMNING	PLATING
MASTIFF	ABIDING	HEALING	TANNING	SLATING
ENFEOFF	GLIDING	SEALING	TINNING	COATING
TAKEOFF	SLIDING	WHALING	WINNING	GRATING
KICKOFF	GELDING	SIBLING	CONNING	PRATING
LIFTOFF	GILDING	CODLING	CUNNING	MEETING
CASTOFF	HILDING	FEELING	PUNNING	WHITING
SHOWOFF	WILDING	CIELING	RUNNING	WRITING
COWCALF	FOLDING	ANGLING	NOONING	MALTING
ONESELF	HOLDING	FAILING	IRONING	BELTING
HIMSELF	BANDING	RAILING	EARNING	FELTING
HERSELF	LANDING	SAILING	WARNING	MELTING
OURSELF	PENDING	WAILING	MORNING	CANTING
THYSELF	BINDING	SMILING	BURNING	TINTING
WERWOLF	FINDING	BOILING	TURNING	BUNTING
THEREOF	WINDING	OAKLING	DAWNING	HUNTING
WHEREOF	WORDING	INKLING	UNDOING	FOOTING
SHADOOF	BLUEING	CALLING	INGOING	PARTING
REPROOF	GOLFING	GALLING	ONGOING	CASTING
WALDORF	ROOFING	WALLING	KEEPING	EASTING
	STAGING	TELLING	WEEPING	LASTING
	HEDGING	YELLING	GRIPING	WASTING
------G	LODGING	FILLING	HELPING	WESTING
	BAGGING	KILLING	LUMPING	POSTING
HANDBAG	LEGGING	MILLING	TAPPING	MATTING
SANDBAG	DIGGING	WILLING	LOPPING	TATTING
MAILBAG	RIGGING	ROLLING	TOPPING	NETTING
FISHFAG	WIGGING	EANLING	CUPPING	PETTING
FILIBEG	HANGING	TANLING	CARPING	SETTING
FORELEG	LONGING	TOOLING	BEARING	FITTING
CORKLEG	FORGING	SAPLING	GEARING	SITTING
PERIWIG	PURGING	FOPLING	HEARING	JOTTING
SHEBANG	ETCHING	DARLING	WEARING	ROTTING
PROBANG	DASHING	CURLING	FLARING	CUTTING
SIAMANG	LASHING	UNSLING	GLARING	FLUTING
TREPANG	WASHING	GOSLING	ROARING	WEAVING
MUSTANG	DISHING	CATLING	SPARING	SHAVING
GINSENG	FISHING	FATLING	STARING	CRAVING
WEBBING	GUSHING	TITLING	SACRING	CARVING
RIBBING	PUSHING	WITLING	VEERING	DRAWING
RUBBING	LATHING	BOWLING	FAIRING	BREWING
FENCING	TITHING	HOWLING	MOORING	SHOWING
MINCING	NOTHING	BEAMING	EARRING	FLOWING
FARCING	SOAKING	FLAMING	WARRING	GLOWING
FORCING	BACKING	FRAMING	HERRING	KNOWING
HEADING	HACKING	SEEMING	FURRING	LAPWING
LEADING	PACKING	TEEMING	GASRING	PRAYING
READING	SACKING	FLEMING	LEASING	UNDYING

CLOYING	TRIUMPH	BLEMISH	ROGUISH
AMAZING	GALUMPH	FLEMISH	SLAVISH
GRAZING	CATARRH	RAMMISH	KNAVISH
ENDLONG	UNLEASH	DIMMISH	PEEVISH
ERELONG	BONEASH	PLANISH	DERVISH
PROLONG	EYELASH	SPANISH	SNOWISH
FURLONG	REFRESH	EVANISH	BABYISH
DAYLONG	NEBBISH	RHENISH	BULRUSH
POPSONG	MOBBISH	PLENISH	OUTRUSH
PAKTONG	RUBBISH	BRINISH	SABBATH
UNWRUNG	TUBBISH	SWINISH	AIRBATH
FIREDOG	FURBISH	MANNISH	BENEATH
BULLDOG	BADDISH	WANNISH	GOLIATH
ROADHOG	FADDISH	FINNISH	WARPATH
WARTHOG	REDDISH	DONNISH	BREADTH
BACKLOG	YIDDISH	DUNNISH	MACBETH
CRANNOG	SWEDISH	NUNNISH	TWELFTH
ICEBERG	WILDISH	MOONISH	TRILITH
LADYBUG	COLDISH	DRONISH	OTOLITH
	HARDISH	TARNISH	STEALTH
	PRUDISH	VARNISH	GREENTH
------H	OGREISH	CORNISH	SEVENTH
	RAFFISH	BURNISH	JACINTH
MESSIAH	HUFFISH	FURNISH	SABAOTH
DELILAH	DOGFISH	DAMPISH	BEEMOTH
CHEETAH	SELFISH	ROMPISH	MAMMOTH
JEHOVAH	WOLFISH	DUMPISH	BETROTH
BUSHWAH	SUNFISH	LUMPISH	INDEPTH
IMPEACH	GARFISH	MUMPISH	UNEARTH
UNTEACH	CATFISH	HIPPISH	REBIRTH
STOMACH	SAWFISH	FOPPISH	AZIMUTH
SPINACH	HAGGISH	WASPISH	BISMUTH
ABROACH	WAGGISH	BEARISH	UNCOUTH
SCREECH	BIGGISH	BOARISH	UNTRUTH
BESEECH	PIGGISH	CHERISH	
OSTRICH	DOGGISH	TIGRISH	
MASTICH	HOGGISH	FAIRISH	------I
DISTICH	MUGGISH	WHORISH	
SQUELCH	LONGISH	BOORISH	ASSAGAI
SQUINCH	HASHISH	MOORISH	ASSEGAI
CRAUNCH	SNAKISH	CURRISH	SAMURAI
STAUNCH	PECKISH	NOURISH	MENISCI
SCRUNCH	SICKISH	SOURISH	EFFENDI
PIBROCH	BUCKISH	GOATISH	WOORALI
NOMARCH	MONKISH	SOFTISH	WOURALI
MONARCH	BOOKISH	WHITISH	ISRAELI
AMBATCH	DARKISH	BRITISH	LAPILLI
UNLATCH	TURKISH	SALTISH	BOUILLI
SCRATCH	DUSKISH	COLTISH	OSMANLI
SPLOTCH	MAWKISH	DOLTISH	TRIPOLI
DEBAUCH	PUBLISH	TARTISH	STIMULI
DEBOUCH	ENGLISH	PETTISH	THALAMI
RETOUCH	HELLISH	WETTISH	SOPRANI
DIPTYCH	DULLISH	SOTTISH	TERMINI
INVEIGH	ABOLISH	RUTTISH	MARTINI
THROUGH	COOLISH	LOUTISH	COLIBRI
BOROUGH	FOOLISH	BRUTISH	WISTITI
PHARAOH	GIRLISH	BEAUISH	CHARQUI
DIGRAPH	GAULISH	ANGUISH	
EPITAPH	STYLISH		

------K	
	HAMMOCK
BESPEAK	HUMMOCK
INBREAK	UNFROCK
UPBREAK	CASSOCK
UNCLOAK	HASSOCK
FINBACK	TUSSOCK
FATBACK	MATTOCK
SETBACK	BUTTOCK
WETBACK	PUTTOCK
CUTBACK	ROEBUCK
POLLACK	SAWBUCK
BARRACK	UPCHUCK
CARRACK	POTLUCK
RANSACK	SCHMUCK
COSSACK	
REDNECK	
WRYNECK	
NIBLICK	
ROLLICK	
GIMMICK	
MIMMICK	
EARPICK	
DERRICK	
SEASICK	
DOGSICK	
AIRSICK	
FOSSICK	
BEDTICK	
SCHTICK	
PEACOCK	
HADDOCK	
PADDOCK	
PIDDOCK	
RUDDOCK	
BURDOCK	
PADLOCK	
WEDLOCK	
SCHLOCK	
HILLOCK	
ROLLOCK	
BULLOCK	
HEMLOCK	
CARLOCK	
FETLOCK	
ROWLOCK	

CALMUCK	LYRICAL	ARSENAL	CAPITAL	TUMBREL
KALMUCK	VESICAL	ORDINAL	MARITAL	MANDREL
UNSTUCK	MUSICAL	VAGINAL	OMENTAL	MONGREL
BEATNIK	OPTICAL	SEMINAL	TRENTAL	QUARREL
SPUTNIK	LEXICAL	NOMINAL	QUINTAL	POITREL
OUTTALK	TOXICAL	RETINAL	FRONTAL	KESTREL
OUTWALK	DECADAL	CORONAL	PIVOTAL	COSTREL
SUFFOLK	OVOIDAL	ETERNAL	CRYPTAL	HANDSEL
NORFOLK	APSIDAL	STERNAL	COASTAL	COUNSEL
BETHINK	COTIDAL	DIURNAL	CRYSTAL	CHESSEL
RETHINK	SCANDAL	JOURNAL	GLOTTAL	TRESSEL
DISLINK	SYNODAL	ECTYPAL	GRADUAL	SCISSEL
BLESBOK	PALUDAL	LIBERAL	SUBDUAL	PRESTEL
BANGKOK	CONCEAL	FEDERAL	LINGUAL	CHATTEL
LOGBOOK	UNIDEAL	SPHERAL	UNEQUAL	CARAVEL
DAYBOOK	CONGEAL	HUMERAL	COEQUAL	UNRAVEL
WETLOOK	OATMEAL	NUMERAL	RORQUAL	SHRIVEL
OUTLOOK	SURREAL	GENERAL	SENSUAL	EMBOWEL
SCHNOOK	LACTEAL	MINERAL	UNUSUAL	ABIGAIL
PARTOOK	GLUTEAL	FUNERAL	FACTUAL	ALLHAIL
TITLARK	ILLEGAL	LATERAL	TACTUAL	HOBNAIL
SKYLARK	EPOCHAL	LITERAL	VICTUAL	TRENAIL
DENMARK	PASCHAL	SEVERAL	VIRTUAL	ENGRAIL
EARMARK	BURGHAL	ENTHRAL	TEXTUAL	ENTRAIL
DISPARK	MARSHAL	ADMIRAL	ASEXUAL	WASSAIL
BULWARK	NARWHAL	RETIRAL	ARRIVAL	OUTSAIL
HAUBERK	STIBIAL	CHLORAL	ESTIVAL	BOBTAIL
BERSERK	GLACIAL	NEMORAL	REVIVAL	WAGTAIL
SELKIRK	SPACIAL	IMMORAL	REMOVAL	PIGTAIL
DYEWORK	SPECIAL	HUMORAL	RENEWAL	FANTAIL
OUTWORK	CRUCIAL	SORORAL	DECIBEL	PINTAIL
DAYWORK	PREDIAL	AURORAL	PEDICEL	CURTAIL
GASMASK	SUNDIAL	MAYORAL	CHANCEL	TRAVAIL
DISMASK	CORDIAL	CENTRAL	TIERCEL	PREVAIL
ODALISK	PALLIAL	VENTRAL	CITADEL	CODICIL
OBELISK	CRANIAL	ROSTRAL	INFIDEL	STENCIL
MOLLUSK	HERNIAL	AUSTRAL	ROUNDEL	COUNCIL
CHABOUK	DECRIAL	LUSTRAL	REMODEL	VERMEIL
VOLAPUK	UXORIAL	NEUTRAL	COWHEEL	STRIGIL
DORHAWK	PATRIAL	DEXTRAL	GENTEEL	CRABOIL
GOSHAWK	SPATIAL	PLEURAL	FINAGEL	GARBOIL
	INITIAL	FIGURAL	EVANGEL	PARBOIL
	NUPTIAL	AUGURAL	HATCHEL	TREFOIL
		NATURAL	SATCHEL	MILFOIL
------L	MARTIAL	SUTURAL	BROTHEL	TURMOIL
	PARTIAL	REVISAL	SPANIEL	DESPOIL
CUBICAL	BESTIAL	REPOSAL	STANIEL	EMBROIL
RADICAL	TRIVIAL	ABYSSAL	CARAMEL	SUBSOIL
MEDICAL	FLUVIAL	REFUSAL	TRAMMEL	TUMBRIL
MAGICAL	PLUVIAL	SPOUSAL	CALOMEL	MANDRIL
LOGICAL	EXUVIAL	AROUSAL	IMPANEL	TENDRIL
ETHICAL	ABAXIAL	PERUSAL	CHANNEL	IMPERIL
HELICAL	COAXIAL	PALATAL	FLANNEL	NOSTRIL
COMICAL	DECIMAL	EDICTAL	COLONEL	UTENSIL
DOMICAL	OPTIMAL	VEGETAL	GRAPNEL	SCISSIL
FINICAL	MAXIMAL	ORBITAL	CHARNEL	JONQUIL
CONICAL	THERMAL	CUBITAL	SCALPEL	PASQUIL
CYNICAL	MIASMAL	RECITAL	APPAREL	BEDEVIL
STOICAL	SEISMAL	DIGITAL	GAMBREL	UNCIVIL
TOPICAL	ABYSMAL	GENITAL	TIMBREL	CHERVIL
TYPICAL	DECANAL			

EYEBALL	PAINFUL	CHRISOM	PALLIUM	PYGMEAN
PINBALL	SKINFUL	TRANSOM	CADMIUM	LINNEAN
METBALL	HELPFUL	EMBOSOM	PREMIUM	PAMPEAN
MISCALL	FEARFUL	IMBOSOM	CRANIUM	PROTEAN
CATCALL	TEARFUL	UNBOSOM	URANIUM	CLACHAN
PITFALL	TACTFUL	BLOSSOM	THORIUM	ARABIAN
OUTFALL	FRETFUL	PHANTOM	YTTRIUM	LESBIAN
DEWFALL	HURTFUL	FIREARM	CAESIUM	GRECIAN
OVERALL	RESTFUL	FOREARM	ELYSIUM	IRIDIAN
INSTALL	WISTFUL	BECHARM	HOODLUM	PRIDIAN
AIRCELL	LUSTFUL	CONFIRM	PABULUM	GORDIAN
RESPELL	PLAYFUL	DIFFORM	OSCULUM	HYGEIAN
INDWELL	BRADAWL	UNIFORM	MINIMUM	RUFFIAN
INKWELL	BARNOWL	TRIFORM	MAXIMUM	BELGIAN
TWIBILL	FERNOWL	OVIFORM	ARCANUM	STYGIAN
ANTHILL		CONFORM	LADANUM	PYTHIAN
SAWMILL		PERFORM	ORGANUM	ITALIAN
DISTILL	------M	LOBWORM	STERNUM	AEOLIAN
INSTILL		LUGWORM	JEJUNUM	PERMIAN
RAGDOLL	GRANDAM	MAWWORM	FULCRUM	IRANIAN
WADMOLL	QUONDAM	SARCASM	HUMDRUM	OXONIAN
REDPOLL	SUNBEAM	FANTASM	EARDRUM	UTOPIAN
LOGROLL	AMALGAM	JUDAISM	DECORUM	DIARIAN
ALCOHOL	GINGHAM	IRICISM	TANTRUM	OVARIAN
MENTHOL	VIETNAM	FASCISM	SISTRUM	IBERIAN
VITRIOL	WOLFRAM	ATHEISM	NOSTRUM	CYPRIAN
TOMFOOL	DIAGRAM	SOPHISM	ROSTRUM	SAURIAN
BANDROL	ANAGRAM	BAALISM	LUSTRUM	ETESIAN
CONTROL	EPIGRAM	REALISM	ELYTRUM	FRISIAN
PARASOL	TRIGRAM	DUALISM	OPOSSUM	PERSIAN
CAPITOL	GROGRAM	ANIMISM	POMATUM	HESSIAN
IMPEARL	PROGRAM	ATOMISM	ERRATUM	RUSSIAN
AXOLOTL	BUCKRAM	COSMISM	STRATUM	ELYSIAN
DEEDFUL	FLOTSAM	PEONISM	SANCTUM	GENTIAN
HEEDFUL	MISDEEM	LIONISM	PINETUM	TERTIAN
NEEDFUL	REQUIEM	ZIONISM	QUANTUM	FUSTIAN
HANDFUL	PROBLEM	HEROISM	OMENTUM	CATALAN
MINDFUL	THEOREM	TOURISM	SCROTUM	ORTOLAN
BODEFUL	MICROHM	PIETISM	FRUSTUM	AMESLAN
TUNEFUL	ACCLAIM	ELITISM	HOMONYM	SANDMAN
HOPEFUL	DECLAIM	EGOTISM	SYNONYM	BONDMAN
CAREFUL	RECLAIM	BAPTISM	PARONYM	WOODMAN
DIREFUL	EXCLAIM	ATAVISM	ANTONYM	GLEEMAN
EASEFUL	INTERIM	MARXISM		FREEMAN
FATEFUL	PILGRIM	ZANYISM		PIKEMAN
HATEFUL	FOGYSIM	TORYISM	------N	FIREMAN
BASHFUL	LEGITIM	MODICUM		FOREMAN
WISHFUL	FREEDOM	SORGHUM	PELICAN	HOSEMAN
RUTHFUL	DUKEDOM	CAMBIUM	AFRICAN	CAVEMAN
PITIFUL	POPEDOM	NIOBIUM	VATICAN	HANGMAN
DUTIFUL	BOREDOM	TERBIUM	RAMADAN	BRAHMAN
PAILFUL	SERFDOM	CALCIUM	OPPIDAN	BUSHMAN
SKILFUL	KINGDOM	STADIUM	ACHAEAN	MILKMAN
TOILFUL	HALIDOM	IRIDIUM	CIRCEAN	LINKMAN
SOULFUL	EARLDOM	RHODIUM	SUBDEAN	BOOKMAN
BRIMFUL	STARDOM	BELGIUM	PANDEAN	WORKMAN
ROOMFUL	HEIRDOM	ELOGIUM	ORPHEAN	COALMAN
HARMFUL	ENVENOM	ISCHIUM	LETHEAN	MAILMAN
MOANFUL	PREDOOM	LITHIUM	UNCLEAN	BELLMAN
GAINFUL	BEDROOM	GALLIUM	CADMEAN	BILLMAN

TOLLMAN	BURTHEN	CAPTAIN	CRISPIN	CHORION
OTTOMAN	BLACKEN	CERTAIN	STEARIN	CARRION
CHAPMAN	SLACKEN	PERTAIN	CHAGRIN	ERASION
SHOPMAN	BRACKEN	CURTAIN	ASPIRIN	SUASION
ALMSMAN	CHICKEN	ABSTAIN	GELATIN	EVASION
KINSMAN	THICKEN	DISTAIN	PENGUIN	ELISION
OARSMAN	QUICKEN	SUSTAIN	BEDOUIN	MANSION
NEWSMAN	DRUNKEN	VERVAIN	PASQUIN	PENSION
DAYSMAN	BETOKEN	JACOBIN	ANGEVIN	TENSION
BOATMAN	HEARKEN	DUSTBIN	MUEZZIN	EROSION
MALTMAN	WOOLLEN	SALICIN	LINCOLN	MERSION
FOOTMAN	SWOLLEN	PALADIN	CONDEMN	VERSION
POSTMAN	FORAMEN	MUEDDIN	CONTEMN	TORSION
DUSTMAN	DURAMEN	STANDIN	BOURBON	PASSION
DECUMAN	REGIMEN	VILLEIN	SILICON	CESSION
INHUMAN	ABDOMEN	MULLEIN	LEXICON	SESSION
SHOWMAN	AGNOMEN	PHONEIN	CELADON	FISSION
SNOWMAN	ALBUMEN	THEREIN	ABANDON	MISSION
DRAYMAN	CERUMEN	WHEREIN	MYLODON	ELUSION
JURYMAN	BITUMEN	PROTEIN	GUERDON	ELATION
EPIZOAN	CHEAPEN	DRIVEIN	BOURDON	ORATION
DEADPAN	STEEPEN	GRIFFIN	SNOWDON	STATION
FIREPAN	SHARPEN	TANGHIN	PIDGEON	OVATION
DISHPAN	WHEATEN	DOLPHIN	WIDGEON	FACTION
OUTSPAN	SWEETEN	DAUPHIN	DUDGEON	PACTION
CATERAN	QUIETEN	XANTHIN	GUDGEON	TACTION
VETERAN	LIGHTEN	CANAKIN	DUNGEON	LECTION
ALCORAN	TIGHTEN	MANAKIN	BURGEON	SECTION
ALKORAN	HEARTEN	LAMBKIN	SURGEON	DICTION
SPORRAN	SMARTEN	WOLFKIN	GALLEON	FICTION
FORTRAN	SHORTEN	MANIKIN	THEREON	UNCTION
ARTISAN	CHASTEN	FINIKIN	WHEREON	COCTION
MAILVAN	GLISTEN	MINIKIN	CHIFFON	AUCTION
MALAYAN	MOISTEN	BUMPKIN	GRIFFON	SUCTION
SARACEN	FLATTEN	PUMPKIN	DECAGON	EDITION
BROADEN	SMITTEN	GHERKIN	NONAGON	COITION
GLADDEN	WRITTEN	REDSKIN	PARAGON	TUITION
TRODDEN	SHOTTEN	DOESKIN	OCTAGON	MENTION
WEALDEN	ENLIVEN	PIGSKIN	HEXAGON	EMOTION
BOUNDEN	BEDIZEN	DOGSKIN	FOURGON	CAPTION
SHEBEEN	DENIZEN	GRISKIN	POLYGON	PORTION
NANKEEN	CITIZEN	MAUDLIN	FASHION	BASTION
FIFTEEN	ARRAIGN	JAVELIN	CUSHION	CAUTION
CANTEEN	CONDIGN	RAVELIN	BILLION	FLEXION
RATTEEN	FOREIGN	MECHLIN	MILLION	FLUXION
SIXTEEN	CONSIGN	CIPOLIN	PILLION	ECHELON
BETWEEN	DISDAIN	LUPULIN	BULLION	MAMELON
STIFFEN	BARGAIN	VITAMIN	CULLION	MOUFLON
SMIDGEN	ENCHAIN	THUMMIN	MULLION	ORGANON
ENDOGEN	UNCHAIN	SUBJOIN	ANTLION	CHIGNON
ZYMOGEN	VILLAIN	CONJOIN	OPINION	LORGNON
ACROGEN	EXPLAIN	DISJOIN	REUNION	RACCOON
BEECHEN	REFRAIN	SIRLOIN	CAMPION	BRIDOON
BIRCHEN	ENGRAIN	PURLOIN	LAMPION	CARDOON
KITCHEN	INGRAIN	SURLOIN	RAMPION	BUFFOON
ROUGHEN	TERRAIN	BENZOIN	TAMPION	DRAGOON
TOUGHEN	MURRAIN	KINGPIN	POMPION	JARGOON
FRESHEN	ENTRAIN	SCULPIN	TOMPION	TYPHOON
HEATHEN	BRITAIN	SKULPIN	PUMPION	BALLOON
EARTHEN	CONTAIN	ATROPIN	CLARION	GALLOON

WALLOON	ADJOURN	AMORINO	OUTCROP	TUBULAR
MIDNOON	SOJOURN	CASSINO	EARDROP	SECULAR
LAMPOON	NOCTURN	JIGABOO	DEWDROP	JOCULAR
HARPOON	SHOTGUN	MANCHOO	CALTROP	MODULAR
MONSOON	PRONOUN	SHAMPOO	MILKSOP	NODULAR
BASSOON	FORERUN	MONTERO	TREETOP	REGULAR
PLATOON	OVERRUN	ALLEGRO	FORETOP	TEGULAR
PONTOON	WHITSUN	ELECTRO	HILLTOP	ANGULAR
CARTOON	HOEDOWN	MAESTRO	OVERTOP	JUGULAR
FESTOON	SUNDOWN	PROVISO	NONSTOP	PILULAR
EPIZOON	UNKNOWN	FURIOSO	EPICARP	TUMULAR
CRAMPON	EMBROWN	CALYPSO	ENCLASP	ANNULAR
SHIPPON	IMBROWN	THERETO	UNCLASP	ZONULAR
CALDRON	UNCROWN	WHERETO	CLOSEUP	LUNULAR
SAFFRON	WIGTOWN	MEMENTO	PUNCHUP	PAPULAR
ANDIRON		PIMENTO	CATCHUP	POPULAR
PIGIRON		TORONTO	KETCHUP	INSULAR
BARIRON	------O	ESPARTO	BREAKUP	TITULAR
ENVIRON		IMPASTO	REGROUP	GRAMMAR
NEUTRON	CURACAO	MULATTO	CHIRRUP	LAMINAR
ELYTRON	NELUMBO	ANNATTO	STIRRUP	LACUNAR
CHEVRON	THEORBO	FAGOTTO		FELSPAR
TREASON	GUANACO	ARNOTTO		SIMITAR
LIAISON	TOBACCO	RISOTTO	------R	COALTAR
STILTON	SIROCCO	RELIEVO		PLANTAR
GLUTTON	MOROCCO	RILIEVO	DRAWBAR	DOGSTAR
HALCYON	PORTICO	MESTIZO	CROWBAR	DAYSTAR
HORIZON	MORISCO	SCHERZO	SIDECAR	SAMOVAR
UNLEARN	AVOCADO		AUTOCAR	POSTWAR
CONCERN	TORNADO		JEMADAR	BLABBER
DISCERN	CRUSADO	------P	CHEDDAR	SLABBER
CITHERN	BRAVADO		JEMIDAR	GRABBER
ZITHERN	TORPEDO	KNEECAP	CUDBEAR	STABBER
LECTERN	UNDERDO	BLUECAP	BUGBEAR	SWABBER
SALTERN	LUMBAGO	OVERLAP	FORBEAR	CLOBBER
LANTERN	CHICAGO	GENIPAP	ANTBEAR	SLOBBER
EASTERN	FARRAGO	BARKEEP	UNCLEAR	BLUBBER
PASTERN	SERPIGO	DEMIREP	NUCLEAR	SLUBBER
WESTERN	PORRIGO	OUTSTEP	SCHMEAR	GRUBBER
CISTERN	PRURIGO	MIDSHIP	BESMEAR	IMBIBER
POSTERN	LENTIGO	GODSHIP	DOGSEAR	CHAMBER
PATTERN	VERTIGO	SONSHIP	OUTWEAR	CLAMBER
BITTERN	HIDALGO	WARSHIP	INSOFAR	CLIMBER
GITTERN	EMBARGO	WORSHIP	VINEGAR	PLUMBER
SILVERN	BOTARGO	HARELIP	REALGAR	SLUMBER
NEWBORN	UNDERGO	EGGFLIP	TUTELAR	OCTOBER
UNICORN	FERRUGO	COWSLIP	BURGLAR	FLEECER
POPCORN	ROSOLIO	PARSNIP	BIFILAR	OFFICER
COEHORN	ANTONIO	EGOTRIP	SIMILAR	ENTICER
LEGHORN	SCORPIO	GASLAMP	BASILAR	PRANCER
BIGHORN	ONTARIO	AIRPUMP	STELLAR	SPENCER
FOGHORN	BEEFALO	MUGWUMP	AXILLAR	BOUNCER
INKHORN	BUFFALO	BELLHOP	AREOLAR	PIERCER
TINHORN	PICCOLO	TOYSHOP	SCHOLAR	ADDUCER
UNSHORN	TREMOLO	DEVELOP	DIPOLAR	REDUCER
FORLORN	PROXIMO	ENVELOP	TEMPLAR	SEDUCER
UNSWORN	CHICANO	SCALLOP	PABULAR	INDUCER
WAYWORN	VOLCANO	SHALLOP	TABULAR	PLEADER
MOWBURN	SOPRANO	SCOLLOP	NEBULAR	TREADER
COTHURN	PIANINO	TROLLOP	LOBULAR	INVADER

BLADDER	STAGGER	SLITHER	TRICKER	JUGGLER
SHEDDER	SWAGGER	PANTHER	STICKER	DANGLER
PLODDER	SNIGGER	SMOTHER	KNOCKER	MANGLER
SCUDDER	TRIGGER	ANOTHER	PLUCKER	BUNGLER
SHUDDER	PLUGGER	SOOTHER	TRUCKER	TRAILER
SECEDER	ARMIGER	BROTHER	STRIKER	DEFILER
BREEDER	CHANGER	FARTHER	STALKER	SPOILER
DECIDER	AVENGER	FURTHER	SKULKER	BROILER
BROIDER	SLINGER	MURTHER	FLANKER	REVILER
DERIDER	BRINGER	MOUTHER	SPANKER	CACKLER
INSIDER	CRINGER	GAMBIER	THINKER	HACKLER
DIVIDER	WRINGER	GLACIER	BLINKER	HECKLER
FIELDER	SWINGER	FANCIER	CLINKER	TICKLER
WIELDER	SPONGER	SOLDIER	DRINKER	BUCKLER
BRANDER	WRONGER	STUDIER	STINKER	SMELLER
STANDER	PLUNGER	CASHIER	CLUNKER	SPELLER
BLENDER	LOUNGER	ATELIER	YOUNKER	QUELLER
SLENDER	CHARGER	DALLIER	SNOOKER	DWELLER
AMENDER	REACHER	COLLIER	STROKER	THILLER
SPENDER	TEACHER	REPLIER	SHIRKER	SPILLER
BLINDER	POACHER	OUTLIER	WHISKER	STILLER
GRINDER	FILCHER	PREMIER	REBUKER	SWILLER
MAUNDER	RANCHER	PANNIER	STEALER	TROLLER
THUNDER	BENCHER	VERNIER	INHALER	SCULLER
BLUNDER	WENCHER	DECRIER	STABLER	CRULLER
PLUNDER	PINCHER	BARRIER	BABBLER	CAJOLER
FOUNDER	MUNCHER	CARRIER	DABBLER	STAPLER
POUNDER	PUNCHER	FARRIER	GABBLER	SAMPLER
ROUNDER	PERCHER	HARRIER	DIBBLER	TIPPLER
WOUNDER	LURCHER	TERRIER	NIBBLER	COUPLER
ASUNDER	CATCHER	WORRIER	COBBLER	SNARLER
BOARDER	HATCHER	CURRIER	GOBBLER	WHIRLER
HOARDER	PATCHER	FURRIER	GAMBLER	PANTLER
DELUDER	WATCHER	COURIER	RAMBLER	HOSTLER
CHOWDER	DITCHER	BRASIER	FUMBLER	BUSTLER
WHENEER	PITCHER	CROSIER	MUMBLER	HUSTLER
PIONEER	BOTCHER	SALTIER	TUMBLER	TATTLER
COMPEER	BUTCHER	RENTIER	GARBLER	SETTLER
WHEREER	BLUCHER	EMPTIER	WARBLER	BRAWLER
CHAFFER	TOUCHER	COTTIER	CIRCLER	CRAWLER
QUAFFER	VOUCHER	CLAVIER	PADDLER	TRAWLER
SCOFFER	WEIGHER	BREVIER	SADDLER	GROWLER
FEOFFER	BURGHER	GLAZIER	WADDLER	PROWLER
PROFFER	LAUGHER	BRAZIER	MEDDLER	DAZZLER
SNUFFER	COUGHER	GRAZIER	PEDDLER	PUZZLER
STUFFER	SMASHER	CROZIER	TODDLER	DREAMER
LUCIFER	FLESHER	SNEAKER	FUDDLER	STEAMER
CONIFER	FRESHER	SPEAKER	PUDDLER	SCHEMER
PORIFER	BLUSHER	BREAKER	DAWDLER	SHAMMER
ROTIFER	FLUSHER	CROAKER	WHEELER	SLAMMER
CHAMFER	CRUSHER	CLACKER	KNEELER	CRAMMER
MANAGER	FEATHER	SMACKER	SPIELER	STAMMER
TANAGER	HEATHER	KNACKER	BAFFLER	SKIMMER
FORAGER	LEATHER	CRACKER	MUFFLER	GLIMMER
RAVAGER	WEATHER	TRACKER	RUFFLER	BRIMMER
DOWAGER	LOATHER	CHECKER	TRIFLER	TRIMMER
VOYAGER	WHETHER	WRECKER	HAGGLER	SWIMMER
PLEDGER	NEITHER	CLICKER	GIGGLER	SCUMMER
DREDGER	THITHER	FLICKER	HIGGLER	DRUMMER
INTEGER	WHITHER	PRICKER	BOGGLER	CHARMER

CLEANER	DROPPER	GREATER	SUMPTER	TROTTER
GLEANER	STOPPER	TREATER	CHARTER	SHUTTER
WAKENER	SCUPPER	SWEATER	STARTER	CLUTTER
COZENER	CRUPPER	RELATER	QUARTER	FLUTTER
THINNER	SHARPER	DILATER	SNORTER	SPUTTER
SKINNER	CHIRPER	BLOATER	FEASTER	STUTTER
SPINNER	USURPER	FLOATER	SHASTER	REFUTER
STUNNER	CLASPER	DOUBTER	PIASTER	SALUTER
WAGONER	GRASPER	EXACTER	BLASTER	SHOUTER
ALMONER	WHISPER	SPECTER	PLASTER	SPOUTER
CROONER	CRISPER	ERECTER	BOASTER	IMPUTER
CORONER	PROSPER	DIMETER	COASTER	RESCUER
LEARNER	SHEARER	AMMETER	ROASTER	SUBDUER
SCORNER	CLEARER	RIVETER	TOASTER	LEAGUER
MOURNER	SWEARER	GRAFTER	FIBSTER	LACQUER
SPURNER	ORDERER	SHIFTER	LOBSTER	CHEQUER
CENTNER	CHEERER	DRIFTER	MOBSTER	CONQUER
VINTNER	FLEERER	GRIFTER	WRESTER	PURSUER
PARTNER	SNEERER	CROFTER	QUESTER	CLEAVER
SPAWNER	STEERER	YACHTER	LEISTER	PALAVER
MISDOER	OFFERER	FIGHTER	BLISTER	WHOEVER
HANAPER	WAGERER	LIGHTER	GLISTER	FOREVER
SCRAPER	ADHERER	RIGHTER	ROISTER	HOWEVER
SLEEPER	CAPERER	PLAITER	TWISTER	CALIVER
CREEPER	CATERER	ARBITER	BOLSTER	DELIVER
STEEPER	UTTERER	RECITER	HOLSTER	MINIVER
SWEEPER	WAVERER	EXCITER	HAMSTER	THRIVER
JUNIPER	REVERER	INDITER	MINSTER	STRIVER
SCALPER	ADMIRER	LIMITER	MONSTER	REVIVER
SCAMPER	DESIRER	JUPITER	PUNSTER	RECOVER
TRAMPER	TABORER	VISITER	BOOSTER	UNCOVER
STAMPER	FLOORER	INVITER	ROOSTER	REMOVER
WHIMPER	SPARRER	PSALTER	TAPSTER	FLYOVER
CRIMPER	STIRRER	SHELTER	HIPSTER	RENEWER
THUMPER	SECURER	SMELTER	BLUSTER	SCREWER
PLUMPER	INJURER	SPELTER	CLUSTER	EMBOWER
STUMPER	SCOURER	SWELTER	FLUSTER	IMBOWER
SCOOPER	INSURER	PHILTER	TRUSTER	WIDOWER
BLOOPER	ASSURER	VAULTER	SHYSTER	ENDOWER
TROOPER	PLEASER	COULTER	CLYSTER	EMPOWER
CLAPPER	GREASER	CHANTER	SCATTER	THROWER
FLAPPER	PRAISER	PLANTER	CHATTER	INDEXER
SNAPPER	BRUISER	GRANTER	SHATTER	DELAYER
TRAPPER	CRUISER	PAINTER	CLATTER	INLAYER
WRAPPER	ADVISER	REINTER	FLATTER	FORAYER
STEPPER	DEVISER	POINTER	PLATTER	STRAYER
CHIPPER	REVISER	PRINTER	SMATTER	ASSAYER
SHIPPER	CHOOSER	STINTER	SPATTER	ESSAYER
WHIPPER	OPPOSER	HAUNTER	WHETTER	METAYER
SKIPPER	EXPOSER	SAUNTER	FLITTER	MONEYER
CLIPPER	COURSER	TAUNTER	GLITTER	ENJOYER
FLIPPER	DRESSER	VAUNTER	SLITTER	CALOYER
SLIPPER	GUESSER	COUNTER	KNITTER	FREEZER
SNIPPER	GLOSSER	GRUNTER	SPITTER	MATADOR
GRIPPER	ACCUSER	SCOOTER	CRITTER	HUMIDOR
TRIPPER	REFUSER	SHOOTER	FRITTER	FEOFFOR
CHOPPER	PERUSER	ADAPTER	QUITTER	OBLIGOR
SHOPPER	DEBATER	CHAPTER	TWITTER	CAMPHOR
WHOPPER	CHEATER	SCEPTER	BLOTTER	SIGNIOR
CROPPER	THEATER	TEMPTER	PLOTTER	WARRIOR

ANNULUS	GRUMOUS	RETREAT	SHERBET	EPAULET
CALAMUS	CHYMOUS	ENTREAT	DECREET	ANNULET
ISTHMUS	HEINOUS	ESTREAT	REGREET	ZONULET
VIDIMUS	OMINOUS	HARDHAT	PLEDGET	RIVULET
TRISMUS	SPINOUS	HIGHHAT	DRUGGET	PLUMMET
BALANUS	RUINOUS	RUNFLAT	MANCHET	GOURMET
TETANUS	POMPOUS	AUTOMAT	CROCHET	CALUMET
ECHINUS	FIBROUS	BUMBOAT	HATCHET	ALKANET
ALUMNUS	HYDROUS	ROWBOAT	LATCHET	DRAGNET
GIBBOUS	ACEROUS	REDCOAT	RATCHET	CABINET
GLEBOUS	ONEROUS	SURCOAT	FITCHET	SATINET
BULBOUS	ODOROUS	QUADRAT	PROPHET	JACONET
GLOBOUS	AMOROUS	MUSKRAT	FRESHET	BARONET
OPACOUS	LEPROUS	HABITAT	EPITHET	CORONET
TALCOUS	CUPROUS	REDOUBT	UNQUIET	BAYONET
ZINCOUS	FERROUS	COMPACT	PLACKET	CLAPNET
SARCOUS	PETROUS	OVERACT	BRACKET	HAIRNET
VISCOUS	NITROUS	REFRACT	THICKET	PARAPET
FUSCOUS	ANUROUS	DETRACT	CRICKET	CRUMPET
RAUCOUS	ACETOUS	RETRACT	PRICKET	TRUMPET
PICEOUS	RIOTOUS	ATTRACT	BROCKET	SNIPPET
HIDEOUS	VACUOUS	EXTRACT	CROCKET	CABARET
ATHEOUS	ARDUOUS	CONTACT	BLANKET	TABARET
TIMEOUS	TENUOUS	INEXACT	TRINKET	MINARET
IGNEOUS	SINUOUS	PANDECT	BRISKET	LAZARET
CEREOUS	FATUOUS	PREFECT	FRISKET	LEVERET
CASEOUS	FULVOUS	CONFECT	MEDALET	SKIRRET
GASEOUS	NERVOUS	PERFECT	DRIBLET	FLEURET
OSSEOUS	GRAMPUS	SUBJECT	DOUBLET	ENGRAFT
PITEOUS	OCTOPUS	PROJECT	CIRCLET	REDIGHT
DUTEOUS	POLYPUS	DIALECT	RUNDLET	SLEIGHT
AQUEOUS	HUMERUS	PRELECT	LOBELET	FREIGHT
NIVEOUS	PYLORUS	DEFLECT	LAKELET	DELIGHT
FUNGOUS	OESTRUS	REFLECT	OSSELET	RELIGHT
AZYGOUS	SILURUS	INFLECT	WAVELET	BENIGHT
TYPHOUS	PAPYRUS	NEGLECT	DOVELET	TONIGHT
DUBIOUS	THYRSUS	COLLECT	LEAFLET	SPRIGHT
VICIOUS	STRATUS	CONNECT	KINGLET	UPRIGHT
TEDIOUS	SANCTUS	RESPECT	RINGLET	INSIGHT
BILIOUS	QUIETUS	INSPECT	WINGLET	UPTIGHT
SIMIOUS	BOLETUS	SUSPECT	NECKLET	DRAUGHT
IMPIOUS	IMPETUS	CORRECT	BOOKLET	FRAUGHT
COPIOUS	ARBUTUS	TRISECT	SKILLET	THOUGHT
CARIOUS	GALLOWS	DISSECT	HORNLET	BROUGHT
VARIOUS	BELLOWS	PROTECT	CACOLET	DROUGHT
SERIOUS	CHLAMYS	PREDICT	TRIOLET	WROUGHT
CURIOUS		VERDICT	CHAPLET	INHABIT
FURIOUS		AFFLICT	TRIPLET	COHABIT
OBVIOUS	------T	INFLICT	TEMPLET	RAREBIT
DEVIOUS		ASTRICT	DROPLET	ADHIBIT
ENVIOUS	DINGBAT	CONVICT	COUPLET	INHIBIT
ANXIOUS	ACROBAT	EXTINCT	SCARLET	COHIBIT
NOXIOUS	WILDCAT	DEFUNCT	STERLET	EXHIBIT
JEALOUS	POLECAT	ADJUNCT	CANTLET	DEFICIT
ZEALOUS	BUSHCAT	CONCOCT	GANTLET	ILLICIT
CALLOUS	COPYCAT	VIADUCT	MANTLET	SOLICIT
VILLOUS	ESCHEAT	SUBDUCT	ROOTLET	PLAUDIT
EMULOUS	THEREAT	OVIDUCT	MARTLET	HOWBEIT
GUMMOUS	WHEREAT	CONDUCT	PARTLET	CONCEIT
PLUMOUS	OVEREAT	PRODUCT	FORTLET	FORFEIT

SURFEIT	OPERANT	GARMENT	WHATNOT	ARBLAST
BENEFIT	VAGRANT	FERMENT	ICEFOOT	BALLAST
MOONLIT	REGRANT	TORMENT	BIGFOOT	OUTLAST
STARLIT	MIGRANT	FITMENT	CHEROOT	TOPMAST
READMIT	SPIRANT	BUTMENT	DISROOT	DURMAST
MANUMIT	WARRANT	PAYMENT	OUTROOT	DISMAST
EXPLOIT	CURRANT	EMINENT	FIREPOT	GYMNAST
DETROIT	ENTRANT	SERPENT	DASHPOT	GABFEST
INTROIT	INTRANT	UNSPENT	GALIPOT	CONFEST
COCKPIT	PEASANT	HORRENT	TALIPOT	SUGGEST
COALPIT	VERSANT	TORRENT	JACKPOT	CONGEST
CLAYPIT	PASSANT	CURRENT	SUNSPOT	UNBLEST
INHERIT	BLATANT	PRESENT	TOSSPOT	EARNEST
DEMERIT	IMITANT	CONSENT	PIERROT	ANAPEST
CULPRIT	SALTANT	DISSENT	DOGTROT	SOPHIST
REVISIT	DISTANT	CONTENT	FOXTROT	REALIST
TRANSIT	INSTANT	PORTENT	PALETOT	DIALIST
DEPOSIT	SEXTANT	UNGUENT	ALIQUOT	DUALIST
REPOSIT	PIQUANT	DILUENT	PERIAPT	CYCLIST
CIRCUIT	SERVANT	SEQUENT	PRECEPT	VIOLIST
BISCUIT	BUOYANT	PREVENT	CONCEPT	CARLIST
CONDUIT	LAMBENT	SOLVENT	UNSWEPT	OCULIST
RECRUIT	NASCENT	RECEIPT	UNKEMPT	STYLIST
NONSUIT	DESCENT	FERVENT	ATTEMPT	CHEMIST
PURSUIT	CREDENT	REPAINT	ACCOMPT	ANIMIST
LAWSUIT	TRIDENT	ATTAINT	EXCERPT	ATOMIST
CHEEZIT	EVIDENT	CATMINT	CORRUPT	PIANIST
ASPHALT	CANDENT	APPOINT	DISRUPT	AGONIST
BAYSALT	PENDENT	REPRINT	DOGCART	ZIONIST
ELFBOLT	ERODENT	IMPRINT	FOUMART	FAUNIST
DEFAULT	PRUDENT	ASQUINT	RAMPART	SOLOIST
ASSAULT	STUDENT	VERMONT	COMPART	TROPIST
CONSULT	REAGENT	AFFRONT	DISPART	HARPIST
PECCANT	COAGENT	UNBURNT	UPSTART	DIARIST
DESCANT	EXIGENT	ROMAUNT	ATHWART	SACRIST
PENDANT	FULGENT	FOXHUNT	FILBERT	QUERIST
GARDANT	TANGENT	ACCOUNT	CONCERT	CHORIST
VERDANT	RINGENT	RECOUNT	CONVERT	FLORIST
MORDANT	PUNGENT	REMOUNT	DESSERT	TOURIST
PAGEANT	TURGENT	DOVECOT	SUBVERT	SUBSIST
ELEGANT	AMBIENT	HARICOT	CULVERT	CONSIST
ENCHANT	ANCIENT	APRICOT	CONVERT	PERSIST
RADIANT	SALIENT	UNBEGOT	PERVERT	STATIST
DEFIANT	LENIENT	MANIHOT	COMFORT	DIETIST
VALIANT	SAPIENT	EYESHOT	COMPORT	PIETIST
RELIANT	PATIENT	MUGSHOT	RAPPORT	ELITIST
VARIANT	MIDLENT	GUNSHOT	SUPPORT	DENTIST
GALLANT	VIOLENT	EARSHOT	PURPORT	EGOTIST
REPLANT	OPULENT	BOWSHOT	DISPORT	BAPTIST
IMPLANT	ODDMENT	GALLIOT	CONSORT	FLUTIST
ADAMANT	CLEMENT	CHARIOT	CONTORT	FUGUIST
CLAMANT	ELEMENT	PATRIOT	BISTORT	CASUIST
DORMANT	SEGMENT	CHEVIOT	DISTORT	ENTWIST
EMANANT	FIGMENT	SANDLOT	RAGWORT	INTWIST
REGNANT	PIGMENT	MELILOT	MUGWORT	UNTWIST
REMNANT	AUGMENT	COPILOT	YOGHURT	COEXIST
PENNANT	RAIMENT	SHALLOT	BOMBAST	MARXIST
RAMPANT	ALIMENT	COMPLOT	OUTCAST	COPYIST
VIBRANT	AILMENT	MARPLOT	ABREAST	AGAINST
HYDRANT	COMMENT	FILEMOT	BELFAST	ALECOST

MIDMOST	MARABOU	FIREBOX	PRIMACY	MUMMIFY
TOPMOST	SAPAJOU	FUSEBOX	TESTACY	CHYMIFY
FARMOST	MANITOU	MAILBOX	PRIVACY	MAGNIFY
OUTMOST	BEBEERU	PILLBOX	SECRECY	DIGNIFY
BEDPOST		GEARBOX	VACANCY	LIGNIFY
COMPOST		PARADOX	INFANCY	SIGNIFY
OUTPOST	------W	EQUINOX	PLIANCY	DAMNIFY
DEFROST		CONFLUX	TENANCY	SCARIFY
PROVOST	JACKDAW	APTERYX	TRUANCY	CLARIFY
ATHIRST	CUMSHAW		DECENCY	SCORIFY
EXHAUST	LOCKJAW		RECENCY	GLORIFY
SAWDUST	CLUBLAW	------Y	LUCENCY	TERRIFY
DISGUST	DEWCLAW		ARDENCY	HORRIFY
ENCRUST	CORNLAW	SICKBAY	PUDENCY	PETRIFY
INCRUST	CATSPAW	FARADAY	REGENCY	NITRIFY
ENTRUST	BANDSAW	GOODDAY	COGENCY	VITRIFY
OTOCYST	HACKSAW	HOLIDAY	URGENCY	FALSIFY
ANALYST	BUCKSAW	WEEKDAY	VALENCY	SALSIFY
BABBITT	FITCHEW	NOONDAY	LATENCY	VERSIFY
BOYCOTT	PREVIEW	TUESDAY	POTENCY	BEATIFY
HALIBUT	PURVIEW	FASTDAY	FLUENCY	GRATIFY
HOLIBUT	FIRENEW	NOSEGAY	IDIOTCY	RECTIFY
HACKBUT	BRANNEW	VIRELAY	THREADY	ACETIFY
SACKBUT	UNSCREW	DISPLAY	ALREADY	CERTIFY
HAIRCUT	RENFREW	OVERLAY	UNREADY	FORTIFY
COCONUT	BESHREW	DEADPAY	SHREDDY	MORTIFY
READOUT	BESTREW	OVERPAY	TRAGEDY	TESTIFY
WITHOUT	RAINBOW	PORTRAY	PERFIDY	JUSTIFY
LOCKOUT	GLASGOW	GAINSAY	SUBSIDY	MYSTIFY
COOKOUT	SOMEHOW	HEARSAY	UNHANDY	BRUTIFY
LOOKOUT	KNOWHOW	OUTSTAY	ANYBODY	SATISFY
WORKOUT	OUTFLOW	URUGUAY	HYMNODY	SCRAGGY
FALLOUT	SHALLOW	RUNAWAY	PROSODY	SPRIGGY
SELLOUT	SWALLOW	CARAWAY	CUSTODY	PRODIGY
WORNOUT	WHITLOW	FARAWAY	UNHARDY	SPRINGY
TURNOUT	EYEBROW	CUTAWAY	DISOBEY	STRINGY
EELPOUT	WINDROW	FLYAWAY	TURNKEY	ANALOGY
SURTOUT	OUTGROW	HEADWAY	FLUNKEY	TRILOGY
BLOWOUT	UPTHROW	ROADWAY	WHISKEY	GEOLOGY
OCCIPUT	SPARROW	FREEWAY	TROLLEY	NEOLOGY
CAJUPUT	DISAVOW	GATEWAY	PARSLEY	BIOLOGY
PRETEXT		GANGWAY	HACKNEY	NOOLOGY
CONTEXT		ARCHWAY	COCKNEY	ZOOLOGY
BETWIXT	------X	HIGHWAY	CHIMNEY	APOLOGY
		PATHWAY	SPINNEY	OROLOGY
	ANTHRAX	RAILWAY	BALONEY	OTOLOGY
------U	OVERTAX	TRAMWAY	SPOONEY	MYOLOGY
	BEESWAX	DOORWAY	BLARNEY	DYSLOGY
MORCEAU	NARTHEX	FOOTWAY	JOURNEY	ALLERGY
BANDEAU	COMPLEX	CARTWAY	TOURNEY	THEURGY
RONDEAU	PERPLEX	WALLABY	CHUTNEY	ZYMURGY
TABLEAU	PERSPEX	LULLABY	PALFREY	LITURGY
ROULEAU	POSTFIX	SQUABBY	COMFREY	BRANCHY
CHATEAU	PHOENIX	SCRUBBY	LAMPREY	PAUNCHY
PLATEAU	PHALANX	SHRUBBY	WHIMSEY	RAUNCHY
FABLIAU	PHARYNX	STANDBY	MALMSEY	CRUNCHY
CAMAIEU	BANDBOX	THEREBY	ODYSSEY	DIARCHY
PURLIEU	SANDBOX	WHEREBY	CURTSEY	ANARCHY
CATECHU	DICEBOX	PRELACY	SPRAYEY	EPARCHY
PARVENU	JUKEBOX	FALLACY	AMPLIFY	STARCHY

SKETCHY	SOUNDLY	NEEDILY	SLEEKLY	UNFITLY
BLOTCHY	UNGODLY	SEEDILY	BLANKLY	SCANTLY
SLOUGHY	THIRDLY	HANDILY	FRANKLY	GIANTLY
ATROPHY	PROUDLY	HARDILY	WRINKLY	SLANTLY
SPLASHY	CRUDELY	TARDILY	STARKLY	FAINTLY
SQUASHY	LARGELY	WORDILY	CLERKLY	SAINTLY
SHEATHY	AGILELY	GAUDILY	BRISKLY	JOINTLY
WREATHY	PRIMELY	FOGGILY	LOCALLY	GAUNTLY
LENGTHY	PRONELY	PITHILY	VOCALLY	BLUNTLY
HEALTHY	SHAPELY	LUCKILY	DUCALLY	INEPTLY
WEALTHY	SPARELY	SULKILY	MODALLY	SMARTLY
SWARTHY	FALSELY	SMOKILY	IDEALLY	INERTLY
DROUTHY	DENSELY	MURKILY	LEGALLY	OVERTLY
STREAKY	TENSELY	DUSKILY	REGALLY	SHORTLY
COLICKY	CLOSELY	HUSKILY	AXIALLY	COURTLY
FINICKY	LOOSELY	GODLILY	PENALLY	BEASTLY
UNLUCKY	TERSELY	SILLILY	FINALLY	GHASTLY
ANOMALY	STATELY	JOLLILY	PAPALLY	THISTLY
AFFABLY	TRITELY	SURLILY	MORALLY	BRISTLY
PLIABLY	ACUTELY	DAYLILY	RURALLY	GRISTLY
AMIABLY	VAGUELY	GRIMILY	NASALLY	GHOSTLY
TUNABLY	BRAVELY	ROOMILY	FATALLY	FIRSTLY
DURABLY	GRAVELY	FUNNILY	VITALLY	STOUTLY
RATABLY	SUAVELY	STONILY	TOTALLY	UNTRULY
NOTABLY	NAIVELY	HAPPILY	EQUALLY	DRIZZLY
MUTABLY	CHIEFLY	WEARILY	SQUALLY	FRIZZLY
EQUABLY	BRIEFLY	CHARILY	USUALLY	GRIZZLY
MOVABLY	FIREFLY	FIERILY	LOYALLY	STREAMY
KNOBBLY	STIFFLY	ANGRILY	ROYALLY	TRIGAMY
STUBBLY	GRUFFLY	FAIRILY	CRUELLY	ZOOGAMY
AUDIBLY	BOATFLY	MERRILY	HAZELLY	EXOGAMY
LEGIBLY	BLOWFLY	SORRILY	SHRILLY	ACADEMY
VISIBLY	SPANGLY	NOISILY	CIVILLY	ALCHEMY
BRAMBLY	SHINGLY	TIPSILY	WOFULLY	THRUMMY
CRUMBLY	DYINGLY	FUSSILY	AWFULLY	ECONOMY
IGNOBLY	LYINGLY	LOFTILY	CLEANLY	ZOONOMY
VOLUBLY	WRONGLY	DIRTILY	UNMANLY	ISONOMY
BROADLY	YOUNGLY	HASTILY	WOMANLY	ANATOMY
TWADDLY	ROUGHLY	NASTILY	HUMANLY	ZOOTOMY
FADEDLY	TOUGHLY	TASTILY	GREENLY	TIFFANY
NAKEDLY	FLESHLY	TESTILY	QUEENLY	TAMMANY
FIXEDLY	FRESHLY	MISTILY	VIXENLY	ROMMANY
MIXEDLY	APISHLY	LUSTILY	PLAINLY	GERMANY
STAIDLY	HARSHLY	RUSTILY	CROSSLY	COMPANY
RABIDLY	DEATHLY	NATTILY	GROSSLY	DITTANY
LUCIDLY	LOATHLY	PETTILY	PIOUSLY	LARCENY
RIGIDLY	FIFTHLY	WITTILY	GREATLY	SPLEENY
VALIDLY	TENTHLY	HEAVILY	EXACTLY	GEOGENY
GELIDLY	NINTHLY	WEEVILY	ERECTLY	BIOGENY
SOLIDLY	MONTHLY	PRIVILY	FLEETLY	ZOOGENY
TIMIDLY	EARTHLY	SHOWILY	SWEETLY	PROGENY
HUMIDLY	SIXTHLY	CRAZILY	QUIETLY	DESTINY
TUMIDLY	SPICILY	DIZZILY	SWIFTLY	CALUMNY
RAPIDLY	SAUCILY	BLEAKLY	LIGHTLY	UNCANNY
VAPIDLY	HEADILY	BLACKLY	NIGHTLY	TYRANNY
VIVIDLY	READILY	SLACKLY	RIGHTLY	BALCONY
WORLDLY	SHADILY	FRECKLY	SIGHTLY	GEOGONY
GRANDLY	GIDDILY	THICKLY	TIGHTLY	ZOOGONY
BLINDLY	MUDDILY	PRICKLY	TACITLY	EUPHONY
ROUNDLY	RUDDILY	QUICKLY	LICITLY	ALIMONY

VOLCANIC	RHETORIC	ADAMITIC	DRUMHEAD
MANGANIC	HISTORIC	EREMITIC	SKINHEAD
MECHANIC	THEATRIC	PALMITIC	OVERHEAD
SHAMANIC	ELECTRIC	GRANITIC	HOGSHEAD
GERMANIC	DIOPTRIC	LIGNITIC	BOLTHEAD
TYMPANIC	MERCURIC	ACONITIC	JOLTHEAD
SULTANIC	TELLURIC	JESUITIC	SOWBREAD
GALVANIC	GEODESIC	COBALTIC	UNTHREAD
PYOGENIC	PHTHISIC	BASALTIC	WELLREAD
ASTHENIC	FORENSIC	PEDANTIC	BESPREAD
HYGIENIC	TRIASSIC	GIGANTIC	BEDSTEAD
HELLENIC	JURASSIC	ATLANTIC	VOLSTEAD
ECUMENIC	POTASSIC	ROMANTIC	JEREMIAD
RABBINIC	SABBATIC	NARCOTIC	OLYMPIAD
SUCCINIC	EMPHATIC	EPULOTIC	VINECLAD
FULMINIC	MURIATIC	HYPNOTIC	FREELOAD
ENCRINIC	PRELATIC	ENZOOTIC	DECKLOAD
TYRANNIC	DRAMATIC	DESPOTIC	OVERLOAD
CARBONIC	HAEMATIC	NEUROTIC	CARTLOAD
DRACONIC	THEMATIC	QUIXOTIC	HIGHROAD
SARDONIC	SIGMATIC	EUPEPTIC	RAILROAD
ISOGONIC	DOGMATIC	ECLIPTIC	TRAMROAD
SIPHONIC	CLIMATIC	ELLIPTIC	TIGHTWAD
EUPHONIC	DALMATIC	SYNOPTIC	SUPERADD
PYTHONIC	AROMATIC	MONASTIC	CHILDBED
CYCLONIC	STOMATIC	DYNASTIC	DEATHBED
MNEMONIC	DERMATIC	MAJESTIC	TWOFACED
PULMONIC	SOCRATIC	DOMESTIC	UNPLACED
GNOMONIC	HIERATIC	AGRESTIC	UNVOICED
HARMONIC	OPERATIC	TUNGSTIC	BROCADED
GEOPONIC	ECSTATIC	SADISTIC	DEGRADED
SUBSONIC	DIDACTIC	THEISTIC	UNHEEDED
DIATONIC	GALACTIC	LOGISTIC	LOPSIDED
PLATONIC	ECLECTIC	MONISTIC	PROVIDED
SUBTONIC	NEARCTIC	EGOISTIC	INTENDED
TECTONIC	DIABETIC	PAPISTIC	UNFUNDED
TEUTONIC	GEODETIC	PORISTIC	SECLUDED
PLUTONIC	EXEGETIC	JURISTIC	SHROUDED
SLAVONIC	JAPHETIC	ARTISTIC	ALMSDEED
EPIPLOIC	PATHETIC	AGNOSTIC	COLESEED
DICHROIC	ESTHETIC	ACROSTIC	FERNSEED
MESOZOIC	ATHLETIC	THROSTIC	BINDWEED
ENTOZOIC	PHYLETIC	ACOUSTIC	DUCKWEED
ETHIOPIC	HERMETIC	MAIEUTIC	LOCOWEED
CYCLOPIC	COSMETIC	TOREUTIC	GOUTWEED
HYDROPIC	FRENETIC	ANALYTIC	TWOEDGED
BARBARIC	MAGNETIC	ORICHALC	SCRAGGED
PINDARIC	PHONETIC	QUIDNUNC	SPRIGGED
TARTARIC	UNPOETIC		UNHANGED
CHOLERIC	HERPETIC		DERANGED
ISOMERIC	DIURETIC	-------D	STRINGED
TURMERIC	APYRETIC		UNTINGED
MESMERIC	DIETETIC	GRANDDAD	ENLARGED
NEOTERIC	EROTETIC	TRINIDAD	ENGORGED
ESOTERIC	HELVETIC	DEADHEAD	DETACHED
EXOTERIC	SINAITIC	FOREHEAD	BREECHED
HYSTERIC	RACHITIC	SOREHEAD	BRANCHED
PODAGRIC	MEPHITIC	BULKHEAD	STARCHED
METEORIC	ENCLITIC	LUNKHEAD	WRETCHED
ENCHORIC	ZEOLITIC	BULLHEAD	CROTCHED

CRUTCHED	STAMENED	MEASURED	INSERTED
UNWASHED	UNOPENED	LEISURED	EXSERTED
POLISHED	RESIGNED	TONSURED	INVERTED
SHEATHED	STRAINED	FEATURED	ASSORTED
UNPATHED	COMBINED	CULTURED	BREASTED
BRANDIED	MARGINED	RAPTURED	UNTASTED
RAREFIED	BUSKINED	VESTURED	BESOTTED
TROPHIED	INCLINED	DECEASED	CORNUTED
UNALLIED	SPAVINED	DISEASED	UNVALUED
CRANNIED	COLUMNED	UNBIASED	DEPRAVED
CANOPIED	GABIONED	LICENSED	DEPRIVED
SALARIED	WEAPONED	COMPOSED	RESOLVED
UNVARIED	SEASONED	UNVERSED	UNPROVED
LIVERIED	UNATONED	ACCURSED	RESERVED
UNBURIED	BLAZONED	RECESSED	WINDOWED
DROPSIED	UNEARNED	EMBOSSED	PILLOWED
UNPITIED	CAVERNED	CONFUSED	UNAVOWED
UNENVIED	UNBURNED	PERTUSED	REFLEXED
FRENZIED	RENOWNED	UNABATED	INFLEXED
UNSLAKED	FRESCOED	GLOBATED	WOOLDYED
UNPACKED	MILLEPED	PLICATED	WALLEYED
UNDECKED	MILLIPED	FALCATED	UNGLAZED
UNCOOKED	PALMIPED	SULCATED	DEEPLAID
UNSEALED	PLUMIPED	FURCATED	HANDMAID
STUBBLED	PINNIPED	GALEATED	BONDMAID
TROUBLED	MULTIPED	PILEATED	MILKMAID
PANICLED	UNWARPED	LINEATED	UNREPAID
BRINDLED	DOGEARED	CILIATED	POSTPAID
TRAVELED	DECLARED	FOLIATED	FORESAID
TRUFFLED	NECTARED	STRIATED	FIRSTAID
SPANGLED	TRUEBRED	INFLATED	UNBERBID
SHINGLED	WELLBRED	OCULATED	PELLUCID
DETAILED	BLOODRED	ANIMATED	UNCANDID
UNSOILED	MEMBERED	PALMATED	SPLENDID
WEEVILED	TIMBERED	PINNATED	MULTIFID
SPECKLED	DODDERED	SERRATED	COVERLID
FRECKLED	POWDERED	IRISATED	RHOMBOID
WRINKLED	COFFERED	AGITATED	CORACOID
UNCALLED	FINGERED	SITUATED	HELICOID
SOCALLED	WICKERED	INDEBTED	CALYCOID
METALLED	TUCKERED	AFFECTED	CONCHOID
LAPELLED	ANTLERED	DEJECTED	TROCHOID
VOWELLED	BANNERED	EXPECTED	SCAPHOID
SCROLLED	MANNERED	TARGETED	TAENIOID
PETIOLED	CORNERED	JACKETED	ALKALOID
STEEPLED	TEMPERED	HELMETED	SEPALOID
CRUMPLED	TATTERED	SIGNETED	PETALOID
UNTITLED	LETTERED	BONNETED	PHYLLOID
BRISTLED	BEAVERED	LAPPETED	COTYLOID
GRIZZLED	QUIVERED	TURRETED	SESAMOID
DIADEMED	CLOVERED	UNSIFTED	PRISMOID
BOTTOMED	FLOWERED	INEDITED	PARANOID
UNHARMED	GASFIRED	SPIRITED	SPHENOID
DEFORMED	INSPIRED	UNSUITED	CORONOID
REFORMED	VERDURED	UNBOLTED	CANCROID
UNFORMED	LABOURED	UNWANTED	DENDROID
COSTUMED	ARBOURED	INDENTED	SPHEROID
TURBANED	COLOURED	ORIENTED	ASTEROID
HARDENED	UNSOURED	DEMENTED	PITYROID
LICHENED	FAVOURED	DEPARTED	NEMATOID

SUCHLIKE	BEARABLE	SCRAMBLE	VOLATILE
STARLIKE	WEARABLE	RESEMBLE	SAXATILE
LADYLIKE	SPARABLE	ENSEMBLE	ERECTILE
TURNPIKE	ADORABLE	ASSEMBLE	STRICKLE
UPSTROKE	EXORABLE	REDOUBLE	UNBUCKLE
EQUIVOKE	RAISABLE	CHASUBLE	SPRINKLE
ARCHDUKE	LAPSABLE	BINNACLE	CANAILLE
FOLKTALE	PASSABLE	PINNACLE	REVEILLE
TELLTALE	IMITABLE	BARNACLE	CHENILLE
PROBABLE	SUITABLE	PENTACLE	PASTILLE
CURBABLE	RENTABLE	TENTACLE	AIGUILLE
PLACABLE	MOOTABLE	OBSTACLE	CARACOLE
PECCABLE	QUOTABLE	BITTACLE	BORECOLE
AMICABLE	PORTABLE	FASCICLE	BUNGHOLE
EDUCABLE	SORTABLE	CAUDICLE	LOOPHOLE
READABLE	TASTABLE	PELLICLE	PORTHOLE
BIDDABLE	TESTABLE	FOLLICLE	BLOWHOLE
VOIDABLE	UNSTABLE	CAULICLE	CABRIOLE
GUIDABLE	ARGUABLE	CURRICLE	GLORIOLE
WELDABLE	VALUABLE	POPSICLE	CAPRIOLE
FUNDABLE	ISSUABLE	VERSICLE	CARRIOLE
FORDABLE	SALVABLE	CANTICLE	SANDMOLE
LAUDABLE	SOLVABLE	DENTICLE	FLAGPOLE
LIKEABLE	PROVABLE	MONTICLE	BEANPOLE
SALEABLE	DRAWABLE	PARTICLE	FUMAROLE
NAMEABLE	KNOWABLE	TESTICLE	FUSAROLE
TAMEABLE	AVOWABLE	CLAVICLE	GIRASOLE
SIZEABLE	SEIZABLE	PEDUNCLE	CAMISOLE
DIGGABLE	BEDABBLE	CARUNCLE	TURNSOLE
WASHABLE	SCRABBLE	TUBERCLE	DIASTOLE
TITHABLE	SQUABBLE	ENCIRCLE	MANCIPLE
SOCIABLE	SCRIBBLE	UNICYCLE	DISCIPLE
RELIABLE	ENFEEBLE	EPICYCLE	MULTIPLE
DENIABLE	FENCIBLE	TRICYCLE	ENSAMPLE
EXPIABLE	VINCIBLE	STRADDLE	REPEOPLE
VARIABLE	RUNCIBLE	UNSADDLE	UNPEOPLE
SATIABLE	FORCIBLE	UNRIDDLE	EGGAPPLE
PITIABLE	MISCIBLE	REKINDLE	EMPURPLE
DUTIABLE	EDUCIBLE	ENKINDLE	IMPURPLE
LEVIABLE	CRUCIBLE	UNMUFFLE	UNCOUPLE
ENVIABLE	INEDIBLE	SEAEAGLE	CENTUPLE
WORKABLE	CREDIBLE	STRUGGLE	SEXTUPLE
SCALABLE	MANDIBLE	ENVEIGLE	SUBTITLE
HEALABLE	VENDIBLE	INVEIGLE	MISTITLE
BAILABLE	ELUDIBLE	TRIANGLE	UNGENTLE
TELLABLE	ELIGIBLE	STRANGLE	EMBATTLE
TILLABLE	EXIGIBLE	ENTANGLE	UNSETTLE
TOLLABLE	TANGIBLE	IMMINGLE	BELITTLE
SYLLABLE	FALLIBLE	PINOCHLE	THROTTLE
VIOLABLE	GULLIBLE	IMMOBILE	MOLECULE
BLAMABLE	TERRIBLE	STROBILE	RIDICULE
FARMABLE	HORRIBLE	IMBECILE	SILICULE
LOANABLE	THURIBLE	DOMICILE	RETICULE
AMENABLE	FEASIBLE	INDOCILE	FLOSCULE
RUINABLE	SENSIBLE	NARGHILE	OPUSCULE
DAMNABLE	PASSIBLE	ZOOPHILE	SCHEDULE
TANNABLE	POSSIBLE	CAMOMILE	GLANDULE
SHAPABLE	PARTIBLE	JUVENILE	SPHERULE
PALPABLE	FLEXIBLE	EOLIPILE	OVERRULE
CULPABLE	PREAMBLE	SCURRILE	FRUSTULE

INCISURE	OPTIMISE	ANNULOSE	REPERUSE
COCKSURE	MAXIMISE	PAPULOSE	ABSTRUSE
REINSURE	PAGANISE	ANKYLOSE	PARALYSE
CYNOSURE	ORGANISE	RACEMOSE	CELIBATE
EXPOSURE	ROMANISE	EXOSMOSE	BILOBATE
REASSURE	WOMANISE	STRUMOSE	ACERBATE
PRESSURE	HUMANISE	SNUBNOSE	INCUBATE
CUBATURE	BOTANISE	DIAGNOSE	DEFECATE
CREATURE	FEMINISE	MONGOOSE	ABDICATE
LIGATURE	LATINISE	MUNGOOSE	DEDICATE
FILATURE	COLONISE	REIMPOSE	MEDICATE
IMMATURE	DEMONISE	WINDROSE	INDICATE
ARMATURE	CANONISE	SUBEROSE	DELICATE
FRACTURE	ETERNISE	TUBEROSE	SILICATE
CINCTURE	IMMUNISE	ROCKROSE	TUNICATE
LINCTURE	PORPOISE	PRIMROSE	LORICATE
TINCTURE	TORTOISE	DEXTROSE	MURICATE
JUNCTURE	POLARISE	COMATOSE	VESICATE
PUNCTURE	HIGHRISE	CERATOSE	URTICATE
JOINTURE	SATIRISE	FRUCTOSE	TRUNCATE
APERTURE	THEORISE	FLEXUOSE	RELOCATE
OVERTURE	MEMORISE	COLLAPSE	ALLOCATE
MOISTURE	VAPORISE	PROLAPSE	ADVOCATE
DATABASE	MOTORISE	REHEARSE	INVOCATE
CARDCASE	COMPRISE	SUBMERSE	CARUCATE
WINGCASE	SURPRISE	DISPERSE	FOREDATE
BOOKCASE	MISPRISE	TRAVERSE	ANTEDATE
SURCEASE	TREATISE	UNIVERSE	VALIDATE
SUBLEASE	PRACTISE	CONVERSE	LAPIDATE
DECREASE	APPETISE	PERVERSE	INUNDATE
INCREASE	AMORTISE	SEAHORSE	POSTDATE
PURCHASE	CHASTISE	WARHORSE	NUCLEATE
IDOCRASE	DISGUISE	DISHORSE	ACULEATE
DIOPTASE	MARQUISE	BATHORSE	PERMEATE
DIASTASE	TELEVISE	PREMORSE	CLYPEATE
TYROLESE	SIDEWISE	RETRORSE	RECREATE
VIENNESE	EDGEWISE	INTRORSE	LAUREATE
GENEVESE	LIKEWISE	EXTRORSE	NAUSEATE
BEPRAISE	LONGWISE	DISBURSE	INDAGATE
APPRAISE	ARCHWISE	WETNURSE	RUNAGATE
SOLECISE	SUCHWISE	DRYNURSE	TIDEGATE
EXERCISE	OVERWISE	RECOURSE	DELEGATE
EXORCISE	PAIRWISE	CUTPURSE	RELEGATE
PARADISE	FLATWISE	CREVASSE	ABNEGATE
MELODISE	CONVULSE	NOBLESSE	OBLIGATE
EULOGISE	CONDENSE	COULISSE	FUMIGATE
ENERGISE	PREPENSE	LACROSSE	IRRIGATE
LOCALISE	PROPENSE	REPOUSSE	LITIGATE
VOCALISE	DISPENSE	APPLAUSE	MITIGATE
IDEALISE	SUSPENSE	DISABUSE	NAVIGATE
LEGALISE	NONSENSE	DANSEUSE	LEVIGATE
ALKALISE	PRETENSE	MASSEUSE	TAILGATE
CANALISE	RESPONSE	TIMEFUSE	TOLLGATE
PENALISE	FLOCCOSE	MADHOUSE	ELONGATE
FINALISE	VARICOSE	ALEHOUSE	ABROGATE
MORALISE	OVERDOSE	DYEHOUSE	DEROGATE
RURALISE	PALUDOSE	TAPHOUSE	ARROGATE
EQUALISE	SPATHOSE	POTHOUSE	SULPHATE
MOBILISE	BOOTHOSE	DORMOUSE	GLACIATE
CIVILISE	DISCLOSE	TITMOUSE	EMACIATE

GLADIATE	GEMINATE	LEVITATE	AMMONITE
PALLIATE	DOMINATE	EDENTATE	MARONITE
SPOLIATE	NOMINATE	ANNOTATE	DISUNITE
INITIATE	RUMINATE	CRISTATE	POLYPITE
BREVIATE	CARINATE	ECOSTATE	SYBARITE
EXUVIATE	UMBONATE	APOSTATE	NAZARITE
ESCALATE	DETONATE	PROSTATE	DENDRITE
CONFLATE	INTONATE	MISSTATE	SIDERITE
SIBILATE	INCHOATE	AMPUTATE	DOLERITE
JUBILATE	CRISPATE	EVACUATE	NEPHRITE
DEPILATE	SEPARATE	GRADUATE	CHLORITE
MUTILATE	CRIBRATE	EVALUATE	MINORITE
OCELLATE	EXECRATE	ADEQUATE	FLUORITE
STELLATE	FULCRATE	EXCAVATE	FAVORITE
ETIOLATE	QUADRATE	SALIVATE	CONTRITE
IMMOLATE	LIBERATE	ACTIVATE	ROBURITE
DESOLATE	LACERATE	TITIVATE	PARASITE
INSOLATE	MACERATE	MOTIVATE	APPOSITE
TINPLATE	ULCERATE	SUBOVATE	OPPOSITE
OMOPLATE	FEDERATE	RENOVATE	CERUSITE
TABULATE	MODERATE	INNOVATE	STEATITE
SUBULATE	TOLERATE	ACERVATE	HEMATITE
MACULATE	NUMERATE	ENERVATE	HEPATITE
PECULATE	GENERATE	ENTRACTE	APPETITE
OSCULATE	VENERATE	AESTHETE	MESQUITE
UNDULATE	LITERATE	OBSOLETE	BRONZITE
MODULATE	EMIGRATE	COMPLETE	ENCEINTE
REGULATE	ASPIRATE	CONCRETE	ANECDOTE
LIGULATE	LEVIRATE	DISCRETE	ANTIDOTE
UNGULATE	DECORATE	MANSUETE	BANKNOTE
SIMULATE	PRIORATE	FLEABITE	CALLNOTE
CUMULATE	PERORATE	BACKBITE	FOOTNOTE
ANNULATE	STUPRATE	JACOBITE	CREASOTE
LUNULATE	OVERRATE	CENOBITE	KREASOTE
COPULATE	FILTRATE	BORACITE	CREOSOTE
POPULATE	CULTRATE	EXPEDITE	KREOSOTE
INSULATE	TARTRATE	GRAPHITE	TRIPTOTE
SQUAMATE	CASTRATE	SULPHITE	MISQUOTE
YOKEMATE	ROSTRATE	CIMOLITE	UNCHASTE
CASEMATE	LUSTRATE	IMPOLITE	DISTASTE
DECIMATE	ACCURATE	UNPOLITE	BARBETTE
ULTIMATE	OBDURATE	AEROLITE	OMELETTE
INTIMATE	INDURATE	PISOLITE	ROULETTE
ESTIMATE	FIGURATE	CRYOLITE	PALMETTE
WORKMATE	DEPURATE	BACULITE	PIANETTE
CHROMATE	SATURATE	CALAMITE	VIGNETTE
AUTOMATE	OBTURATE	ISLAMITE	BRUNETTE
SHIPMATE	TRACTATE	DYNAMITE	ANISETTE
HELPMATE	PUNCTATE	SODOMITE	GRISETTE
MESSMATE	ERUCTATE	DOLOMITE	CASSETTE
PLAYMATE	HEBETATE	CHROMITE	SEPTETTE
IMPANATE	VEGETATE	MELANITE	SESTETTE
ALIENATE	DUBITATE	BASANITE	COQUETTE
STAGNATE	MEDITATE	STIBNITE	CORVETTE
UNCINATE	DIGITATE	SELENITE	GARROTTE
ORDINATE	COGITATE	DEFINITE	SUBACUTE
PAGINATE	MILITATE	INFINITE	ABSOLUTE
VAGINATE	CAPITATE	MELINITE	RESOLUTE
ECHINATE	IRRITATE	BUFONITE	OBVOLUTE
LAMINATE	HESITATE	LIMONITE	REVOLUTE

TEACHING	KINGLING	CHARMING	LUSTRING
BUNCHING	BUNGLING	ALARMING	ENDURING
CATCHING	SHEILING	ASSUMING	ALLURING
FETCHING	WEAKLING	GREENING	BANXRING
WITCHING	TACKLING	WAKENING	DEBASING
NOTCHING	TICKLING	GRAINING	PLEASING
TOUCHING	DUCKLING	TRAINING	PHRASING
SLASHING	SUCKLING	GROINING	UPRISING
SWASHING	TINKLING	STUNNING	IMPOSING
BLUSHING	DARKLING	LEARNING	COURSING
CRUSHING	DIALLING	YEARNING	BLESSING
SCATHING	SMELLING	MOURNING	DRESSING
LOATHING	SPELLING	BROWNING	PRESSING
TEETHING	DUELLING	CROWNING	CROSSING
CLOTHING	DWELLING	SEAGOING	TRUSSING
SOOTHING	SWELLING	OUTGOING	ACCUSING
FARTHING	CHILLING	SCRAPING	CHEATING
SOUTHING	SHILLING	SLEEPING	TREATING
ANYTHING	DRILLING	SWEEPING	FLOATING
SNEAKING	FRILLING	STAMPING	EXACTING
SPEAKING	GRILLING	WHOMPING	SHEETING
CROAKING	QUILLING	THUMPING	FLEETING
BLACKING	TROLLING	STOOPING	GREETING
SMACKING	WEANLING	TRAPPING	SWEETING
PRICKING	YEANLING	WRAPPING	RIVETING
TRICKING	TWINLING	CHIPPING	SHAFTING
SHOCKING	DUMPLING	SHIPPING	YACHTING
STOCKING	RIPPLING	WHIPPING	FIGHTING
STRIKING	COUPLING	SKIPPING	LIGHTING
STALKING	YEARLING	CLIPPING	EXCITING
BEANKING	SNARLING	DRIPPING	VOMITING
SPANKING	STARLING	TRIPPING	VISITING
THINKING	STERLING	CHOPPING	INVITING
SHEALING	STIRLING	DROPPING	QUILTING
STEALING	NURSLING	STOPPING	VAULTING
STABLING	GNATLING	GRASPING	PAINTING
LAMBLING	BEETLING	GROUPING	PRINTING
RAMBLING	BANTLING	UNCARING	TAUNTING
HUMBLING	FOOTLING	SHEARING	MOUNTING
MUMBLING	NESTLING	CLEARING	GRUNTING
TUMBLING	TATTLING	SWEARING	SHOOTING
MARBLING	WATTLING	CHEERING	TEMPTING
DOUBLING	SETTLING	STEERING	SHIRTING
MEDDLING	BRAWLING	OFFERING	SPORTING
MIDDLING	TRAWLING	CATERING	COASTING
PUDDLING	SCOWLING	WATERING	FROSTING
SEEDLING	GROWLING	COVERING	FLATTING
HANDLING	GRAYLING	LOWERING	PLATTING
KINDLING	DAZZLING	TOWERING	KNITTING
FONDLING	GLOAMING	ASPIRING	SCOUTING
BARDLING	SCHEMING	RETIRING	THIEVING
LORDLING	SKIMMING	UNTIRING	THRIVING
STEELING	SLIMMING	COLORING	SHELVING
CAGELING	BRIMMING	FLOORING	BEESWING
ATHELING	TRIMMING	UPSPRING	LEFTWING
HIRELING	SWIMMING	STARRING	INLAYING
RUFFLING	BECOMING	UNERRING	ASSAYING
TRIFLING	INCOMING	WHIRRING	EDIFYING
GIGGLING	ONCOMING	STIRRING	OUTLYING
BOGGLING	BLOOMING	UNSTRING	DAIRYING

NOTIONAL	FORESTAL	MUSCATEL	EARSHELL
OPTIONAL	REMITTAL	IMMANUEL	MISSPELL
MATRONAL	REBUTTAL	DISHEVEL	FORETELL
SEASONAL	RESIDUAL	SEALEVEL	TUBEWELL
PERSONAL	DIVIDUAL	BERGMEHL	FAREWELL
CANTONAL	PUNCTUAL	TREENAIL	DRAWWELL
HIBERNAL	HABITUAL	HANGNAIL	HANDBILL
INFERNAL	EVENTUAL	DOORNAIL	TIMEBILL
MATERNAL	BISEXUAL	HANDRAIL	DUCKBILL
PATERNAL	UPHEAVAL	MONORAIL	HORNBILL
INTERNAL	MEDIEVAL	WINDSAIL	BOATBILL
EXTERNAL	PRIMEVAL	FORESAIL	PLAYBILL
TRIBUNAL	CARNIVAL	DOVETAIL	SANDHILL
COMMUNAL	DEPRIVAL	COCKTAIL	DUNGHILL
WOODCOAL	AESTIVAL	CATSTAIL	DOWNHILL
CHARCOAL	FESTIVAL	DAFFODIL	FOOTHILL
ENTOZOAL	SURVIVAL	SALADOIL	OVERKILL
CEREBRAL	REPROVAL	SPIKEOIL	WINDMILL
DIHEDRAL	APPROVAL	SPERMOIL	TIDEMILL
VISCERAL	INTERVAL	TRAINOIL	CANEMILL
DIPTERAL	REVIEWAL	CARAPOIL	BONEMILL
GUTTERAL	BESTOWAL	FAUTEUIL	SILKMILL
PODAGRAL	DEFRAYAL	TRANQUIL	WOOLMILL
INTEGRAL	BETRAYAL	SEADEVIL	CORNMILL
URETHRAL	CONVEYAL	ALGUAZIL	CLAYMILL
TEMPORAL	DISLOYAL	HANDBALL	MINIPILL
CORPORAL	CAPSIZAL	TIMEBALL	MANDRILL
PECTORAL	CASCABEL	FIREBALL	CLAPSILL
SECTORAL	MUSCADEL	BASEBALL	GOODWILL
DOCTORAL	ASPHODEL	PUFFBALL	SELFWILL
PASTORAL	COGWHEEL	HIGHBALL	CLODPOLL
LITTORAL	PINWHEEL	HEELBALL	BEADROLL
SPECTRAL	NEWSREEL	CORNBALL	BANKROLL
TELLURAL	WHEATEEL	TRAPBALL	PLIMSOLL
MACRURAL	PARALLEL	SOFTBALL	SKUAGULL
CAESURAL	BECHAMEL	SPITBALL	NUMSKULL
CULTURAL	PHILOMEL	FOOTBALL	BELLPULL
GESTURAL	HYDROMEL	DUSTBALL	PROTOCOL
REPRISAL	FONTANEL	SNOWBALL	BASSVIOL
PROPOSAL	SENTINEL	BIRDCALL	METHANOL
DISPOSAL	CRACKNEL	ROLLCALL	CESSPOOL
PETROSAL	SCRANNEL	DEADFALL	SESSPOOL
REVERSAL	UNKENNEL	LANDFALL	SKINWOOL
COLOSSAL	MANGONEL	WINDFALL	CONYWOOL
ESPOUSAL	PETRONEL	RAINFALL	ENTRESOL
CAROUSAL	SHRAPNEL	DOWNFALL	CLAYMARL
PARIETAL	ESTOPPEL	FOOTFALL	KEELHAUL
VARIETAL	WHIMBREL	WINDGALL	OVERHAUL
SKELETAL	SPANDREL	SPURGALL	DREADFUL
DECRETAL	TAFFEREL	TOWNHALL	FRAUDFUL
HOSPITAL	DOGGEREL	PALLMALL	PEACEFUL
DETRITAL	MACKEREL	ENTHRALL	GRACEFUL
REQUITAL	PICKEREL	CORNWALL	VOICEFUL
BIDENTAL	COCKEREL	CARRYALL	FORCEFUL
CLIENTAL	DOTTEREL	DUMBBELL	PRIDEFUL
ORIENTAL	SQUIRREL	HAREBELL	VENGEFUL
PARENTAL	CHAPTREL	BLUEBELL	GUILEFUL
TEETOTAL	MINSTREL	DOORBELL	SHAMEFUL
IMMORTAL	CAROUSEL	RAKEHELL	BLAMEFUL
PEDESTAL	BROCATEL	EGGSHELL	CRIMEFUL

SCHOLIUM	PUBLICAN	SOCINIAN	BEADSMAN
ENCOMIUM	ANGLICAN	ARMINIAN	HEADSMAN
CHROMIUM	GALLICAN	BACONIAN	SEEDSMAN
PHORMIUM	PEMMICAN	CATONIAN	LANDSMAN
DIDYMIUM	AMERICAN	FAVONIAN	BONDSMAN
GERANIUM	ETRUSCAN	DEVONIAN	HERDSMAN
TITANIUM	ACARIDAN	BEZONIAN	BEDESMAN
SELENIUM	HARRIDAN	DIGYNIAN	SIDESMAN
HYMENIUM	ARCHAEAN	OLYMPIAN	DALESMAN
AMMONIUM	SPELAEAN	THESPIAN	SALESMAN
VELARIUM	LINNAEAN	MALARIAN	TALISMAN
SOLARIUM	JACOBEAN	AGRARIAN	TACKSMAN
AQUARIUM	CETACEAN	ROSARIAN	MARKSMAN
VIVARIUM	CADUCEAN	CAMBRIAN	HELMSMAN
DELIRIUM	PERIGEAN	ALGERIAN	DOOMSMAN
CIBORIUM	NYMPHEAN	VALERIAN	CLANSMAN
EMPORIUM	DRYCLEAN	AUSTRIAN	GOWNSMAN
INDUSIUM	CERULEAN	SILURIAN	TOWNSMAN
SOLATIUM	HYMENEAN	ASSYRIAN	OVERSMAN
LIXIVIUM	EBURNEAN	EURASIAN	CHESSMAN
DILUVIUM	EUROPEAN	EPHESIAN	PRESSMAN
ALLUVIUM	TRAPPEAN	MILESIAN	HUNTSMAN
TANTALUM	CESAREAN	ARTESIAN	SCOTSMAN
VEXILLUM	NAZAREAN	PARISIAN	STUNTMAN
DATEPLUM	EMPYREAN	PRUSSIAN	SUBHUMAN
SPECULUM	COTQUEAN	HORATIAN	TALLYMAN
VINCULUM	TOBOGGAN	ALSATIAN	DAIRYMAN
VASCULUM	CARDIGAN	VENETIAN	FERRYMAN
PENDULUM	MICHIGAN	NICOTIAN	SAUCEPAN
COAGULUM	MULLIGAN	ERASTIAN	BRINEPAN
OLIBANUM	YATAGHAN	MORAVIAN	MARZIPAN
GALBANUM	MAGICIAN	BATAVIAN	TRAGOPAN
LAUDANUM	LOGICIAN	DILUVIAN	LUTHERAN
TYMPANUM	MUSICIAN	PERUVIAN	DIOCESAN
DUODENUM	OPTICIAN	VESUVIAN	PARMESAN
SPHAGNUM	ARCADIAN	INDIAMAN	PARTISAN
GLUCINUM	ORCADIAN	CHINAMAN	TARLATAN
ALUMINUM	CANADIAN	FREEDMAN	PAKISTAN
THORINUM	COMEDIAN	PLACEMAN	AUGUSTAN
PLATINUM	ASCIDIAN	SPACEMAN	BRAKEVAN
LABURNUM	OPHIDIAN	LIEGEMAN	CORDOVAN
ALBURNUM	MERIDIAN	BARGEMAN	WESLEYAN
KHARTOUM	OBSIDIAN	BRAKEMAN	BARTIZAN
CEREBRUM	GUARDIAN	NOBLEMAN	PARTIZAN
VARIORUM	PLEBEIAN	RIFLEMAN	MENHADEN
PLECTRUM	GRAAFIAN	FUGLEMAN	UNBIDDEN
SPECTRUM	PELAGIAN	HORSEMAN	EMBOLDEN
ADIANTUM	GEORGIAN	NORSEMAN	BEHOLDEN
LOMENTUM	NOACHIAN	COACHMAN	UNBURDEN
MOMENTUM	DELPHIAN	HENCHMAN	ABERDEEN
TOMENTUM	PARTHIAN	WATCHMAN	SPALPEEN
FACTOTUM	SCYTHIAN	FRESHMAN	SEAGREEN
TEETOTUM	HEGELIAN	WHEELMAN	SHAGREEN
RESIDUUM	CIVILIAN	DRAGOMAN	SAPGREEN
	BOHEMIAN	SPEARMAN	NINETEEN
	TURANIAN	ALDERMAN	EIGHTEEN
-------N	TITANIAN	SUPERMAN	THIRTEEN
	ATHENIAN	WATERMAN	FOURTEEN
SUBURBAN	ARMENIAN	CHAIRMAN	OVERWEEN
BARBICAN	SIRENIAN	MOTORMAN	CYANOGEN

HYDROGEN	MOLESKIN	SCULLION	DURATION
NITROGEN	FORESKIN	ACROMION	GYRATION
GROSCHEN	BUCKSKIN	DOMINION	NATATION
WATERHEN	SEALSKIN	TRUNNION	CITATION
LENGTHEN	SWANSKIN	SEAONION	DOTATION
SMOOTHEN	BEARSKIN	DISUNION	NOTATION
UNSHAKEN	GOATSKIN	CHAMPION	POTATION
MISTAKEN	FORMALIN	SCORPION	ROTATION
STRICKEN	ZEPPELIN	DECURION	MUTATION
SHRUNKEN	FRANKLIN	OCCASION	NUTATION
UNSPOKEN	MANDOLIN	ABRASION	EQUATION
UNBROKEN	PANGOLIN	INVASION	TAXATION
MAGDALEN	GLOBULIN	ADHESION	VEXATION
CYCLAMEN	BENJAMIN	INHESION	FIXATION
GRAVAMEN	SAINFOIN	COHESION	LUXATION
FRESHMEN	TERRAPIN	DECISION	REACTION
SPECIMEN	THOLEPIN	INCISION	INACTION
COGNOMEN	UNDERPIN	EXCISION	FRACTION
CRAGSMEN	MANDARIN	DERISION	TRACTION
UNSHAPEN	GLYCERIN	IRRISION	EXACTION
CHILDREN	CULVERIN	REVISION	EJECTION
BRETHREN	VERATRIN	DIVISION	ELECTION
THREATEN	MOCCASIN	EMULSION	FLECTION
HEIGHTEN	DAMASSIN	AVULSION	ERECTION
BRIGHTEN	ASSASSIN	EVULSION	FRICTION
FRIGHTEN	DOGLATIN	SCANSION	EVICTION
STRAITEN	HAEMATIN	SPONSION	SANCTION
UNFASTEN	BULLETIN	EMERSION	FUNCTION
TUNGSTEN	BLOCKTIN	AVERSION	JUNCTION
CHRISTEN	REPLEVIN	EVERSION	DELETION
HENEQUEN	MYRMIDON	SCISSION	AMBITION
UNSHAVEN	MASTODON	EMISSION	ADDITION
CAMPAIGN	MELODEON	OMISSION	SEDITION
REASSIGN	BLUDGEON	AFFUSION	AUDITION
DEMIJOHN	BOURGEON	EFFUSION	VOLITION
REORDAIN	STURGEON	INFUSION	IGNITION
CHAPLAIN	LUNCHEON	DELUSION	MONITION
COMPLAIN	PUNCHEON	ALLUSION	MUNITION
MORTMAIN	PANTHEON	ILLUSION	POSITION
AIRDRAIN	CAMELEON	LIBATION	PETITION
SUZERAIN	NAPOLEON	VACATION	FRUITION
QUATRAIN	MEZEREON	LOCATION	DEVOTION
RESTRAIN	ENNEAGON	VOCATION	GUMPTION
DISTRAIN	TETRAGON	SEDATION	ADOPTION
PLANTAIN	PENTAGON	IDEATION	ERUPTION
MAINTAIN	HEPTAGON	CREATION	EXERTION
FOUNTAIN	MARTAGON	LEGATION	ABORTION
MOUNTAIN	PARERGON	NEGATION	EGESTION
CORDWAIN	ANTIPHON	LIGATION	QUESTION
COXSWAIN	COLOPHON	AVIATION	LOCUTION
CLAVECIN	MARATHON	ABLATION	ABLUTION
CERULEIN	COERCION	OBLATION	DILUTION
CHOWMEIN	RELIGION	DELATION	SOLUTION
PARAFFIN	FALCHION	RELATION	OBLIVION
CAPUCHIN	APHELION	DILATION	DILUVION
MUTCHKIN	GANGLION	ILLATION	ALLUVION
CANNIKIN	PAVILION	VENATION	GONFALON
PANNIKIN	SCALLION	DONATION	MOUFFLON
CIDERKIN	STALLION	LUNATION	CARILLON
LAMBSKIN	TRILLION	AERATION	PROPYLON

CINNAMON	FREEBORN	KANGAROO	PAWNSHOP
SEALEMON	HOMEBORN	BUCKAROO	SLOPSHOP
UNCOMMON	BASEBORN	WANDEROO	ESCALLOP
GONFANON	TRUEBORN	COCKATOO	SLIPSLOP
RIGADOON	WELLBORN	RANCHERO	WARWHOOP
DOUBLOON	TWINBORN	SOMBRERO	LOLLIPOP
SHALLOON	SEAACORN	MAESTOSO	ROOTCROP
EPIPLOON	SEEDCORN	VIRTUOSO	RAINDROP
FORENOON	CAVICORN	SARGASSO	TEARDROP
TEASPOON	SHOEHORN	STACCATO	SNOWDROP
EGGSPOON	BULLHORN	LITERATO	SWEETSOP
MACAROON	LANTHORN	GRAFFITO	BLACKTOP
PICAROON	POSTHORN	MOSQUITO	PERICARP
QUADROON	HAWTHORN	HEREUNTO	ENDOCARP
OCTOROON	TIMEWORN	CONCERTO	XYLOCARP
POLTROON	CAREWORN	HITHERTO	AUTOHARP
DUCATOON	TOILWORN	STILETTO	ACORNCUP
SPONTOON	WELLWORN	PALMETTO	POPGROUP
SPITTOON	OVERWORN	LIBRETTO	RUNNERUP
ENTOZOON	TACITURN	FALSETTO	
POLYZOON	DOWNTURN		
HEREUPON	OVERTURN		------R
FANFARON	FLASHGUN	------P	
SQUADRON	HOMESPUN		CINNABAR
DIHEDRON	FINESPUN	HANDICAP	MOTORCAR
CHALDRON	SHEEPRUN	BLACKCAP	HAVILDAR
CAULDRON	SHOWDOWN	FOOLSCAP	CALENDAR
PAULDRON	DISCROWN	DOGCHEAP	ZAMINDAR
VIGNERON	CAPETOWN	OVERLEAP	ZEMINDAR
CHAPERON	DOWNTOWN	FALLTRAP	CAVEBEAR
GRIDIRON	POSTTOWN	CLAPTRAP	OVERBEAR
CASTIRON		SKINDEEP	SPURGEAR
OXYMORON		DOGSLEEP	FOOTGEAR
ELECTRON	------O	OVERSTEP	OVERHEAR
PLASTRON		DOORSTEP	REAPPEAR
UNREASON	FLAMENCO	FOOTSTEP	EELSPEAR
DIAPASON	ELDORADO	HEADSHIP	WHEATEAR
GRANDSON	COLORADO	HARDSHIP	BURNTEAR
WHORESON	COMMANDO	WARDSHIP	FORSWEAR
EMPOISON	INNUENDO	LORDSHIP	OUTSWEAR
IMPRISON	WELLTODO	FIRESHIP	KNITWEAR
GARRISON	PLUMBAGO	KINGSHIP	FOOTWEAR
JETTISON	SANTIAGO	DEANSHIP	LEAPYEAR
LEWISSON	IMPETIGO	CLANSHIP	AGARAGAR
ADVOWSON	FANDANGO	TRANSHIP	FAMILIAR
SHERATON	CONTANGO	TOWNSHIP	PECULIAR
SKELETON	FLAMINGO	HEROSHIP	UNIFILAR
PLANKTON	ARPEGGIO	HEIRSHIP	LAMELLAR
KINGSTON	BORACHIO	LADYSHIP	BACILLAR
UNBUTTON	SERAGLIO	LANDSLIP	MEDULLAR
EMBLAZON	INTAGLIO	SNOWSLIP	ALVEOLAR
FOREWARN	ROSOGLIO	HANDGRIP	VARIOLAR
TARAFERN	CURCULIO	OUTSTRIP	PETIOLAR
LEATHERN	LOTHARIO	SELFHELP	PREMOLAR
NORTHERN	SCENARIO	FIREDAMP	UNIPOLAR
SOUTHERN	MACHISMO	HEADLAMP	EXEMPLAR
QUARTERN	FILIPINO	DAVYLAMP	GLOBULAR
SLATTERN	PEPERINO	FEEDPUMP	PIACULAR
STUBBORN	KAKEMONO	WORKSHOP	ORACULAR
DEADBORN	BALLYHOO	DRAMSHOP	SACCULAR

SPECULAR	SQUANDER	STARCHER	WHIFFLER
ACICULAR	DEFENDER	THATCHER	SCUFFLER
SPICULAR	OFFENDER	SNATCHER	SHUFFLER
CALCULAR	ENGENDER	SKETCHER	SNUFFLER
CIRCULAR	CALENDER	TWITCHER	WRIGGLER
VASCULAR	KALENDER	SCUTCHER	SMUGGLER
MUSCULAR	ATTENDER	PLOUGHER	WRANGLER
PENDULAR	EXTENDER	DECIPHER	RETAILER
SINGULAR	LAVENDER	THRASHER	ENTAILER
CELLULAR	CYLINDER	POLISHER	COMPILER
NUMMULAR	REMINDER	FINISHER	BEGUILER
GRANULAR	SECONDER	PUNISHER	STICKLER
SCAPULAR	REFUNDER	PERISHER	TRUCKLER
STIPULAR	FLOUNDER	RAVISHER	CABALLER
CONSULAR	REGARDER	BREATHER	LIBELLER
CAPSULAR	RETARDER	AWEATHER	MODELLER
FISTULAR	REWARDER	REGATHER	REPELLER
PUSTULAR	IMBORDER	TOGETHER	LEVELLER
VALVULAR	SUBORDER	PACIFIER	REVELLER
COLUMNAR	RECORDER	CODIFIER	JEWELLER
SUBLUNAR	DISORDER	MODIFIER	CAVILLER
WILDBOAR	MARAUDER	VILIFIER	ENROLLER
CALCSPAR	OBTRUDER	TYPIFIER	STROLLER
FELDSPAR	INTRUDER	VERIFIER	CONSOLER
SCIMITAR	REINDEER	PURIFIER	TRAMPLER
LOADSTAR	FUSILEER	CLOTHIER	SCRUPLER
LODESTAR	ENGINEER	ESPALIER	WRESTLER
GUICOWAR	DOMINEER	GASALIER	WHISTLER
SCRUBBER	MUTINEER	CAVALIER	EPISTLER
DECEMBER	OVERSEER	GASELIER	PRATTLER
REMEMBER	MULETEER	HOTELIER	SCRAWLER
NOVEMBER	CHAUFFER	LIVELIER	SCREAMER
ENCUMBER	CRUCIFER	COMPLIER	STREAMER
CUCUMBER	MAMMIFER	SUPPLIER	GOSSAMER
REJOICER	THURIFER	OCCUPIER	REDEEMER
BALANCER	TRANSFER	CROUPIER	DULCIMER
ROMANCER	PILLAGER	QUARRIER	EMBALMER
SILENCER	VILLAGER	FRONTIER	THRUMMER
DIVORCER	RUMMAGER	COURTIER	WELCOMER
TRADUCER	TEENAGER	SQUEAKER	MISNOMER
PRODUCER	VINTAGER	HAYMAKER	RANSOMER
CRUSADER	COTTAGER	PARTAKER	CUSTOMER
CONCEDER	BESIEGER	ATTACKER	AFFIRMER
OUTRIDER	ENDANGER	MIMICKER	DEFORMER
CONSIDER	ARRANGER	ONLOOKER	REFORMER
OUTSIDER	STRANGER	REMARKER	INFORMER
PROVIDER	REVENGER	REPEALER	PERFUMER
BEWILDER	MALINGER	REVEALER	CONSUMER
BEHOLDER	SPRINGER	FRIBBLER	CHICANER
UPHOLDER	STRINGER	QUIBBLER	PROFANER
SHOULDER	ENLARGER	TREMBLER	BEMOANER
SMOULDER	SCOURGER	GRUMBLER	LARCENER
OLEANDER	BLEACHER	STUMBLER	PARCENER
BILANDER	PREACHER	TROUBLER	GARDENER
INLANDER	BROACHER	TWADDLER	CONGENER
COLANDER	STANCHER	WHEEDLER	WARRENER
UPLANDER	TRENCHER	CHANDLER	SOFTENER
ISLANDER	QUENCHER	SWINDLER	WHITENER
DEMANDER	CLINCHER	TEASELER	FASTENER
POMANDER	SEARCHER	TRAVELER	HASTENER

CALIPERS	CLUELESS	GLADNESS	PUNINESS
TROUSERS	WAVELESS	VOIDNESS	ROPINESS
CLEAVERS	LOVELESS	BALDNESS	WARINESS
TWEAZERS	MOVELESS	MILDNESS	EERINESS
TWEEZERS	LEAFLESS	WILDNESS	AIRINESS
UPSTAIRS	SELFLESS	BOLDNESS	MIRINESS
OUTDOORS	ROOFLESS	COLDNESS	WIRINESS
SCISSORS	WINGLESS	KINDNESS	EASINESS
ALLFOURS	SONGLESS	FONDNESS	ROSINESS
SUBCLASS	PATHLESS	GOODNESS	BUSINESS
OUTCLASS	PITHLESS	HARDNESS	DEWINESS
WINDLASS	RUTHLESS	LOUDNESS	WAXINESS
EYEGLASS	BODILESS	LEWDNESS	SEXINESS
EGGGLASS	PITILESS	NICENESS	HAZINESS
SPYGLASS	RECKLESS	WIDENESS	LAZINESS
OVERPASS	LUCKLESS	NUDENESS	MAZINESS
TRESPASS	SAILLESS	RUDENESS	WEAKNESS
SEAGRASS	TAILLESS	FREENESS	SICKNESS
RYEGRASS	VEILLESS	RIFENESS	MEEKNESS
DOGGRASS	SKILLESS	SAFENESS	LANKNESS
PRINCESS	TOILLESS	SAGENESS	RANKNESS
CHIEFESS	SOULLESS	HUGENESS	DARKNESS
IDEALESS	BEAMLESS	LIKENESS	REALNESS
TOMBLESS	SEAMLESS	HALENESS	EVILNESS
HEADLESS	STEMLESS	PALENESS	TALLNESS
LEADLESS	BRIMLESS	IDLENESS	FELLNESS
DEEDLESS	HARMLESS	VILENESS	DULLNESS
HEEDLESS	TERMLESS	SOLENESS	FULLNESS
NEEDLESS	FORMLESS	GAMENESS	COOLNESS
LANDLESS	PLANLESS	LAMENESS	FOULNESS
MINDLESS	GAINLESS	SAMENESS	SLIMNESS
WINDLESS	PAINLESS	TAMENESS	GRIMNESS
FOODLESS	RAINLESS	SANENESS	PRIMNESS
WORDLESS	REINLESS	FINENESS	TRIMNESS
FADELESS	CHINLESS	RIPENESS	CALMNESS
TIDELESS	SKINLESS	BARENESS	WARMNESS
TREELESS	MOONLESS	RARENESS	FIRMNESS
LIFELESS	HELPLESS	SORENESS	GLUMNESS
EDGELESS	FEARLESS	PURENESS	LEANNESS
RULELESS	TEARLESS	BASENESS	MEANNESS
FAMELESS	STARLESS	WISENESS	KEENNESS
NAMELESS	PEERLESS	LATENESS	OPENNESS
TAMELESS	HAIRLESS	MUTENESS	EVENNESS
TIMELESS	STIRLESS	BLUENESS	VAINNESS
HOMELESS	TACTLESS	TRUENESS	THINNESS
FUMELESS	SALTLESS	DEAFNESS	CANONESS
MANELESS	TINTLESS	SMUGNESS	BARONESS
TONELESS	KNOTLESS	SNUGNESS	DEEPNESS
TUNELESS	BOOTLESS	RICHNESS	DAMPNESS
SHOELESS	SPOTLESS	ARCHNESS	DEARNESS
HOPELESS	HURTLESS	MUCHNESS	NEARNESS
CARELESS	MASTLESS	HIGHNESS	FAIRNESS
TIRELESS	RESTLESS	RASHNESS	POORNESS
CORELESS	LISTLESS	RACINESS	SOURNESS
CURELESS	FLAWLESS	TIDINESS	NEATNESS
BASELESS	VIEWLESS	INKINESS	FLATNESS
NOSELESS	GLIBNESS	UGLINESS	MEETNESS
DATELESS	DUMBNESS	OILINESS	DEFTNESS
MATELESS	NUMBNESS	WILINESS	SOFTNESS
NOTELESS	DEADNESS	HOLINESS	SALTNESS

RESTRICT	DRIFTNET	ROCKSALT	ASPIRANT
DISTRICT	STRUMPET	HOMEFELT	ROBORANT
SUCCINCT	CELLARET	UNSPOILT	IGNORANT
PRECINCT	BANNERET	AIRBUILT	ABERRANT
DISTINCT	FLOWERET	BIRDBOLT	FIGURANT
INSTINCT	ANCHORET	RINGBOLT	PHEASANT
CONJUNCT	CARBURET	DEMIVOLT	PLEASANT
DISJUNCT	TABOURET	CATAPULT	PUISSANT
AQUEDUCT	THICKSET	CORYBANT	RECUSANT
USUFRUCT	QUICKSET	COSECANT	HABITANT
OBSTRUCT	MARMOSET	ABDICANT	OSCITANT
INSTRUCT	SHARPSET	INDICANT	EXCITANT
ALPHABET	SOMERSET	VESICANT	MILITANT
SCILICET	AIRSHAFT	TOXICANT	IRRITANT
PARAKEET	AIRCRAFT	ABRADANT	HESITANT
LORIKEET	UNTHRIFT	ABUNDANT	VISITANT
DISCREET	ROODLOFT	SERGEANT	EQUITANT
BYSTREET	COCKLOFT	SERJEANT	EXULTANT
PLANCHET	SAILLOFT	RECREANT	CONSTANT
RICOCHET	STRAIGHT	OBLIGANT	DEBUTANT
CROTCHET	SEAFIGHT	LITIGANT	ADJUTANT
DISQUIET	GUNFIGHT	MITIGANT	EVACUANT
UPMARKET	TWILIGHT	ARROGANT	PURSUANT
CLOUDLET	FANLIGHT	BACCHANT	RELEVANT
BRACELET	SUNLIGHT	PENCHANT	ADJACENT
LANCELET	GASLIGHT	MERCHANT	INDECENT
SPIKELET	WAXLIGHT	COUCHANT	RETICENT
PLUMELET	DAYLIGHT	ELEPHANT	INNOCENT
CORSELET	SKYLIGHT	INHALANT	ACESCENT
MANTELET	MIDNIGHT	EXHALANT	CRESCENT
PAMPHLET	AFFRIGHT	SIBILANT	ABDUCENT
BROOKLET	OUTRIGHT	JUBILANT	ADDUCENT
CROWNLET	EYESIGHT	VIGILANT	DECADENT
COVERLET	AIRTIGHT	EGGPLANT	ACCIDENT
CROSSLET	UNBOUGHT	SUPPLANT	OCCIDENT
PLANTLET	UNSOUGHT	AIRPLANT	INCIDENT
FRONTLET	PORTRAIT	AMBULANT	STRIDENT
GAUNTLET	DISTRAIT	OSCULANT	RESIDENT
WRISTLET	PROHIBIT	PETULANT	SCANDENT
TROUTLET	POSTOBIT	CLAIMANT	IMPUDENT
GLOBULET	CUCURBIT	COTENANT	COREGENT
CARCANET	IMPLICIT	COVENANT	INDIGENT
BURGANET	EXPLICIT	STAGNANT	DILIGENT
SARCENET	ACCREDIT	PREGNANT	EMULGENT
STAKENET	BULLSHIT	POIGNANT	PLANGENT
SARSENET	RECOMMIT	ORDINANT	EMERGENT
PURSENET	INTROMIT	DOMINANT	GRADIENT
TABBINET	INTERMIT	RUMINANT	OBEDIENT
BOBBINET	TRANSMIT	ABSONANT	APERIENT
MUSLINET	WELLKNIT	RESONANT	NUTRIENT
CLARINET	SLIMEPIT	ASSONANT	PRURIENT
BASSINET	BRINEPIT	FLIPPANT	ESURIENT
MARTINET	DECREPIT	OCCUPANT	SENTIENT
TRAILNET	TOADSPIT	QUADRANT	QUOTIENT
TRAWLNET	TURNSPIT	TOLERANT	SERVIENT
FALCONET	SANSCRIT	GENERANT	REDOLENT
DRAGONET	INSPIRIT	ALTERANT	INDOLENT
SALMONET	SANSKRIT	FLAGRANT	INSOLENT
CANZONET	BOWSPRIT	FRAGRANT	FECULENT
SCOOPNET	SWIMSUIT	EMIGRANT	ESCULENT

LUCULENT	IMPOTENT	RESCRIPT	ETHICIST
TEMULENT	EXISTENT	CONTEMPT	EXORCIST
VIRULENT	DEFLUENT	CONSUMPT	MELODIST
PURULENT	REFLUENT	BANKRUPT	MONODIST
LIGAMENT	AFFLUENT	EUCALYPT	PARODIST
FILAMENT	EFFLUENT	PUSHCART	DITHEIST
ARMAMENT	INFLUENT	DUSTCART	CANOEIST
ORNAMENT	FREQUENT	BRAGGART	PACIFIST
BODEMENT	ELOQUENT	FOREPART	DRUGGIST
VEHEMENT	WARPAINT	REDSTART	OOLOGIST
TENEMENT	ACQUAINT	STALWART	EULOGIST
BASEMENT	CALAMINT	MALAPERT	PSYCHIST
CASEMENT	CONJOINT	INEXPERT	BUDDHIST
EASEMENT	DISJOINT	REINSERT	STOCKIST
PAVEMENT	PINPOINT	REASSERT	ARBALIST
MOVEMENT	DEWPOINT	TEESHIRT	VOCALIST
FRAGMENT	DRYPOINT	OUTSKIRT	IDEALIST
LODGMENT	MISPRINT	REIMPORT	FINALIST
JUDGMENT	AQUATINT	PASSPORT	ANNALIST
PEDIMENT	HOMODONT	REEXPORT	PAPALIST
SEDIMENT	CONFRONT	PILEWORT	MORALIST
RUDIMENT	SUNBURNT	COLEWORT	FATALIST
REGIMENT	DISCOUNT	LUNGWORT	VITALIST
LINIMENT	MISCOUNT	DROPWORT	LOYALIST
MUNIMENT	VISCOUNT	SALTWORT	ROYALIST
ORPIMENT	SURMOUNT	GOUTWORT	NOVELIST
BAILMENT	DISMOUNT	YOGHOURT	PUGILIST
SHIPMENT	SEDERUNT	TYPECAST	NIHILIST
AVERMENT	MASSICOT	FORECAST	HOMILIST
ABETMENT	MASTICOT	WORMCAST	CIVILIST
OINTMENT	WAINSCOT	DOWNCAST	SICKLIST
SORTMENT	UNFORGOT	OVERCAST	DUELLIST
VESTMENT	WHITEHOT	STEDFAST	REENLIST
ABUTMENT	CASESHOT	HOLDFAST	SCIOLIST
DOCUMENT	BUCKSHOT	MAKEFAST	FABULIST
TEGUMENT	SNAPSHOT	ELEGIAST	POPULIST
ARGUMENT	CACHALOT	BOOTLAST	BIGAMIST
MONUMENT	ESCHALOT	FOREMAST	OPTIMIST
REMANENT	POLYGLOT	HALFMAST	MAXIMIST
IMMANENT	BERGAMOT	SEACOAST	PSALMIST
IMMINENT	HUGUENOT	ANTEPAST	ALARMIST
DEPONENT	JACKBOOT	CONTRAST	ORGANIST
OPPONENT	SNOWBOOT	IMMODEST	ROMANIST
EXPONENT	CLUBFOOT	SLUGFEST	HUMANIST
ILLSPENT	BAREFOOT	MANIFEST	SATANIST
MISSPENT	FLATFOOT	TEACHEST	BOTANIST
APPARENT	CROWFOOT	ROUGHEST	LUTANIST
DEFERENT	OFFSHOOT	FARTHEST	ALIENIST
AFFERENT	ALUMROOT	FURTHEST	LUTENIST
EFFERENT	BEETROOT	BUDAPEST	FEMINIST
ADHERENT	ENTREPOT	INTEREST	LATINIST
INHERENT	HOTCHPOT	AFFOREST	HEDONIST
COHERENT	FLESHPOT	ENFOREST	UNIONIST
REVERENT	GALLIPOT	FOOTREST	COLONIST
RACKRENT	STOCKPOT	CONQUEST	DEMONIST
CORNRENT	STINKPOT	REINVEST	CANONIST
BESPRENT	WATERPOT	HEBRAIST	ARSONIST
QUITRENT	STARSPOT	ULTRAIST	SAXONIST
APPETENT	TRANSEPT	CLUBBIST	JINGOIST
PENITENT	ADSCRIPT	SOLECIST	CENTOIST

MIGHTILY	RUEFULLY	DIRECTLY	SCRUTINY
GUILTILY	WILFULLY	STRICTLY	TWOPENNY
FAULTILY	MANFULLY	UNMEETLY	SIXPENNY
SCANTILY	FITFULLY	SECRETLY	THEOGONY
DAINTILY	ARTFULLY	SLIGHTLY	SYMPHONY
JAUNTILY	LAWFULLY	KNIGHTLY	CUSHIONY
HEARTILY	JOYFULLY	BRIGHTLY	HEGEMONY
FROSTILY	UNSEEMLY	STRAITLY	CEREMONY
CRUSTILY	INFIRMLY	ADROITLY	ACRIMONY
TRUSTILY	YEOMANLY	OCCULTLY	AGRIMONY
PRETTILY	HIDDENLY	PLIANTLY	ANTIMONY
SMUTTILY	SUDDENLY	DECENTLY	SCAMMONY
PLAGUILY	MAIDENLY	RECENTLY	MONOTONY
SCURVILY	WOODENLY	ARDENTLY	GLUTTONY
BIWEEKLY	BROKENLY	UNGENTLY	POLYGYNY
VERBALLY	SULLENLY	COGENTLY	WHITEBOY
RASCALLY	ROTTENLY	URGENTLY	DOUGHBOY
FEUDALLY	HEAVENLY	SILENTLY	CABINBOY
LINEALLY	UNEVENLY	MOMENTLY	PAPERBOY
FRUGALLY	SLOVENLY	ABSENTLY	CHOIRBOY
LABIALLY	BRAZENLY	LATENTLY	BILLYBOY
FACIALLY	MALIGNLY	INTENTLY	CORDUROY
SOCIALLY	BENIGNLY	POTENTLY	PADUASOY
RADIALLY	UNGAINLY	FLUENTLY	ORTHOEPY
FILIALLY	COUSINLY	QUAINTLY	UROSCOPY
GENIALLY	SOLEMNLY	PROMPTLY	REOCCUPY
VENIALLY	COMMONLY	ABRUPTLY	LAPIDARY
AERIALLY	MATRONLY	THWARTLY	QUANDARY
SERIALLY	WANTONLY	EXPERTLY	BOUNDARY
JOVIALLY	MONOPOLY	COVERTLY	PLAGIARY
FORMALLY	ROLYPOLY	MODESTLY	VESPIARY
NORMALLY	MULTIPLY	PRIESTLY	TERTIARY
DISMALLY	MISAPPLY	HONESTLY	BESTIARY
SIGNALLY	LINEARLY	AUGUSTLY	BREVIARY
CARNALLY	BEGGARLY	UNJUSTLY	TUTELARY
SPIRALLY	VULGARLY	DEVOUTLY	BURGLARY
CHORALLY	OCULARLY	HOLLOWLY	PUPILARY
FLORALLY	LUBBERLY	NARROWLY	CALAMARY
PLURALLY	TENDERLY	REFLEXLY	ROSEMARY
CAUSALLY	GINGERLY	CONVEXLY	COSTMARY
MENTALLY	FATHERLY	ENDOGAMY	VICENARY
MORTALLY	MOTHERLY	XENOGAMY	CATENARY
FESTALLY	FORMERLY	MONOGAMY	ORDINARY
DISTALLY	MANNERLY	MISOGAMY	CULINARY
BRUTALLY	PROPERLY	POLYGAMY	LAMINARY
MANUALLY	WINTERLY	TOPONOMY	SEMINARY
ANNUALLY	EASTERLY	AGRONOMY	LUMINARY
CASUALLY	MASTERLY	AUTONOMY	STANNARY
VISUALLY	WESTERLY	TAXONOMY	CORONARY
ACTUALLY	SISTERLY	BLOSSOMY	POLYPARY
RITUALLY	LATTERLY	LOBOTOMY	HONARARY
MUTUALLY	BITTERLY	HOMONYMY	NUMERARY
SEXUALLY	CLEVERLY	PARONYMY	CINERARY
SOWBELLY	SILVERLY	METONYMY	LITERARY
KERNELLY	UNFAIRLY	MAHOGANY	CONTRARY
GRAVELLY	REMISSLY	EPIPHANY	EMISSARY
SNIVELLY	ODIOUSLY	ONTOGENY	GLOSSARY
WOEFULLY	FAMOUSLY	VILLAINY	COMETARY
IREFULLY	JOYOUSLY	SUNSHINY	MONETARY
USEFULLY	ABJECTLY	IGNOMINY	MILITARY

SOLITARY	FRUITERY	GEOLATRY	FELICITY
LIMITARY	PSALTERY	ZOOLATRY	TONICITY
SANITARY	SMELTERY	BARRATRY	BASICITY
SALUTARY	ADULTERY	GADGETRY	VELOCITY
FEBRUARY	LIENTERY	MUSKETRY	FEROCITY
STATUARY	PLASTERY	TOILETRY	ATROCITY
OBITUARY	BLISTERY	VARLETRY	SCARCITY
MORTUARY	BLUSTERY	SYMMETRY	ASTUCITY
SALIVARY	SHATTERY	GEOMETRY	QUIDDITY
JANIZARY	FLATTERY	BIOMETRY	HEREDITY
RIBALDRY	SLUTTERY	COQUETRY	LUCIDITY
HERALDRY	THIEVERY	JESUITRY	RIGIDITY
MONANDRY	DELIVERY	CHOULTRY	ALGIDITY
WIZARDRY	RECOVERY	PEDANTRY	VALIDITY
SLOBBERY	VASSALRY	INFANTRY	GELIDITY
SNOBBERY	CHIVALRY	TENANTRY	SOLIDITY
PLUMBERY	HOSTELRY	ERRANTRY	TIMIDITY
CHANCERY	YEOMANRY	ZEALOTRY	HUMIDITY
BLADDERY	WARDENRY	HARLOTRY	TUMIDITY
BROIDERY	FALCONRY	ANCESTRY	RAPIDITY
THUNDERY	PIGEONRY	TAPESTRY	SAPIDITY
CHIEFERY	BLAZONRY	FORESTRY	CUPIDITY
SAVAGERY	ALLEGORY	REGISTRY	ACRIDITY
DRUDGERY	CATEGORY	TANISTRY	VIRIDITY
WHIGGERY	SEIGNORY	MINISTRY	FLUIDITY
THUGGERY	ADVISORY	PAPISTRY	LIVIDITY
SNUGGERY	INFUSORY	INDUSTRY	VELLEITY
ORANGERY	DELUSORY	SULPHURY	LOCALITY
PATCHERY	ILLUSORY	BISTOURY	VOCALITY
WITCHERY	LIBATORY	TREASURY	MODALITY
BOTCHERY	SUDATORY	OUTLAWRY	IDEALITY
BUTCHERY	ALEATORY	PORPHYRY	LEGALITY
FEATHERY	NEGATORY	DOCIMASY	REGALITY
LEATHERY	NUGATORY	EUPHRASY	BANALITY
SMITHERY	DILATORY	PHANTASY	VENALITY
SMOTHERY	FILATORY	APOSTASY	FINALITY
SOLDIERY	SANATORY	PROPHESY	TONALITY
COLLIERY	MINATORY	COURTESY	MORALITY
FARRIERY	GYRATORY	PLEURISY	FATALITY
FURRIERY	NATATORY	GEOGNOSY	NATALITY
TRICKERY	CITATORY	EPILEPSY	VITALITY
CROCKERY	ROTATORY	JEALOUSY	TOTALITY
SADDLERY	LAVATORY	ENTREATY	EQUALITY
JUGGLERY	FERETORY	SOBRIETY	FIDELITY
RAILLERY	AUDITORY	SUBTLETY	DEBILITY
DROLLERY	VOMITORY	ENTIRETY	MOBILITY
SCULLERY	FUMITORY	ALMIGHTY	NOBILITY
CAJOLERY	MONITORY	DRAUGHTY	FACILITY
CREAMERY	PUNITORY	DROUGHTY	DOCILITY
FLUMMERY	PETITORY	ACERBITY	NIHILITY
BLOOMERY	GOSSIPRY	AUDACITY	HUMILITY
GREENERY	MISCARRY	SAGACITY	SENILITY
REFINERY	ALEBERRY	FUGACITY	VIRILITY
SWANNERY	BILBERRY	TENACITY	MOTILITY
TRUMPERY	MULBERRY	CAPACITY	FUTILITY
SLIPPERY	BARBERRY	RAPACITY	CIVILITY
FRIPPERY	DEWBERRY	FERACITY	SEDULITY
LAMASERY	COWBERRY	VERACITY	CALAMITY
CHEATERY	BAYBERRY	VORACITY	ENORMITY
CEMETERY	IDOLATRY	VIVACITY	URBANITY

--------A	TRABECULA	INSOMNIAC	BRITANNIC
	FEBRICULA	SYMPOSIAC	THEOGONIC
HARMONICA	CAMPANULA	DIONYSIAC	CINCHONIC
ARACHNIDA	PENINSULA	BRICABRAC	SYMPHONIC
ASAFETIDA	TARANTULA	PTOLEMAIC	PYRRHONIC
MEMORANDA	MELODRAMA	ALGEBRAIC	GNATHONIC
CRUSTACEA	MONODRAMA	CHOLERAIC	HEGEMONIC
HYDRANGEA	MYRIORAMA	PHARISAIC	PNEUMONIC
DIARRHOEA	COSMORAMA	PYRAMIDIC	MACARONIC
OTORRHOEA	EXANTHEMA	ICELANDIC	SEMITONIC
APOCRYPHA	EMPHYSEMA	PSALMODIC	MONOTONIC
EUPHORBIA	PENULTIMA	SPASMODIC	EMBRYONIC
APOTHECIA	CARCINOMA	RHAPSODIC	CAINOZOIC
PARAPODIA	HYDROSOMA	SUDORIFIC	KAINOZOIC
NEURALGIA	ZERODERMA	CALORIFIC	ORTHOEPIC
NOSTALGIA	EMPYREUMA	COLORIFIC	ANTHROPIC
SPORANGIA	LOUISIANA	VAPORIFIC	PHILIPPIC
BATRACHIA	PUZZOLANA	SOPORIFIC	SACCHARIC
DIDELPHIA	MARIHUANA	STRATEGIC	THEANDRIC
AUSTRALIA	MARIJUANA	NEURALGIC	CYLINDRIC
CACHAEMIA	PHENOMENA	NOSTALGIC	LIENTERIC
LEUKAEMIA	CASUARINA	PEDAGOGIC	CHIVALRIC
CHOLAEMIA	BALLERINA	DEMAGOGIC	ALLEGORIC
MONOMANIA	SIGNORINA	THEOLOGIC	PAREGORIC
CATAMENIA	ARGENTINA	LETHARGIC	CAMPHORIC
STRYCHNIA	POLLYANNA	DEMIURGIC	BISHOPRIC
PNEUMONIA	DULCAMARA	STOMACHIC	GERIATRIC
PRINCIPIA	SOLFATARA	MONARCHIC	DIAMETRIC
AMBLYOPIA	AMBULACRA	EPITAPHIC	SYMMETRIC
URTICARIA	CLEPSYDRA	DIDELPHIC	GEOMETRIC
ARAUCARIA	CARNIVORA	TRILITHIC	ISOMETRIC
LACUNARIA	PALAESTRA	NEOLITHIC	OBSTETRIC
CINERARIA	ORCHESTRA	OENANTHIC	ECCENTRIC
MILITARIA	BRACHYURA	EVANGELIC	EXCENTRIC
RANCHERIA	APPALOOSA	PARABOLIC	CATOPTRIC
CAFETERIA	BABIRUSSA	METABOLIC	SULPHURIC
INFUSORIA	CHIPOLATA	ALCOHOLIC	PANEGYRIC
PORPHYRIA	INAMORATA	VITRIOLIC	INTRINSIC
DYSCRASIA	INCOGNITA	DIASTOLIC	EXTRINSIC
ANALGESIA	MINNESOTA	EPISTOLIC	FOLKMUSIC
DYSPEPSIA	PARAMATTA	APOSTOLIC	ACROBATIC
ECLAMPSIA	CHERIMOYA	HYDRAULIC	LYMPHATIC
PERIPETIA	INFLUENZA	SALICYLIC	SCHEMATIC
PHILOMELA		PYROXYLIC	CINEMATIC
VENEZUELA		PANORAMIC	KINEMATIC
SHANGRILA	--------B	TAXONOMIC	PRAGMATIC
TALEGALLA		TRIATOMIC	ENIGMATIC
VARICELLA	DITHYRAMB	MONATOMIC	STIGMATIC
COLUMELLA	TOOTHCOMB	EPIDERMIC	ZEUGMATIC
SABADILLA	COCKSCOMB	SYNONYMIC	ASTHMATIC
CEBADILLA	HONEYCOMB	METONYMIC	GRAMMATIC
CEVADILLA	CURRYCOMB	INORGANIC	ZYGOMATIC
SAPODILLA	DISENTOMB	MESSIANIC	IDIOMATIC
CAMARILLA	ALTARTOMB	BRAHMANIC	AXIOMATIC
GUERRILLA		PURITANIC	CHROMATIC
SCINTILLA		PYROGENIC	AUTOMATIC
CARAMBOLA	--------C	CRYOGENIC	SPERMATIC
HYPERBOLA		JACOBINIC	MIASMATIC
SCAGLIOLA	TACAMAHAC	TRICLINIC	PLASMATIC
VIBRACULA	EGOMANIAC	ISOCLINIC	PRISMATIC

95

TRAUMATIC	ELOHISTIC	UNCLOUDED	FORENAMED
RHEUMATIC	SOPHISTIC	FULLSPEED	CONFIRMED
PNEUMATIC	REALISTIC	FILIGREED	UNFEIGNED
APLANATIC	DUALISTIC	CHICKWEED	ENGRAINED
QUADRATIC	BALLISTIC	DYERSWEED	INGRAINED
ANASTATIC	STYLISTIC	DRIFTWEED	UNTRAINED
STALACTIC	ANIMISTIC	UNENGAGED	UNSTAINED
SYNTACTIC	AGONISTIC	UNFLEDGED	UNDEFINED
DIALECTIC	PATRISTIC	BOWLEGGED	UNREFINED
ANALECTIC	HEURISTIC	UNAVENGED	ABANDONED
SUBARCTIC	STATISTIC	UNMATCHED	CUSHIONED
ANTARCTIC	PIETISTIC	UNWATCHED	MULLIONED
ASYNDETIC	EGOTISTIC	DEBAUCHED	OPINIONED
ENERGETIC	CASUISTIC	UNTOUCHED	BASTIONED
PROPHETIC	ATAVISTIC	UNWEIGHED	GALLOONED
DIATHETIC	ENCAUSTIC	UNABASHED	CHEVRONED
APATHETIC	METHYSTIC	BLOODSHED	HIGHTONED
SYNTHETIC	SCORBUTIC	FURNISHED	UNLEARNED
AESTHETIC	TRACHYTIC	WATERSHED	CONCERNED
HOMILETIC	EPIPHYTIC	UNSCATHED	UNADORNED
SPLENETIC	ZOOPHYTIC	UNSTUDIED	UNCROWNED
PHRENETIC	PARALYTIC	QUALIFIED	PORTICOED
THRENETIC	CHARABANC	DIGNIFIED	UNSTAMPED
DIANOETIC	OPODELDOC	GLORIFIED	DEVELOPED
THEORETIC		PETRIFIED	SCALLOPED
COPESETIC		VITRIFIED	DEWLAPPED
JACOBITIC		CERTIFIED	QUADRUPED
CYNEGITIC	--------D	UNSULLIED	FLAPEARED
PROCLITIC		PANOPLIED	CROPEARED
IMPOLITIC	ROUNDHEAD	BALCONIED	CROSSBRED
PISOLITIC	THICKHEAD	UNWEARIED	CALIBERED
SYBARITIC	BLOCKHEAD	DRAPERIED	CHAMBERED
DIACRITIC	CROSSHEAD	PILLORIED	BLADDERED
DENDRITIC	BLACKLEAD	ECSTASIED	GLANDERED
NEPHRITIC	OUTSPREAD	UNTRACKED	FEATHERED
ARTHRITIC	ROADSTEAD	WRYNECKED	WEATHERED
PLEURITIC	HOMESTEAD	FETLOCKED	CROSIERED
ASPHALTIC	FARMSTEAD	CASSOCKED	CHECKERED
GEOMANTIC	CROSSROAD	UNTHANKED	WHISKERED
AUTHENTIC	MEGAFARAD	TENTACLED	SLIPPERED
PSYCHOTIC	HAMADRYAD	FASCICLED	TROUSERED
SYMBIOTIC	UNPLUMBED	TUBERCLED	UNWATERED
PATRIOTIC	FLOWERBED	UNBRIDLED	CHARTERED
EXOSMOTIC	CHUBFACED	UNRUFFLED	SCATTERED
EPIZOOTIC	BALDFACED	HOBNAILED	CHEQUERED
SCLEROTIC	BOLDFACED	UNSPOILED	UNEXPIRED
CHLOROTIC	BAREFACED	SANDALLED	UNDESIRED
AMAUROTIC	BENEFICED	FUNNELLED	UNTUTORED
EMBRYOTIC	SURPLICED	BARRELLED	UNINJURED
EPILEPTIC	UNNOTICED	LAURELLED	ENAMOURED
PROLEPTIC	AFFIANCED	CHISELLED	UNASSURED
DYSPEPTIC	BIGHEADED	TASSELLED	CINCTURED
CATHARTIC	PIGHEADED	TRAVELLED	CIVILISED
BOMBASTIC	UNDECIDED	PENCILLED	ORGANISED
SARCASTIC	UNDIVIDED	UNSKILLED	SURPRISED
ORGIASTIC	PRETENDED	WEEVILLED	PRACTISED
INELASTIC	DIAMONDED	EMBATTLED	UNADVISED
GYMNASTIC	UNBOUNDED	UNSETTLED	UNOPPOSED
FANTASTIC	UNFOUNDED	UNDREAMED	UNEXPOSED
ATHEISTIC	UNWOUNDED	UNASHAMED	SUBMERSED
	UNGUARDED		

UNBIASSED	HAMFISTED	THRESHOLD	HETEROPOD
CONFESSED	EXHAUSTED	BLACKBAND	GASTROPOD
PROFESSED	UNSPOTTED	BRASSBAND	CARPETROD
UNBLESSED	UNDILUTED	WAISTBAND	DISREGARD
ADDRESSED	INVOLUTED	WRISTBAND	INTERLARD
UNDRESSED	UNSUBDUED	BELLYBAND	SPIKENARD
DEPRESSED	CONTINUED	AFOREHAND	CARDBOARD
UNCROSSED	TRINERVED	UNDERHAND	SIDEBOARD
DEDICATED	UNENDOWED	RIGHTHAND	BASEBOARD
TUNICATED	EAGLEEYED	SHORTHAND	DASHBOARD
MURICATED	HACKNEYED	COURTHAND	BACKBOARD
TRUNCATED	BLEAREYED	FIRSTHAND	BUCKBOARD
FLOREATED	PALFREYED	CLEVELAND	BILLBOARD
EMACIATED	UNALLOYED	CRASHLAND	CLAPBOARD
FASCIATED	CIVILIZED	DREAMLAND	CHIPBOARD
UNRELATED	ORGANIZED	GREENLAND	SHIPBOARD
OCELLATED	CREAMLAID	FAIRYLAND	STARBOARD
STELLATED	NURSEMAID	REPRIMAND	OVERBOARD
TUBULATED	HOUSEMAID	FIREBRAND	FOOTBOARD
UNDULATED	DAIRYMAID	DUSTBRAND	DARTBOARD
TEGULATED	AFORESAID	QUICKSAND	SAFEGUARD
ANGULATED	APARTHEID	AMPERSAND	FIREGUARD
LUNULATED	QUADRIFID	WITHSTAND	BODYGUARD
CASEMATED	CHRYSALID	TRANSCEND	BOULEVARD
VAGINATED	PITHECOID	REPREHEND	EARTHWARD
ECHINATED	MENISCOID	APPREHEND	NORTHWARD
LAMINATED	PTERYGOID	PENFRIEND	SOUTHWARD
LACERATED	SCORPIOID	BOYFRIEND	AFTERWARD
CAMERATED	CORALLOID	RECOMMEND	NIGHTWARD
DECORATED	METALLOID	GAVELKIND	GRAVEYARD
ZERORATED	MONGOLOID	WOMANKIND	CLOTHYARD
ROSTRATED	VARIOLOID	WHIRLWIND	STOCKYARD
DIGITATED	CELLULOID	DACHSHUND	STEELYARD
TORQUATED	ARACHNOID	DUMBFOUND	COURTYARD
REDOUBTED	PLATINOID	HOREHOUND	HAPHAZARD
UNDOUBTED	SALMONOID	BUCKHOUND	SWINEHERD
DEFLECTED	ELLIPSOID	HOARHOUND	BLACKBIRD
RINGLETED	HAEMATOID	DEERHOUND	BOWERBIRD
CORONETED	TREMATOID	GRAYHOUND	DICKYBIRD
PARAPETED	DERMATOID	GREYHOUND	DECACHORD
DELIGHTED	THANATOID	FOOTPOUND	HEXACHORD
INHIBITED	PLANETOID	WHOLEFOOD	MONOCHORD
CONCEITED	GRANITOID	CHILDHOOD	CATCHWORD
UNLIMITED	ICHTHYOID	THANEHOOD	WATCHWORD
UNMERITED	TRAPEZOID	FALSEHOOD	BACKSWORD
UNVISITED	TRICUSPID	HARDIHOOD	CROSSWORD
UNINVITED	PERFERVID	WOMANHOOD	OVERCLOUD
ENCHANTED	MINEFIELD	QUEENHOOD	OVERCROWD
GARMENTED	COALFIELD	ADULTHOOD	
CONTENTED	CORNFIELD	SAINTHOOD	
UNTAINTED	STEPCHILD	WIDOWHOOD	--------E
UNJOINTED	OVERBUILD	LIFEBLOOD	
APPOINTED	STONECOLD	EAGLEWOOD	PETECHIAE
UNSTINTED	BLINDFOLD	COPSEWOOD	BRANCHIAE
UNDAUNTED	THREEFOLD	TOUCHWOOD	VERTEBRAE
FINFOOTED	SEVENFOLD	BRUSHWOOD	VIBRISSAE
CONCERTED	SHEEPFOLD	UNDERWOOD	ASTROLABE
CONTORTED	EIGHTFOLD	ALOESWOOD	SUBSCRIBE
DISTORTED	LEASEHOLD	DRIFTWOOD	PRESCRIBE
CONGESTED	HOUSEHOLD	PHYLLOPOD	PROSCRIBE

INTERFACE
ABOUTFACE
BLONDLACE
FIREPLACE
INTERLACE
AEROSPACE
TIMEPIECE
COWARDICE
PREJUDICE
BOXOFFICE
SACRIFICE
FISHSLICE
PRECIPICE
LIQUORICE
ARMISTICE
INJUSTICE
IMPEDANCE
CLOGDANCE
AVOIDANCE
FOLKDANCE
ABUNDANCE
VENGEANCE
ARROGANCE
PERCHANCE
MISCHANCE
DALLIANCE
APPLIANCE
SEMBLANCE
FREELANCE
SIBILANCE
VIGILANCE
DEMILANCE
AMBULANCE
PETULANCE
ORDINANCE
DOMINANCE
ASSONANCE
CLEARANCE
CUMBRANCE
TOLERANCE
UTTERANCE
SEVERANCE
FRAGRANCE
IGNORANCE
ABERRANCE
ENDURANCE
INSURANCE
ASSURANCE
PLEASANCE
OBEISANCE
PUISSANCE
RECUSANCE
SUBSTANCE
QUITTANCE
PURSUANCE
GRIEVANCE
RELEVANCE
ALLOWANCE
ANNOYANCE
RETICENCE

INNOCENCE
ACESCENCE
DECADENCE
ACCIDENCE
INCIDENCE
RESIDENCE
IMPUDENCE
INDIGENCE
DILIGENCE
EMERGENCE
NESCIENCE
OBEDIENCE
PRURIENCE
ESURIENCE
REDOLENCE
INDOLENCE
INSOLENCE
FECULENCE
TEMULENCE
VIRULENCE
PURULENCE
VEHEMENCE
IMMANENCE
IMMINENCE
HALFPENCE
FOURPENCE
DEFERENCE
REFERENCE
INFERENCE
ADHERENCE
INHERENCE
COHERENCE
REVERENCE
APPETENCE
PENITENCE
IMPOTENCE
EXISTENCE
AFFLUENCE
EFFLUENCE
INFLUENCE
ELOQUENCE
PRONOUNCE
WORKFORCE
REINFORCE
ACQUIESCE
INTUMESCE
REPRODUCE
INTRODUCE
BARRICADE
CAVALCADE
MOTORCADE
AMBUSCADE
ORANGEADE
LAMPSHADE
MARMALADE
EVERGLADE
FUSILLADE
ESPLANADE
PROMENADE
COLONNADE

GASCONADE
CANNONADE
CARRONADE
CASSONADE
COTTONADE
GALLOPADE
ANTITRADE
OVERTRADE
PALLISADE
RETROCEDE
INTERCEDE
MILLEPEDE
CENTIPEDE
SUPERSEDE
FUNGICIDE
GERMICIDE
VERMICIDE
VULPICIDE
PARRICIDE
MATRICIDE
PATRICIDE
FOETICIDE
PESTICIDE
PHOSPHIDE
LANDSLIDE
BACKSLIDE
BROADSIDE
ALONGSIDE
RIVERSIDE
FLOODTIDE
SUBDIVIDE
HYDROXIDE
DEMIMONDE
INCOMMODE
INTERNODE
ELECTRODE
TREMATODE
INTERLUDE
DESUETUDE
LONGITUDE
AMPLITUDE
PLENITUDE
MAGNITUDE
LIPPITUDE
TURPITUDE
LASSITUDE
BEATITUDE
PLATITUDE
GRATITUDE
RECTITUDE
MULTITUDE
CERTITUDE
FORTITUDE
VASTITUDE
SERVITUDE
BUMBLEBEE
DISPONDEE
MORTGAGEE
DEBAUCHEE
CONFIRMEE

MAHARANEE
CONSIGNEE
FANCYFREE
CORALTREE
FRUITTREE
FRICASSEE
SUBLESSEE
TENNESSEE
ADDRESSEE
DEDICATEE
GUARANTEE
PRESENTEE
MUFFETTEE
COMMITTEE
VOUCHSAFE
RECHAUFFE
AFTERLIFE
CASEKNIFE
JACKKNIFE
HOUSEWIFE
APPENDAGE
BRONZEAGE
DISENGAGE
SHRINKAGE
VASSALAGE
CARTILAGE
HYPALLAGE
SCRIMMAGE
SCRUMMAGE
ORPHANAGE
MISMANAGE
CAREENAGE
SIPHONAGE
GABIONAGE
ESPIONAGE
COMMONAGE
MATRONAGE
PATRONAGE
PARSONAGE
PERSONAGE
FRONTPAGE
CELLARAGE
DISPARAGE
PILFERAGE
BROKERAGE
COOPERAGE
PORTERAGE
OSSIFRAGE
SAXIFRAGE
ANCHORAGE
FACTORAGE
DEMURRAGE
ARBITRAGE
ENCOURAGE
ENTOURAGE
PASTURAGE
KNIGHTAGE
HERMITAGE
ADVANTAGE
CLIENTAGE

PARENTAGE	FAIRYTALE	TOLERABLE	IMMUTABLE
REPORTAGE	CLUBBABLE	NUMERABLE	REPUTABLE
KENTLEDGE	CLIMBABLE	GENERABLE	IMPUTABLE
KNOWLEDGE	MEDICABLE	VENERABLE	SCRUTABLE
CAMBRIDGE	REVOCABLE	SUPERABLE	RESCUABLE
CARTRIDGE	DECIDABLE	MISERABLE	SUBDUABLE
PARTRIDGE	AVOIDABLE	ALTERABLE	INEQUABLE
FOREJUDGE	DIVIDABLE	UTTERABLE	UNEQUABLE
SACRILEGE	WIELDABLE	SEVERABLE	CLEAVABLE
SORTILEGE	MOULDABLE	ADMIRABLE	DERIVABLE
PRIVILEGE	AMENDABLE	EXPIRABLE	REVIVABLE
DISOBLIGE	WOUNDABLE	DESIRABLE	REMOVABLE
LONGRANGE	GUARDABLE	MEMORABLE	IMMOVABLE
REARRANGE	DELUDABLE	HONORABLE	RENEWABLE
CHALLENGE	PEACEABLE	VAPORABLE	ALLOWABLE
SURCHARGE	TRACEABLE	SECURABLE	REPAYABLE
DISCHARGE	AGREEABLE	ENDURABLE	ENJOYABLE
OVERGORGE	GAUGEABLE	FIGURABLE	FREEZABLE
VERMIFUGE	MALLEABLE	INSURABLE	COERCIBLE
FEBRIFUGE	PERMEABLE	ASSURABLE	IRASCIBLE
TOOTHACHE	SHAPEABLE	SATURABLE	ADDUCIBLE
HEARTACHE	INEFFABLE	EXCISABLE	DEDUCIBLE
MOUSTACHE	LITIGABLE	DEMISABLE	REDUCIBLE
BELLYACHE	NAVIGABLE	ADVISABLE	INDUCIBLE
AVALANCHE	LEVIGABLE	DEVISABLE	INAUDIBLE
RECHERCHE	REACHABLE	DEPOSABLE	ILLEGIBLE
DYSTROPHE	TEACHABLE	IMPOSABLE	DIRIGIBLE
UNSHEATHE	MATCHABLE	OPPOSABLE	FRANGIBLE
INBREATHE	TOUCHABLE	CLASSABLE	INDELIBLE
INWREATHE	WEIGHABLE	ACCUSABLE	DIVISIBLE
UNWREATHE	LAUGHABLE	EXCUSABLE	INVISIBLE
MENAGERIE	UNAMIABLE	REFUSABLE	OMISSIBLE
GAUCHERIE	SPEAKABLE	DEBATABLE	PLAUSIBLE
DIABLERIE	BREAKABLE	UNEATABLE	INFUSIBLE
SPARTERIE	THINKABLE	CREATABLE	AVERTIBLE
BRIDECAKE	DRINKABLE	PALATABLE	DISSEMBLE
CREAMCAKE	EXHALABLE	DILATABLE	INSOLUBLE
FRUITCAKE	AVAILABLE	DOUBTABLE	SPECTACLE
HANDSHAKE	UNTAMABLE	TRACTABLE	ADMINICLE
SNOWFLAKE	CLAIMABLE	VEGETABLE	CHRONICLE
CANEBRAKE	ESTIMABLE	TIMETABLE	VENTRICLE
CORNCRAKE	FLAMMABLE	COVETABLE	CARBUNCLE
SHELDRAKE	RESUMABLE	HABITABLE	SIPHUNCLE
WAPENTAKE	ALIENABLE	EXCITABLE	CORPUSCLE
UNDERTAKE	DISENABLE	COGITABLE	ASTRADDLE
KITTIWAKE	UNTENABLE	LIMITABLE	MANHANDLE
GRAYWACKE	PREGNABLE	IGNITABLE	PANHANDLE
HITCHHIKE	DRAINABLE	HERITABLE	CLIENTELE
CHILDLIKE	TRAINABLE	VERITABLE	RESHUFFLE
DEATHLIKE	DEFINABLE	IRRITABLE	PORBEAGLE
WOMANLIKE	UNTUNABLE	EQUITABLE	BALDEAGLE
UNWARLIKE	INCAPABLE	GRANTABLE	BEDRAGGLE
HANDSPIKE	ESCAPABLE	PRINTABLE	BESPANGLE
ARTICHOKE	GRASPABLE	TURNTABLE	RECTANGLE
SUNSTROKE	REPARABLE	COUNTABLE	PENTANGLE
TRITICALE	SEPARABLE	DENOTABLE	SURCINGLE
FULLSCALE	EXECRABLE	ADAPTABLE	COMMINGLE
GALINGALE	LACERABLE	TEMPTABLE	RECONCILE
RATIONALE	REFERABLE	CONSTABLE	CROCODILE
WHOLESALE	INFERABLE	REFUTABLE	MEANWHILE

ERSTWHILE	BLASPHEME	METALLINE	SAXOPHONE
FACSIMILE	ENTHYMEME	VITELLINE	CHAPERONE
CHAMOMILE	QUICKLIME	COROLLINE	TOMBSTONE
CAMPANILE	PANTOMIME	SIBYLLINE	CURBSTONE
STOCKPILE	AFORETIME	BANDOLINE	GLADSTONE
EXPANSILE	FLEXITIME	MANDOLINE	LOADSTONE
EXTENSILE	ORIFLAMME	CRINOLINE	SANDSTONE
VIBRATILE	PROGRAMME	UNDERLINE	LODESTONE
PULSATILE	UNWELCOME	INTERLINE	FREESTONE
VERSATILE	METRONOME	COASTLINE	MILESTONE
INDUCTILE	AQUADROME	WAISTLINE	LIMESTONE
INFANTILE	VELODROME	MASCULINE	COPESTONE
DRAINTILE	AERODROME	JESSAMINE	BLUESTONE
INFERTILE	LITHESOME	UNDERMINE	HAILSTONE
EXSERTILE	WHOLESOME	DETERMINE	MILLSTONE
TURNSTILE	LOATHSOME	MEZZANINE	BRIMSTONE
UNSHACKLE	TOOTHSOME	FALCONINE	WHINSTONE
BESPECKLE	WEARISOME	SATURNINE	MOONSTONE
EARCOCKLE	TRICKSOME	SUBALPINE	TURNSTONE
PARBUCKLE	LIGHTSOME	CISALPINE	BUHRSTONE
BAGATELLE	HEARTSOME	PORCUPINE	WHETSTONE
GRISAILLE	HARMOTOME	MARGARINE	SAILBORNE
QUADRILLE	MICROTOME	SUBMARINE	MELBOURNE
AMPHIBOLE	PERISTOME	NECTARINE	IMPORTUNE
ROCAMBOLE	DISINHUME	ESTUARINE	OPPORTUNE
CARAMBOLE	FILOPLUME	ALIZARINE	BRAKESHOE
HYPERBOLE	HURRICANE	COLUBRINE	HORSESHOE
GIRANDOLE	SUGARCANE	BERBERINE	MISTLETOE
CREEPHOLE	SALANGANE	GLYCERINE	LANDSCAPE
RANTIPOLE	CYMOPHANE	TANGERINE	BROOMRAPE
RIGMAROLE	MONOPLANE	BUTTERINE	VIDEOTAPE
BANDEROLE	AEROPLANE	VICTORINE	SELLOTAPE
CASSEROLE	MARCHPANE	VERATRINE	STOVEPIPE
PRINCIPLE	DAMASCENE	VULTURINE	PITCHPIPE
DISPEOPLE	DROPSCENE	LIMOUSINE	DRAINPIPE
CRABAPPLE	POLYTHENE	INFANTINE	BLASTPIPE
PINEAPPLE	MAGDALENE	GALANTINE	PINSTRIPE
QUADRUPLE	ACETYLENE	EGLANTINE	TELESCOPE
QUINTUPLE	WOLVERENE	LEVANTINE	ENGISCOPE
DISMANTLE	SUPERVENE	BYZANTINE	PERISCOPE
TEAKETTLE	INTERVENE	ARGENTINE	BAROSCOPE
VESTIBULE	CHAMPAGNE	VALENTINE	HOROSCOPE
FASCICULE	COLUMBINE	LACERTINE	GYROSCOPE
POETICULE	CONCUBINE	ASBESTINE	ENGYSCOPE
MONTICULE	THYLACINE	CELESTINE	INTERLOPE
HOMUNCULE	MUSCADINE	FORESTINE	PHALAROPE
MAJUSCULE	GRENADINE	INTESTINE	TIGHTROPE
MINUSCULE	CELANDINE	GRAPEVINE	ARCHETYPE
GALLINULE	ALMANDINE	BOMBAZINE	CHEMITYPE
SLIDERULE	SECUNDINE	ORGANZINE	HELIOTYPE
MICROPYLE	GABARDINE	BLADEBONE	PHONOTYPE
DECASTYLE	SUPERFINE	WHALEBONE	FERROTYPE
LIFESTYLE	ABORIGINE	AITCHBONE	PHOTOTYPE
PERISTYLE	AIRENGINE	CHEEKBONE	PROTOTYPE
HYPOSTYLE	GASENGINE	WOEBEGONE	FIELDFARE
POLYSTYLE	MOONSHINE	HEADPHONE	NIGHTMARE
BAMBOOZLE	BREADLINE	TELEPHONE	CHINAWARE
SCHNOZZLE	INQUILINE	AUDIPHONE	ESCLANDRE
BLACKGAME	CABALLINE	XYLOPHONE	INSINCERE
MELODRAME	CORALLINE	HOMOPHONE	ADIPOCERE

BELVEDERE	MINIATURE	FORMALISE	BELLICOSE
INTERFERE	PRELATURE	NORMALISE	VORTICOSE
SOMEWHERE	PREMATURE	PLURALISE	FRUTICOSE
ELSEWHERE	CRENATURE	TANTALISE	VERRUCOSE
CAPONIERE	SIGNATURE	BRUTALISE	GRANDIOSE
BRASSIERE	CONNATURE	VISUALISE	FORECLOSE
CASSIMERE	SERRATURE	SEXUALISE	PAPILLOSE
PERSEVERE	DICTATURE	STABILISE	CELLULOSE
SEPULCHRE	CURVATURE	STERILISE	GRANULOSE
SOLITAIRE	DEPICTURE	FOSSILISE	FISTULOSE
CEASEFIRE	STRICTURE	FERTILISE	ANCHYLOSE
DEATHFIRE	STRUCTURE	METALLISE	LACRIMOSE
CROSSFIRE	GARNITURE	SYMBOLISE	LACRYMOSE
COACHHIRE	FURNITURE	EUPHEMISE	CALABOOSE
YORKSHIRE	SEPULTURE	SYSTEMISE	JUXTAPOSE
SCRUTOIRE	DEBENTURE	VICTIMISE	DECOMPOSE
TRANSPIRE	INDENTURE	ECONOMISE	SUPERPOSE
REINSPIRE	CALENTURE	EPITOMISE	INTERPOSE
ACROSPIRE	ADVENTURE	VULCANISE	INDISPOSE
GRANDSIRE	RECAPTURE	MECHANISE	TRANSPOSE
CHOKEBORE	ENRAPTURE	GALVANISE	SQUARROSE
HELLEBORE	SCRIPTURE	OXYGENISE	CESPITOSE
FOURSCORE	SCULPTURE	RECOGNISE	TOMENTOSE
STEVEDORE	DEPARTURE	SOLEMNISE	SCHISTOSE
COMMODORE	COVERTURE	TYRANNISE	SILIQUOSE
THEREFORE	DEPASTURE	CARBONISE	QUARTZOSE
WHEREFORE	IMPOSTURE	HARMONISE	RACEHORSE
SEMAPHORE	ADMIXTURE	SERMONISE	CARTHORSE
GONOPHORE	MANOEUVRE	PATRONISE	DRAYHORSE
GYNOPHORE	MELAPHYRE	MODERNISE	DEXTRORSE
SOPHOMORE	BRIEFCASE	EQUIPOISE	REIMBURSE
NEVERMORE	CRANKCASE	TURQUOISE	CONCOURSE
SINGAPORE	STAIRCASE	BARBARISE	DISCOURSE
MADREPORE	DISPLEASE	VULGARISE	PAILLASSE
EXTEMPORE	CINGALESE	SUMMARISE	RETROUSSE
DRUGSTORE	MANGANESE	MESMERISE	MENOPAUSE
HERBIVORE	POLONAISE	PULVERISE	SELFABUSE
CARNIVORE	DISPRAISE	DEODORISE	INTERFUSE
DECAMETRE	OSTRACISE	AUTHORISE	TRANSFUSE
DECIMETRE	IMPRECISE	GLAMORISE	CLUBHOUSE
KILOMETRE	ITALICISE	TEMPORISE	DEADHOUSE
SALTPETRE	PUBLICISE	TERRORISE	BAKEHOUSE
DECALITRE	ANGLICISE	FACTORISE	WAREHOUSE
DECILITRE	CRITICISE	EMPHASISE	WORKHOUSE
JOBCENTRE	SUBSIDISE	DRAMATISE	FARMHOUSE
CONCENTRE	LIQUIDISE	DOGMATISE	CHOPHOUSE
FAITHCURE	DEOXIDISE	CLIMATISE	FLOPHOUSE
PROCEDURE	METHODISE	MAGNETISE	BEERHOUSE
PREFIGURE	ANALOGISE	SENSITISE	POORHOUSE
CONFIGURE	EPILOGISE	HYPNOTISE	ALMSHOUSE
DISFIGURE	SYLLOGISE	EXPERTISE	BOATHOUSE
CANNELURE	APOLOGISE	ADVERTISE	PENTHOUSE
CHEVELURE	CATECHISE	IMPROVISE	OASTHOUSE
ADMEASURE	FRANCHISE	SUPERVISE	PLAYHOUSE
EMBRASURE	VERBALISE	CLOCKWISE	FISHLOUSE
ENCLOSURE	VANDALISE	OTHERWISE	BOOKLOUSE
INCLOSURE	FEUDALISE	CROSSWISE	DEERMOUSE
COMPOSURE	SOCIALISE	SLANTWISE	TRILOBATE
DISPOSURE	SERIALISE	COASTWISE	STYLOBATE
PLICATURE	ANIMALISE	CORYMBOSE	REPROBATE

APPROBATE	FUSTIGATE	DOORPLATE	DESTINATE
DESICCATE	PROROGATE	LEGISLATE	FESTINATE
EXSICCATE	SURROGATE	TRANSLATE	PULVINATE
DEPRECATE	OBJURGATE	CLAYSLATE	CARBONATE
IMPRECATE	EXPURGATE	EJACULATE	DIACONATE
ERADICATE	SUBJUGATE	SPECULATE	MUCRONATE
PREDICATE	CONJUGATE	SPICULATE	PERSONATE
VINDICATE	CORRUGATE	CALCULATE	INCARNATE
SYNDICATE	EXARCHATE	INOCULATE	ALTERNATE
VELLICATE	CALIPHATE	CIRCULATE	TRIBUNATE
IMPLICATE	PHOSPHATE	ACIDULATE	COADUNATE
DUPLICATE	BILABIATE	PENDULATE	FORTUNATE
EXPLICATE	OFFICIATE	COAGULATE	DISSIPATE
FORNICATE	ENUNCIATE	LINGULATE	INCULPATE
FABRICATE	ASSOCIATE	STIMULATE	EXCULPATE
IMBRICATE	IRRADIATE	FORMULATE	SYNCOPATE
LUBRICATE	IMMEDIATE	GRANULATE	APOCOPATE
METRICATE	DIMIDIATE	STIPULATE	EXTIRPATE
INTRICATE	REPUDIATE	CONSULATE	DISPARATE
EXTRICATE	RETALIATE	CAPSULATE	CELEBRATE
CORTICATE	AFFILIATE	SPATULATE	CALIBRATE
MASTICATE	HUMILIATE	GRATULATE	ADUMBRATE
RUSTICATE	DEFOLIATE	POSTULATE	LUCUBRATE
DEFALCATE	BIFOLIATE	PUSTULATE	DESECRATE
INCULCATE	EXFOLIATE	STALEMATE	THIRDRATE
BISULCATE	LACINIATE	INCREMATE	DEHYDRATE
SUFFOCATE	VICARIATE	SUBLIMATE	VISCERATE
COLLOCATE	INEBRIATE	ACCLIMATE	VIZIERATE
DISLOCATE	FIMBRIATE	COLLIMATE	GLOMERATE
EMBROCATE	EXCORIATE	REANIMATE	ENUMERATE
CONVOCATE	ELUTRIATE	INANIMATE	ITINERATE
DEMARCATE	INFURIATE	PROXIMATE	EXONERATE
ALTERCATE	LUXURIATE	CHECKMATE	TEMPERATE
BIFURCATE	INSATIATE	CLASSMATE	COOPERATE
EXPISCATE	NOVITIATE	SULTANATE	DESPERATE
OBFUSCATE	NEGOTIATE	OXYGENATE	PULSERATE
CORUSCATE	ALLEVIATE	DESIGNATE	REITERATE
MANDUCATE	LIXIVIATE	TURBINATE	INTEGRATE
DEPREDATE	CEPHALATE	VACCINATE	REMIGRATE
ELUCIDATE	CORRELATE	RUNCINATE	IMMIGRATE
CANDIDATE	VENTILATE	CIRCINATE	DENIGRATE
CUSPIDATE	UMBELLATE	FASCINATE	DEATHRATE
LIQUIDATE	APPELLATE	EVAGINATE	BIRTHRATE
DEOXIDATE	VACILLATE	ORIGINATE	ELABORATE
FECUNDATE	OSCILLATE	MACHINATE	PERFORATE
OBCORDATE	PAPILLATE	DECLINATE	MELIORATE
ENUCLEATE	TITILLATE	RECLINATE	DEFLORATE
COCHLEATE	DECOLLATE	POLLINATE	EVAPORATE
DELINEATE	CUCULLATE	STAMINATE	CORPORATE
CONCREATE	CHOCOLATE	ELIMINATE	DOCTORATE
PROCREATE	PERCOLATE	CRIMINATE	PASTORATE
BRACTEATE	URCEOLATE	CULMINATE	UNDERRATE
PROPAGATE	LINEOLATE	FULMINATE	PENETRATE
FLOODGATE	FAVEOLATE	ABOMINATE	IMPETRATE
VARIEGATE	PETIOLATE	GERMINATE	ARBITRATE
SEGREGATE	OSTIOLATE	TERMINATE	PROSTRATE
AGGREGATE	INVIOLATE	VERMINATE	FIRSTRATE
COLLIGATE	FISHPLATE	ACUMINATE	FRUSTRATE
CASTIGATE	BOOKPLATE	PECTINATE	PANDURATE
INSTIGATE	DIALPLATE	OBSTINATE	SUPPURATE

MICTURATE	VULPINITE	DESTITUTE	REMISSIVE
TRITURATE	BELEMNITE	INSTITUTE	DIFFUSIVE
INSENSATE	MAMMONITE	MICROCYTE	RECLUSIVE
DECUSSATE	MORMONITE	HALOPHYTE	SECLUSIVE
HUMECTATE	ANHYBRITE	AEROPHYTE	INCLUSIVE
CREPITATE	HYPOCRITE	ENTOPHYTE	EXCLUSIVE
STIPITATE	OZOCERITE	PROSELYTE	PRELUSIVE
PALPITATE	OZOKERITE	COLLEAGUE	COLLUSIVE
NICTITATE	PRETERITE	PEDAGOGUE	OBTRUSIVE
GRAVITATE	ERYTHRITE	DEMAGOGUE	INTRUSIVE
ORIENTATE	METEORITE	SYNAGOGUE	COMBATIVE
POTENTATE	ANCHORITE	DECALOGUE	PROBATIVE
CONNOTATE	FULGURITE	CATALOGUE	SICCATIVE
DEVASTATE	FAVOURITE	HOMOLOGUE	FRICATIVE
INTESTATE	MARCASITE	SINOLOGUE	EDUCATIVE
REINSTATE	REQUISITE	MONOLOGUE	PURGATIVE
OVERSTATE	EXQUISITE	OVERVALUE	MEDIATIVE
SAGITTATE	COMPOSITE	TECHNIQUE	TALKATIVE
PERMUTATE	BIPARTITE	EQUIVOQUE	COLLATIVE
DECIDUATE	MUSCOVITE	ARABESQUE	EMULATIVE
ATTENUATE	QUARTZITE	BURLESQUE	CALMATIVE
EXTENUATE	BACCHANTE	GROTESQUE	FORMATIVE
INSINUATE	VIGILANTE	ODALISQUE	LUCRATIVE
INFATUATE	FIGURANTE	CHIBOUQUE	OPERATIVE
PUNCTUATE	DEBUTANTE	OVERISSUE	ITERATIVE
FLUCTUATE	ASYMPTOTE	BICONCAVE	NARRATIVE
HABITUATE	MONOPTOTE	MISBEHAVE	PULSATIVE
EVENTUATE	FORETASTE	BONDSLAVE	CAUSATIVE
AGGRAVATE	ESTAFETTE	PALSGRAVE	IMITATIVE
CULTIVATE	COURGETTE	SEMIBREVE	TENTATIVE
CAPTIVATE	OUBLIETTE	YESTEREVE	HORTATIVE
BINERVATE	SERVIETTE	DIVORCIVE	PRIVATIVE
INNERVATE	NOVELETTE	CONDUCIVE	DEFECTIVE
RECURVATE	EPAULETTE	GERUNDIVE	EFFECTIVE
INCURVATE	LORGNETTE	UNDECEIVE	INFECTIVE
PARACLETE	WAGONETTE	OVERDRIVE	OBJECTIVE
COLUMBITE	SALOPETTE	ASSUASIVE	ADJECTIVE
TRILOBITE	CIGARETTE	PERVASIVE	SELECTIVE
COENOBITE	SOUBRETTE	REPULSIVE	DIRECTIVE
FROSTBITE	USHERETTE	IMPULSIVE	DETECTIVE
CHALYBITE	MAJORETTE	EXPULSIVE	INVECTIVE
EXTRADITE	AMOURETTE	REVULSIVE	DEDUCTIVE
RECONDITE	POUSSETTE	DIVULSIVE	SEDUCTIVE
APHRODITE	QUINTETTE	EXPANSIVE	INDUCTIVE
MALACHITE	QUARTETTE	DEFENSIVE	DEPLETIVE
SOCIALITE	PIROUETTE	OFFENSIVE	EXPLETIVE
ISRAELITE	PLAQUETTE	EXPENSIVE	ACCRETIVE
CARMELITE	BRIQUETTE	INTENSIVE	DECRETIVE
CORALLITE	ETIQUETTE	OSTENSIVE	SECRETIVE
SATELLITE	BANQUETTE	EXTENSIVE	EXCRETIVE
COCCOLITE	STATUETTE	EXPLOSIVE	TRADITIVE
SCAPOLITE	ATTRIBUTE	PURPOSIVE	PRIMITIVE
COPROLITE	PROSECUTE	CORROSIVE	DORMITIVE
NATROLITE	PERSECUTE	ASPERSIVE	COGNITIVE
CELLULITE	PARACHUTE	DETERSIVE	APERITIVE
GRANULITE	DISSOLUTE	RECURSIVE	NUTRITIVE
BEDLAMITE	CONVOLUTE	EXCURSIVE	SENSITIVE
DIATOMITE	TRANSMUTE	IMPASSIVE	FACTITIVE
VULCANITE	COMMINUTE	RECESSIVE	PARTITIVE
MANGANITE	DISREPUTE	EXCESSIVE	INTUITIVE

INCENTIVE	ANATOMIZE	FOOLPROOF	VETCHLING
RETENTIVE	EPITOMIZE	RUSTPROOF	EARTHLING
ATTENTIVE	VULCANIZE		CRACKLING
INVENTIVE	MECHANIZE		CHICKLING
PLAINTIVE	GALVANIZE	--------G	TWINKLING
PROMOTIVE	OXYGENIZE		SPARKLING
DECEPTIVE	HELLENIZE	CARPETBAG	APPALLING
RECEPTIVE	PLATINIZE	WHIRLIGIG	MODELLING
INCEPTIVE	SOLEMNIZE	CHAINGANG	PANELLING
IRRUPTIVE	TYRANNIZE	BOOMERANG	LEVELLING
ASSERTIVE	CARBONIZE	REJOICING	TOWELLING
DIGESTIVE	HARMONIZE	DEGRADING	THRILLING
EXECUTIVE	SERMONIZE	EXCEEDING	UNWILLING
EVOLUTIVE	MATRONIZE	UNHEEDING	SCHOOLING
REFLEXIVE	PATRONIZE	CONFIDING	STRIPLING
EQUIVALVE	MODERNIZE	UNBENDING	SHEARLING
STOCKDOVE	BARBARIZE	REGARDING	UNDERLING
CREAMWOVE	VULGARIZE	REWARDING	SCANTLING
BATTLEAXE	SUMMARIZE	ACCORDING	STARTLING
OSTRACIZE	TARTARIZE	WELLBEING	COURTLING
PUBLICIZE	MESMERIZE	SWINGEING	WRESTLING
ANGLICIZE	PAUPERIZE	SPRINGING	FIRSTLING
CRITICIZE	NEOTERIZE	BELONGING	TROUTLING
HYBRIDIZE	CAUTERIZE	PREACHING	SCREAMING
SUBSIDIZE	SILVERIZE	BREECHING	REDEEMING
DEOXIDIZE	PULVERIZE	SEARCHING	BESEEMING
METHODIZE	DEODORIZE	SCORCHING	REFORMING
DIALOGIZE	AUTHORIZE	CHURCHING	PRESUMING
ANALOGIZE	TERRORIZE	THATCHING	CONSUMING
EPILOGIZE	CICATRIZE	STITCHING	UNMEANING
SYLLOGIZE	MARTYRIZE	SLOUCHING	MADDENING
NEOLOGIZE	EMPHASIZE	THRASHING	GARDENING
APOLOGIZE	MEDIATIZE	THRESHING	DEAFENING
CATECHIZE	DRAMATIZE	PUNISHING	AWAKENING
VERBALIZE	DOGMATIZE	RAVISHING	SICKENING
FEUDALIZE	CLIMATIZE	SHEATHING	HAPPENING
LABIALIZE	AROMATIZE	BREATHING	SOFTENING
SOCIALIZE	MAGNETIZE	SOMETHING	FASTENING
ANIMALIZE	SONNETIZE	PLAYTHING	DESIGNING
NORMALIZE	SENSITIZE	HAYMAKING	RETAINING
SIGNALIZE	NARCOTIZE	FINICKING	EXAMINING
CARNALIZE	HYPNOTIZE	UNWINKING	ADJOINING
PLURALIZE	REBAPTIZE	PROVOKING	BEGINNING
TANTALIZE		REVEALING	JAWBONING
BRUTALIZE		SHAMBLING	RECKONING
VISUALIZE	--------F	BRAMBLING	REASONING
SEXUALIZE		TREMBLING	SEASONING
STABILIZE	STONEDEAF	SCUMBLING	LIGHTNING
SYPHILIZE	CORALREEF	WHEEDLING	FOREGOING
STERILIZE	DISBELIEF	WORLDLING	STRAPPING
FOSSILIZE	MISBELIEF	BRANDLING	ENDEARING
SUBTILIZE	BASRELIEF	SWINDLING	SEAFARING
FERTILIZE	PIKESTAFF	FOUNDLING	WAYFARING
METALLIZE	PLAINTIFF	UNFEELING	UNSPARING
SYMBOLIZE	FISTICUFF	SHAVELING	TIMBERING
FORMULIZE	FOODSTUFF	SHUFFLING	SOLDERING
EUPHEMIZE	BOOKSHELF	FLEDGLING	WANDERING
SYSTEMIZE	EARTHWOLF	SMUGGLING	VENEERING
VICTIMIZE	BOMBPROOF	SHINGLING	GOFFERING
ECONOMIZE	FIREPROOF	YOUNGLING	SUFFERING

FINGERING	IMPROVING	POLYGRAPH	FIFTEENTH
LINGERING	OBSERVING	ENDOLYMPH	SIXTEENTH
GATHERING	DESERVING	PARANYMPH	TEREBINTH
WITHERING	FOLLOWING	ENDOMORPH	LABYRINTH
WUTHERING	UNKNOWING	NEWSFLASH	BILLIONTH
TEMPERING	RIGHTWING	GATECRASH	MILLIONTH
SIMPERING	UNVARYING	SUCCOTASH	COLOCYNTH
COPPERING	UNPITYING	WHITEWASH	OSTROGOTH
FALTERING	DIPHTHONG	BRAINWASH	CERECLOTH
CENTERING	CACHOLONG	COLORWASH	DISHCLOTH
WESTERING	BINTURONG	REFURBISH	SACKCLOTH
LETTERING	UNDERHUNG	CLACKDISH	NECKCLOTH
MUTTERING	GROUNDHOG	HOUNDFISH	FOOTCLOTH
SILVERING	COFFEEBUG	BLACKFISH	TOLLBOOTH
FLOWERING	CLARETJUG	UNSELFISH	FORETOOTH
INQUIRING		DEVILFISH	BUCKTOOTH
TAILORING		JELLYFISH	BONEEARTH
FLAVORING	--------H	BACKSHISH	STALWORTH
OFFSPRING		BUCKSHISH	OUTGROWTH
DAYSPRING	ALLELUIAH	ESTABLISH	
ABHORRING	MAHARAJAH	REPUBLISH	
RECURRING	SHILLELAH	DISRELISH	--------I
HAMSTRING	OVERREACH	UNENGLISH	
BOWSTRING	SASSENACH	EMBELLISH	DZIGGETAI
MURMURING	SLOWCOACH	SQUEAMISH	JABORANDI
LABOURING	COCKROACH	SPLEENISH	LOTOPHAGI
COLOURING	SANDARACH	REPLENISH	PATCHOULI
UNCEASING	HEMISTICH	KITTENISH	CHARIVARI
PROMISING	GOLDFINCH	PREMONISH	SPAGHETTI
SURMISING	CHAFFINCH	REFURNISH	
SUNRISING	BELLPUNCH	GIBBERISH	
REPEATING	CHILIARCH	QUAKERISH	--------K
ANIMATING	MATRIARCH	LICKERISH	
AFFECTING	PATRIARCH	COPPERISH	BEEFSTEAK
PARGETING	DEADMARCH	BITTERISH	PICKABACK
MARKETING	DISCHURCH	CLEVERISH	HUCKABACK
FILLETING	OVERMATCH	LIQUORISH	HORSEBACK
JENNETING	SASQUATCH	VAPOURISH	HUNCHBACK
CARPETING	BOMBKETCH	VULTURISH	HATCHBACK
VELVETING	FORASMUCH	YELLOWISH	FLASHBACK
UPLIFTING	DISAVOUCH	PRETTYISH	GREENBACK
WEIGHTING	FERMANAGH	MACINTOSH	PAPERBACK
REVOLTING	BOBSLEIGH	BLOODBATH	BUSHWHACK
INSULTING	OVERWEIGH	PHILOMATH	APPLEJACK
FLAUNTING	EDINBURGH	AFTERMATH	BLACKJACK
EXCEPTING	CHINCOUGH	HOMEOPATH	BONEBLACK
DIVERTING	PARAGRAPH	OSTEOPATH	SHOEBLACK
REPORTING	TELEGRAPH	HUNDREDTH	COALBLACK
UNRESTING	EIDOGRAPH	NINETIETH	HAVERSACK
BESETTING	IDEOGRAPH	EIGHTIETH	THUMBTACK
BEFITTING	OLEOGRAPH	TWENTIETH	PINCHBECK
UNFITTING	IDIOGRAPH	THIRTIETH	RAINCHECK
UNWITTING	ALLOGRAPH	COCCOLITH	ROUGHNECK
ENGRAVING	HOLOGRAPH	RHINOLITH	BREAKNECK
BELIEVING	XYLOGRAPH	GOLDSMITH	SHIPWRECK
RELIEVING	HOMOGRAPH	LOCKSMITH	SKINFLICK
FORGIVING	MONOGRAPH	IRONSMITH	TOOTHPICK
MISGIVING	BAROGRAPH	THEREWITH	GOLDBRICK
LAWGIVING	CEROGRAPH	WHEREWITH	FIREBRICK
REVOLVING	AUTOGRAPH	FORTHWITH	BATHBRICK

RIKSTRICK	ZUMBOORUK	BACKPEDAL	ENCHORIAL
BRAINSICK		REGICIDAL	AUTHORIAL
CRABSTICK		HOMICIDAL	CENSORIAL
BUFFSTICK	--------L	FETICIDAL	SENSORIAL
DRUMSTICK		PYRAMIDAL	TONSORIAL
CHAPSTICK	HEBRAICAL	DISCOIDAL	CURSORIAL
SLAPSTICK	MONADICAL	LITHOIDAL	FACTORIAL
BAILIWICK	VERIDICAL	CYCLOIDAL	RECTORIAL
BLACKCOCK	JURIDICAL	COLLOIDAL	SECTORIAL
POPPYCOCK	DRUIDICAL	SIGMOIDAL	PICTORIAL
HOLLYHOCK	SYNODICAL	ETHMOIDAL	SUCTORIAL
CHUBBLOCK	PARODICAL	PREBENDAL	EDITORIAL
MATCHLOCK	MIRIFICAL	DECAPODAL	RAPTORIAL
INTERLOCK	ILLOGICAL	ANTIPODAL	SARTORIAL
FLINTLOCK	ENERGICAL	BEAUIDEAL	TEXTORIAL
ANTIKNOCK	PSYCHICAL	LARYNGEAL	MERCURIAL
FEEDSTOCK	GRAPHICAL	COCCYGEAL	CENTURIAL
BANKSTOCK	UNETHICAL	PIECEMEAL	GYMNASIAL
OVERSTOCK	UMBILICAL	COCHINEAL	AMBROSIAL
EIDERDUCK	DYNAMICAL	SEXAPPEAL	PRIMATIAL
DECOYDUCK	ENDEMICAL	NECTAREAL	SCIENTIAL
WOODCHUCK	POLEMICAL	MARMOREAL	ESSENTIAL
AWESTRUCK	ORGANICAL	CORPOREAL	POTENTIAL
FENUGREEK	SATANICAL	PURPUREAL	IMPARTIAL
EMBERWEEK	BOTANICAL	POPLITEAL	CELESTIAL
BOLSHEVIK	GALENICAL	STOMACHAL	PREPUTIAL
BEANSTALK	ARSENICAL	MONARCHAL	CONVIVIAL
FOOTSTALK	TECHNICAL	SENESCHAL	EFFLUVIAL
BOARDWALK	DOMINICAL	TRIUMPHAL	VIGESIMAL
CROSSWALK	LACONICAL	CATARRHAL	EPIDERMAL
TOWNSFOLK	CANONICAL	BETROTHAL	SUBNORMAL
RIVERBANK	SPHERICAL	AZIMUTHAL	BAPTISMAL
PICKTHANK	NUMERICAL	MICROBIAL	LACHRYMAL
CLOVEPINK	GENERICAL	ADVERBIAL	BACCHANAL
DEADDRUNK	EMPIRICAL	CONNUBIAL	FOGSIGNAL
SPRINGBOK	SATIRICAL	TRIFACIAL	MEDICINAL
STORYBOOK	WHIMSICAL	EDIFICIAL	OFFICINAL
FLESHHOOK	DROPSICAL	FINANCIAL	SYNCLINAL
SHEEPHOOK	CLASSICAL	GERUNDIAL	ISOCLINAL
DISEMBARK	UNMUSICAL	EPISODIAL	REGIMINAL
FLOODMARK	SCIATICAL	PROSODIAL	ABDOMINAL
TRADEMARK	FANATICAL	CUSTODIAL	BINOMINAL
BENCHMARK	HEPATICAL	COLLEGIAL	DOCTRINAL
BIRTHMARK	PIRATICAL	VESTIGIAL	MATUTINAL
WATERMARK	PRACTICAL	PETECHIAL	DECAGONAL
PITCHFORK	MIMETICAL	BRANCHIAL	OCTAGONAL
FIELDWORK	GENETICAL	BRONCHIAL	HEXAGONAL
SPADEWORK	HERETICAL	PAROCHIAL	POLYGONAL
FRAMEWORK	POLITICAL	TRINOMIAL	TORSIONAL
HOUSEWORK	PYRITICAL	CONGENIAL	PASSIONAL
PATCHWORK	LEVITICAL	VICENNIAL	SESSIONAL
EARTHWORK	IDENTICAL	TRIENNIAL	STATIONAL
HANDIWORK	IDIOTICAL	PERENNIAL	FACTIONAL
BRICKWORK	SCEPTICAL	OCTENNIAL	SECTIONAL
CLOCKWORK	ERISTICAL	SEXENNIAL	FICTIONAL
CROWNWORK	INDEXICAL	MARSUPIAL	EMOTIONAL
GUESSWORK	QUIZZICAL	ACTUARIAL	FLUXIONAL
FROSTWORK	PROVENCAL	SUBAERIAL	EMBRYONAL
FANCYWORK	EQUIVOCAL	VIZIERIAL	POLYZONAL
BERGAMASK	ARCHDUCAL	UNISERIAL	HODIERNAL

FRATERNAL	PERPETUAL	FIREDRILL	PICTOGRAM
COETERNAL	SPIRITUAL	CROWQUILL	HISTOGRAM
NOCTURNAL	ACCENTUAL	CATCHPOLL	DISESTEEM
ANTIPAPAL	UNISEXUAL	COURTROLL	STRATAGEM
MUNICIPAL	MEDIAEVAL	CHOKEFULL	JERUSALEM
PRINCIPAL	PRIMAEVAL	CHOCKFULL	DIAPHRAGM
EPISCOPAL	RETRIEVAL	APRILFOOL	EPIPHRAGM
PALPEBRAL	GENITIVAL	DAYSCHOOL	QUITCLAIM
VERTEBRAL	DISPROVAL	WHIRLPOOL	BROADBRIM
TRIHEDRAL	DISAVOWAL	LIVERPOOL	OVERWHELM
CATHEDRAL	PORTRAYAL	TOADSTOOL	MICROFILM
ILLIBERAL	PENNONCEL	FALDSTOOL	STOCKHOLM
BICAMERAL	BUFFWHEEL	CAMPSTOOL	PRINCEDOM
EPHEMERAL	DASHWHEEL	FOOTSTOOL	BUMBLEDOM
PUERPERAL	CARTWHEEL	CATERWAUL	POLYPIDOM
BILATERAL	UNGENTEEL	UNHEEDFUL	RASCALDOM
BILITERAL	CASTSTEEL	REMINDFUL	CUCKOLDOM
TRIFLORAL	ARCHANGEL	UNMINDFUL	MARTYRDOM
ELECTORAL	SCHLEMIEL	REGARDFUL	HOUSEROOM
CHAPARRAL	DOGKENNEL	CHANCEFUL	CRUSHROOM
DIAMETRAL	PERSONNEL	CHANGEFUL	CLOAKROOM
CADASTRAL	PIMPERNEL	SCATHEFUL	CHECKROOM
ANCESTRAL	SCOUNDREL	REBUKEFUL	CLASSROOM
FENESTRAL	GROUNDSEL	UNHOPEFUL	ELBOWROOM
SINISTRAL	BLACKMAIL	REPOSEFUL	THEREFROM
CLOISTRAL	SHAVETAIL	HEALTHFUL	DAIRYFARM
CLAUSTRAL	DISENTAIL	PLENTIFUL	FIREALARM
PALUSTRAL	NONPAREIL	BOUNTIFUL	PACHYDERM
INAUGURAL	ALMONDOIL	BEAUTIFUL	PERISPERM
UNNATURAL	MULTIFOIL	UNDUTIFUL	ENDOSPERM
APPRAISAL	CASTOROIL	SHOVELFUL	DISAFFIRM
SURPRISAL	TORMENTIL	UNSKILFUL	BACCIFORM
COMMENSAL	DAREDEVIL	SPLEENFUL	SACCIFORM
REHEARSAL	DEMIDEVIL	WONDERFUL	PISCIFORM
DISPERSAL	PUNCHBALL	MASTERFUL	CRUCIFORM
UNIVERSAL	BLACKBALL	PRAYERFUL	CORDIFORM
SUCCURSAL	STICKBALL	COLOURFUL	CUNEIFORM
DISMISSAL	EIGHTBALL	FORGETFUL	FUNGIFORM
REPERUSAL	FANCYBALL	POCKETFUL	VILLIFORM
ANTENATAL	WATERFALL	BUCKETFUL	VERMIFORM
DIALECTAL	NIGHTFALL	REGRETFUL	ACINIFORM
BUSHMETAL	MUSICHALL	FRIGHTFUL	FIBRIFORM
BELLMETAL	GUILDHALL	DECEITFUL	CAPRIFORM
OCCIPITAL	DANCEHALL	RESENTFUL	MITRIFORM
BICIPITAL	CLOTHHALL	SORROWFUL	VITRIFORM
PLACENTAL	FORESTALL	PROCONSUL	TAURIFORM
ELEMENTAL	BOOKSTALL		BURSIFORM
SEGMENTAL	REINSTALL		MULTIFORM
PIGMENTAL	DEATHBELL	--------M	DENTIFORM
ALIMENTAL	ALARMBELL		LENTIFORM
ANECDOTAL	BOMBSHELL	COMMENDAM	RESTIFORM
ANTIDOTAL	HARDSHELL	COFFERDAM	CYSTIFORM
SUBCOSTAL	UNDERSELL	AMSTERDAM	SCUTIFORM
COMMITTAL	SPEEDWELL	COLDCREAM	UNGUIFORM
ACQUITTAL	BRIDEWELL	PHAENOGAM	LARVIFORM
EPIPHYTAL	CROSSBILL	CRYPTOGAM	MISINFORM
BILINGUAL	CROWSBILL	PENTAGRAM	TRANSFORM
CONTINUAL	CHURCHILL	CABLEGRAM	CAIRNGORM
MENSTRUAL	TREADMILL	RADIOGRAM	BARNSTORM
EFFECTUAL	OVERSPILL	PHONOGRAM	SNOWSTORM

BLINDWORM	DARWINISM	PROOEMIUM	HERCULEAN
EARTHWORM	RIBBONISM	GELSEMIUM	MISDEMEAN
CATAPLASM	MAMMONISM	GERMANIUM	MELIBOEAN
ENDOPLASM	MORMONISM	RUTHENIUM	CYCLOPEAN
ECTOPLASM	PLATONISM	ASPLENIUM	CORNOPEAN
OSTRACISM	MODERNISM	ALUMINIUM	CAESAREAN
GOTHICISM	COMMUNISM	ZIRCONIUM	NECTAREAN
ANGLICISM	VOODOOISM	EUPHONIUM	TARTAREAN
GALLICISM	DICHROISM	HARMONIUM	CERBEREAN
ETHNICISM	HYLOZOISM	PLUTONIUM	CYTHEREAN
PHYSICISM	BARBARISM	ENTROPIUM	EPICUREAN
CRITICISM	VULGARISM	MARSUPIUM	SUFFRAGAN
CELTICISM	GARGARISM	HERBARIUM	PTARMIGAN
EROTICISM	CAESARISM	ELATERIUM	GLAMORGAN
MYSTICISM	PANDERISM	BACTERIUM	ASTRAKHAN
WITTICISM	QUAKERISM	TRIFORIUM	LEVIATHAN
HYBRIDISM	ISOMERISM	SENSORIUM	AMPHIBIAN
METHODISM	MESMERISM	COLLYRIUM	MICROBIAN
YANKEEISM	MANNERISM	GYMNASIUM	PHENICIAN
PARSEEISM	PAUPERISM	MAGNESIUM	PATRICIAN
ORANGEISM	NEOTERISM	SYMPOSIUM	PHYSICIAN
TRITHEISM	ESOTERISM	POTASSIUM	TACTICIAN
PANTHEISM	LISTERISM	STRONTIUM	DIETICIAN
EGOTHEISM	HETAIRISM	DELIQUIUM	MORTICIAN
FALANGISM	VAMPIRISM	EFFLUVIUM	CONFUCIAN
SYLLOGISM	TERRORISM	TRAPEZIUM	TRAGEDIAN
NEOLOGISM	EPICURISM	FLABELLUM	HEBRIDIAN
MONACHISM	DEFEATISM	FLAGELLUM	QUOTIDIAN
CATECHISM	DOGMATISM	ROSTELLUM	DRAVIDIAN
MASOCHISM	MAGNETISM	SCUTELLUM	PROSODIAN
ANARCHISM	EREMITISM	SPIRILLUM	CUSTODIAN
CHURCHISM	JESUITISM	RETICULUM	COLLEGIAN
FETISHISM	OCCULTISM	OPERCULUM	NORWEGIAN
CABBALISM	TARANTISM	CAPITULUM	NEOLOGIAN
TRIBALISM	NARCOTISM	DIACHYLUM	PELASGIAN
VERBALISM	HYPNOTISM	CONUNDRUM	SELACHIAN
RASCALISM	DESPOTISM	PYRETHRUM	MAMMALIAN
VANDALISM	QUIZOTISM	INDECORUM	CASTALIAN
FEUDALISM	REBAPTISM	COLOSTRUM	CARNELIAN
NEPHALISM	MONKEYISM	ULTIMATUM	CORNELIAN
RACIALISM	MACROCOSM	ARBORETUM	VIRGILIAN
SOCIALISM	MICROCOSM	EQUISETUM	REPTILIAN
ANIMALISM	CATACLYSM	ASPHALTUM	CASTILIAN
FORMALISM	TARAXACUM	SARMENTUM	MONGOLIAN
PLURALISM	COLCHICUM	CONTINUUM	VULCANIAN
CASUALISM	CREDENDUM	MENSTRUUM	TASMANIAN
RITUALISM	ATHENAEUM	PSEUDONYM	DARWINIAN
SYMBOLISM	PETROLEUM	HETERONYM	CHTHONIAN
EUPHEMISM	MAUSOLEUM	CRYPTONYM	CHELONIAN
EXTREMISM	CALCANEUM		PLUTONIAN
PESSIMISM	COLOSSEUM		NEWTONIAN
VOLCANISM	ENDOSTEUM	--------N	SLAVONIAN
VULCANISM	BUBBLEGUM		AMAZONIAN
MECHANISM	COLUMBIUM	DOMINICAN	SATURNIAN
FENIANISM	YTTERBIUM	ANTELUCAN	NEPTUNIAN
SHAMANISM	GYNOECIUM	MAHOMEDAN	TRIGYNIAN
GALVANISM	PALLADIUM	OSTRACEAN	ETHIOPIAN
JANSENISM	SPORIDIUM	SADDUCEAN	FALLOPIAN
CRETINISM	CONTAGIUM	MANICHEAN	BARBARIAN
CALVINISM	MAGNALIUM	MAUSOLEAN	CERCARIAN

BULGARIAN	DEATHSMAN	BOATSWAIN	COTILLION
VULGARIAN	GROOMSMAN	COTTONGIN	ANTHEMION
HUNGARIAN	STEERSMAN	BALDACHIN	COMPANION
TOPIARIAN	CRAFTSMAN	SPILLIKIN	COMMUNION
PALMARIAN	DRAFTSMAN	GRIMALKIN	CRITERION
LIBRARIAN	YACHTSMAN	TOURMALIN	CENTURION
SECTARIAN	POINTSMAN	ADRENALIN	PRECISION
DIETARIAN	SPORTSMAN	DIGITALIN	CONCISION
UNITARIAN	SELECTMAN	HOBGOBLIN	COLLISION
ESTUARIAN	FELLOWMAN	METHEGLIN	PREVISION
DIMYARIAN	CLERGYMAN	FRANCOLIN	PROVISION
CIMMERIAN	LIVERYMAN	TARPAULIN	REPULSION
HESPERIAN	QUARRYMAN	SAINTFOIN	IMPULSION
GREGORIAN	WHERRYMAN	CHINCAPIN	EXPULSION
VICTORIAN	FRYINGPAN	CHINKAPIN	REVULSION
NESTORIAN	CATAMARAN	BREASTPIN	DIVULSION
HISTORIAN	COURTESAN	SAFETYPIN	EXPANSION
TELLURIAN	CHARLATAN	SACCHARIN	RECENSION
CAUCASIAN	MAHOMETAN	WISCONSIN	ASCENSION
MAGNESIAN	SAMARITAN	TRAVERTIN	DIMENSION
CARTESIAN	SACRISTAN	HARLEQUIN	INTENSION
DIONYSIAN	ORANGUTAN	BRICKKILN	EXTENSION
DALMATIAN	FORBIDDEN	CHAWBACON	IMPLOSION
CHRISTIAN	BEDRIDDEN	SUBDEACON	EXPLOSION
VITRUVIAN	UNTRODDEN	BASILICON	CORROSION
MYROBALAN	DISBURDEN	EIRENICON	IMMERSION
POLICEMAN	CARRAGEEN	GERFALCON	ASPERSION
ORANGEMAN	PALANKEEN	JERFALCON	DETERSION
SCYTHEMAN	DAMASKEEN	GYRFALCON	REVERSION
STABLEMAN	EVERGREEN	COTYLEDON	DIVERSION
MIDDLEMAN	VELVETEEN	ZEUGLODON	INVERSION
SICKLEMAN	SEVENTEEN	IGUANODON	RECURSION
GENTLEMAN	HALLOWEEN	GLYPTODON	INCURSION
ENGINEMAN	OESTROGEN	BOMBARDON	EXCURSION
EXCISEMAN	UNBURTHEN	HYPOGAEON	IMPASSION
FRENCHMAN	OUTSPOKEN	HABERGEON	ACCESSION
CHURCHMAN	FORETOKEN	TRUNCHEON	RECESSION
SCOTCHMAN	LOVETOKEN	SCUTCHEON	SECESSION
PLOUGHMAN	GENTLEMEN	CHAMELEON	EGRESSION
SCHOOLMAN	MISSHAPEN	ENDECAGON	OBSESSION
PATROLMAN	ENLIGHTEN	DODECAGON	ADMISSION
MUSSULMAN	FLYBITTEN	BANDWAGON	DEMISSION
RIBBONMAN	UNWRITTEN	TRILITHON	REMISSION
FOREWOMAN	FORGOTTEN	OSTRACION	DIFFUSION
FISHWOMAN	HALFDOZEN	SUSPICION	SUFFUSION
WORKWOMAN	CHAMPAIGN	COLLODION	CONFUSION
CHARWOMAN	SOVEREIGN	ACCORDION	PROFUSION
KINSWOMAN	UNDERSIGN	CONTAGION	OCCLUSION
CELLARMAN	APPLEJOHN	SUBREGION	SECLUSION
FISHERMAN	PREORDAIN	STANCHION	EXCLUSION
HAMMERMAN	CHILBLAIN	PYGMALION	COLLUSION
EALDORMAN	PORCELAIN	BATTALION	PROLUSION
COLOURMAN	DOWNTRAIN	DANDELION	OBTRUSION
GUARDSMAN	CONSTRAIN	PARHELION	DETRUSION
SWORDSMAN	CHIEFTAIN	ANTHELION	INTRUSION
TRIBESMAN	UNCERTAIN	POSTILION	EXTRUSION
TRADESMAN	ASCERTAIN	MEDALLION	CONTUSION
BRIDESMAN	APPERTAIN	REBELLION	PERTUSION
SPOKESMAN	ENTERTAIN	DECILLION	PROBATION
STATESMAN	COCKSWAIN	MODILLION	PLACATION

PLICATION	CAUSATION	NUTRITION	JEFFERSON
FALCATION	LACTATION	DENTITION	FOSTERSON
SULCATION	DICTATION	PARTITION	AUTOMATON
AVOCATION	AGITATION	INTUITION	ASYNDETON
EVOCATION	IMITATION	DETENTION	SIMPLETON
FURCATION	SALTATION	RETENTION	BADMINTON
EDUCATION	MENTATION	INTENTION	UNCONCERN
GRADATION	FLOTATION	ATTENTION	SUBALTERN
OXIDATION	QUOTATION	INVENTION	MISGOVERN
EXUDATION	HORTATION	COMMOTION	EARTHBORN
PURGATION	GESTATION	PROMOTION	STILLBORN
RADIATION	ARCUATION	DECEPTION	FIRSTBORN
MEDIATION	VALUATION	RECEPTION	BREADCORN
FILIATION	SINUATION	INCEPTION	LONGICORN
FOLIATION	LIQUATION	EXCEPTION	CAPRICORN
EXPIATION	SITUATION	COEMPTION	SERRICORN
VARIATION	ELEVATION	EXEMPTION	CLAVICORN
STRIATION	PRIVATION	IRRUPTION	BROOMCORN
SATIATION	SALVATION	DESERTION	BUGLEHORN
VITIATION	NERVATION	INSERTION	KRUMMHORN
DEVIATION	REDACTION	ASSERTION	GREENHORN
CHELATION	DEFECTION	APPORTION	ALPENHORN
DEFLATION	REFECTION	INTORTION	BUCKTHORN
REFLATION	AFFECTION	EXTORTION	HEARTBURN
INFLATION	INFECTION	DIGESTION	ABOUTTURN
COLLATION	ABJECTION	INCAUTION	FINEDRAWN
VIOLATION	OBJECTION	EXECUTION	SHAKEDOWN
ISOLATION	DEJECTION	ELOCUTION	TOUCHDOWN
ADULATION	REJECTION	POLLUTION	BREAKDOWN
EMULATION	INJECTION	EVOLUTION	EIDERDOWN
OVULATION	SELECTION	REFLEXION	SWANSDOWN
CREMATION	DIRECTION	INFLEXION	COUNTDOWN
ANIMATION	RESECTION	CONNEXION	NIGHTGOWN
GEMMATION	BISECTION	PREFIXION	OVERBLOWN
SUMMATION	DETECTION	DEFLUXION	WELLKNOWN
FORMATION	ADDICTION	EFFLUXION	HALFCROWN
EMANATION	INDICTION	INFLUXION	OVERGROWN
CRENATION	DECOCTION	PADEMELON	
COGNATION	ABDUCTION	DECATHLON	
URINATION	ADDUCTION	SEMICOLON	--------O
RUINATION	DEDUCTION	DIACHYLON	
DAMNATION	REDUCTION	PERSIMMON	
PHONATION	SEDUCTION	DISCOMMON	BECCAFICO
PRONATION	INDUCTION	ICHNEUMON	CALAMANCO
CARNATION	DEPLETION	OLECRANON	BASTINADO
VERNATION	REPLETION	PANTALOON	CARBONADO
PALPATION	ACCRETION	HONEYMOON	DESPERADO
LIBRATION	SECRETION	AFTERNOON	MUSCOVADO
VIBRATION	EXCRETION	MUSKETOON	SFORZANDO
OPERATION	TRADITION	HYDROZOON	CRESCENDO
ITERATION	RENDITION	PROTOZOON	DECKCARGO
MIGRATION	CONDITION	THEREUPON	CAPRICCIO
ADORATION	PERDITION	WHEREUPON	PASTICCIO
NARRATION	ERUDITION	TRIHEDRON	SOLFEGGIO
SERRATION	COALITION	EPHEMERON	PISTACHIO
TITRATION	ABOLITION	BRANDIRON	IMBROGLIO
PULSATION	INANITION	CRAMPIRON	PUNCTILIO
SENSATION	COGNITION	FREEMASON	PORTFOLIO
CASSATION	DETRITION	CAPARISON	ARMADILLO
CESSATION	ATTRITION	ENCRIMSON	DUODECIMO
			SIXTEENMO

CAMPANERO	AFTERCROP	GEOMANCER	IMPEACHER
PIZZICATO	EAVESDROP	SENTENCER	STOMACHER
OBBLIGATO	UNDERPROP	DENOUNCER	BESEECHER
INAMORATO	SARCOCARP	RENOUNCER	SCRATCHER
INCOGNITO	COFFEECUP	ANNOUNCER	STRETCHER
CONTRALTO	BUTTERCUP	IMPLEADER	DEBAUCHER
ESPERANTO	CLARETCUP	SERENADER	TRIUMPHER
THEREINTO		PERSUADER	REFRESHER
WHEREINTO		SUCCEEDER	FURBISHER
WHEREUNTO	--------R	COWFEEDER	FLYFISHER
MANIFESTO		EMBROIDER	PUBLISHER
LARGHETTO	BEVELGEAR	GASHOLDER	GARNISHER
LAZARETTO	TROCHLEAR	CORIANDER	TARNISHER
	TRILINEAR	ICELANDER	VARNISHER
	COLLINEAR	LOWLANDER	BURNISHER
--------P	DISAPPEAR	COMMANDER	FURNISHER
	FISHSPEAR	GERMANDER	NOURISHER
DIRTCHEAP	UNDERWEAR	GOOSANDER	GODFATHER
DRAINTRAP	LIGHTYEAR	BYSTANDER	FORGATHER
JOCKSTRAP	CANESUGAR	CULLENDER	GODMOTHER
BOOBYTRAP	DATESUGAR	SUSPENDER	FINANCIER
SARANWRAP	COLCOTHAR	SURRENDER	BRIGADIER
OVERSLEEP	CONCILIAR	PRETENDER	GRENADIER
CASSAREEP	CLAUSALAR	CONTENDER	CUSTODIER
SKINNYDIP	TESSELLAR	BARTENDER	STUPEFIER
SPACESHIP	TONSILLAR	PROVENDER	LIQUEFIER
JUDGESHIP	DOGCOLLAR	REMAINDER	CRUCIFIER
THANESHIP	TUBICOLAR	ATTAINDER	MOLLIFIER
RAJAHSHIP	MOLECULAR	REJOINDER	NULLIFIER
CLERKSHIP	ORBICULAR	ABSCONDER	AMPLIFIER
RIVALSHIP	PEDICULAR	IMPOUNDER	MAGNIFIER
DEVILSHIP	VEHICULAR	EXPOUNDER	SCARIFIER
STEAMSHIP	FUNICULAR	MAILORDER	CLARIFIER
VICARSHIP	UTRICULAR	GUNPOWDER	FALSIFIER
SIZARSHIP	AURICULAR	TABASHEER	VERSIFIER
ELDERSHIP	VESICULAR	BANDOLEER	GRATIFIER
USHERSHIP	ARTICULAR	BUCCANEER	RECTIFIER
OWNERSHIP	AVUNCULAR	CANNONEER	CERTIFIER
PRIORSHIP	BILOCULAR	PRIVATEER	FORTIFIER
MAJORSHIP	BINOCULAR	TARGETEER	TESTIFIER
MINORSHIP	OPERCULAR	RACKETEER	JUSTIFIER
TUTORSHIP	FLOSCULAR	SONNETEER	SERASKIER
AUGURSHIP	GLANDULAR	PUPPETEER	CHEVALIER
CADETSHIP	IRREGULAR	GARRETEER	CORDELIER
GIANTSHIP	STELLULAR	PROFITEER	GONDOLIER
SAINTSHIP	MANIPULAR	PULPITEER	COSTUMIER
COUNTSHIP	UNPOPULAR	VOLUNTEER	PONTONIER
ABBOTSHIP	CAPITULAR	GAZETTEER	CHAINPIER
COURTSHIP	FLUORSPAR	MORTGAGER	PACEMAKER
ENVOYSHIP	REGISTRAR	OUTRIGGER	HOMEMAKER
HORSEWHIP	GIBRALTAR	EXCHANGER	SHOEMAKER
FINGERTIP	DESCRIBER	PHALANGER	BOOKMAKER
CHOKEDAMP	DISMEMBER	PASSENGER	BOOTMAKER
AFTERDAMP	SEPTEMBER	MESSENGER	STAYMAKER
CHAINPUMP	OUTNUMBER	SCAVENGER	SPINNAKER
CHINASHOP	BOXNUMBER	DERRINGER	CARETAKER
SWEETSHOP	PERTURBER	SCROUNGER	JAYWALKER
REDEVELOP	DISTURBER	HOROLOGER	DIESINKER
BELLYFLOP	DISGRACER	HAMBURGER	GASCOOKER
COCKAHOOP	ARTIFICER	LIMBURGER	BERSERKER

SCRIBBLER	WALLPAPER	DISGUISER	RECRUITER
SCRAMBLER	NEWSPAPER	MERGANSER	DRYSALTER
STRAGGLER	INNKEEPER	CONDENSER	DEFAULTER
STRUGGLER	BOXKEEPER	DISPENSER	CONSULTER
WASSAILER	SANDPIPER	REHEARSER	ENCHANTER
DESPOILER	DISTEMPER	DISPERSER	WARRANTER
SPRINKLER	DEVELOPER	TRAVERSER	AUGMENTER
CUDGELLER	KIDNAPPER	CANVASSER	COMMENTER
PROPELLER	DISPAUPER	WITNESSER	CARPENTER
GOSPELLER	CUPBEARER	ADDRESSER	DISSENTER
TRAVELLER	CALENDRER	REPRESSER	PREVENTER
SNIVELLER	CHAMBERER	ENGROSSER	MIDWINTER
DRIVELLER	SLUMBERER	FIREEATER	FOXHUNTER
SHOVELLER	BROIDERER	BEEFEATER	ENCOUNTER
GROVELLER	SLANDERER	GASHEATER	CORRUPTER
INDWELLER	MAUNDERER	TWOSEATER	SUBVERTER
DISTILLER	THUNDERER	PYROLATER	CONVERTER
THROTTLER	BLUNDERER	DESOLATER	PERVERTER
EMBEZZLER	PLUNDERER	BACKWATER	SUPPORTER
DECLAIMER	CHAFFERER	JERKWATER	ALABASTER
PARTTIMER	PROFFERER	CHARACTER	PAYMASTER
MIDSUMMER	SWAGGERER	ATTRACTER	POETASTER
CONFIRMER	FURTHERER	PERFECTER	SUGGESTER
CONFORMER	STAMMERER	RESPECTER	TRIMESTER
PERFORMER	WHIMPERER	SPHINCTER	PROTESTER
SHEBEENER	WHISPERER	CONCOCTER	SEQUESTER
STIFFENER	FRUITERER	CRICKETER	HARVESTER
KITCHENER	ADULTERER	TRINKETER	YOUNGSTER
SWEETENER	POULTERER	PARAMETER	SOPHISTER
CHASTENER	SAUNTERER	HEXAMETER	FILLISTER
ENLIVENER	CHARTERER	TELEMETER	GANNISTER
SCRIVENER	PLASTERER	PERIMETER	CHORISTER
ARRAIGNER	ROISTERER	TASIMETER	BARRISTER
FOREIGNER	SCATTERER	PEDOMETER	TRICKSTER
CONSIGNER	CHATTERER	HODOMETER	UPHOLSTER
BARGAINER	FLATTERER	RHEOMETER	THROWSTER
EXPLAINER	SMATTERER	AREOMETER	BESPATTER
ENGRAINER	SPUTTERER	ERIOMETER	MUSKETTER
CONTAINER	STUTTERER	KILOMETER	OUTFITTER
ABSTAINER	DELIVERER	ATMOMETER	PERMITTER
SUSTAINER	RECOVERER	ZYMOMETER	BEDSITTER
COALMINER	CONSPIRER	MANOMETER	GARROTTER
PURLOINER	PREFERRER	BAROMETER	BOGBUTTER
CONTEMNER	CONFERRER	AEROMETER	PRESBYTER
ALECONNER	HARBOURER	PYROMETER	BELEAGUER
DUNGEONER	SUCCOURER	GASOMETER	INTRIGUER
FASHIONER	CLAMOURER	OPTOMETER	HARANGUER
PENSIONER	TREASURER	VOLTMETER	CONTINUER
STATIONER	REINSURER	VOLUMETER	EXCHEQUER
PORTIONER	PURCHASER	TRUMPETER	RECONQUER
CAUTIONER	APPRAISER	BANQUETER	WHICHEVER
HARPOONER	EXORCISER	HEREAFTER	RETRIEVER
DETHRONER	MORALISER	FREIGHTER	GEARLEVER
DISCERNER	EQUALISER	SLAUGHTER	WHOSOEVER
EASTERNER	CIVILISER	INHABITER	HOWSOEVER
WESTERNER	ORGANISER	EXHIBITER	PERCEIVER
SOJOURNER	POLARISER	BACKBITER	REDELIVER
COPARTNER	THEORISER	FORFEITER	CONTRIVER
LANDOWNER	PRACTISER	DYNAMITER	CATSILVER
SANDPAPER	APPETISER	EXPLOITER	VOICEOVER

SPILLOVER	GLADIATOR	EXPOSITOR	WESTWARDS
CROSSOVER	SPOLIATOR	GUARANTOR	ANTIPODES
PRESERVER	INITIATOR	WARRANTOR	PHALANGES
CONSERVER	ESCALATOR	PRECENTOR	CACOETHES
VANCOUVER	MUTILATOR	TORMENTOR	NEPENTHES
SAFFLOWER	IMMOLATOR	LOCOMOTOR	CONGERIES
SUNFLOWER	DESOLATOR	VASOMOTOR	MYSTERIES
SWALLOWER	PECULATOR	PRECEPTOR	VARIETIES
LAWNMOWER	MODULATOR	RECEIPTOR	CALVITIES
OVERPOWER	REGULATOR	COADJUTOR	SEVENTIES
BELLTOWER	SIMULATOR	DISSEIZOR	INGLUVIES
DISPLAYER	INSULATOR	BUCENTAUR	ISOSCELES
RATEPAYER	DECIMATOR	BUTTERBUR	STRANGLES
PORTRAYER	ALIENATOR	CHAUFFEUR	SOMETIMES
GAINSAYER	NOMINATOR	RACONTEUR	SCARPINES
JOURNEYER	RUMINATOR	DAYLABOUR	PORTICOES
DESTROYER	RESONATOR	NEIGHBOUR	TORNADOES
IDEALIZER	DETONATOR	SPLENDOUR	TORPEDOES
MORALIZER	SEPARATOR	BEHAVIOUR	VOLCANOES
CIVILIZER	LIBERATOR	CORNFLOUR	PETTITOES
ORGANIZER	MODERATOR	TRICOLOUR	SCANSORES
ROMANIZER	TOLERATOR	DISCOLOUR	WALDENSES
POLARIZER	NUMERATOR	DEMEANOUR	ELEVENSES
THEORIZER	GENERATOR	DISHONOUR	INCUBUSES
APPETIZER	VENERATOR	ENDEAVOUR	GALLOWSES
BULLDOZER	DECORATOR	DISFAVOUR	OPTIMATES
FANCYFAIR	DEPURATOR	EXEQUATUR	OURSELVES
CANECHAIR	SPECTATOR		PHALANXES
BATHCHAIR	HESITATOR		FLESHINGS
DECKCHAIR	ANNOTATOR	--------S	RIDDLINGS
EASYCHAIR	GRADUATOR		SCUMMINGS
DISREPAIR	EXCAVATOR	CANDLEMAS	TRAPPINGS
RESERVOIR	RENOVATOR	MARTINMAS	BEESTINGS
EMBRACEOR	INNOVATOR	CHRISTMAS	BIESTINGS
POSTERIOR	REFRACTOR	HALLOWMAS	PROBOSCIS
FIFEMAJOR	DETRACTOR	DINOCERAS	CHRYSALIS
DRUMMAJOR	RETRACTOR	SASSAFRAS	DIGITALIS
ANTICHLOR	EXTRACTOR	ECONOMICS	AMARYLLIS
COUNCILOR	PROJECTOR	MECHANICS	ACROPOLIS
MONSIGNOR	PRELECTOR	GNOMONICS	EPIDERMIS
CONQUEROR	DEFLECTOR	HARMONICS	MACARONIS
SUSPENSOR	REFLECTOR	GEOPONICS	DEINORNIS
PRECURSOR	COLLECTOR	TECTONICS	AEPYORNIS
SUCCESSOR	CONNECTOR	HYSTERICS	BOURGEOIS
PROCESSOR	INSPECTOR	DIOPTRICS	ALLANTOIS
CONFESSOR	CORRECTOR	DRAMATICS	EPHEMERIS
PROFESSOR	PROSECTOR	DOGMATICS	VERDIGRIS
AGGRESSOR	DISSECTOR	DIDACTICS	AMBERGRIS
DEPRESSOR	PROTECTOR	EXEGETICS	PARABASIS
OPPRESSOR	PREDICTOR	ATHLETICS	PSORIASIS
POSSESSOR	CONDUCTOR	PHONETICS	DIATHESIS
INCUBATOR	INHABITOR	DIETETICS	SYNTHESIS
DEDICATOR	INHIBITOR	ACOUSTICS	PARENESIS
INDICATOR	EXHIBITOR	HIGHLANDS	DIAERESIS
ADVOCATOR	CAPACITOR	BACKWOODS	APHERESIS
EMENDATOR	SOLICITOR	BILLIARDS	SYNERESIS
ESCHEATOR	ADMONITOR	HOMEWARDS	SYNIZESIS
ABNEGATOR	APPARITOR	BACKWARDS	SILICOSIS
ALLIGATOR	INHERITOR	DOWNWARDS	PSYCHOSIS
NAVIGATOR	DEPOSITOR	EASTWARDS	CIRRHOSIS

SYMBIOSIS	GRACELESS	NIGHTLESS	CLOSENESS
ANKYLOSIS	VOICELESS	SIGHTLESS	LOOSENESS
EXOSMOSIS	PRICELESS	LIMITLESS	TERSENESS
MELANOSIS	JUICELESS	FRUITLESS	WHITENESS
DIAGNOSIS	FORCELESS	GUILTLESS	TRITENESS
PROGNOSIS	TRUCELESS	FAULTLESS	WASTENESS
SCLEROSIS	GUIDELESS	PLANTLESS	ACUTENESS
CHLOROSIS	SMOKELESS	SCENTLESS	VAGUENESS
AMAUROSIS	GUILELESS	TAINTLESS	GRAVENESS
HALITOSIS	SHAMELESS	POINTLESS	STIFFNESS
PROLEPSIS	BLAMELESS	STINTLESS	BLUFFNESS
EPIPHYSIS	CRIMELESS	FRONTLESS	GRUFFNESS
SYMPHYSIS	PLUMELESS	DAUNTLESS	WRONGNESS
APOPHYSIS	RHYMELESS	COUNTLESS	YOUNGNESS
PARALYSIS	SPINELESS	HEARTLESS	ROUGHNESS
CATALYSIS	SHAPELESS	CRESTLESS	TOUGHNESS
ATMOLYSIS	SHORELESS	TRUSTLESS	FRESHNESS
PHLEBITIS	CEASELESS	SPOUTLESS	APISHNESS
RHACHITIS	NOISELESS	SINEWLESS	HARSHNESS
SPLENITIS	PULSELESS	MONEYLESS	CAITHNESS
PHRENITIS	SENSELESS	SULTANESS	SPICINESS
RETINITIS	CAUSELESS	BROADNESS	JUICINESS
ENTERITIS	HOUSELESS	NAKEDNESS	SAUCINESS
NEPHRITIS	TASTELESS	TIREDNESS	HEADINESS
ARTHRITIS	VALUELESS	FIXEDNESS	READINESS
GASTRITIS	ISSUELESS	STAIDNESS	SHADINESS
PLEURITIS	GRAVELESS	RABIDNESS	GIDDINESS
HEPATITIS	NERVELESS	LUCIDNESS	MUDDINESS
CERATITIS	BRIEFLESS	RIGIDNESS	RUDDINESS
KERATITIS	REACHLESS	SOLIDNESS	NEEDINESS
PAROTITIS	MATCHLESS	TIMIDNESS	SEEDINESS
PARATAXIS	FLESHLESS	TUMIDNESS	HANDINESS
BOONDOCKS	DEATHLESS	RAPIDNESS	SANDINESS
GANGLIONS	FAITHLESS	VAPIDNESS	WINDINESS
FIREIRONS	TOOTHLESS	TEPIDNESS	MOODINESS
SIDEBURNS	MIRTHLESS	FETIDNESS	WOODINESS
INNUENDOS	WORTHLESS	LIVIDNESS	HARDINESS
AMIDSHIPS	TRUTHLESS	VIVIDNESS	TARDINESS
BLEACHERS	FANCILESS	BLANDNESS	WORDINESS
CALLIPERS	MERCILESS	GRANDNESS	CURDINESS
MESSIEURS	PENNILESS	BLINDNESS	GAUDINESS
SECATEURS	TRACKLESS	ROUNDNESS	BAWDINESS
HIGHCLASS	FLECKLESS	SOUNDNESS	LEAFINESS
WINEGLASS	STALKLESS	WEIRDNESS	HUFFINESS
BELLGLASS	THANKLESS	PROUDNESS	PUFFINESS
ISINGLASS	DREAMLESS	CRUDENESS	TURFINESS
ENCOMPASS	BRAINLESS	LARGENESS	FOGGINESS
COALBRASS	STAINLESS	LITHENESS	DINGINESS
BLUEGRASS	CROWNLESS	STALENESS	ITCHINESS
EMBARRASS	SLEEPLESS	NOBLENESS	WASHINESS
THUMBLESS	ORDERLESS	WHOLENESS	FISHINESS
THROBLESS	CHEERLESS	AMPLENESS	BUSHINESS
DREADLESS	WATERLESS	PRONENESS	PITHINESS
CHILDLESS	DOWERLESS	SPARENESS	LEAKINESS
BOUNDLESS	POWERLESS	AWARENESS	SHAKINESS
SOUNDLESS	ODOURLESS	WHERENESS	FLAKINESS
BLOODLESS	DOUBTLESS	OBESENESS	ROCKINESS
BEARDLESS	CRAFTLESS	FALSENESS	LUCKINESS
CLOUDLESS	SHIFTLESS	DENSENESS	MILKINESS
PLACELESS	DRIFTLESS	TENSENESS	SILKINESS

BULKINESS	PETTINESS	BLUNTNESS	LIMACEOUS
SULKINESS	WITTINESS	SMARTNESS	POMACEOUS
SMOKINESS	GOUTINESS	ALERTNESS	VINACEOUS
DUSKINESS	HEAVINESS	INERTNESS	CERACEOUS
HUSKINESS	SHOWINESS	SHORTNESS	ROSACEOUS
SCALINESS	CRAZINESS	MOISTNESS	CETACEOUS
MEALINESS	DIZZINESS	CURSTNESS	SETACEOUS
GODLINESS	BLEAKNESS	STOUTNESS	SILICEOUS
SILLINESS	BLACKNESS	GLUEYNESS	PUMICEOUS
JOLLINESS	SLACKNESS	READDRESS	SERICEOUS
MANLINESS	THICKNESS	LAUNDRESS	UNTIMEOUS
EARLINESS	QUICKNESS	FOUNDRESS	CUTANEOUS
BURLINESS	SLEEKNESS	OVERDRESS	ERRONEOUS
CURLINESS	BLANKNESS	SORCERESS	CINEREOUS
SURLINESS	CRANKNESS	PANDERESS	ARBOREOUS
LOWLINESS	FRANKNESS	MURDERESS	RIGHTEOUS
SLIMINESS	BRISKNESS	QUAKERESS	PLENTEOUS
GRIMINESS	VOCALNESS	COHEIRESS	BOUNTEOUS
FILMINESS	EQUALNESS	AUTHORESS	COURTEOUS
GUMMINESS	SMALLNESS	TAILORESS	BEAUTEOUS
ROOMINESS	CHILLNESS	VICTORESS	ANALOGOUS
RAININESS	STILLNESS	DOCTORESS	AMORPHOUS
SPININESS	WOFULNESS	DROPPRESS	SCIRRHOUS
SUNNINESS	AWFULNESS	STOPPRESS	BIBACIOUS
STONINESS	SOLEMNESS	CREATRESS	BODACIOUS
TAWNINESS	CLEANNESS	TRAITRESS	AUDACIOUS
DOWNINESS	HUMANNESS	MONITRESS	SAGACIOUS
PULPINESS	GREENNESS	TEMPTRESS	FUGACIOUS
HAPPINESS	BROWNNESS	REPOSSESS	SALACIOUS
NAPPINESS	DEACONESS	PRIESTESS	TENACIOUS
SAPPINESS	PYTHONESS	EDELWEISS	CAPACIOUS
WEARINESS	PATRONESS	ALBATROSS	RAPACIOUS
CHARINESS	CHEAPNESS	REPERCUSS	FERACIOUS
HOARINESS	STEEPNESS	PANTALETS	VERACIOUS
FIERINESS	PLUMPNESS	ENTREMETS	VORACIOUS
HAIRINESS	SHARPNESS	UMBILICUS	VIVACIOUS
SORRINESS	CRISPNESS	CERATODUS	DIOECIOUS
NOISINESS	CLEARNESS	AREOPAGUS	JUDICIOUS
PROSINESS	UNHARNESS	ASPARAGUS	OFFICIOUS
TIPSINESS	SOBERNESS	AMIANTHUS	MALICIOUS
MASSINESS	QUEERNESS	SARTORIUS	DELICIOUS
MOSSINESS	EAGERNESS	SPHACELUS	FEROCIOUS
FUSSINESS	OTHERNESS	STROBILUS	ATROCIOUS
LOUSINESS	GOVERNESS	MALLEOLUS	CONSCIOUS
MEATINESS	CRASSNESS	GLADIOLUS	ASTUCIOUS
SLATINESS	CROSSNESS	GAUDEAMUS	INSIDIOUS
LOFTINESS	GROSSNESS	IGNORAMUS	INVIDIOUS
SOOTINESS	GREATNESS	NYSTAGMUS	MELODIOUS
EMPTINESS	EXACTNESS	GINGLYMUS	EGREGIOUS
DIRTINESS	ERECTNESS	COTHURNUS	RELIGIOUS
HASTINESS	FLEETNESS	FRUTICOUS	INGENIOUS
NASTINESS	SWEETNESS	VERRUCOUS	SELENIOUS
TESTINESS	QUIETNESS	HAZARDOUS	ARSENIOUS
MISTINESS	SWIFTNESS	EPIGAEOUS	FELONIOUS
FUSTINESS	LIGHTNESS	PLUMBEOUS	PECUNIOUS
LUSTINESS	RIGHTNESS	FABACEOUS	VICARIOUS
RUSTINESS	TIGHTNESS	SEBACEOUS	NEFARIOUS
FATTINESS	UNFITNESS	MICACEOUS	BIFARIOUS
NATTINESS	SCANTNESS	TUFACEOUS	MALARIOUS
JETTINESS	FAINTNESS	FILACEOUS	IMPERIOUS

DELIRIOUS	BARBAROUS	AMPHIOXUS	STREAMLET
LABORIOUS	DEIPAROUS	EMBERDAYS	FLAGEOLET
NOTORIOUS	UNIPAROUS	HENDIADYS	CABRIOLET
INCURIOUS	OVIPAROUS		ESTAMINET
INJURIOUS	NECTAROUS		CLARIONET
PENURIOUS	TARTAROUS	--------T	SWIMMERET
LUXURIOUS	TENEBROUS		SPINNERET
VEXATIOUS	SLUMBROUS	TITTLEBAT	INTERPRET
FRACTIOUS	LUDICROUS	CONCORDAT	SULPHURET
FACETIOUS	DIANDROUS	BLOODHEAT	SUMMERSET
AMBITIOUS	ANHYDROUS	SUPERHEAT	SOBRIQUET
SEDITIOUS	ENHYDROUS	BUCKWHEAT	WOODCRAFT
BUMPTIOUS	CANCEROUS	MINCEMEAT	RUNECRAFT
OBLIVIOUS	PONDEROUS	FORCEMEAT	KINGCRAFT
LIXIVIOUS	MURDEROUS	HORSEMEAT	MAKESHIFT
OBNOXIOUS	OVIFEROUS	FLESHMEAT	GEARSHIFT
ANOMALOUS	OVIGEROUS	SWEETMEAT	SPINDRIFT
APETALOUS	DANGEROUS	COCKLEHAT	CANDYTUFT
TROUBLOUS	LECHEROUS	HOUSEBOAT	COCKFIGHT
CAUTELOUS	CANKEROUS	DREAMBOAT	BULLFIGHT
LIBELLOUS	TRIMEROUS	FERRYBOAT	HEADLIGHT
APHYLLOUS	DIPTEROUS	PETTICOAT	LIMELIGHT
VARIOLOUS	DEXTEROUS	DRESSCOAT	HIGHLIGHT
FRIVOLOUS	PULVEROUS	GREATCOAT	JACKLIGHT
GLOBULOUS	RANCOROUS	WAISTCOAT	MOONLIGHT
CALCULOUS	INODOROUS	NANNYGOAT	LAMPLIGHT
CREDULOUS	CLAMOROUS	CUTTHROAT	STARLIGHT
ACIDULOUS	GLAMOROUS	PLUTOCRAT	FOOTLIGHT
PENDULOUS	FLAVOROUS	DANDIPRAT	SPOTLIGHT
TREMULOUS	MONSTROUS	HELIOSTAT	GOODNIGHT
GRANULOUS	MERCUROUS	SELFDOUBT	OVERNIGHT
CRAPULOUS	FURFUROUS	DISAFFECT	FORTNIGHT
QUERULOUS	FULGUROUS	DISINFECT	EYEBRIGHT
GARRULOUS	MACRUROUS	IMPERFECT	DOWNRIGHT
FISTULOUS	VULTUROUS	INTERJECT	COPYRIGHT
PUSTULOUS	VENTUROUS	GENUFLECT	HINDSIGHT
EXOGAMOUS	RAPTUROUS	INTELLECT	FORESIGHT
UNANIMOUS	MOMENTOUS	RECOLLECT	OVERSIGHT
ANONYMOUS	TOMENTOUS	REINSPECT	ONSLAUGHT
EPONYMOUS	SCHISTOUS	MISDIRECT	METHOUGHT
EROGENOUS	INNOCUOUS	INCORRECT	UNTHOUGHT
EXOGENOUS	DECIDUOUS	RESURRECT	INWROUGHT
OXYGENOUS	ASSIDUOUS	INTERSECT	UNWROUGHT
LICHENOUS	AMBIGUOUS	ARCHITECT	FARSOUGHT
TENDINOUS	IRRIGUOUS	INTERDICT	CENTREBIT
ULIGINOUS	INGENUOUS	CONSTRICT	DEVILSBIT
CRIMINOUS	STRENUOUS	BYPRODUCT	DISCREDIT
VERMINOUS	CONGRUOUS	CONSTRUCT	DISCOMFIT
ALUMINOUS	IMPETUOUS	VIDELICET	PRETERMIT
FIBRINOUS	SUMPTUOUS	SUGARBEET	WHODUNNIT
PLATINOUS	LONGEVOUS	CROWSFEET	MALADROIT
GLUTINOUS	ACCLIVOUS	PACKSHEET	CHERRYPIT
TYRANNOUS	DECLIVOUS	PARRAKEET	AFFIDAVIT
TRIGONOUS	THESAURUS	AIRJACKET	HEARTFELT
UNISONOUS	CONSENSUS	EELBASKET	ROOSEVELT
POISONOUS	NARCISSUS	TIERCELET	MOLLYBOLT
CAVERNOUS	APPARATUS	TONGUELET	DIFFICULT
ALBURNOUS	SALERATUS	SPRINGLET	HYDROPULT
EPIGYNOUS	SUBSULTUS	BRANCHLET	DESICCANT
TRIGYNOUS	COMPLEXUS	SURMULLET	EXSICCANT

PREDICANT	INCESSANT	PRESCIENT	ANNULMENT
MENDICANT	COMBATANT	EXPEDIENT	ALIGNMENT
APPLICANT	EXPECTANT	RESILIENT	ADORNMENT
LUBRICANT	RELUCTANT	EMOLLIENT	EQUIPMENT
CORUSCANT	CREPITANT	EBULLIENT	DEBARMENT
CONFIDANT	ANNUITANT	RECIPIENT	DEFERMENT
DEMANDANT	RESULTANT	INCIPIENT	DETERMENT
ASCENDANT	REPENTANT	EXCIPIENT	INTERMENT
DEFENDANT	IMPORTANT	TRANSIENT	AMASSMENT
DEPENDANT	RESISTANT	IMPATIENT	TREATMENT
APPENDANT	ASSISTANT	PREVALENT	ENACTMENT
INTENDANT	EXECUTANT	UNIVALENT	EJECTMENT
ATTENDANT	POLLUTANT	PESTILENT	REVETMENT
REDUNDANT	DISPUTANT	EXCELLENT	REFITMENT
REGARDANT	ATTENUANT	REPELLENT	ALLOTMENT
ACCORDANT	FLUCTUANT	IMPELLENT	APARTMENT
PROCREANT	GALLIVANT	ATTOLLENT	EMOLUMENT
MISCREANT	OBSERVANT	SOMNOLENT	ENDOWMENT
TERMAGANT	CHATOYANT	TURBULENT	EMBAYMENT
INELEGANT	COGNIZANT	SUCCULENT	ALLAYMENT
TRENCHANT	DECUMBENT	TRUCULENT	REPAYMENT
SYCOPHANT	RECUMBENT	CRAPULENT	ENJOYMENT
IRRADIANT	INCUMBENT	CORPULENT	PERMANENT
BRILLIANT	ABSORBENT	FLATULENT	PROMINENT
COMPLIANT	SUBJACENT	FUNDAMENT	CONTINENT
SUPPLIANT	CONTICENT	LINEAMENT	PERTINENT
INEBRIANT	DEMULCENT	FIRMAMENT	ABSTINENT
LUXURIANT	RENASCENT	SACRAMENT	COMPONENT
ASSAILANT	ALBESCENT	TESTAMENT	PROPONENT
UNGALLANT	PUBESCENT	AMENDMENT	SECERNENT
APPELLANT	QUIESCENT	AGREEMENT	DIFFERENT
COALPLANT	CANESCENT	JUDGEMENT	DETERRENT
COAGULANT	SENESCENT	INCLEMENT	ABHORRENT
STIMULANT	VIRESCENT	IMPLEMENT	DECURRENT
POSTULANT	DEHISCENT	ATONEMENT	RECURRENT
AFFIRMANT	PRECEDENT	SCAPEMENT	EXCURRENT
INFORMANT	DIFFIDENT	ELOPEMENT	REPRESENT
SUBTENANT	CONFIDENT	DECREMENT	COMPETENT
INDIGNANT	PRESIDENT	RECREMENT	PREPOTENT
MALIGNANT	DISSIDENT	INCREMENT	ADVERTENT
BENIGNANT	PROVIDENT	EXCREMENT	RESISTENT
REPUGNANT	SPLENDENT	INUREMENT	INSISTENT
OPPUGNANT	DEPENDENT	ERASEMENT	REMITTENT
EXAMINANT	IMPENDENT	AMUSEMENT	DIFFLUENT
GERMINANT	CORRODENT	ABATEMENT	CONFLUENT
UNISONANT	IMPRUDENT	STATEMENT	CONGRUENT
CONSONANT	BANKAGENT	AMAZEMENT	OBSTRUENT
DISSONANT	NEGLIGENT	FEOFFMENT	RESOLVENT
CELEBRANT	INDULGENT	PARCHMENT	INSOLVENT
EXUBERANT	REFULGENT	CATCHMENT	COMPLAINT
ITINERANT	EFFULGENT	HATCHMENT	RESTRAINT
COOPERANT	COTANGENT	ABASHMENT	DISTRAINT
INTEGRANT	IMPINGENT	CONDIMENT	SKINFLINT
IMMIGRANT	STRINGENT	MERRIMENT	FLAYFLINT
DEODORANT	DETERGENT	WORRIMENT	SPEARMINT
CORMORANT	DIVERGENT	DETRIMENT	FISHJOINT
PENETRANT	RESURGENT	NUTRIMENT	BALLPOINT
OBSCURANT	INSURGENT	SENTIMENT	REAPPOINT
COGNISANT	DEFICIENT	DEVILMENT	VIEWPOINT
CORPOSANT	EFFICIENT	ENROLMENT	BLUEPRINT

117

NEWSPRINT	PUBLICIST	MAMMONIST	--------W
FOOTPRINT	PHYSICIST	GNOMONIST	
MEZZOTINT	BALLADIST	HARMONIST	WAPENSHAW
FOREFRONT	METHODIST	PLATONIST	HERONSHAW
PARAMOUNT	PROSODIST	PLUTONIST	INTERVIEW
CATAMOUNT	TALMUDIST	MODERNIST	CORKSCREW
BLOODSHOT	PANTHEIST	COMMUNIST	FIDDLEBOW
SLINGSHOT	MASSAGIST	EUCHARIST	EYESHADOW
CHAINSHOT	DIALOGIST	CATHARIST	BOWWINDOW
UNDERSHOT	ANALOGIST	SUMMARIST	BAYWINDOW
HEPTAGLOT	ECOLOGIST	GUITARIST	RAREESHOW
UNDERPLOT	GEOLOGIST	MESMERIST	DEATHBLOW
GUILLEMOT	NEOLOGIST	MANNERIST	AFTERGLOW
BANDICOOT	BIOLOGIST	MEMOIRIST	ODDFELLOW
BIRDSFOOT	ZOOLOGIST	TERRORIST	SCARECROW
COLTSFOOT	APOLOGIST	COLOURIST	DOWNTHROW
CROWSFOOT	OTOLOGIST	POSTURIST	OVERTHROW
OVERSHOOT	THEURGIST	LIMPWRIST	
BRIERROOT	LITURGIST	GEODESIST	
ARROWROOT	CATECHIST	DEFEATIST	--------X
COFFEEPOT	MASOCHIST	PRELATIST	
FLOWERPOT	ANARCHIST	DRAMATIST	EARTHFLAX
HOTTENTOT	FETISHIST	DOGMATIST	PROTHORAX
INTERCEPT	CABBALIST	EXEGETIST	MULTIPLEX
SUBSCRIPT	CYMBALIST	CORNETIST	DECOMPLEX
PRESCRIPT	HERBALIST	DECRETIST	MIDDLESEX
CONSCRIPT	VERBALIST	SCIENTIST	DICTATRIX
INTERRUPT	FEUDALIST	ARCHIVIST	TESTATRIX
INCORRUPT	NEPHALIST	PENTECOST	DIRECTRIX
UNCORRUPT	RACIALIST	SOUTHMOST	EXECUTRIX
LIONHEART	SOCIALIST	STERNMOST	BALLOTBOX
EXTROVERT	FORMALIST	UNDERMOST	HETERODOX
MISREPORT	CARNALIST	INNERMOST	POMPHOLYX
DAVENPORT	PLURALIST	UPPERMOST	
DEVONPORT	ACTUALIST	AFTERMOST	
TRANSPORT	RITUALIST	UTTERMOST	--------Y
LIVERWORT	BICYCLIST	OUTERMOST	
GLASSWORT	PROFILIST	LOWERMOST	DAPPLEBAY
FORECOURT	BLACKLIST	HOLOCAUST	ALACKADAY
BROADCAST	MEDALLIST	HYPOCAUST	BOXINGDAY
BEANFEAST	METALLIST	ANTITRUST	YESTERDAY
NORTHEAST	SYMBOLIST	SPOROCYST	WEDNESDAY
SOUTHEAST	TRIGAMIST	COSMONAUT	CHINACLAY
REDBREAST	ALCHEMIST	ASTRONAUT	BRICKCLAY
STEADFAST	EXTREMIST	CANDLENUT	ROUNDELAY
BREAKFAST	PESSIMIST	BRAZILNUT	SWORDPLAY
SCHOLIAST	ECONOMIST	BUTTERNUT	HORSEPLAY
ENCOMIAST	ANATOMIST	HEREABOUT	INTERPLAY
ECTOBLAST	EPITOMIST	WALKABOUT	THEREAWAY
BEECHMAST	ZOOTOMIST	DISHCLOUT	BREAKAWAY
DISHONEST	VOLCANIST	DOWNSPOUT	THROWAWAY
BIRDSNEST	MECHANIST	BULLTROUT	INTRICACY
CROWSNEST	SOPRANIST		IMMEDIACY
BUCHAREST	GALVANIST		SUPREMACY
DISFOREST	HELLENIST	--------U	DIPLOMACY
BLOODTEST	JANSENIST		CONTUMACY
NORTHWEST	MACHINIST	TROUSSEAU	OBSTINACY
SOUTHWEST	VIOLINIST	IMPROMPTU	MOBOCRACY
MOSAICIST	CALVINIST		THEOCRACY
BIBLICIST	COLUMNIST		DEMOCRACY

AUTOCRACY	TETRALOGY	AGREEABLY	HAGGARDLY
PROCURACY	SYMBOLOGY	PERMEABLY	NIGGARDLY
INTESTACY	MUSCOLOGY	INEFFABLY	DASTARDLY
COLONELCY	PHYCOLOGY	LAUGHABLY	AWKWARDLY
SERGEANCY	OSTEOLOGY	ESTIMABLY	FROWARDLY
RECREANCY	EUCHOLOGY	DEFINABLY	OUTWARDLY
SIBILANCY	PATHOLOGY	REPARABLY	WAYWARDLY
PETULANCY	LITHOLOGY	SEPARABLY	STRANGELY
THEOMANCY	ANTHOLOGY	EXECRABLY	SUBTILELY
STAGNANCY	MYTHOLOGY	TOLERABLY	FERTILELY
PREGNANCY	SOCIOLOGY	VENERABLY	HOSTILELY
POIGNANCY	HAGIOLOGY	MISERABLY	SERVILELY
FLIPPANCY	OPHIOLOGY	ADMIRABLY	SUPREMELY
OCCUPANCY	SEMIOLOGY	DESIRABLY	EXTREMELY
FLAGRANCY	AETIOLOGY	INCURABLY	SUBLIMELY
FRAGRANCY	PHILOLOGY	ENDURABLY	NOISOMELY
OSCITANCY	COSMOLOGY	ADVISABLY	IRKSOMELY
MILITANCY	ETYMOLOGY	EXCUSABLY	FULSOMELY
HESITANCY	POENOLOGY	PALATABLY	CONTUMELY
CONSTANCY	ICHNOLOGY	HERITABLY	MUNDANELY
ADJUTANCY	ETHNOLOGY	VERITABLY	PROFANELY
RELEVANCY	HYMNOLOGY	IRRITABLY	OBSCENELY
INDECENCY	ICONOLOGY	EQUITABLY	GENUINELY
INNOCENCY	PHONOLOGY	IMMUTABLY	UNSHAPELY
RESIDENCY	TROPOLOGY	DERIVABLY	SINCERELY
EMERGENCY	NECROLOGY	IMMOVABLY	AUSTERELY
PRURIENCY	MICROLOGY	ALLOWABLY	OBSCURELY
ESURIENCY	HYDROLOGY	IRASCIBLY	LEISURELY
REDOLENCY	CHIROLOGY	ILLEGIBLY	PRECISELY
PURULENCY	COPROLOGY	INDELIBLY	CONCISELY
VEHEMENCY	PETROLOGY	DIVISIBLY	IMMENSELY
IMMANENCY	ASTROLOGY	INVISIBLY	INTENSELY
INHERENCY	NEUROLOGY	PLAUSIBLY	VERBOSELY
RENITENCY	HYETOLOGY	POLITICLY	PURPOSELY
IMPOTENCY	HISTOLOGY	CRABBEDLY	OPEROSELY
FREQUENCY	TAUTOLOGY	DECIDEDLY	ADVERSELY
CAPTAINCY	THEOMACHY	GUARDEDLY	REVERSELY
SURGEONCY	LOGOMACHY	STUDIEDLY	DIVERSELY
BARONETCY	ENTELECHY	IMPLIEDLY	INVERSELY
DISEMBODY	OLIGARCHY	HURRIEDLY	PROFUSELY
EVERYBODY	TETRARCHY	CROOKEDLY	RECLUSELY
CHIROPODY	PENTARCHY	ASHAMEDLY	RADIATELY
FOOLHARDY	HEPTARCHY	FEIGNEDLY	MEDIATELY
BEERMONEY	POLYARCHY	REFINEDLY	PHILATELY
DECALCIFY	ARCHDUCHY	LEARNEDLY	PALMATELY
PREACHIFY	EPIGRAPHY	RETIREDLY	PINNATELY
SPEECHIFY	GEOGRAPHY	ASSUREDLY	PRIVATELY
EXEMPLIFY	BIOGRAPHY	ADVISEDLY	ERUDITELY
INDEMNIFY	ZOOGRAPHY	BLESSEDLY	OBLIQUELY
PERSONIFY	OROGRAPHY	LIMITEDLY	BRUSQUELY
CHONDRIFY	MYOGRAPHY	POINTEDLY	CONCAVELY
ELECTRIFY	THEOSOPHY	DEVOTEDLY	SUASIVELY
DEVITRIFY	TELEPATHY	REPUTEDLY	EVASIVELY
DIVERSIFY	ANTIPATHY	UNMIXEDLY	PENSIVELY
OBJECTIFY	IDIOPATHY	FLACCIDLY	MASSIVELY
REFORTIFY	ALLOPATHY	SQUALIDLY	PASSIVELY
COCKNEYFY	UNHEALTHY	CUCKOLDLY	ABUSIVELY
ODONTALGY	SEAWORTHY	UNWORLDLY	FURTIVELY
GENEALOGY	PEACEABLY	HUSBANDLY	FESTIVELY
MAMMALOGY	TRACEABLY	UNSOUNDLY	RESTIVELY

COSTIVELY	SOTTISHLY	NOMINALLY	SIMILARLY
DRAGONFLY	BRUTISHLY	ETERNALLY	SCHOLARLY
BUTTERFLY	ROGUISHLY	DIURNALLY	TABULARLY
ABIDINGLY	SLAVISHLY	LIBERALLY	SECULARLY
WINDINGLY	KNAVISHLY	NUMERALLY	JOCULARLY
LONGINGLY	PEEVISHLY	GENERALLY	REGULARLY
SIGHINGLY	SEVENTHLY	LATERALLY	POPULARLY
GUSHINGLY	BIMONTHLY	LITERALLY	INSULARLY
PUSHINGLY	UNEARTHLY	SEVERALLY	TITULARLY
MOCKINGLY	UNCOUTHLY	IMMORALLY	SLENDERLY
FEELINGLY	UNHANDILY	CENTRALLY	WEATHERLY
RAILINGLY	SCRAGGILY	NEUTRALLY	BROTHERLY
WAILINGLY	STARCHILY	NATURALLY	NORTHERLY
SMILINGLY	SKETCHILY	CAPITALLY	SOUTHERLY
WILLINGLY	NOTAPHILY	GRADUALLY	SOLDIERLY
SEEMINGLY	LENGTHILY	UNEQUALLY	QUARTERLY
MEANINGLY	HEALTHILY	COEQUALLY	ENDLESSLY
WHININGLY	WEALTHILY	SENSUALLY	GODLESSLY
WINNINGLY	UNLUCKILY	UNUSUALLY	USELESSLY
CUNNINGLY	SUBFAMILY	VIRTUALLY	AIMLESSLY
WARNINGLY	UNHAPPILY	TEXTUALLY	SINLESSLY
WEEPINGLY	PRIMARILY	GENTEELLY	WITLESSLY
GRIPINGLY	SUMMARILY	UNCIVILLY	ARTLESSLY
LIMPINGLY	PLENARILY	HEEDFULLY	LAWLESSLY
GROPINGLY	CURSORILY	NEEDFULLY	JOYLESSLY
CARPINGLY	SAVOURILY	MINDFULLY	EXPRESSLY
GASPINGLY	THRIFTILY	WAKEFULLY	GIBBOUSLY
SPARINGLY	WEIGHTILY	BALEFULLY	PITEOUSLY
STARINGLY	FLIGHTILY	DOLEFULLY	DUTEOUSLY
JEERINGLY	HAUGHTILY	BANEFULLY	DUBIOUSLY
VEERINGLY	NAUGHTILY	TUNEFULLY	VICIOUSLY
ADORINGLY	DOUGHTILY	HOPEFULLY	TEDIOUSLY
AMUSINGLY	THIRSTILY	CAREFULLY	COPIOUSLY
MELTINGLY	CUBICALLY	DIREFULLY	VARIOUSLY
LASTINGLY	RADICALLY	FATEFULLY	SERIOUSLY
FITTINGLY	MEDICALLY	HATEFULLY	CURIOUSLY
WITTINGLY	MAGICALLY	BASHFULLY	FURIOUSLY
CUTTINGLY	LOGICALLY	PITIFULLY	OBVIOUSLY
GLOWINGLY	ETHICALLY	DUTIFULLY	DEVIOUSLY
KNOWINGLY	COMICALLY	SKILFULLY	ENVIOUSLY
COAXINGLY	FINICALLY	HARMFULLY	ANXIOUSLY
DENYINGLY	CONICALLY	PAINFULLY	NOXIOUSLY
PITYINGLY	CYNICALLY	FEARFULLY	JEALOUSLY
AMAZINGLY	STOICALLY	TACTFULLY	ZEALOUSLY
PRUDISHLY	TOPICALLY	FRETFULLY	CALLOUSLY
SELFISHLY	TYPICALLY	HURTFULLY	EMULOUSLY
WOLFISHLY	BASICALLY	RESTFULLY	HEINOUSLY
WAGGISHLY	MUSICALLY	WISTFULLY	OMINOUSLY
MAWKISHLY	OPTICALLY	LUSTFULLY	RUINOUSLY
HELLISHLY	LEXICALLY	PLAYFULLY	POMPOUSLY
FOOLISHLY	ILLEGALLY	UNIFORMLY	ONEROUSLY
STYLISHLY	SPECIALLY	UNCLEANLY	ODOROUSLY
SWINISHLY	CORDIALLY	RUFFIANLY	AMOROUSLY
ROMPISHLY	SPATIALLY	WORKMANLY	RIOTOUSLY
LUMPISHLY	INITIALLY	UNWOMANLY	ARDUOUSLY
MUMPISHLY	MARTIALLY	INHUMANLY	SINUOUSLY
FOPPISHLY	PARTIALLY	DRUNKENLY	NERVOUSLY
WASPISHLY	TRIVIALLY	CERTAINLY	COMPACTLY
BOORISHLY	DECIMALLY	FORLORNLY	PERFECTLY
PETTISHLY	THERMALLY	OLIGOPOLY	CORRECTLY

UNQUIETLY	COLOPHONY	ARBITRARY	PREDATORY
SPRIGHTLY	POLYPHONY	ADVERSARY	MANDATORY
UPRIGHTLY	MATRIMONY	ACCESSARY	LAUDATORY
UNSIGHTLY	PATRIMONY	NECESSARY	FEUDATORY
ILLICITLY	PARSIMONY	MANDATARY	PREFATORY
PECCANTLY	TESTIMONY	PROLETARY	PURGATORY
VERDANTLY	SYNCHRONY	PLANETARY	EXPIATORY
ELEGANTLY	PHILOGYNY	SECRETARY	CREMATORY
RADIANTLY	ERRANDBOY	TERMITARY	SIGNATORY
DEFIANTLY	STABLEBOY	DIGNITARY	DAMNATORY
VALIANTLY	PLOUGHBOY	SIGNITARY	CULPATORY
GALLANTLY	SCHOOLBOY	PITUITARY	LIBRATORY
RAMPANTLY	MISEMPLOY	SEDENTARY	VIBRATORY
DISTANTLY	PHOTOCOPY	MOMENTARY	MIGRATORY
INSTANTLY	TELESCOPY	VOLUNTARY	PULSATORY
PIQUANTLY	HOROSCOPY	TRIBUTARY	DICTATORY
EVIDENTLY	ALLOTROPY	RESIDUARY	SALTATORY
PENDENTLY	PREOCCUPY	RELIQUARY	HORTATORY
PRUDENTLY	PHONOTYPY	ANTIQUARY	GUSTATORY
PUNGENTLY	PHOTOTYPY	ELECTUARY	ELEVATORY
ANCIENTLY	COLUMBARY	SANCTUARY	OLFACTORY
SALIENTLY	FORMICARY	SUMPTUARY	REFECTORY
LENIENTLY	DROMEDARY	CASSOWARY	DIRECTORY
SAPIENTLY	LEGENDARY	COXCOMBRY	EMUNCTORY
PATIENTLY	ZEMINDARY	CUCKOLDRY	DEPLETORY
VIOLENTLY	SECONDARY	HUSBANDRY	EXPLETORY
OPULENTLY	TRACHEARY	POLYANDRY	DECRETORY
CLEMENTLY	JUDICIARY	SHRUBBERY	SECRETORY
EMINENTLY	FIDUCIARY	EMBRACERY	EXCRETORY
CURRENTLY	AUXILIARY	MIDWIFERY	PELLITORY
PRESENTLY	PECUNIARY	BLEACHERY	DORMITORY
FERVENTLY	ANCILLARY	TREACHERY	TERRITORY
CORRUPTLY	ARMILLARY	PERIPHERY	DESULTORY
UNCOURTLY	CAPILLARY	CHANDLERY	INVENTORY
EARNESTLY	PAPILLARY	JEWELLERY	SCRIPTORY
PATCHOULY	MAXILLARY	ARTILLERY	OFFERTORY
SHALLOWLY	VEXILLARY	GOSSAMERY	REPERTORY
COMPLEXLY	COROLLARY	PERFUMERY	LOVESTORY
DICHOGAMY	MEDULLARY	CHICANERY	EXECUTORY
BLASPHEMY	EXEMPLARY	MACHINERY	STATUTORY
ASTRONOMY	CALCULARY	MILLINERY	BLAEBERRY
VASECTOMY	NUMMULARY	COCOONERY	NASEBERRY
OSTEOTOMY	FORMULARY	MESENTERY	BLUEBERRY
DICHOTOMY	SCAPULARY	DYSENTERY	HACKBERRY
LITHOTOMY	CARTULARY	SPLINTERY	CRANBERRY
CYSTOTOMY	CUSTOMARY	DICASTERY	RASPBERRY
PHYTOTOMY	INFIRMARY	MONASTERY	BEARBERRY
TAXIDERMY	MERCENARY	DISCOVERY	CROWBERRY
THEOPHANY	DUODENARY	ENGLISHRY	PAEDIATRY
ACCOMPANY	MILLENARY	GIMMICKRY	TRINKETRY
HISTOGENY	CENTENARY	HEATHENRY	TELEMETRY
PHYTOGENY	SEPTENARY	HUNKYDORY	ASYMMETRY
MOONSHINY	IMAGINARY	AMPHIGORY	AEROMETRY
TRUEPENNY	LEGIONARY	SEIGNIORY	HOROMETRY
HALFPENNY	VISIONARY	VAINGLORY	GASOMETRY
CALCEDONY	PULMONARY	PROVISORY	MARQUETRY
COSMOGONY	SUBLUNARY	ACCESSORY	PARQUETRY
TELEPHONY	ITINERARY	REMISSORY	CIRCUITRY
ANTIPHONY	VULNERARY	DIMISSORY	PAGEANTRY
CACOPHONY	TEMPORARY	PROBATORY	GALLANTRY

---------A

ANTARCTICA
SAUROPSIDA
PROPAGANDA
CORRIGENDA
ARTHROPODA
GONORRHOEA
JINRIKISHA
XENOPHOBIA
ORTHOPEDIA
CYCLOPEDIA
CASSIOPEIA
PARAPLEGIA
CARDIALGIA
GASTRALGIA
SATURNALIA
PENETRALIA
HYPERDULIA
MELANAEMIA
OPHTHALMIA
ANGLOMANIA
DIPSOMANIA
EROTOMANIA
CALIFORNIA
CORNUCOPIA
NYCTALOPIA
EMMETROPIA
SIGILLARIA
DIPHTHERIA
GLUCOSURIA
HAEMATURIA
PHLEGMASIA
EUTHANASIA
FRAMBOESIA
YUGOSLAVIA
CINDERELLA
GRANADILLA
SEGUIDILLA
CHINCHILLA
CASCARILLA
GORGONZOLA
SARCOLEMMA
STAPHYLOMA
PARENCHYMA
QUADRUMANA
PHAGEDAENA
SCARLATINA
CONCERTINA
BELLADONNA
CORDILLERA
CINECAMERA
SCORZONERA
COLEOPTERA
PHYLLOXERA
DISCOPHORA
CTENOPHORA
ASPIDISTRA
ENDOPLEURA
BABIROUSSA

VERTEBRATA
COMEDIETTA
COLEORHIZA

---------B

UNDERSHRUB

---------C

GENETHLIAC
SACROILIAC
MONOMANIAC
PYROMANIAC
ORTHOPEDIC
TENEBRIFIC
FRIGORIFIC
SCIENTIFIC
ODONTALGIC
LITHOLOGIC
MYTHOLOGIC
SOCIOLOGIC
ETHNOLOGIC
TAUTOLOGIC
OLIGARCHIC
HEPTARCHIC
EPIGRAPHIC
BIOGRAPHIC
THEOSOPHIC
TRIMORPHIC
ZOOMORPHIC
PROGNATHIC
TELEPATHIC
IDIOPATHIC
ALLOPATHIC
FELSPATHIC
MEGALITHIC
MONOLITHIC
HELMINTHIC
ENCEPHALIC
NAPHTHALIC
PHILATELIC
BIMETALLIC
HYPERBOLIC
ISODYNAMIC
COSMORAMIC
CHERUBIMIC
OPHTHALMIC
ASTRONOMIC
LOXODROMIC
TAXIDERMIC
HYPODERMIC
DIATHERMIC
EMBOLISMIC
PATRONYMIC
METRONYMIC
THEOPHANIC
ALDERMANIC

TALISMANIC
PYTHOGENIC
PHOTOGENIC
SPLANCHNIC
GANGLIONIC
HISTRIONIC
ENHARMONIC
ELECTRONIC
ULTRASONIC
SUPERSONIC
HYPERSONIC
SUPERTONIC
PALAEOZOIC
TELESCOPIC
HOROSCOPIC
POLYCARPIC
CONGENERIC
MESENTERIC
DYSENTERIC
METAPHORIC
PHOSPHORIC
PERCHLORIC
UNHISTORIC
PAEDIATRIC
HEXAMETRIC
ASYMMETRIC
BAROMETRIC
PYROMETRIC
VOLUMETRIC
CONCENTRIC
GEOCENTRIC
EGOCENTRIC
EPIGASTRIC
METAPHYSIC
PANCREATIC
ACROAMATIC
MATHEMATIC
EMBLEMATIC
SYSTEMATIC
PHLEGMATIC
ASTIGMATIC
DIPLOMATIC
ACHROMATIC
ENDERMATIC
SCHISMATIC
NUMISMATIC
MORGANATIC
DEMOCRATIC
AUTOCRATIC
AEROSTATIC
SUBAQUATIC
CATALECTIC
APOPLECTIC
EPIDEICTIC
APODEICTIC
ALPHABETIC
APOLOGETIC
CATECHETIC
ANTITHETIC
EPENTHETIC

ARITHMETIC	---------D	BAREBACKED
EPIGENETIC		HUMPBACKED
SYNGENETIC	FIGUREHEAD	LANDLOCKED
CYBERNETIC	MAIDENHEAD	UNPROVOKED
ANCHORETIC	LOGGERHEAD	UNREPEALED
BRONCHITIC	COPPERHEAD	UNTROUBLED
ISRAELITIC	JOLTERHEAD	SPECTACLED
SYPHILITIC	LETTERHEAD	CARBUNCLED
VARIOLITIC	DEATHSHEAD	UNRIVALLED
COPROLITIC	SWEETBREAD	TRAMMELLED
TYMPANITIC	SHORTBREAD	CHANNELLED
ENCRINITIC	WIDESPREAD	DUCKBILLED
UNROMANTIC	BRIDLEROAD	TENDRILLED
CRESCENTIC	MICROFARAD	UNSCHOOLED
ENDOSMOTIC	SHAMEFACED	PRINCIPLED
ESCHAROTIC	CREAMFACED	AFORENAMED
ECCOPROTIC	POKERFACED	UNREDEEMED
ASYMPTOTIC	UNBALANCED	ACCUSTOMED
CARBAZOTIC	HARDHEADED	UNREFORMED
CATALEPTIC	BAREHEADED	FRIGHTENED
ANTISEPTIC	LONGHEADED	UNLEAVENED
STOCHASTIC	COOLHEADED	FATBRAINED
ANACLASTIC	UNPROVIDED	UNSTRAINED
SCHOLASTIC	FREEHANDED	UNCONFINED
ANAPLASTIC	FOREHANDED	UNIMAGINED
DOCIMASTIC	EVENHANDED	UNEXAMINED
PLEONASTIC	LEFTHANDED	DETERMINED
EPISPASTIC	UNDEFENDED	TRUNNIONED
SOLECISTIC	UNATTENDED	SQUADRONED
DITHEISTIC	BASEMINDED	UNSEASONED
PHLOGISTIC	OPENMINDED	UNGOVERNED
EULOGISTIC	FAIRMINDED	MAXILLIPED
BUDDHISTIC	UNSECONDED	UNPREPARED
ERETHISTIC	CONFOUNDED	UNNUMBERED
IDEALISTIC	UNGROUNDED	DISORDERED
FATALISTIC	REDBLOODED	UNFATHERED
PUGILISTIC	UNREGARDED	UNHAMPERED
NIHILISTIC	UNREWARDED	UNTEMPERED
SCIOLISTIC	UNRECORDED	REGISTERED
SIMPLISTIC	INTERBREED	CLOISTERED
OPTIMISTIC	CROSSBREED	UNFETTERED
APHORISTIC	COTTONSEED	UNLETTERED
HUMORISTIC	KERCHIEFED	LONGHAIRED
FUTURISTIC	MIDDLEAGED	FAIRHAIRED
LINGUISTIC	DISENGAGED	UNIMPAIRED
EUPHUISTIC	UNABRIDGED	UNINSPIRED
ALTRUISTIC	UNREVENGED	UNEXPLORED
ESSAYISTIC	UNATTACHED	UNRESTORED
DIAGNOSTIC	UNSMIRCHED	UNDETERRED
GEOGNOSTIC	FARFETCHED	UNCOLOURED
DIACAUSTIC	UNPOLISHED	UNHONOURED
DIACOUSTIC	UNFINISHED	UNMEASURED
EPIGLOTTIC	ASTONISHED	STRUCTURED
AERONAUTIC	UNPUNISHED	DEBENTURED
ENTOPHYTIC	ABLEBODIED	ENRAPTURED
CAOUTCHOUC	SIMPLIFIED	SCULPTURED
	CLASSIFIED	DISPLEASED
	STRATIFIED	MISADVISED
	SANCTIFIED	UNLICENSED
	PROPERTIED	UNINCLOSED

BRILLIANCE	EXPEDIENCE	INFINITUDE
COMPLIANCE	RESILIENCE	CRASSITUDE
SUPPLIANCE	EBULLIENCE	SPISSITUDE
LUXURIANCE	EXPERIENCE	EXACTITUDE
FERDELANCE	TRANSIENCE	INAPTITUDE
SUSTENANCE	IMPATIENCE	TRANSFEREE
CONVENANCE	PREVALENCE	ALMONDTREE
PROVENANCE	PESTILENCE	BOTTLETREE
MALIGNANCE	EXCELLENCE	DRAGONTREE
REPUGNANCE	REPELLENCE	COTTONTREE
UNISONANCE	CONDOLENCE	BUTTERTREE
CONSONANCE	SOMNOLENCE	COVENANTEE
DISSONANCE	TURBULENCE	CHIMPANZEE
GOVERNANCE	SUCCULENCE	BOWIEKNIFE
APPEARANCE	TRUCULENCE	CLASPKNIFE
EXUBERANCE	CRAPULENCE	BRIGANDAGE
HINDERANCE	CORPULENCE	IMPOUNDAGE
SUFFERANCE	FLATULENCE	HEMORRHAGE
TEMPERANCE	RECOMMENCE	REMARRIAGE
DEFEASANCE	PERMANENCE	ASSEMBLAGE
EXPECTANCE	PROMINENCE	PERSIFLAGE
RELUCTANCE	CONTINENCE	CAMOUFLAGE
REPENTANCE	PERTINENCE	AFTERIMAGE
ACCEPTANCE	ABSTINENCE	PILGRIMAGE
IMPORTANCE	THREEPENCE	VILLEINAGE
RESISTANCE	PREFERENCE	TELPHERAGE
ASSISTANCE	DIFFERENCE	HARBOURAGE
ADMITTANCE	CONFERENCE	DISCOURAGE
REMITTANCE	ABHORRENCE	SURPLUSAGE
CONNIVANCE	OCCURRENCE	FREIGHTAGE
OBSERVANCE	RECURRENCE	EXPLOITAGE
CONVEYANCE	COMPETENCE	PERCENTAGE
SURVEYANCE	ADVERTENCE	OVERBRIDGE
COGNIZANCE	CONFLUENCE	FOOTBRIDGE
DECUMBENCE	CONGRUENCE	DRAWBRIDGE
RENASCENCE	CONNIVENCE	BLANCMANGE
ALBESCENCE	RECRUDESCE	PREARRANGE
PUBESCENCE	CONVALESCE	DISARRANGE
QUIESCENCE	EFFLORESCE	MISARRANGE
DEHISCENCE	DELIQUESCE	CONSTRINGE
PRECEDENCE	EFFERVESCE	PERSTRINGE
DIFFIDENCE	NIGHTSHADE	OVERCHARGE
CONFIDENCE	CUSTOMMADE	CENTRIFUGE
SUBSIDENCE	PASQUINADE	SUBTERFUGE
DISSIDENCE	MASQUERADE	SYNECDOCHE
PROVIDENCE	TARDIGRADE	APOSTROPHE
ASCENDENCE	CENTIGRADE	PHILOSOPHE
DEPENDENCE	RETROGRADE	BIJOUTERIE
IMPRUDENCE	BALUSTRADE	BRUSQUERIE
NEGLIGENCE	VELOCIPEDE	KNOBKERRIE
INDULGENCE	SORORICIDE	CHEESECAKE
REFULGENCE	FRATRICIDE	SWEEPSTAKE
EFFULGENCE	HUMBERSIDE	EARTHQUAKE
DETERGENCE	MERSEYSIDE	PRIESTLIKE
DIVERGENCE	EASTERTIDE	CHRISTLIKE
RESURGENCE	NATIONWIDE	UNLADYLIKE
UPSURGENCE	INQUIETUDE	BUSHSHRIKE
DEFICIENCE	CONSUETUDE	BACKSTROKE
PRESCIENCE	SOLICITUDE	MARTINGALE
CONSCIENCE	SIMILITUDE	ASCRIBABLE

CONFUTABLE	REFLEXIBLE	BLITHESOME
COMMUTABLE	INFLEXIBLE	MEDDLESOME
COMPUTABLE	REASSEMBLE	METTLESOME
DISPUTABLE	DISENNOBLE	BURDENSOME
STATUTABLE	DISSOLUBLE	CHROMOSOME
UNARGUABLE	TABERNACLE	CUMBERSOME
INVALUABLE	RECEPTACLE	HUMOURSOME
ACHIEVABLE	GRANDUNCLE	BRIGHTSOME
BELIEVABLE	SEMICIRCLE	IMPOSTHUME
RELIEVABLE	ENTEROCELE	CELLOPHANE
DECEIVABLE	BOONDOGGLE	HYDROPHANE
RECEIVABLE	QUADRANGLE	ELECAMPANE
FORGIVABLE	AUTOMOBILE	WINDOWPANE
CULTIVABLE	DISCOPHILE	TRAMONTANE
INSOLVABLE	PAEDOPHILE	CISMONTANE
UNPROVABLE	AUDIOPHILE	ANTHRACENE
APPROVABLE	NECROPHILE	PARASELENE
OBSERVABLE	WORTHWHILE	CONTRAVENE
REVIEWABLE	PREHENSILE	CHATELAINE
CONVEYABLE	FLUVIATILE	PSITTACINE
EMPLOYABLE	RETRACTILE	PLASTICINE
SQUEEZABLE	PROJECTILE	KINCARDINE
OXIDIZABLE	PRODUCTILE	FIREENGINE
REALIZABLE	MERCANTILE	AEROENGINE
COGNIZABLE	BISSEXTILE	CATARRHINE
INVINCIBLE	RAMSHACKLE	EARTHSHINE
ENFORCIBLE	CORNCOCKLE	TOURMALINE
PRODUCIBLE	BESPRINKLE	DISINCLINE
INCREDIBLE	PERIWINKLE	ROSANILINE
EXTENDIBLE	JARGONELLE	STREAMLINE
CORRODIBLE	DEMOISELLE	TRAMPOLINE
INCLUDIBLE	IMMORTELLE	DISCIPLINE
INELIGIBLE	DESHABILLE	STRYCHNINE
NEGLIGIBLE	DISHABILLE	UNFEMININE
CORRIGIBLE	VAUDEVILLE	COWDIEPINE
INTANGIBLE	BARCAROLLE	COWRIEPINE
INFALLIBLE	BUTTONHOLE	SACCHARINE
REFERRIBLE	EYELETHOLE	AQUAMARINE
INFERRIBLE	PARTICIPLE	ADULTERINE
DEFEASIBLE	ADAMSAPPLE	SAPPHIRINE
EXPANSIBLE	DISENTITLE	LACUSTRINE
DEFENSIBLE	FORECASTLE	TAMBOURINE
INSENSIBLE	DEADNETTLE	AVANTURINE
OSTENSIBLE	CASEBOTTLE	AVENTURINE
EXTENSIBLE	BLUEBOTTLE	BRIGANTINE
REVERSIBLE	VENTRICULE	ADAMANTINE
IMPASSIBLE	ANIMALCULE	QUARANTINE
ACCESSIBLE	TETRASTYLE	TRIDENTINE
ADMISSIBLE	PENTASTYLE	BARKENTINE
REMISSIBLE	SUMMERTIME	TURPENTINE
IMPOSSIBLE	DINNERTIME	FLORENTINE
DIFFUSIBLE	DECIGRAMME	GUILLOTINE
COMPATIBLE	KILOGRAMME	VESPERTINE
EFFECTIBLE	GASTRONOME	PREDESTINE
DEDUCTIBLE	PALINDROME	PHILISTINE
INVENTIBLE	HIPPODROME	ENSANGUINE
REVERTIBLE	MONOCHROME	MARGRAVINE
DIGESTIBLE	POLYCHROME	ABERDEVINE
COMESTIBLE	FROLICSOME	COMEDIENNE
RESISTIBLE	UNHANDSOME	PARISIENNE

TRIFOLIATE	TRIPINNATE	FELICITATE
CALUMNIATE	PASSIONATE	EXCOGITATE
REPATRIATE	TRITERNATE	HABILITATE
EXPATRIATE	ANTICIPATE	DEBILITATE
LICENTIATE	EMANCIPATE	FACILITATE
ABBREVIATE	CONSTIPATE	DECAPITATE
ASPHYXIATE	EPISCOPATE	TRIDENTATE
CHEAPSKATE	EXHILARATE	UNICOSTATE
ASSIBILATE	VERTEBRATE	TRICOSTATE
INVIGILATE	CONSECRATE	UNDERSTATE
ANNIHILATE	SECONDRATE	INTERSTATE
ASSIMILATE	DELIBERATE	INADEQUATE
FLABELLATE	DILACERATE	COLLIQUATE
CANCELLATE	EXULCERATE	MENSTRUATE
FLAGELLATE	EVISCERATE	EFFECTUATE
CRENELLATE	DESIDERATE	PERPETUATE
TESSELLATE	IMMODERATE	ACCENTUATE
DISTILLATE	VOCIFERATE	DEACTIVATE
PISTILLATE	EXAGGERATE	REACTIVATE
LANCEOLATE	ACCELERATE	INCOMPLETE
VITRIOLATE	DECELERATE	BENEDICITE
APOSTOLATE	DEGENERATE	PLEBISCITE
EARTHPLATE	REGENERATE	AREOPAGITE
IMMACULATE	INCINERATE	ISHMAELITE
PANICULATE	REMUNERATE	CARNALLITE
GENICULATE	EXASPERATE	THEODOLITE
AURICULATE	RECUPERATE	ACTINOLITE
VESICULATE	VITUPERATE	STAUROLITE
RETICULATE	INVETERATE	CHRYSOLITE
ARTICULATE	OBLITERATE	GRAPTOLITE
EMASCULATE	ALLITERATE	TOPAZOLITE
INOSCULATE	ILLITERATE	PREADAMITE
ACCUMULATE	ADULTERATE	STALAGMITE
MANIPULATE	ASSEVERATE	INDEFINITE
DEPOPULATE	DEFLAGRATE	UNDERWRITE
CAPITULATE	CHURCHRATE	PORPHYRITE
AMALGAMATE	DEASPIRATE	PERQUISITE
DESQUAMATE	PERSPIRATE	STALACTITE
DISANIMATE	DUUMVIRATE	TRIPARTITE
LEGITIMATE	EDULCORATE	TROTSKYITE
GUESTIMATE	STERCORATE	CONFIDANTE
CONSUMMATE	INVIGORATE	DILETTANTE
BICHROMATE	CAMPHORATE	PIANOFORTE
REJUVENATE	AMELIORATE	TOOTHPASTE
IMPREGNATE	DECOLORATE	AFTERTASTE
DERACINATE	ELECTORATE	FOURCHETTE
VATICINATE	PERPETRATE	CASSOLETTE
INORDINATE	INFILTRATE	MARIONETTE
COORDINATE	CALYPTRATE	MIGNONETTE
INVAGINATE	FENESTRATE	MAISONETTE
EMARGINATE	MAGISTRATE	LEADERETTE
DESALINATE	BIROSTRATE	CHEMISETTE
EFFEMINATE	ILLUSTRATE	SILHOUETTE
INSEMINATE	INACCURATE	EPROUVETTE
DENOMINATE	INAUGURATE	CONTRIBUTE
INNOMINATE	SULPHURATE	DISTRIBUTE
ILLUMINATE	MARQUISATE	IRRESOLUTE
CHLORINATE	COMPENSATE	SUBSTITUTE
PALATINATE	INSPISSATE	CONSTITUTE
GELATINATE	CAPACITATE	PROSTITUTE

TROGLODYTE	ABROGATIVE	QUANTITIVE
LITHOPHYTE	PALLIATIVE	CONSULTIVE
MICROPHYTE	INITIATIVE	PENDENTIVE
HYDROPHYTE	CORELATIVE	PRESENTIVE
PROTOPHYTE	REGULATIVE	PREVENTIVE
DISEMBOGUE	CUMULATIVE	LOCOMOTIVE
SIALAGOGUE	COPULATIVE	PERCEPTIVE
CHOLAGOGUE	NOMINATIVE	SUSCEPTIVE
MYSTAGOGUE	INCHOATIVE	RESUMPTIVE
SIALOGOGUE	REPARATIVE	ASSUMPTIVE
UNDERVALUE	EXECRATIVE	ABSORPTIVE
MOZAMBIQUE	FEDERATIVE	CORRUPTIVE
COMMUNIQUE	GENERATIVE	DISRUPTIVE
CATAFALQUE	IMPERATIVE	SUPPORTIVE
ROMANESQUE	ALTERATIVE	DISTORTIVE
STATUESQUE	DECORATIVE	SUGGESTIVE
INTERWEAVE	PEJORATIVE	CONGESTIVE
DISENSLAVE	FIGURATIVE	PERSISTIVE
ARCHITRAVE	MATURATIVE	EXHAUSTIVE
DISBELIEVE	ACCUSATIVE	DIMINUTIVE
MISBELIEVE	VEGETATIVE	CLACKVALVE
PERSUASIVE	EXCITATIVE	DISAPPROVE
DISSUASIVE	MEDITATIVE	ANTIFREEZE
INDECISIVE	COGITATIVE	DEEPFREEZE
COMPULSIVE	DENOTATIVE	FANATICIZE
PROPULSIVE	IMPUTATIVE	SCEPTICIZE
CONVULSIVE	DERIVATIVE	CHLORIDIZE
SUSPENSIVE	RELAXATIVE	GORMANDIZE
DISTENSIVE	REFRACTIVE	AGGRANDIZE
RESPONSIVE	DETRACTIVE	PSALMODIZE
DISPERSIVE	RETRACTIVE	RHAPSODIZE
SUBVERSIVE	ATTRACTIVE	JEOPARDIZE
PERVERSIVE	EXTRACTIVE	BASTARDIZE
DISCURSIVE	SUBJECTIVE	THEOLOGIZE
SUCCESSIVE	REFLECTIVE	LETHARGIZE
CONCESSIVE	INFLECTIVE	SCANDALIZE
REDRESSIVE	COLLECTIVE	SPECIALIZE
REGRESSIVE	CONNECTIVE	BESTIALIZE
AGGRESSIVE	RESPECTIVE	ETERNALIZE
DIGRESSIVE	CORRECTIVE	LIBERALIZE
DEPRESSIVE	PROTECTIVE	FEDERALIZE
REPRESSIVE	CONVECTIVE	GENERALIZE
IMPRESSIVE	PREDICTIVE	MINERALIZE
OPPRESSIVE	VINDICTIVE	LITERALIZE
EXPRESSIVE	AFFLICTIVE	DEMORALIZE
POSSESSIVE	INFLICTIVE	CENTRALIZE
SUBMISSIVE	ADJUNCTIVE	NEUTRALIZE
PERMISSIVE	CONDUCTIVE	NATURALIZE
DISMISSIVE	PRODUCTIVE	PALATALIZE
SUCCUSSIVE	COMPLETIVE	CAPITALIZE
CONCUSSIVE	DISCRETIVE	DEVITALIZE
PERCUSSIVE	EXHIBITIVE	SENSUALIZE
DISCUSSIVE	DEFINITIVE	EVANGELIZE
APPLAUSIVE	INFINITIVE	VOLATILIZE
PRECLUSIVE	ADMONITIVE	ALCOHOLIZE
CONCLUSIVE	TRANSITIVE	VITRIOLIZE
PROTRUSIVE	APPOSITIVE	MONOPOLIZE
INCUBATIVE	EXPOSITIVE	EPISTOLIZE
INDICATIVE	REPETITIVE	MACADAMIZE
RECREATIVE	APPETITIVE	LEGITIMIZE

DRAMATICAL	MANAGERIAL	DEVOTIONAL
CLIMATICAL	IMMATERIAL	ERUPTIONAL
SOCRATICAL	IMMEMORIAL	SYNCHRONAL
DIDACTICAL	SPONSORIAL	ISOCHRONAL
DIABETICAL	GRESSORIAL	IMPERSONAL
HERMETICAL	INFUSORIAL	CANDLECOAL
FRENETICAL	SENATORIAL	CANNELCOAL
PHONETICAL	NATATORIAL	METACARPAL
UNPOETICAL	EQUATORIAL	ARCHETYPAL
DIETETICAL	TINCTORIAL	INVOLUCRAL
EXEGITICAL	PROCTORIAL	DECAHEDRAL
MEPHITICAL	MONITORIAL	OCTAHEDRAL
APOLITICAL	INDUSTRIAL	HEXAHEDRAL
EREMITICAL	SOLSTITIAL	HEMIHEDRAL
UNCRITICAL	CREDENTIAL	POLYHEDRAL
JESUITICAL	EVIDENTIAL	UNILATERAL
PEDANTICAL	PRUDENTIAL	TRILATERAL
ELLIPTICAL	TANGENTIAL	COLLATERAL
AUTOPTICAL	TORRENTIAL	TRILITERAL
LOGISTICAL	COLLOQUIAL	PERIPTERAL
PAPISTICAL	QUADRIVIAL	SEPULCHRAL
ANALYTICAL	DUODECIMAL	HYPAETHRAL
RECIPROCAL	MILLESIMAL	DECEMVIRAL
HEBDOMADAL	CENTESIMAL	ORCHESTRAL
SEPTICIDAL	HYPODERMAL	CAMPESTRAL
RHOMBOIDAL	DIATHERMAL	PROCEDURAL
HELICOIDAL	GEOTHERMAL	INTRAMURAL
LAMBDOIDAL	ISOTHERMAL	EXTRAMURAL
CONCHOIDAL	PHANTASMAL	CONNATURAL
SPHENOIDAL	EMBOLISMAL	STRUCTURAL
SPHEROIDAL	PAROXYSMAL	SCRIPTURAL
ASTEROIDAL	PHENOMENAL	SCULPTURAL
PHALANGEAL	SUPRARENAL	BRACHYURAL
PHARYNGEAL	ABORIGINAL	SUPERVISAL
PERITONEAL	ANTICLINAL	TRANSPOSAL
PERIOSTEAL	TRIGEMINAL	METATARSAL
COMMONWEAL	SUBLIMINAL	DUNIWASSAL
FEBRIFUGAL	COGNOMINAL	CUCURBITAL
HIERARCHAL	PRONOMINAL	CONGENITAL
ACRONYCHAL	ENDOCRINAL	ENCRINITAL
APOCRYPHAL	INTESTINAL	QUADRANTAL
PROVERBIAL	TETRAGONAL	APLACENTAL
INJUDICIAL	PENTAGONAL	ACCIDENTAL
BENEFICIAL	HEPTAGONAL	OCCIDENTAL
UNOFFICIAL	ANTIPHONAL	INCIDENTAL
ARTIFICIAL	OBSIDIONAL	NIDAMENTAL
PROVINCIAL	OCCASIONAL	LIGAMENTAL
ANTISOCIAL	DIVISIONAL	ORNAMENTAL
COMMERCIAL	VOCATIONAL	ATRAMENTAL
PRIMORDIAL	CREATIONAL	TENEMENTAL
EPITHELIAL	RELATIONAL	FRAGMENTAL
POLYNOMIAL	IRRATIONAL	RUDIMENTAL
SELFDENIAL	GYRATIONAL	REGIMENTAL
CATAMENIAL	ROTATIONAL	DOCUMENTAL
MILLENNIAL	FRACTIONAL	MONUMENTAL
CENTENNIAL	FRICTIONAL	HORIZONTAL
SEPTENNIAL	FUNCTIONAL	SACERDOTAL
CEREMONIAL	ADDITIONAL	HOLOPHOTAL
ANTIMONIAL	VOLITIONAL	INDIVIDUAL
GLOSSARIAL	POSITIONAL	SUBLINGUAL

TRILINGUAL	RESPECTFUL	CLASSICISM
CONSENSUAL	DELIGHTFUL	FANATICISM
CONTACTUAL	THOUGHTFUL	ASCETICISM
UNPUNCTUAL	CONCEITFUL	SCEPTICISM
CONVENTUAL	UNEVENTFUL	GNOSTICISM
CONCEPTUAL	DISGUSTFUL	SCOTTICISM
CONTEXTUAL	CHLOROPHYL	BRIGANDISM
HOMOSEXUAL		LOLLARDISM
ADJECTIVAL		HYLOTHEISM
WITHDRAWAL	---------M	HENOTHEISM
PENNYROYAL		MONOTHEISM
ENDORHIZAL	COLLARBEAM	POLYTHEISM
TREADWHEEL	MAINSTREAM	MICROSEISM
BEVELWHEEL	SLIPSTREAM	GEOPHAGISM
CROWNWHEEL	PHANEROGAM	DEMAGOGISM
MANCHINEEL	BIRMINGHAM	PARALOGISM
KRIEGSPIEL	STEREOGRAM	MONARCHISM
ANTECHAPEL	CARDIOGRAM	DIMORPHISM
DISAPPAREL	SPHENOGRAM	RADICALISM
COLDCHISEL	CHRONOGRAM	SURREALISM
BOMBVESSEL	DENDROGRAM	SPECIALISM
DISEMBOWEL	CRYPTOGRAM	NOMINALISM
FINGERNAIL	POSTMORTEM	JOURNALISM
DAGGLETAIL	APOPHTHEGM	LIBERALISM
BLUEPENCIL	SUBKINGDOM	FEDERALISM
CINQUEFOIL	COCKNEYDOM	LITERALISM
DISEMBROIL	COFFEEROOM	CHLORALISM
COWCHERVIL	BRIDEGROOM	HUMORALISM
CANNONBALL	DININGROOM	CENTRALISM
BASKETBALL	LIVINGROOM	NATURALISM
VOLLEYBALL	SCHOOLROOM	CAPITALISM
BREASTWALL	DISEMBOSOM	REVIVALISM
DIVINGBELL	ECHINODERM	EVANGELISM
ACORNSHELL	BLASTODERM	METABOLISM
CRANESBILL	ANGIOSPERM	ALCOHOLISM
COFFEEMILL	GYMNOSPERM	VATICANISM
GROUNDSILL	SCHOOLTERM	LESBIANISM
STANDSTILL	CALYCIFORM	RUFFIANISM
CLOSESTOOL	GLANDIFORM	BRAHMANISM
COTTONWOOL	CYATHIFORM	PURITANISM
EUCALYPTOL	MONILIFORM	FEMININISM
SCHOOLGIRL	STELLIFORM	CHAUVINISM
CHORUSGIRL	POCULIFORM	ANTAGONISM
UNGRACEFUL	COTYLIFORM	CINCHONISM
REVENGEFUL	CRIBRIFORM	PYRRHONISM
THIMBLEFUL	DENDRIFORM	EUDEMONISM
PURPOSEFUL	ETHERIFORM	GEOTROPISM
REMORSEFUL	STRATIFORM	PLAGIARISM
UNGRATEFUL	DIGITIFORM	MONETARISM
DESPITEFUL	LINGUIFORM	MILITARISM
MEANINGFUL	CHLOROFORM	GRANGERISM
UNFAITHFUL	BRAINSTORM	COTTIERISM
UNTRUTHFUL	CANKERWORM	EUHEMERISM
UNMERCIFUL	ENTHUSIASM	POLYMERISM
UNTHANKFUL	ICONOCLASM	SPOONERISM
DISDAINFUL	PROTOPLASM	AMATEURISM
WORSHIPFUL	PHARISAISM	NARCISSISM
TUMBLERFUL	LAMBDACISM	PRAGMATISM
SUCCESSFUL	LACONICISM	TRAUMATISM
NEGLECTFUL	EMPIRICISM	RHEUMATISM

SEPARATISM	FRANCISCAN	CHAIRWOMAN
MODERATISM	CHIMNEYCAN	BONDSWOMAN
SYNCRETISM	MOHAMMEDAN	SALESWOMAN
SYBARITISM	ARACHNIDAN	MIDSHIPMAN
PARASITISM	COFFEEBEAN	COUNTERMAN
PATRIOTISM	RUNNERBEAN	GROUNDSMAN
ANABAPTISM	CRUSTACEAN	SUPERHUMAN
ABSOLUTISM	THEODICEAN	HIGHWAYMAN
PANSLAVISM	CESTIODEAN	JOURNEYMAN
POSITIVISM	ANTIPODEAN	NURSERYMAN
FLUNKEYISM	TELEOSTEAN	COUNTRYMAN
COCKNEYISM	PHOENICIAN	BIPARTISAN
MEERSCHAUM	TECHNICIAN	NEAPOLITAN
LEBENSRAUM	POLITICIAN	GARGANTUAN
STUMBLEBUM	BEAUTICIAN	HANDMAIDEN
MEMORANDUM	CISTERCIAN	ROSEGARDEN
REFERENDUM	THEOLOGIAN	BEARGARDEN
PERITONEUM	BATRACHIAN	CASEHARDEN
PERIOSTEUM	EUSTACHIAN	OVERBURDEN
EUPHORBIUM	MALPIGHIAN	WINDSCREEN
APOTHECIUM	EPITAPHIAN	FIRESCREEN
ANDROECIUM	DIDELPHIAN	UNFORESEEN
COMPENDIUM	CORINTHIAN	MANGOSTEEN
PARAPODIUM	MIDLOTHIAN	COPENHAGEN
EPITHELIUM	AUSTRALIAN	STRENGTHEN
PROSCENIUM	ABYSSINIAN	DISBURTHEN
DELPHINIUM	ELEUSINIAN	FINESPOKEN
TRICLINIUM	CALEDONIAN	FAIRSPOKEN
MILLENNIUM	BABYLONIAN	DEATHTOKEN
STRAMONIUM	CICERONIAN	CHAPFALLEN
HONORARIUM	CAMERONIAN	CHOPFALLEN
SANITARIUM	DECAGYNIAN	CATECHUMEN
OPPROBRIUM	HEXAGYNIAN	FORECHOSEN
ACROTERIUM	CATENARIAN	STRAIGHTEN
SUDATORIUM	TRACTARIAN	DISHEARTEN
SANATORIUM	VEGETARIAN	PINEMARTEN
MORATORIUM	SANITARIAN	FLEABITTEN
PRAETORIUM	DECANDRIAN	YESTEREVEN
AUDITORIUM	OCTANDRIAN	UNFORGIVEN
DIGITORIUM	HEXANDRIAN	FOREORDAIN
PANCRATIUM	CHAUCERIAN	UNDERDRAIN
NASTURTIUM	INFUSORIAN	OVERSTRAIN
CEREBELLUM	STENTORIAN	BLOODSTAIN
HAUSTELLUM	PEDESTRIAN	BRIDLEREIN
TROPAEOLUM	EQUESTRIAN	RAGAMUFFIN
ACETABULUM	CENTAURIAN	ENKEPHALIN
VIBRACULUM	ATHANASIAN	PENICILLIN
CURRICULUM	CIRCENSIAN	BOOKMUSLIN
MOLYBDENUM	DICKENSIAN	TENDERLOIN
AMBULACRUM	PARNASSIAN	CORKINGPIN
SIMULACRUM	CARTHUSIAN	FREEMARTIN
INVOLUCRUM	SUBCLAVIAN	CHAMBERTIN
KETTLEDRUM	MILITIAMAN	BONESPAVIN
SUBSTRATUM	HUSBANDMAN	ARCHDEACON
	SURFACEMAN	CATHOLICON
	SERVICEMAN	ARMAGEDDON
---------N	GARBAGEMAN	ACOTYLEDON
	ENGLISHMAN	DIPROTODON
REPUBLICAN	COUNCILMAN	CURMUDGEON
COPERNICAN	NOBLEWOMAN	CLAYPIGEON

ALTERATION	EXCAVATION	AMMUNITION
EMIGRATION	SALIVATION	APPARITION
ADMIRATION	DERIVATION	CONTRITION
ASPIRATION	ACTIVATION	TRANSITION
EXPIRATION	TITIVATION	DEPOSITION
DECORATION	MOTIVATION	REPOSITION
COLORATION	RENOVATION	IMPOSITION
ABERRATION	INNOVATION	APPOSITION
FILTRATION	STARVATION	OPPOSITION
CASTRATION	ENERVATION	EXPOSITION
LUSTRATION	RELAXATION	REPETITION
INDURATION	INDEXATION	CONTENTION
FIGURATION	ANNEXATION	ABSTENTION
ABJURATION	DENIZATION	DISTENTION
OBJURATION	AREFACTION	SUBVENTION
ADJURATION	REFRACTION	PREVENTION
DEPURATION	INFRACTION	CONVENTION
MATURATION	DETRACTION	LOCOMOTION
SATURATION	RETRACTION	CONCEPTION
OBTURATION	ATTRACTION	PERCEPTION
IONISATION	EXTRACTION	ASCRIPTION
ACCUSATION	CONFECTION	REDEMPTION
DILATATION	PERFECTION	RESUMPTION
FLOATATION	SUBJECTION	ASSUMPTION
ERUCTATION	PROJECTION	EXCERPTION
VEGETATION	BYELECTION	ABSORPTION
HABITATION	DEFLECTION	CORRUPTION
DUBITATION	REFLECTION	DISRUPTION
RECITATION	INFLECTION	PROPORTION
EXCITATION	COLLECTION	CONTORTION
MEDITATION	CONNECTION	DISTORTION
DIGITATION	INSPECTION	SUGGESTION
COGITATION	CORRECTION	CONGESTION
LIMITATION	SUBSECTION	EXHAUSTION
SANITATION	TRISECTION	COMBUSTION
CAPITATION	DISSECTION	PRECAUTION
IRRITATION	PROTECTION	ALLOCUTION
HESITATION	CONVECTION	ABSOLUTION
VISITATION	PREDICTION	RESOLUTION
EQUITATION	AFFLICTION	DEVOLUTION
LEVITATION	INFLICTION	REVOLUTION
INVITATION	CONVICTION	INVOLUTION
EXALTATION	EXTINCTION	DIMINUTION
EXULTATION	ADJUNCTION	COMPLEXION
PLANTATION	INJUNCTION	ENCEPHALON
DENOTATION	CONCOCTION	WATERMELON
ANNOTATION	SUBDUCTION	PENTATHLON
ADAPTATION	CONDUCTION	BACKGAMMON
TEMPTATION	PRODUCTION	PHENOMENON
FLIRTATION	COMPLETION	CHAMPIGNON
CRUSTATION	CONCRETION	TABLESPOON
REFUTATION	DISCRETION	COURTBARON
SALUTATION	ADHIBITION	DECAHEDRON
DEPUTATION	INHIBITION	OCTAHEDRON
REPUTATION	EXHIBITION	HEXAHEDRON
AMPUTATION	EXPEDITION	HEMIHEDRON
IMPUTATION	EBULLITION	OCTOHEDRON
EVACUATION	DEMOLITION	POLYHEDRON
GRADUATION	DEFINITION	QUERCITRON
EVALUATION	ADMONITION	COMPARISON

BOMBARDIER	ROADRUNNER	DROSOMETER
HALBERDIER	FORERUNNER	HYPSOMETER
SANCTIFIER	PETITIONER	PHOTOMETER
STULTIFIER	QUESTIONER	PIEZOMETER
BEAUTIFIER	EMBLAZONER	HYPERMETER
CHANDELIER	NORTHERNER	PACHYMETER
MULTIPLIER	SOUTHERNER	THEREAFTER
CHIFFONIER	OVERTURNER	GUNFIGHTER
PLUMASSIER	CHURCHGOER	DUMBWAITER
CUIRASSIER	SKYSCRAPER	TYPEWRITER
PERRUQUIER	GAMEKEEPER	TROCHANTER
MATCHMAKER	BOOKKEEPER	SUPPLANTER
CLOCKMAKER	GOALKEEPER	COVENANTER
DRESSMAKER	SHOPKEEPER	RESIDENTER
UNDERTAKER	DOORKEEPER	ORNAMENTER
PAINSTAKER	BUCKJUMPER	FREQUENTER
NUTCRACKER	INTERLOPER	CALCSINTER
WOODPECKER	WORSHIPPER	BOOKHUNTER
TRAFFICKER	CLODHOPPER	RENCOUNTER
LUMPSUCKER	REMEMBERER	DISCOUNTER
HITCHHIKER	MALINGERER	FREEBOOTER
COALBUNKER	CLOISTERER	HELICOPTER
BILLBROKER	DISCOVERER	HYMENOPTER
PAWNBROKER	DEFLOWERER	FORECASTER
WHOLESALER	ADVENTURER	NEWSCASTER
DISSEMBLER	MANOEUVRER	HEADMASTER
CHRONICLER	STABILISER	RINGMASTER
PANHANDLER	ADVERTISER	COALMASTER
RECONCILER	TRANSPOSER	POSTMASTER
BASEBALLER	DISCOURSER	MANCHESTER
FOOTBALLER	REPROBATER	ADMINISTER
MARSHALLER	DESECRATER	ENCLOISTER
VICTUALLER	BILGEWATER	FOURPOSTER
TRAMMELLER	FRESHWATER	FILIBUSTER
BOOKSELLER	BREAKWATER	DEADLETTER
BESTSELLER	TETRAMETER	LOVELETTER
FORETELLER	VOLTAMETER	BONESETTER
STENCILLER	PENTAMETER	BABYSITTER
WEEDKILLER	ACIDIMETER	BOGTROTTER
CONTROLLER	PLANIMETER	WOODCUTTER
POURPARLER	DENSIMETER	FILECUTTER
DAYDREAMER	GRAVIMETER	CORKCUTTER
BECHEDEMER	PLEXIMETER	AMBIDEXTER
BLASPHEMER	TACHOMETER	COALHEAVER
DISCLAIMER	BATHOMETER	BRAINFEVER
DROPHAMMER	RADIOMETER	CANTILEVER
CLAWHAMMER	AUDIOMETER	WHENSOEVER
WINDJAMMER	EUDIOMETER	WHATSOEVER
ASTRONOMER	GONIOMETER	PEARLDIVER
BABYFARMER	OPSIOMETER	UNDERCOVER
COPARCENER	CYCLOMETER	REDISCOVER
THREATENER	ANEMOMETER	CHANGEOVER
CAMPAIGNER	PLANOMETER	FISHCARVER
COMPLAINER	CLINOMETER	WALLFLOWER
RESTRAINER	PHONOMETER	BELLFLOWER
DISTRAINER	MICROMETER	CORNFLOWER
MAINTAINER	HYDROMETER	CROWFLOWER
CORDWAINER	HYGROMETER	PLATELAYER
FORTYNINER	SPIROMETER	BRICKLAYER
EMISCANNER	PULSOMETER	SOOTHSAYER

EPENTHESIS	SEARCHLESS	INWARDNESS
HYPOTHESIS	CHURCHLESS	ABSURDNESS
EPIGENESIS	BREATHLESS	SHREWDNESS
PANGENESIS	REMEDILESS	SCARCENESS
BIOGENESIS	SYSTEMLESS	FIERCENESS
APHAERESIS	FATHOMLESS	SPRUCENESS
AMANUENSIS	RANSOMLESS	SAVAGENESS
THROMBOSIS	BOTTOMLESS	BLITHENESS
APOTHEOSIS	MOTIONLESS	STABLENESS
ENANTIOSIS	SEASONLESS	FEEBLENESS
ENDOSMOSIS	COLLARLESS	EDIBLENESS
ECCHYMOSIS	CUMBERLESS	NIMBLENESS
HAEMATOSIS	FATHERLESS	HUMBLENESS
ASBESTOSIS	MOTHERLESS	DOUBLENESS
ECTHLIPSIS	DINNERLESS	FACILENESS
TRACHEITIS	SUPPERLESS	FICKLENESS
LARYNGITIS	MASTERLESS	SUPPLENESS
BRONCHITIS	SISTERLESS	SUBTLENESS
CEPHALITIS	FETTERLESS	GENTLENESS
TONSILITIS	ANSWERLESS	LITTLENESS
TYMPANITIS	PRAYERLESS	INSANENESS
CEREBRITIS	COLOURLESS	SERENENESS
STOMATITIS	SAVOURLESS	DIVINENESS
DERMATITIS	EFFECTLESS	SQUARENESS
EPIGLOTTIS	OBJECTLESS	SOMBRENESS
CHOPSTICKS	THRIFTLESS	MEAGRENESS
CANONICALS	FLIGHTLESS	ENTIRENESS
MUSSULMANS	SPIRITLESS	SECURENESS
AFTERPAINS	RESULTLESS	DEMURENESS
MALAPROPOS	TENANTLESS	MATURENESS
RHINOCEROS	RELENTLESS	MOROSENESS
PETTICHAPS	PARENTLESS	COARSENESS
PETTYCHAPS	EFFORTLESS	HOARSENESS
ALEXANDERS	CHRISTLESS	SPARSENESS
DOWNSTAIRS	SHADOWLESS	AVERSENESS
DOUBLEBASS	MARROWLESS	OBTUSENESS
THIRDCLASS	PUBLICNESS	SEDATENESS
FIRSTCLASS	JAGGEDNESS	OBLATENESS
FIBREGLASS	DOGGEDNESS	INNATENESS
PLEXIGLASS	RUGGEDNESS	POLITENESS
BEARDGRASS	WICKEDNESS	FINITENESS
BROMEGRASS	SEAREDNESS	REMOTENESS
COUCHGRASS	SACREDNESS	CHASTENESS
AFTERGRASS	CURSEDNESS	MINUTENESS
STEWARDESS	ROOTEDNESS	ASTUTENESS
SHIELDLESS	AMAZEDNESS	NATIVENESS
FRIENDLESS	MORBIDNESS	ACTIVENESS
GROUNDLESS	TURBIDNESS	STANCHNESS
REGARDLESS	RANCIDNESS	MODISHNESS
CHANGELESS	CANDIDNESS	MULISHNESS
SCATHELESS	SORDIDNESS	MOPISHNESS
THRONELESS	TURGIDNESS	UPPISHNESS
LUSTRELESS	PALLIDNESS	GARISHNESS
TONGUELESS	STOLIDNESS	BOYISHNESS
VIRTUELESS	TORPIDNESS	SMOOTHNESS
SLEEVELESS	STUPIDNESS	SCABBINESS
SPEECHLESS	FLORIDNESS	FLABBINESS
BRANCHLESS	TORRIDNESS	CHUBBINESS
STANCHLESS	FERVIDNESS	STEADINESS
QUENCHLESS	UNKINDNESS	SPEEDINESS

UNTIDINESS	WATERINESS	PROPERNESS
MOULDINESS	STARRINESS	BETTERNESS
BLOODINESS	PALTRINESS	BITTERNESS
STURDINESS	SULTRINESS	CLEVERNESS
CLOUDINESS	UNEASINESS	UNFAIRNESS
STUFFINESS	GREASINESS	REMISSNESS
SHAGGINESS	QUEASINESS	ODIOUSNESS
FLAGGINESS	CHEESINESS	POROUSNESS
CRAGGINESS	CLUMSINESS	JOYOUSNESS
GROGGINESS	GLASSINESS	ABJECTNESS
SPONGINESS	GRASSINESS	SELECTNESS
POACHINESS	GLOSSINESS	DIRECTNESS
TETCHINESS	DROSSINESS	STRICTNESS
PITCHINESS	DROWSINESS	SECRETNESS
TOUCHINESS	SWEATINESS	SLIGHTNESS
DAUPHINESS	SLEETINESS	BRIGHTNESS
TRASHINESS	CRAFTINESS	ADROITNESS
FLESHINESS	MIGHTINESS	EYEWITNESS
MARSHINESS	GUILTINESS	EARWITNESS
FILTHINESS	FAULTINESS	OCCULTNESS
FROTHINESS	SCANTINESS	RECENTNESS
EARTHINESS	DAINTINESS	SILENTNESS
WORTHINESS	FLINTINESS	PROMPTNESS
TRICKINESS	HEARTINESS	ABRUPTNESS
STICKINESS	YEASTINESS	EXPERTNESS
CHALKINESS	FROSTINESS	ROBUSTNESS
FRISKINESS	CRUSTINESS	AUGUSTNESS
DEADLINESS	TRUSTINESS	SALLOWNESS
KINDLINESS	PRETTINESS	YELLOWNESS
GOODLINESS	GRITTINESS	HOLLOWNESS
LORDLINESS	KNOTTINESS	CONVEXNESS
LIKELINESS	SMUTTINESS	NIGHTDRESS
TIMELINESS	SCURVINESS	COURTDRESS
COMELINESS	GENIALNESS	MANAGERESS
HOMELINESS	JOVIALNESS	FRUITERESS
LONELINESS	DISMALNESS	ADULTERESS
LIVELINESS	SHRILLNESS	RETROGRESS
LOVELINESS	WOEFULNESS	TRANSGRESS
KINGLINESS	USEFULNESS	DECOMPRESS
SICKLINESS	RUEFULNESS	DICTATRESS
CHILLINESS	WILFULNESS	DIRECTRESS
SEEMLINESS	MANFULNESS	SEDUCTRESS
UNHOLINESS	SINFULNESS	INVENTRESS
PORTLINESS	FITFULNESS	ANCESTRESS
COSTLINESS	ARTFULNESS	SEMPSTRESS
UNRULINESS	LAWFULNESS	MULATTRESS
CREAMINESS	JOYFULNESS	DISPOSSESS
DREAMINESS	HIDDENNESS	INTERCROSS
STEAMINESS	SUDDENNESS	CRISSCROSS
CLAMMINESS	BROKENNESS	FOOTLIGHTS
GLOOMINESS	SULLENNESS	GRASSROOTS
BRAININESS	BARRENNESS	HEREABOUTS
BRAWNINESS	ROTTENNESS	DIPLODOCUS
SLOPPINESS	UNEVENNESS	CORYPHAEUS
BLEARINESS	BRAZENNESS	OESOPHAGUS
DREARINESS	COMMONNESS	POLYANTHUS
SUGARINESS	MODERNNESS	PROTHALLUS
UNWARINESS	SCRIMPNESS	FASCICULUS
TAWDRINESS	WILDERNESS	DIDUNCULUS
CHEERINESS	TENDERNESS	STRABISMUS

CONVERGENT	DENOUEMENT	INSTRUMENT
SUFFICIENT	EVOLVEMENT	PREPAYMENT
PROFICIENT	ABRIDGMENT	DEFRAYMENT
OMNISCIENT	ADJUDGMENT	DEPLOYMENT
INGREDIENT	DETACHMENT	EMPLOYMENT
DISSILIENT	ATTACHMENT	PREEMINENT
CONVENIENT	ENRICHMENT	INCOHERENT
PERCIPIENT	FAMISHMENT	IRREVERENT
SUSCIPIENT	BANISHMENT	CONCURRENT
PARTURIENT	PUNISHMENT	PERCURRENT
ASSENTIENT	RAVISHMENT	IMPENITENT
PERCUTIENT	AMBUSHMENT	MALCONTENT
DISCUTIENT	IMPEDIMENT	DISCONTENT
NONCHALENT	EMBODIMENT	ARMIPOTENT
AMBIVALENT	HABILIMENT	IGNIPOTENT
EQUIVALENT	COMPLIMENT	OMNIPOTENT
GRAVEOLENT	EXPERIMENT	SUBSISTENT
MALEVOLENT	EMBANKMENT	CONSISTENT
BENEVOLENT	INSTALMENT	PERSISTENT
FLOCCULENT	ENTAILMENT	COEXISTENT
FRAUDULENT	FULFILMENT	INFREQUENT
MEDICAMENT	INSTILMENT	SUBSEQUENT
PARLIAMENT	ASSIGNMENT	CONSEQUENT
LOCULAMENT	ORDAINMENT	DELINQUENT
TOURNAMENT	OBTAINMENT	INELOQUENT
ENTOMBMENT	DETAINMENT	DISSOLVENT
BENUMBMENT	ATTAINMENT	CIRCUMVENT
RETARDMENT	ENJOINMENT	CONSTRAINT
DEFACEMENT	CANTONMENT	PEPPERMINT
EFFACEMENT	GOVERNMENT	STANDPOINT
ENLACEMENT	DISOWNMENT	EMBONPOINT
SOLACEMENT	RESHIPMENT	DISAPPOINT
ENTICEMENT	DECAMPMENT	DIPHYODONT
AMERCEMENT	ENCAMPMENT	TANTAMOUNT
SEDUCEMENT	ESCARPMENT	CANNONSHOT
INDUCEMENT	RECOUPMENT	COMPATRIOT
ENGAGEMENT	ENDEARMENT	BREASTKNOT
MANAGEMENT	WILDERMENT	SQUAREROOT
OBLIGEMENT	WONDERMENT	CHAMBERPOT
REGALEMENT	PREFERMENT	BEAUTYSPOT
BABBLEMENT	BETTERMENT	NYMPHOLEPT
RABBLEMENT	HARASSMENT	TYPESCRIPT
DEFILEMENT	ASSESSMENT	TRANSCRIPT
REVILEMENT	EMBOSSMENT	POSTSCRIPT
COMPLEMENT	INDICTMENT	MANUSCRIPT
SUPPLEMENT	INFEFTMENT	SWEETHEART
BATTLEMENT	COMMITMENT	PRECONCERT
SETTLEMENT	RELENTMENT	DISCONCERT
EPAULEMENT	RESENTMENT	ANIMADVERT
EBOULEMENT	ANOINTMENT	CONTROVERT
PUZZLEMENT	DEPARTMENT	BLACKSHIRT
REFINEMENT	DEPORTMENT	UNDERSHIRT
ESCAPEMENT	ASSORTMENT	DISCOMFORT
RETIREMENT	ARRESTMENT	SPOILSPORT
ALLUREMENT	DIVESTMENT	SPLEENWORT
DEBASEMENT	INVESTMENT	BUTTERWORT
INCASEMENT	ENLISTMENT	ADDERSWORT
INCITEMENT	ADJUSTMENT	ECCLESIAST
EXCITEMENT	ENCYSTMENT	ENTHUSIAST
INDITEMENT	INTEGUMENT	OSTEOBLAST

INTENDANCY	TOXICOLOGY	CHANGEABLY
REDUNDANCY	BALNEOLOGY	UNSOCIABLY
SYCOPHANCY	CONCHOLOGY	UNDENIABLY
IRRADIANCY	PSYCHOLOGY	INVARIABLY
CAPNOMANCY	GRAPHOLOGY	REMARKABLY
NECROMANCY	MORPHOLOGY	PRESUMABLY
HYDROMANCY	EXOBIOLOGY	IMAGINABLY
CHIROMANCY	SEMEIOLOGY	ABOMINABLY
OPPUGNANCY	BIBLIOLOGY	PARDONABLY
EXUBERANCY	CRANIOLOGY	REASONABLY
EXPECTANCY	PHYSIOLOGY	SEASONABLY
RELUCTANCY	ENTOMOLOGY	IMPALPABLY
ACCEPTANCY	SEISMOLOGY	COMPARABLY
DECUMBENCY	PHRENOLOGY	PREFERABLY
RECUMBENCY	TECHNOLOGY	SUFFERABLY
INCUMBENCY	DEMONOLOGY	ANSWERABLY
ABSORBENCY	CHRONOLOGY	DEPLORABLY
PRECEDENCY	ESCAPOLOGY	PERDURABLY
PRESIDENCY	DENDROLOGY	COLOURABLY
DEPENDENCY	ONEIROLOGY	HONOURABLY
REFULGENCY	GLOSSOLOGY	FAVOURABLY
STRINGENCY	SOMATOLOGY	MEASURABLY
DETERGENCY	TERATOLOGY	CENSURABLY
DIVERGENCY	ODONTOLOGY	DELECTABLY
DEFICIENCY	DEONTOLOGY	CREDITABLY
EFFICIENCY	EGYPTOLOGY	PROFITABLY
EXPEDIENCY	CRYPTOLOGY	HOSPITABLY
RESILIENCY	GLOTTOLOGY	CHARITABLY
EBULLIENCY	EMBRYOLOGY	UNSUITABLY
RECIPIENCY	BRACHYLOGY	LAMENTABLY
TRANSIENCY	METALLURGY	ACCEPTABLY
EXCELLENCY	DRAMATURGY	DETESTABLY
REPELLENCY	MATRIARCHY	DISPUTABLY
TURBULENCY	PATRIARCHY	STATUTABLY
SUCCULENCY	TELEGRAPHY	OBSERVABLY
TRUCULENCY	PASIGRAPHY	COGNIZABLY
FLATULENCY	CACOGRAPHY	INCREDIBLY
DECURRENCY	IDEOGRAPHY	INTANGIBLY
INSOLVENCY	OREOGRAPHY	INFALLIBLY
CHAPLAINCY	LOGOGRAPHY	INSENSIBLY
BANKRUPTCY	HOLOGRAPHY	OSTENSIBLY
SALMAGUNDY	XYLOGRAPHY	ACCESSIBLY
UNDERSTUDY	DEMOGRAPHY	COMPATIBLY
DISCJOCKEY	TOPOGRAPHY	ABSORBEDLY
DOGPARSLEY	TYPOGRAPHY	WRETCHEDLY
COWPARSLEY	HOROGRAPHY	DEFORMEDLY
BLOODMONEY	AUTOGRAPHY	CONSUMEDLY
PETROMONEY	POLYGRAPHY	DESIGNEDLY
STRATHSPEY	PHILOSOPHY	DECLAREDLY
DAPPLEGREY	HOMEOPATHY	COMPOSEDLY
DISQUALIFY	OSTEOPATHY	CONFUSEDLY
PRESIGNIFY	HYDROPATHY	REPEATEDLY
SACCHARIFY	NEUROPATHY	AFFECTEDLY
DISSATISFY	ROADWORTHY	DEJECTEDLY
HIPPOPHAGY	NOTEWORTHY	SPIRITEDLY
BIBLIOPEGY	IMPROBABLY	UNWONTEDLY
MINERALOGY	IMPLACABLY	ADMITTEDLY
MALACOLOGY	DESPICABLY	BESOTTEDLY
MUSICOLOGY	FORMIDABLY	POLLUTEDLY
LEXICOLOGY	NOTICEABLY	DEPRAVEDLY

ESPECIALLY	DOUBTFULLY	PERILOUSLY
JUDICIALLY	RIGHTFULLY	FABULOUSLY
OFFICIALLY	FRUITFULLY	SEDULOUSLY
REMEDIALLY	BOASTFULLY	POPULOUSLY
BIENNIALLY	TRUSTFULLY	INFAMOUSLY
NOTARIALLY	ALDERMANLY	VENOMOUSLY
IMPERIALLY	MISTAKENLY	ENORMOUSLY
MATERIALLY	UNCOMMONLY	RAVENOUSLY
INFORMALLY	STUBBORNLY	LUMINOUSLY
ABNORMALLY	TACITURNLY	MUTINOUSLY
ORIGINALLY	MELANCHOLY	CUMBROUSLY
MARGINALLY	FAMILIARLY	WONDROUSLY
CRIMINALLY	PECULIARLY	NUMEROUSLY
DIAGONALLY	GLOBULARLY	GENEROUSLY
NATIONALLY	ORACULARLY	DECOROUSLY
RATIONALLY	CIRCULARLY	RIGOROUSLY
OPTIONALLY	SINGULARLY	VIGOROUSLY
PERSONALLY	DECEMBERLY	VALOROUSLY
MATERNALLY	DISORDERLY	DOLOROUSLY
INTERNALLY	UNFATHERLY	TIMOROUSLY
EXTERNALLY	UNMOTHERLY	HUMOROUSLY
CORPORALLY	CAVALIERLY	SONOROUSLY
SPECTRALLY	UNMANNERLY	COVETOUSLY
BINAURALLY	IMPROPERLY	VIRTUOUSLY
GUTTURALLY	DAUGHTERLY	TORTUOUSLY
PUNCTUALLY	SINISTERLY	GRIEVOUSLY
HABITUALLY	UNSISTERLY	ABSTRACTLY
EVENTUALLY	DEBONAIRLY	INDIRECTLY
DISLOYALLY	INFERIORLY	SUCCINCTLY
UNDERBELLY	ANTERIORLY	DISTINCTLY
PARALLELLY	EXTERIORLY	CONJUNCTLY
ROCKABILLY	HEEDLESSLY	DISCREETLY
TRANQUILLY	LIFELESSLY	IMPLICITLY
DREADFULLY	NAMELESSLY	EXPLICITLY
FRAUDFULLY	HOPELESSLY	ABUNDANTLY
PEACEFULLY	CARELESSLY	RECREANTLY
GRACEFULLY	RUTHLESSLY	ARROGANTLY
FORCEFULLY	PITILESSLY	VIGILANTLY
VENGEFULLY	RECKLESSLY	PETULANTLY
SHAMEFULLY	LUCKLESSLY	STAGNANTLY
BLAMEFULLY	HARMLESSLY	POIGNANTLY
GRATEFULLY	FEARLESSLY	RESONANTLY
TASTEFULLY	PEERLESSLY	FLIPPANTLY
WASTEFULLY	BOOTLESSLY	TOLERANTLY
WRONGFULLY	SPOTLESSLY	FLAGRANTLY
WATCHFULLY	RESTLESSLY	FRAGRANTLY
WRATHFULLY	GORGEOUSLY	IGNORANTLY
FAITHFULLY	EDACIOUSLY	PLEASANTLY
SLOTHFULLY	SPACIOUSLY	PUISSANTLY
MIRTHFULLY	GRACIOUSLY	CONSTANTLY
YOUTHFULLY	SPECIOUSLY	ADJACENTLY
TRUTHFULLY	PRECIOUSLY	INDECENTLY
FANCIFULLY	LUSCIOUSLY	INNOCENTLY
MERCIFULLY	STUDIOUSLY	IMPUDENTLY
THANKFULLY	GLORIOUSLY	DILIGENTLY
SCORNFULLY	UXORIOUSLY	EMERGENTLY
MOURNFULLY	SPURIOUSLY	OBEDIENTLY
CHEERFULLY	FACTIOUSLY	INSOLENTLY
POWERFULLY	CAPTIOUSLY	LUCULENTLY
BLISSFULLY	CAUTIOUSLY	VIRULENTLY

PURULENTLY	CAUTIONARY	SALUTATORY
VEHEMENTLY	FLUXIONARY	DETRACTORY
APPARENTLY	QUATERNARY	TRAJECTORY
INHERENTLY	DISPENSARY	CORRECTORY
COHERENTLY	COMMISSARY	COMPLETORY
FREQUENTLY	HEREDITARY	SUPPLETORY
ELOQUENTLY	INSANITARY	INHIBITORY
CONJOINTLY	DEPOSITARY	EXHIBITORY
IMMODESTLY	ELEMENTARY	PLAUDITORY
MANIFESTLY	ALIMENTARY	ADMONITORY
CRYPTOGAMY	COMMENTARY	TRANSITORY
CHIROGNOMY	INSALUTARY	REPOSITORY
GASTRONOMY	VOLUPTUARY	EXPOSITORY
MONOCHROMY	EMBROIDERY	CONSULTORY
POLYCHROMY	BEWITCHERY	PROMONTORY
MASTECTOMY	DEBAUCHERY	PEREMPTORY
STRABOTOMY	DISTILLERY	CLERESTORY
PHLEBOTOMY	TOMFOOLERY	PREHISTORY
TRICHOTOMY	STATIONERY	CONSISTORY
OVARIOTOMY	BUFFOONERY	CLEARSTORY
HYMENOTOMY	LAMPOONERY	ABSOLUTORY
ENTEROTOMY	DRYSALTERY	INTERMARRY
NEPHROTOMY	EFFRONTERY	CLOUDBERRY
EMBRYOTOMY	BAPTISTERY	GOOSEBERRY
MISCELLANY	UPHOLSTERY	BLACKBERRY
ORGANOGENY	PRESBYTERY	ELDERBERRY
EMBRYOGENY	REDELIVERY	STRAWBERRY
PYROTECHNY	COMPULSORY	BIRDCHERRY
THREEPENNY	SUSPENSORY	PSYCHIATRY
PINCHPENNY	RESPONSORY	MARIOLATRY
CATCHPENNY	PRECURSORY	ICONOLATRY
PICKANINNY	POSSESSORY	NECROLATRY
CHALCEDONY	PROMISSORY	ASTROLATRY
DEATHAGONY	DISMISSORY	PLANIMETRY
SANCTIMONY	DEDICATORY	ANEMOMETRY
RADIOSCOPY	VESICATORY	MICROMETRY
URINOSCOPY	INVOCATORY	HYPSOMETRY
MICROSCOPY	AMENDATORY	BATHYMETRY
OVERCANOPY	EMENDATORY	MERCHANTRY
APOTHECARY	OBLIGATORY	PHEASANTRY
PREBENDARY	DEROGATORY	PLEASANTRY
SUBSIDIARY	INITIATORY	CANTERBURY
INCENDIARY	SIBILATORY	PARONOMASY
CARPELLARY	DEPILATORY	LACKADAISY
FRITILLARY	AMBULATORY	MINSTRELSY
PISTILLARY	OSCULATORY	INSOBRIETY
VOCABULARY	UNDULATORY	EFFICACITY
CHARTULARY	REGULATORY	INCAPACITY
SEXAGENARY	SIMULATORY	INFELICITY
OCTOGENARY	COPULATORY	SIMPLICITY
VETERINARY	DEFAMATORY	COMPLICITY
SANGUINARY	EXECRATORY	ENDEMICITY
PENSIONARY	LIBERATORY	CANONICITY
PASSIONARY	EXPIRATORY	SPHERICITY
CESSIONARY	LABORATORY	CENTRICITY
MISSIONARY	ADJURATORY	PLACTICITY
STATIONARY	DEPURATORY	ELASTICITY
FACTIONARY	EXCUSATORY	CAUSTICITY
DICTIONARY	EXCITATORY	FLACCIDITY
TUITIONARY	INVITATORY	SQUALIDITY

----------A	----------C	PANHELLENIC
		THEOTECHNIC
BIBLIOTHECA	PERICARDIAC	PYROTECHNIC
GLYPTOTHECA	ENDOCARDIAC	POLYTECHNIC
ASSAFOETIDA	DIPSOMANIAC	CHALCEDONIC
BRACHIOPODA	APHRODISIAC	MICROSCOPIC
COLLECTANEA	CLOGALMANAC	HYGROSCOPIC
LEUCORRHOEA	DITHYRAMBIC	NYCTITROPIC
AMENORRHOEA	HYDROPHOBIC	STEREOTYPIC
IPECACUANHA	ORTHOPAEDIC	CENTROBARIC
CHILOGNATHA	CYCLOPAEDIC	HEMISPHERIC
AGORAPHOBIA	CEPHALALGIC	ATMOSPHERIC
ANGLOPHOBIA	EMMENAGOGIC	PHYLACTERIC
HYDROPHOBIA	PSYCHOLOGIC	CLIMACTERIC
CYCLOPAEDIA	MORPHOLOGIC	PREHISTORIC
PSEUDOPODIA	PHYSIOLOGIC	PSYCHIATRIC
MONODELPHIA	DEMONOLOGIC	GRAVIMETRIC
GLOSSOLALIA	CHRONOLOGIC	CLINOMETRIC
BACCHANALIA	EMBRYOLOGIC	ECONOMETRIC
PSYCHEDELIA	DRAMATURGIC	MICROMETRIC
MEMORABILIA	PARAGRAPHIC	HYDROMETRIC
HAEMOPHILIA	TELEGRAPHIC	HYGROMETRIC
NECROPHILIA	IDEOGRAPHIC	BARYCENTRIC
MELANCHOLIA	HOLOGRAPHIC	PERIGASTRIC
SEPTICAEMIA	XYLOGRAPHIC	CACOGASTRIC
NYMPHOMANIA	DEMOGRAPHIC	HYPOGASTRIC
BIBLIOMANIA	MONOGRAPHIC	ERYTHEMATIC
MEGALOMANIA	TOPOGRAPHIC	PROBLEMATIC
AMOENOMANIA	TYPOGRAPHIC	THEOREMATIC
KLEPTOMANIA	AUTOGRAPHIC	DICHROMATIC
HEMERALOPIA	APOSTROPHIC	PHANTOMATIC
CALCEOLARIA	PHILOSOPHIC	SYMPTOMATIC
ALBUMINURIA	METAMORPHIC	CHARISMATIC
AUSTRALASIA	IDIOMORPHIC	OCHLOCRATIC
PARONOMASIA	HOMOMORPHIC	HIPPOCRATIC
ANTONOMASIA	MONOMORPHIC	PLUTOCRATIC
ANAESTHESIA	POLYMORPHIC	BIQUADRATIC
DIFFERENTIA	PHILOMATHIC	CATHEDRATIC
SCANDINAVIA	HYDROPATHIC	MAGISTRATIC
CHRYSOCOLLA	MICROLITHIC	HYDROSTATIC
TEREBRATULA	PSYCHEDELIC	PARALLACTIC
EPITHELIOMA	ARCHANGELIC	ACATALECTIC
PROSENCHYMA	ITHYPHALLIC	PALAEARCTIC
AMPHISBAENA	MELANCHOLIC	STRATEGETIC
PROLEGOMENA	UNAPOSTOLIC	SYMPATHETIC
COCHINCHINA	SOMNAMBULIC	PARENTHETIC
GLOBIGERINA	CRYPTOGAMIC	ANAESTHETIC
BURNTSIENNA	EPITHALAMIC	DIAMAGNETIC
ABRACADABRA	AERODYNAMIC	MYTHOPOETIC
SCOLOPENDRA	LOGARITHMIC	DIAPHORETIC
LEPIDOPTERA	TELEGRAMMIC	ANTIPYRETIC
MONOTREMATA	GASTRONOMIC	PERIPATETIC
CONTRAYERVA	POLYCHROMIC	ANTHRACITIC
	ADIATHERMIC	ONIROCRITIC
	ENDOSPERMIC	HYPERCRITIC
----------B	CATACLYSMIC	PORPHYRITIC
	CHARLATANIC	STALACTITIC
CALLINGCRAB	HYDROCYANIC	PERISTALTIC
	PHAGEDAENIC	SYCOPHANTIC
	CALISTHENIC	NECROMANTIC

CHIROMANTIC	UNPUBLISHED	COMPLICATED
ANACREONTIC	UNABOLISHED	ELASTICATED
MACROBIOTIC	UNBLEMISHED	DILAPIDATED
UNPATRIOTIC	UNTARNISHED	UNMITIGATED
ANASTOMOTIC	UNVARNISHED	FASTIGIATED
ANAPLEROTIC	UNFURNISHED	UNMUTILATED
APOCALYPTIC	DEEPMOUTHED	TESSELLATED
SCHOLIASTIC	UNSPECIFIED	CASTELLATED
ENCOMIASTIC	UNQUALIFIED	LANCEOLATED
HOMOPLASTIC	UNDIGNIFIED	GENICULATED
CEROPLASTIC	PERSONIFIED	RETICULATED
ANTISPASTIC	COUNTRIFIED	ARTICULATED
METHODISTIC	DIVERSIFIED	FORAMINATED
PANTHEISTIC	UNSATISFIED	OPINIONATED
DIALOGISTIC	WHISKEYFIED	CONSTIPATED
EPILOGISTIC	PREOCCUPIED	VERTEBRATED
SYLLOGISTIC	BUNCHBACKED	UNASPIRATED
DYSLOGISTIC	HUNCHBACKED	DISAFFECTED
MASOCHISTIC	CROOKBACKED	UNCONNECTED
CABBALISTIC	UNCONCEALED	UNSUSPECTED
UNREALISTIC	FOURWHEELED	UNCORRECTED
ANOMALISTIC	UNTRAVELLED	UNPROTECTED
RITUALISTIC	UNFULFILLED	UNINHABITED
EUPHEMISTIC	DISGRUNTLED	UNINHIBITED
PESSIMISTIC	CLOSEHAULED	UNSOLICITED
HELLENISTIC	UNRECLAIMED	UNWARRANTED
CALVINISTIC	UNCONFIRMED	UNFERMENTED
MODERNISTIC	UNPERFORMED	INTERRUPTED
COMMUNISTIC	ENLIGHTENED	COLDHEARTED
EUCHARISTIC	CONSTRAINED	KINDHEARTED
CATACAUSTIC	DISINCLINED	TRUEHEARTED
HERMENEUTIC	TRUNCHEONED	HALFHEARTED
TROGLODYTIC	UNPARAGONED	WEAKHEARTED
	DIMENSIONED	UNCONVERTED
	IMPASSIONED	UNPERVERTED
----------D	CARNATIONED	UNSUPPORTED
	AFFECTIONED	TRANSPORTED
GINGERBREAD	CONDITIONED	UNCONTESTED
CLEANLIMBED	INTENTIONED	CLOSEFISTED
UNDISTURBED	UNCONCERNED	UNEXHAUSTED
DOUBLEFACED	STEREOTYPED	MALADJUSTED
BRAZENFACED	DISTEMPERED	CARBURETTED
EXPERIENCED	SEQUESTERED	UNCOMMITTED
UNSENTENCED	HIGHPOWERED	UNCIVILIZED
UNANNOUNCED	SELFCENTRED	INORGANIZED
ADDLEHEADED	UNHARBOURED	CHAMBERMAID
LEVELHEADED	TRICOLOURED	HELMINTHOID
CLEARHEADED	DISCOLOURED	ENCEPHALOID
ARROWHEADED	SELFASSURED	CRYSTALLOID
CURLYHEADED	UNTINCTURED	ELEPHANTOID
CLOSEHANDED	UNEXERCISED	BLEACHFIELD
RIGHTHANDED	UNORGANISED	SCHOOLCHILD
EMPTYHANDED	UNPRACTISED	SWITZERLAND
COLDBLOODED	UNDISGUISED	COUNTERMAND
WARMBLOODED	UNDISCLOSED	SUPERINTEND
CHICKENFEED	BOTTLENOSED	COLOURBLIND
DOUBLEEDGED	UNSURPASSED	SPLITSECOND
CROSSLEGGED	EMBARRASSED	SUPERABOUND
BANDYLEGGED	UNWITNESSED	ABOVEGROUND
ESTABLISHED	UNREDRESSED	UNDERGROUND

BROTHERHOOD	ACQUITTANCE	FANFARONADE
BRANCHIOPOD	CONTINUANCE	DIGITIGRADE
DIVININGROD	IRRELEVANCE	PLANTIGRADE
COMPASSCARD	CONTRIVANCE	RODOMONTADE
SUBSTANDARD	FLAMBOYANCE	BACILLICIDE
COOLTANKARD	COMPLACENCE	TYRANNICIDE
NOTICEBOARD	MALEFICENCE	INSECTICIDE
CENTREBOARD	BENEFICENCE	INFANTICIDE
DIVINGBOARD	MUNIFICENCE	LIBERTICIDE
SWITCHBOARD	ERUBESCENCE	THALIDOMIDE
BATTENBOARD	IRIDESCENCE	COUNTRYSIDE
THITHERWARD	CANDESCENCE	WHITSUNTIDE
BUTCHERBIRD	TURGESCENCE	DISQUIETUDE
HARPSICHORD	COALESCENCE	DECREPITUDE
	OPALESCENCE	PULCHRITUDE
	ADOLESCENCE	VICISSITUDE
----------E	EVANESCENCE	INGRATITUDE
	TORPESCENCE	PROMPTITUDE
SUPERSCRIBE	EXCRESCENCE	INCERTITUDE
BUFFALOROBE	FLORESCENCE	CABBAGETREE
COMMONPLACE	VITRESCENCE	BUTTERKNIFE
MARKETPLACE	PUTRESCENCE	VAGABONDAGE
CENTREPIECE	LACTESCENCE	HAEMORRHAGE
MANTELPIECE	ANTECEDENCE	MISCARRIAGE
MASTERPIECE	COINCIDENCE	CONCUBINAGE
COACHOFFICE	DESPONDENCE	CHAPERONAGE
MALPRACTICE	RESPONDENCE	LIFEPEERAGE
SELFSERVICE	SELFDEFENCE	HUCKSTERAGE
PERTURBANCE	CONTINGENCE	SEIGNIORAGE
DISTURBANCE	SUBMERGENCE	ACKNOWLEDGE
MISGUIDANCE	CONVERGENCE	CHAINBRIDGE
CONCORDANCE	OMNISCIENCE	INTERCHANGE
DISCORDANCE	PREAUDIENCE	SHORTCHANGE
MORRISDANCE	CONSILIENCE	UNDERCHARGE
INSOUCIANCE	DISSILIENCE	THAUMATURGE
MESALLIANCE	CONVENIENCE	BONNETROUGE
MISALLIANCE	PERCIPIENCE	SCHOTTISCHE
OVERBALANCE	AMBIVALENCE	CATASTROPHE
NONCHALANCE	EQUIVALENCE	ANTISTROPHE
RESEMBLANCE	MALEVOLENCE	CAMARADERIE
PERFORMANCE	BENEVOLENCE	GENDARMERIE
MAINTENANCE	FLOCCULENCE	BOURGEOISIE
COUNTENANCE	FRAUDULENCE	RATTLESNAKE
DISCREPANCE	INCOHERENCE	WORKMANLIKE
COMEUPPANCE	IRREVERENCE	DEATHSTROKE
FORBEARANCE	CONCURRENCE	CHIPPENDALE
REMEMBRANCE	IMPENITENCE	FARTHINGALE
ENCUMBRANCE	OMNIPOTENCE	NIGHTINGALE
FURTHERANCE	SUBSISTENCE	DESCRIBABLE
INTOLERANCE	CONSISTENCE	PERTURBABLE
DELIVERANCE	PERSISTENCE	PRACTICABLE
DISENTRANCE	COEXISTENCE	IRREVOCABLE
REASSURANCE	SUBSEQUENCE	CONFISCABLE
MALFEASANCE	CONSEQUENCE	PERSUADABLE
MISFEASANCE	CROWNPRINCE	UNAVOIDABLE
RENAISSANCE	PRECOGNOSCE	DESCENDABLE
INHABITANCE	SUPERINDUCE	COMMENDABLE
EXORBITANCE	REINTRODUCE	REPLACEABLE
INHERITANCE	FIREBRIGADE	SERVICEABLE
OUTDISTANCE	SWITCHBLADE	ENFORCEABLE

DIVORCEABLE	INNUMERABLE	CONTESTABLE
UNWEDGEABLE	REMUNERABLE	FORGETTABLE
UNSHAKEABLE	VITUPERABLE	REGRETTABLE
DISLIKEABLE	INALTERABLE	IRREFUTABLE
IMPERMEABLE	UNALTERABLE	INSCRUTABLE
UNMITIGABLE	UNUTTERABLE	CONTINUABLE
INNAVIGABLE	CONQUERABLE	PERPETUABLE
IMPEACHABLE	DELIVERABLE	RETRIEVABLE
UNREACHABLE	RECOVERABLE	CONCEIVABLE
UNTEACHABLE	PERSPIRABLE	PERCEIVABLE
UNTOUCHABLE	UNDESIRABLE	CONTRIVABLE
PUBLISHABLE	PREFERRABLE	DISSOLVABLE
ABOLISHABLE	CONFERRABLE	IRREMOVABLE
NOURISHABLE	UNENDURABLE	PRESERVABLE
APPRECIABLE	PLEASURABLE	CONSERVABLE
LIQUEFIABLE	INCREASABLE	ORGANIZABLE
ACIDIFIABLE	PURCHASABLE	CONVINCIBLE
MAGNIFIABLE	CHASTISABLE	PUTRESCIBLE
VITRIFIABLE	INADVISABLE	COGNOSCIBLE
RECTIFIABLE	UNADVISABLE	IRREDUCIBLE
CERTIFIABLE	CONDENSABLE	DESCENDIBLE
FORTIFIABLE	DISPENSABLE	REFRANGIBLE
JUSTIFIABLE	CONVERSABLE	DISCERNIBLE
CONCILIABLE	COMPASSABLE	PERSUASIBLE
PROPITIABLE	DISCUSSABLE	INDIVISIBLE
REPLEVIABLE	INEXCUSABLE	CONVULSIBLE
UNSPEAKABLE	ESCHEATABLE	SUBSENSIBLE
UNBREAKABLE	ENTREATABLE	DISTENSIBLE
UNTHINKABLE	UNPALATABLE	RESPONSIBLE
CONCEALABLE	REDOUBTABLE	COLLAPSIBLE
CONGEALABLE	REFRACTABLE	REPRESSIBLE
UNAVAILABLE	RETRACTABLE	IMPRESSIBLE
COMPELLABLE	INTRACTABLE	EXPRESSIBLE
DISTILLABLE	UNTRACTABLE	PERMISSIBLE
TRISYLLABLE	ATTRACTABLE	COMPOSSIBLE
RECLAIMABLE	COLLECTABLE	PROTRUSIBLE
INESTIMABLE	RESPECTABLE	EXTRACTIBLE
INFLAMMABLE	CORRECTABLE	PERFECTIBLE
CONFIRMABLE	PREDICTABLE	DISSECTIBLE
CONFORMABLE	COFFEETABLE	CONDUCTIBLE
PERFORMABLE	INHABITABLE	PERCEPTIBLE
INALIENABLE	INDUBITABLE	SUSCEPTIBLE
IMPREGNABLE	HEREDITABLE	CORRUPTIBLE
EXPLAINABLE	FORFEITABLE	CONVERTIBLE
CONTAINABLE	INCOGITABLE	PERVERTIBLE
SUSTAINABLE	ILLIMITABLE	SUGGESTIBLE
INDEFINABLE	INDOMITABLE	EXHAUSTIBLE
UNDEFINABLE	EXPLOITABLE	COMBUSTIBLE
DENOMINABLE	INHERITABLE	CONCEPTACLE
CONDEMNABLE	INEQUITABLE	CONVENTICLE
FASHIONABLE	CORBELTABLE	INTERMEDDLE
MENTIONABLE	FERMENTABLE	HORNSWOGGLE
TREASONABLE	PRESENTABLE	DISENTANGLE
INESCAPABLE	PREVENTABLE	INTERMINGLE
DEVELOPABLE	UNPRINTABLE	BIBLIOPHILE
UNFLAPPABLE	ACCOUNTABLE	CONTRACTILE
IRREPARABLE	ATTEMPTABLE	PROTRACTILE
INSEPARABLE	DINNERTABLE	HONEYSUCKLE
INEXECRABLE	COMFORTABLE	PENNONCELLE
INTOLERABLE	SUPPORTABLE	CHANTERELLE

TESTICULATE	PHOSPHORATE	INOBTRUSIVE
UNGUICULATE	DETERIORATE	UNOBTRUSIVE
PEDUNCULATE	COMMEMORATE	DEPRECATIVE
CARUNCULATE	INCORPORATE	ERADICATIVE
TUBERCULATE	EXPECTORATE	PREDICATIVE
TRIANGULATE	DIRECTORATE	VINDICATIVE
STRANGULATE	CONCENTRATE	IMPLICATIVE
DISSIMULATE	ORCHESTRATE	APPLICATIVE
CAMPANULATE	SEQUESTRATE	DUPLICATIVE
PENINSULATE	DEMONSTRATE	EXPLICATIVE
ENCAPSULATE	REMONSTRATE	LUBRICATIVE
EXPOSTULATE	EXTRAVASATE	SUFFOCATIVE
DEPHLEGMATE	SUPERFETATE	PROVOCATIVE
PENULTIMATE	RESUSCITATE	ELUCIDATIVE
GUESSTIMATE	PREMEDITATE	RETARDATIVE
APPROXIMATE	REGURGITATE	PROPAGATIVE
POMEGRANATE	INGURGITATE	PREROGATIVE
CONCATENATE	DECREPITATE	ENUNCIATIVE
RATIOCINATE	PRECIPITATE	ASSOCIATIVE
SUBORDINATE	NECESSITATE	RETALIATIVE
CONTAMINATE	INDECIDUATE	CORRELATIVE
DISSEMINATE	INDIVIDUATE	APPELLATIVE
RECRIMINATE	HETEROCLITE	SUPERLATIVE
INCRIMINATE	TOXOPHILITE	LEGISLATIVE
PREDOMINATE	CROCIDOLITE	SPECULATIVE
DETERMINATE	METEOROLITE	CALCULATIVE
INTERMINATE	ICHTHYOLITE	CIRCULATIVE
EXTERMINATE	SUBURBANITE	COAGULATIVE
MANDARINATE	CASSITERITE	STIMULATIVE
DEFIBRINATE	LABRADORITE	AFFIRMATIVE
PEREGRINATE	DECOMPOSITE	REFORMATIVE
ASSASSINATE	MONOPHYSITE	IMAGINATIVE
AGGLUTINATE	POCOCURANTE	ORIGINATIVE
PARIPINNATE	AGUARDIENTE	CRIMINATIVE
BICARBONATE	CASTINGVOTE	CARMINATIVE
FRACTIONATE	SUFFRAGETTE	GERMINATIVE
FUNCTIONATE	HISTORIETTE	TERMINATIVE
IMPERSONATE	FLANNELETTE	ALTERNATIVE
CONSTERNATE	LAUNDERETTE	NUNCUPATIVE
UNFORTUNATE	LEATHERETTE	DECLARATIVE
IMPORTUNATE	VINAIGRETTE	PREPARATIVE
PARTICIPATE	ELECTROCUTE	COMPARATIVE
EQUILIBRATE	THALLOPHYTE	EXONERATIVE
REVERBERATE	ELECTROLYTE	INOPERATIVE
PROTUBERATE	EMMENAGOGUE	COOPERATIVE
INCARCERATE	DISCONTINUE	REITERATIVE
CONFEDERATE	DISCOTHEQUE	ELABORATIVE
CONSIDERATE	PICTURESQUE	PERFORATIVE
PROLIFERATE	SOLDATESQUE	EVAPORATIVE
REFRIGERATE	GIGANTESQUE	RESTORATIVE
AGGLOMERATE	MISCONSTRUE	PENETRATIVE
INTEMPERATE	PRECONCEIVE	SUPPURATIVE
DEPAUPERATE	MISCONCEIVE	ADVERSATIVE
COMMISERATE	INOFFENSIVE	EXPECTATIVE
CONFLAGRATE	INEXPENSIVE	QUALITATIVE
DECEMVIRATE	COEXTENSIVE	GRAVITATIVE
TRIUMVIRATE	PROGRESSIVE	FACULTATIVE
COLLABORATE	COMPRESSIVE	CONNOTATIVE
CORROBORATE	SUPPRESSIVE	DEHORTATIVE
IMPERFORATE	TRANSFUSIVE	EXHORTATIVE

COMMUTATIVE
DISPUTATIVE
INSINUATIVE
OBSERVATIVE
RADIOACTIVE
RETROACTIVE
DIFFRACTIVE
PROTRACTIVE
ABSTRACTIVE
INEFFECTIVE
PROSPECTIVE
PERSPECTIVE
BENEDICTIVE
RESTRICTIVE
DISTINCTIVE
INSTINCTIVE
SUBJUNCTIVE
CONJUNCTIVE
DISJUNCTIVE
OBSTRUCTIVE
DESTRUCTIVE
INSTRUCTIVE
PROHIBITIVE
PRETERITIVE
ACQUISITIVE
INQUISITIVE
INSENSITIVE
PREPOSITIVE
COMPETITIVE
SUBSTANTIVE
INATTENTIVE
DESCRIPTIVE
INSCRIPTIVE
PRESUMPTIVE
CONSUMPTIVE
RETRIBUTIVE
ATTRIBUTIVE
CONSECUTIVE
INSTITUTIVE
CIRCUMVOLVE
BOXINGGLOVE
COUNTERMOVE
MICROGROOVE
CATHOLICIZE
GOURMANDIZE
MYTHOLOGIZE
ETYMOLOGIZE
TAUTOLOGIZE
ETHEREALIZE
IMPERIALIZE
MATERIALIZE
ARTERIALIZE
MEMORIALIZE
PERSONALIZE
EXTERNALIZE
GUTTURALIZE
ORIENTALIZE
IMMORTALIZE
CRYSTALLIZE
HYPERBOLIZE

TUBERCULIZE
AMERICANIZE
EUROPEANIZE
DISORGANIZE
PLEBEIANIZE
NITROGENIZE
DEFIBRINIZE
DECARBONIZE
EMULSIONIZE
FRACTIONIZE
SYNCHRONIZE
FAMILIARIZE
FORMULARIZE
DEPAUPERIZE
PHOSPHORIZE
EXTEMPORIZE
HYPOTHESIZE
EMBLEMATIZE
SYSTEMATIZE
ACCLIMATIZE
DIPLOMATIZE
DEMOCRATIZE
HYPOSTATIZE
DEMAGNETIZE
PROSELYTIZE
SOLILOQUIZE

----------F

NECKERCHIEF
BULLETPROOF

----------G

UNITPRICING
PRONOUNCING
MINDREADING
RICEPUDDING
PLUMPUDDING
HANGGLIDING
BACKSLIDING
SCAFFOLDING
OUTSTANDING
UNOFFENDING
BOOKBINDING
FACTFINDING
SURROUNDING
SIGHTSEEING
ENCOURAGING
DISOBLIGING
BELLRINGING
FARREACHING
UNFLINCHING
EYECATCHING
ASTONISHING
FLOURISHING
LANGUISHING
MERRYMAKING

STOCKTAKING
UNDERTAKING
PAINSTAKING
BACKPACKING
UNSHRINKING
GOODLOOKING
HARDWORKING
MARSHALLING
VICTUALLING
MISSPELLING
BOOKSELLING
COUNSELLING
CHITTERLING
PROGRAMMING
MISBECOMING
FORTHCOMING
SHORTCOMING
UNPRESUMING
OVERWEENING
REAWAKENING
THREATENING
FRIGHTENING
CHRISTENING
QUESTIONING
UNREASONING
FOREWARNING
CHURCHGOING
BOOKKEEPING
SHOPKEEPING
SHOWJUMPING
KNEECAPPING
OVERBEARING
CONSIDERING
BEWILDERING
ENGINEERING
DOMINEERING
INGATHERING
UNFALTERING
MINISTERING
PERSEVERING
WEDDINGRING
CHECKSTRING
UNMURMURING
OFFSCOURING
DISPLEASING
TANTALISING
UMPROMISING
ADVERTISING
DISTRESSING
SUFFOCATING
HUMILIATING
UNDEVIATING
VACILLATING
OSCILLATING
CALCULATING
CIRCULATING
STIMULATING
LANCINATING
FASCINATING
FULMINATING

ALTERNATING
PENETRATING
INSINUATING
FLUCTUATING
AGGRAVATING
CAPTIVATING
DISTRACTING
CONFLICTING
CAMPMEETING
DISQUIETING
BULLBAITING
BEARBAITING
DISPIRITING
HANDWRITING
TYPEWRITING
UNRELENTING
OILPAINTING
FREEBOOTING
EVERLASTING
INTERESTING
UNRESISTING
UNBEFITTING
UNREMITTING
WOODCUTTING
UNFORGIVING
UNOBSERVING
UNDESERVING
BASTARDWING
OVERFLOWING
BRICKLAYING
LONGPLAYING
SOOTHSAYING
PATRONIZING
TEMPORIZING
MONOPHTHONG

---------- H

SYMPOSIARCH
BOXINGMATCH
SONOFABITCH
CHAINSTITCH
CESAREWITCH
DOUBLEDUTCH
EAVESTROUGH
CARDIOGRAPH
SEISMOGRAPH
CHRONOGRAPH
CRYPTOGRAPH
HORSERADISH
CHAFINGDISH
BELLOWSFISH
PHOTOFINISH
NIGHTMARISH
ISRAELITISH
DISTINGUISH
HANDBREADTH
COPPERSMITH
SILVERSMITH

SEVENTEENTH
CHEESECLOTH
CABBAGEMOTH
CLOTHESMOTH
CHISELTOOTH
THENCEFORTH
UNDERGROWTH
AFTERGROWTH

---------- I

CUIRBOUILLI
MISSISSIPPI

---------- K

DOUBLESPEAK
TECHNOSPEAK
BIOFEEDBACK
DIAMONDBACK
STICKLEBACK
QUARTERBACK
STEEPLEJACK
JUMPINGJACK
CRACKERJACK
LEATHERNECK
CANDLESTICK
DOUBLEQUICK
SHUTTLECOCK
COUNTRYROCK
HIDEANDSEEK
KITCHENSINK
COUNTERSINK
COOKERYBOOK
COUNTERMARK
COUNTERWORK
CHEQUERWORK
VACUUMFLASK

---------- L

PHARISAICAL
COXCOMBICAL
SPASMODICAL
RHAPSODICAL
STRATEGICAL
PEDAGOGICAL
MYCOLOGICAL
IDEOLOGICAL
THEOLOGICAL
AEROLOGICAL
HOROLOGICAL
NOSOLOGICAL
ONTOLOGICAL
LETHARGICAL
CHIRURGICAL
MONARCHICAL

EVANGELICAL
PARABOLICAL
EPISTOLICAL
BIOCHEMICAL
METONYMICAL
PURITANICAL
UNCANONICAL
THRASONICAL
SUBTROPICAL
NEOTROPICAL
ANTITYPICAL
CYLINDRICAL
ALLEGORICAL
CATEGORICAL
PLETHORICAL
DIAMETRICAL
SYMMETRICAL
GEOMETRICAL
ISOMETRICAL
OBSTETRICAL
ECCENTRICAL
PANEGYRICAL
NONSENSICAL
INTRINSICAL
EXTRINSICAL
GEOPHYSICAL
KINEMATICAL
PRAGMATICAL
ENIGMATICAL
STIGMATICAL
GRAMMATICAL
IDIOMATICAL
PRISMATICAL
STALACTICAL
IMPRACTICAL
UNPRACTICAL
SYNTACTICAL
DIALECTICAL
ENERGETICAL
PROPHETICAL
AESTHETICAL
HOMILETICAL
THEORETICAL
JACOBITICAL
DIACRITICAL
NEPHRITICAL
PLEURITICAL
PARASITICAL
ANECDOTICAL
PROLEPTICAL
SARCASTICAL
FANTASTICAL
SOPHISTICAL
STATISTICAL
PIETISTICAL
EGOTISTICAL
EPIPHYTICAL
PARADOXICAL
UNEQUIVOCAL
DIPHYCERCAL

SESQUIPEDAL	INESSENTIAL	INFRACOSTAL
FRATRICIDAL	UNESSENTIAL	SUPRACOSTAL
ELLIPSOIDAL	COESSENTIAL	PENTECOSTAL
PLANETOIDAL	PENITENTIAL	INTERCOSTAL
TRAPEZOIDAL	EXISTENTIAL	TRANSMITTAL
PERITONAEAL	INFLUENTIAL	AUDIOVISUAL
OESOPHAGEAL	ANTENUPTIAL	INEFFECTUAL
RECTILINEAL	SEXAGESIMAL	UNSPIRITUAL
MULTILINEAL	SUPERNORMAL	TRANSSEXUAL
CURVILINEAL	RURIDECANAL	NOMINATIVAL
INCORPOREAL	LATITUDINAL	INFINITIVAL
COUNTERSEAL	ATTITUDINAL	DISAPPROVAL
DIPHTHONGAL	PROVISIONAL	BUCKETWHEEL
CENTRIFUGAL	DIMENSIONAL	BREASTWHEEL
MATRIARCHAL	OBSESSIONAL	BLOODVESSEL
THEREWITHAL	PROBATIONAL	COUNTERVAIL
WHEREWITHAL	EDUCATIONAL	COUNTERFOIL
NEANDERTHAL	GRADATIONAL	DISENTHRALL
MULTIRACIAL	OPERATIONAL	WHIPOORWILL
PREJUDICIAL	SENSATIONAL	COCKANDBULL
SACRIFICIAL	DIRECTIONAL	XANTHOPHYLL
SUPERFICIAL	INDUCTIONAL	CHLOROPHYLL
QUINCUNCIAL	TRADITIONAL	BOARDSCHOOL
INTERMEDIAL	CONDITIONAL	NIGHTSCHOOL
PERICARDIAL	INTUITIONAL	CHOLESTEROL
PRIMIGENIAL	INTENTIONAL	SELFCONTROL
MATRIMONIAL	UNEMOTIONAL	DANCINGGIRL
PATRIMONIAL	EXCEPTIONAL	AMPLEXICAUL
TESTIMONIAL	EVOLUTIONAL	DISGRACEFUL
PARTICIPIAL	UNIPERSONAL	RESOURCEFUL
SECRETARIAL	TRIPERSONAL	DISTASTEFUL
RECTISERIAL	SEMPITERNAL	REPROACHFUL
MULTISERIAL	ENNEAHEDRAL	UNHEALTHFUL
MAGISTERIAL	TETRAHEDRAL	TEASPOONFUL
MINISTERIAL	ICOSAHEDRAL	DISTRESSFUL
SEIGNIORIAL	ANTIFEDERAL	DISTRUSTFUL
ACCESSORIAL	EQUILATERAL	MISTRUSTFUL
INSESSORIAL	PROTECTORAL	CHRYSOBERYL
ASSESSORIAL	CONIROSTRAL	PTERODACTYL
PISCATORIAL	BEHAVIOURAL	
PURGATORIAL	COMMISSURAL	
MEDIATORIAL	CONJECTURAL	----------M
DICTATORIAL	REAPPRAISAL	
DIRECTORIAL	TRANSVERSAL	BLOODSTREAM
TERRITORIAL	HYPOGLOSSAL	BLOCKSYSTEM
INVENTORIAL	EXOSKELETAL	CABBAGEPALM
REPORTORIAL	CENTRIPETAL	OFFICIALDOM
EXECUTORIAL	CONSONANTAL	CHRISTENDOM
TRIMESTRIAL	IMPLACENTAL	WAITINGROOM
TERRESTRIAL	FUNDAMENTAL	DISACCUSTOM
EQUINOCTIAL	FIRMAMENTAL	ACINACIFORM
TRIBUNITIAL	SACRAMENTAL	CORALLIFORM
SUBSTANTIAL	TESTAMENTAL	LAMELLIFORM
RESIDENTIAL	IMPLEMENTAL	DOLABRIFORM
OBEDIENTIAL	RECREMENTAL	CEREBRIFORM
EXPONENTIAL	INCREMENTAL	CRATERIFORM
DEFERENTIAL	DETRIMENTAL	SCALPRIFORM
REFERENTIAL	NUTRIMENTAL	PANDURIFORM
INFERENTIAL	SENTIMENTAL	GRANITIFORM
REVERENTIAL	CONTINENTAL	TRAPEZIFORM

CABBAGEWORM	OPPORTUNISM	ABECEDARIAN
DEMONIACISM	MALAPROPISM	ZOANTHARIAN
CATHOLICISM	HEMIHEDRISM	MILLENARIAN
HIBERNICISM	CONSUMERISM	CENTENARIAN
ESOTERICISM	PYTHAGORISM	SABBATARIAN
EXOTERICISM	ASTIGMATISM	UNSECTARIAN
ECLECTICISM	FAVOURITISM	PROLETARIAN
ATHLETICISM	PROSELYTISM	EGALITARIAN
ROMANTICISM	EXCLUSIVISM	UTILITARIAN
MONASTICISM	PERITONAEUM	TRINITARIAN
AGNOSTICISM	SUCCEDANEUM	LIBERTARIAN
VAGABONDISM	INTERMEDIUM	ANTIQUARIAN
SADDUCEEISM	ANTEPENDIUM	ALEXANDRIAN
ABSENTEEISM	PERICARDIUM	PURGATORIAN
HIERARCHISM	ENDOCARDIUM	ZOROASTRIAN
ZOOMORPHISM	FLORILEGIUM	HOLOTHURIAN
ISOMORPHISM	PERICRANIUM	HOMOIOUSIAN
PROGNATHISM	CONDOMINIUM	UNCHRISTIAN
CANNIBALISM	ARCHEGONIUM	LILLIPUTIAN
CLERICALISM	PELARGONIUM	GENTLEWOMAN
OFFICIALISM	PANDEMONIUM	CHURCHWOMAN
COLONIALISM	SYLLABARIUM	WASHERWOMAN
IMPERIALISM	COLUMBARIUM	BUSINESSMAN
MATERIALISM	PLANETARIUM	CONGRESSMAN
REGIONALISM	EQUILIBRIUM	DRAUGHTSMAN
NATIONALISM	MEGATHERIUM	MERCHANTMAN
RATIONALISM	DINOTHERIUM	DOWNTRODDEN
PERSONALISM	CREMATORIUM	SMOKESCREEN
PATERNALISM	EPIGASTRIUM	CHOIRSCREEN
EXTERNALISM	INTERREGNUM	BOTTLEGREEN
COMMUNALISM	ANTIRRHINUM	OXYHYDROGEN
CEREBRALISM	MEDIASTINUM	CRESTFALLEN
ORIENTALISM	CANDELABRUM	GENTLEWOMEN
TEETOTALISM	DESIDERATUM	CONGRESSMEN
MEDIEVALISM		FOUNTAINPEN
PARALLELISM		LEPIDOSIREN
BIMETALLISM	----------N	FORESHORTEN
HYPERBOLISM		MISBEGOTTEN
ANGLICANISM	ARCHIMEDEAN	UNFORGOTTEN
AMERICANISM	SPRINGCLEAN	CLEANSHAVEN
PLEBEIANISM	HYPERBOREAN	COUNTERSIGN
PELAGIANISM	PYTHAGOREAN	ARCHVILLAIN
BOHEMIANISM	BARRELORGAN	CHAMBERLAIN
SOCINIANISM	ELIZABETHAN	LEGERDEMAIN
ARMINIANISM	ACADEMICIAN	HAEMOGLOBIN
AGRARIANISM	MECHANICIAN	PODOPHYLLIN
ERASTIANISM	RHETORICIAN	CATERCOUSIN
MORAVIANISM	ELECTRICIAN	HYDROCARBON
LUTHERANISM	MAGNETICIAN	ONOMASTICON
WESLEYANISM	ACOUSTICIAN	DICOTYLEDON
PHENOMENISM	ROSICRUCIAN	NICKELODEON
DETERMINISM	ANGLOINDIAN	ANACOLUTHON
LIBERTINISM	CAROLINGIAN	RAPSCALLION
RELIGIONISM	MYTHOLOGIAN	QUADRILLION
HISTRIONISM	PHILOLOGIAN	QUINTILLION
REVISIONISM	SATURNALIAN	SLUMGULLION
EUDAEMONISM	CROCODILIAN	ORCHESTRION
ANACHRONISM	SMITHSONIAN	IMPRECISION
SYNCHRONISM	PENTAGYNIAN	SUPERVISION
ISOCHRONISM	AESCULAPIAN	PROGRESSION

CELEBRATION	LAMENTATION	TRANSACTION
CEREBRATION	CEMENTATION	PROSPECTION
CALIBRATION	FOMENTATION	VENESECTION
ADUMBRATION	OSTENTATION	VIVISECTION
OBSECRATION	CONNOTATION	MALEDICTION
DESECRATION	ACCEPTATION	VALEDICTION
DEHYDRATION	IMPARTATION	BENEDICTION
CANCERATION	DEHORTATION	DERELICTION
BOTHERATION	EXHORTATION	CONFLICTION
GLOMERATION	DEPORTATION	RESTRICTION
ENUMERATION	IMPORTATION	DISTINCTION
EXONERATION	ASPORTATION	MALFUNCTION
COOPERATION	EXPORTATION	CONJUNCTION
DESPERATION	DEVASTATION	DISJUNCTION
REITERATION	INFESTATION	COMPUNCTION
INTEGRATION	MOLESTATION	OBSTRUCTION
REMIGRATION	OBTESTATION	DESTRUCTION
IMMIGRATION	DETESTATION	INSTRUCTION
DENIGRATION	ATTESTATION	PROHIBITION
RESPIRATION	AEROSTATION	EXTRADITION
INSPIRATION	ENCYSTATION	RECONDITION
ELABORATION	CONFUTATION	RECOGNITION
PERFORATION	COMMUTATION	PREMONITION
MELIORATION	PERMUTATION	PRETERITION
DEFLORATION	COMPUTATION	INNUTRITION
DEPLORATION	DISPUTATION	MICTURITION
IMPLORATION	DEVALUATION	PARTURITION
EXPLORATION	REVALUATION	ACQUISITION
EVAPORATION	ATTENUATION	REQUISITION
CORPORATION	EXTENUATION	INQUISITION
RESTORATION	INSINUATION	PREPOSITION
PENETRATION	INFATUATION	COMPOSITION
ARBITRATION	PUNCTUATION	PROPOSITION
PROSTRATION	FLUCTUATION	SUPPOSITION
FRUSTRATION	HABITUATION	DISPOSITION
PROCURATION	AGGRAVATION	COMPETITION
OBSCURATION	DEPRAVATION	BIPARTITION
FULGURATION	DEPRIVATION	DEGLUTITION
CONJURATION	CULTIVATION	INATTENTION
MURMURATION	AESTIVATION	CONTRAPTION
COLOURATION	INNERVATION	DESCRIPTION
SUPPURATION	OBSERVATION	INSCRIPTION
MENSURATION	RESERVATION	PRESUMPTION
TRITURATION	INCURVATION	CONSUMPTION
UTILISATION	REALIZATION	REINSERTION
DECUSSATION	SOLMIZATION	REASSERTION
ABLACTATION	ATOMIZATION	DEMIBASTION
AFFECTATION	LABEFACTION	INDIGESTION
DELECTATION	TABEFACTION	RETRIBUTION
HUMECTATION	CALEFACTION	ATTRIBUTION
EXPECTATION	TUMEFACTION	CONSECUTION
CREPITATION	BENEFACTION	PROSECUTION
PALPITATION	RAREFACTION	PERSECUTION
JACTITATION	INTERACTION	DISSOLUTION
NICTITATION	DIFFRACTION	CONVOLUTION
GRAVITATION	SUBTRACTION	COMMINUTION
OCCULTATION	CONTRACTION	DESTITUTION
RECANTATION	PROTRACTION	RESTITUTION
INCANTATION	ABSTRACTION	INSTITUTION
INDENTATION	DISTRACTION	GENUFLEXION

CRUCIFIXION
TRANSFIXION
ENNEAHEDRON
TETRAHEDRON
ICOSAHEDRON
EXOSKELETON
ULTRAMODERN
LAMELLICORN

---------O

AMONTILLADO
RALLENTANDO
DECRESCENDO
ARCHIPELAGO
INTERNUNCIO
BRAGGADOCIO
VIOLONCELLO
CHIAROSCURO
CONTRABASSO
SWEETPOTATO
RIFACIMENTO
ALTORILIEVO
CAVORILIEVO

---------P

COMPOSTHEAP
THUNDERCLAP
STEWARDSHIP
JUSTICESHIP
COMRADESHIP
TRUSTEESHIP
APOSTLESHIP
LECTURESHIP
PRELATESHIP
PRIMATESHIP
SHERIFFSHIP
MESSIAHSHIP
MARSHALSHIP
GENERALSHIP
ADMIRALSHIP
WORKMANSHIP
SHOWMANSHIP
DENIZENSHIP
CITIZENSHIP
CAPTAINSHIP
SURGEONSHIP
SCHOLARSHIP
SOLDIERSHIP
PREMIERSHIP
PARTNERSHIP
SPONSORSHIP
CREATORSHIP
CURATORSHIP
ELECTORSHIP
PROCTORSHIP
AUDITORSHIP

HEROWORSHIP
STUDENTSHIP
PROVOSTSHIP
VICEROYSHIP
RUBBERSTAMP
BRINESHRIMP
WHISTLESTOP

---------R

LIQUIDAMBAR
RECTILINEAR
CURVILINEAR
INTERLINEAR
ANCHOVYPEAR
BARLEYSUGAR
VERISIMILAR
CATERPILLAR
PETRODOLLAR
CIRCUMPOLAR
SUBGLOBULAR
SPECTACULAR
ADMINICULAR
VENTRICULAR
ANIMALCULAR
CARBUNCULAR
INTEROCULAR
CREPUSCULAR
CORPUSCULAR
EQUIANGULAR
RECTANGULAR
MULTANGULAR
PENTANGULAR
UNICELLULAR
SUBSCAPULAR
PROCONSULAR
UNIVALVULAR
TRANSCRIBER
ANTECHAMBER
DISENCUMBER
NECROMANCER
CONVEYANCER
GREENGROCER
CHEERLEADER
HOMESTEADER
MASQUERADER
GALLBLADDER
SHAREHOLDER
LEASEHOLDER
HOUSEHOLDER
STOCKHOLDER
SMALLHOLDER
GERRYMANDER
JERRYMANDER
WITHSTANDER
REPREHENDER
MONEYLENDER
RECOMMENDER
COMETFINDER

CHILDMINDER
BELLFOUNDER
CURRYPOWDER
CHANTICLEER
MOUNTAINEER
ELECTIONEER
CROTCHETEER
PAMPHLETEER
FORAMINIFER
PETTIFOGGER
CLIFFHANGER
OPERASINGER
MINNESINGER
RIGHTWINGER
SCAREMONGER
WHOREMONGER
CHRONOLOGER
BACKBENCHER
DOOMWATCHER
XYLOGRAPHER
MONOGRAPHER
TOPOGRAPHER
TYPOGRAPHER
PHILOSOPHER
HABERDASHER
GATECRASHER
ESTABLISHER
REPLENISHER
GRANDFATHER
SOMEWHITHER
GRANDMOTHER
STEPBROTHER
LAMMERGEIER
AMELANCHIER
ACCOMPANIER
GONFALONIER
BULLTERRIER
ARQUEBUSIER
LOUDSPEAKER
WINDBREAKER
BUSHWHACKER
FIRECRACKER
BILLSTICKER
DOORKNOCKER
BLOODSUCKER
DEERSTALKER
FLOORWALKER
FREETHINKER
CHAINSMOKER
STOCKBROKER
FAITHHEALER
SIDEWHEELER
BLACKMAILER
HOSPITALLER
TEETOTALLER
FORESTALLER
RATHSKELLER
CAVEDWELLER
COMPTROLLER
COALTRIMMER

GASTRONOMER	FRANKFURTER	ACCELERATOR
TRANSFORMER	BROADCASTER	VITUPERATOR
CONTRAVENER	CRITICASTER	DEFLAGRATOR
ENTERTAINER	BURGOMASTER	CONSPIRATOR
MULESKINNER	SCOUTMASTER	PERPETRATOR
BREADWINNER	WESTMINSTER	INFILTRATOR
FRONTRUNNER	PATERNOSTER	ILLUSTRATOR
TRUNCHEONER	FILLIBUSTER	INAUGURATOR
PARISHIONER	BLOCKBUSTER	SULPHURATOR
REVERSIONER	DISEMBITTER	TOTALISATOR
PROBATIONER	TRANSMITTER	COMPENSATOR
EXTORTIONER	SURREBUTTER	AUSCULTATOR
EXECUTIONER	YELLOWFEVER	COMMENTATOR
CATERCORNER	DISBELIEVER	DISSERTATOR
STOREKEEPER	MISBELIEVER	CONTINUATOR
HOUSEKEEPER	WHERESOEVER	CONSERVATOR
LIGHTKEEPER	WHICHSOEVER	CONSTRICTOR
PARATROOPER	THANKSGIVER	CONSTRUCTOR
HANDICAPPER	QUACKSALVER	LITHOTRITOR
COALWHIPPER	QUICKSILVER	CARBURETTOR
TEENYBOPPER	INTERVIEWER	CONTRIBUTOR
WEENYBOPPER	CAULIFLOWER	DISTRIBUTOR
GRASSHOPPER	GILLYFLOWER	PROSTITUTOR
CARDSHARPER	CANDLEPOWER	CONNOISSEUR
STEREOTYPER	GORMANDIZER	LITTERATEUR
PHILANDERER	THEOLOGIZER	SLAVELABOUR
SLAUGHTERER	SYMPATHIZER	MULTICOLOUR
UPHOLSTERER	MINERALIZER	WATERCOLOUR
TRANSFERRER	NEUTRALIZER	PROTOMARTYR
DAYLABOURER	MONOPOLIZER	
HAIRDRESSER	SCRUTINIZER	
WINDCHEATER	CONTRATENOR	----------S
BIBLIOLATER	PREDECESSOR	
BARLEYWATER	INTERCESSOR	BIODYNAMICS
CONSTRUCTER	ADJUDICATOR	CATAPHONICS
ALKALIMETER	PACIFICATOR	HISTRIONICS
POLARIMETER	EQUIVOCATOR	ELECTRONICS
CALORIMETER	CONFISCATOR	ULTRASONICS
COLORIMETER	DILAPIDATOR	PAEDIATRICS
SPEEDOMETER	COMMENDATOR	CLIOMETRICS
SWINGOMETER	PROMULGATOR	METAPHYSICS
CRANIOMETER	COMPURGATOR	MATHEMATICS
PLUVIOMETER	DENUNCIATOR	INFORMATICS
THERMOMETER	ANNUNCIATOR	NUMISMATICS
SEISMOMETER	CONCILIATOR	AEROSTATICS
SALINOMETER	CALUMNIATOR	APOLOGETICS
ACTINOMETER	PROPITIATOR	CATECHETICS
CHRONOMETER	ABBREVIATOR	CYBERNETICS
SPHEROMETER	NOMENCLATOR	LINGUISTICS
SCLEROMETER	INVIGILATOR	DIAGNOSTICS
CHLOROMETER	ANNIHILATOR	AERONAUTICS
INTERPRETER	ACCUMULATOR	NETHERLANDS
HEREINAFTER	MANIPULATOR	HEAVENWARDS
BULLFIGHTER	DEPOPULATOR	PROBOSCIDES
MOONLIGHTER	VATICINATOR	CANTHARIDES
GODDAUGHTER	DENOMINATOR	SUPERFICIES
UNDERWRITER	ILLUMINATOR	SWEEPSTAKES
REPRESENTER	EMANCIPATOR	PHILIPPINES
TELEPRINTER	CONSECRATOR	PERIPHRASES
TRANSPORTER	EXAGGERATOR	PARENTHESES

IGNORAMUSES	MEANINGLESS	IMMENSENESS
TABLETENNIS	PASSIONLESS	INTENSENESS
ICHTHYORNIS	SLUMBERLESS	VERBOSENESS
AVOIRDUPOIS	SHELTERLESS	OPEROSENESS
CEPHALASPIS	HARBOURLESS	ADVERSENESS
PHTHIRIASIS	SUCCOURLESS	DIFFUSENESS
PERIPHRASIS	FLAVOURLESS	PROFUSENESS
ANTIPHRASIS	DELIGHTLESS	MEDIATENESS
PARENTHESIS	THOUGHTLESS	OBLIQUENESS
METAGENESIS	COMFORTLESS	BRUSQUENESS
ABIOGENESIS	EXHAUSTLESS	FORGIVENESS
GAMOGENESIS	CRABBEDNESS	PENSIVENESS
HOMOGENESIS	GUARDEDNESS	PASSIVENESS
MONOGENESIS	PARCHEDNESS	ABUSIVENESS
ONTOGENESIS	CROOKEDNESS	AMATIVENESS
CYTOGENESIS	RETIREDNESS	RESTIVENESS
POLYGENESIS	ASSUREDNESS	COSTIVENESS
TELEKINESIS	ADVISEDNESS	NOTHINGNESS
APOSIOPESIS	EXPOSEDNESS	WILLINGNESS
CATACHRESIS	BLESSEDNESS	FADDISHNESS
DIAPHORESIS	POINTEDNESS	REDDISHNESS
NECROBIOSIS	STINTEDNESS	PRUDISHNESS
ANASTOMOSIS	STUNTEDNESS	SELFISHNESS
DIARTHROSIS	DEVOTEDNESS	WAGGISHNESS
ENARTHROSIS	FLACCIDNESS	BOOKISHNESS
APONEUROSIS	SQUALIDNESS	MAWKISHNESS
EREMACAUSIS	LANGUIDNESS	HELLISHNESS
HAEMOPTYSIS	UNSOUNDNESS	FOOLISHNESS
PHARYNGITIS	AWKWARDNESS	GIRLISHNESS
TONSILLITIS	FROWARDNESS	STYLISHNESS
PNEUMONITIS	FORWARDNESS	SWINISHNESS
PERITONITIS	WAYWARDNESS	DAMPISHNESS
BLEPHARITIS	STRANGENESS	ROMPISHNESS
SCLEROTITIS	PLIABLENESS	LUMPISHNESS
PHYLLOTAXIS	AMIABLENESS	MUMPISHNESS
TENTERHOOKS	TENABLENESS	FOPPISHNESS
THEATRICALS	TUNABLENESS	WASPISHNESS
SMITHEREENS	NOTABLENESS	BOORISHNESS
RESPONSIONS	MUTABLENESS	GOATISHNESS
WELLINGTONS	EQUABLENESS	SOTTISHNESS
CONTRETEMPS	MOVABLENESS	BRUTISHNESS
TRICERATOPS	AUDIBLENESS	KNAVISHNESS
MIDDLECLASS	VISIBLENESS	PEEVISHNESS
BOTTLEGLASS	IGNOBLENESS	UNCOUTHNESS
CHEVALGLASS	VOLUBLENESS	SHRUBBINESS
GALLOWGLASS	SUBTILENESS	THREADINESS
COTTONGRASS	BRITTLENESS	UNREADINESS
CLOVERGRASS	SUBLIMENESS	SCRUFFINESS
CANARYGRASS	NOISOMENESS	SCRAGGINESS
SHEPHERDESS	IRKSOMENESS	SPRINGINESS
ARCHDUCHESS	FULSOMENESS	STRINGINESS
TRAFFICLESS	WINSOMENESS	STARCHINESS
DEFENCELESS	LISSOMENESS	SKETCHINESS
NONETHELESS	PROFANENESS	LENGTHINESS
MEASURELESS	OBSCENENESS	HEALTHINESS
FEATURELESS	GENUINENESS	WEALTHINESS
PASTURELESS	AUSTERENESS	SWARTHINESS
PURPOSELESS	OBSCURENESS	UNLUCKINESS
REVERSELESS	PRECISENESS	WORLDLINESS
REMORSELESS	CONCISENESS	UNGODLINESS

SHAPELINESS
STATELINESS
LOATHLINESS
EARTHLINESS
PRICKLINESS
CLEANLINESS
UNMANLINESS
WOMANLINESS
ORDERLINESS
SIGHTLINESS
SAINTLINESS
COURTLINESS
BEASTLINESS
GHASTLINESS
BRISTLINESS
GHOSTLINESS
UNHAPPINESS
SCRAPPINESS
SHOWERINESS
FLOWERINESS
CURSORINESS
ELUSORINESS
SAVOURINESS
TRICKSINESS
FIDGETINESS
THRIFTINESS
WEIGHTINESS
FLIGHTINESS
HAUGHTINESS
NAUGHTINESS
DOUGHTINESS
ANTIQUINESS
SHADOWINESS
SEASICKNESS
CUBICALNESS
LOGICALNESS
FINICALNESS
TRIVIALNESS
LITERALNESS
NATURALNESS
GENTEELNESS
HEEDFULNESS
NEEDFULNESS
MINDFULNESS
WAKEFULNESS
BALEFULNESS
DOLEFULNESS
HOPEFULNESS
CAREFULNESS
DIREFULNESS
HATEFULNESS
BASHFULNESS
WISHFULNESS
PITIFULNESS
DUTIFULNESS
SKILFULNESS
SOULFULNESS
HARMFULNESS
GAINFULNESS
PAINFULNESS

HELPFULNESS
FEARFULNESS
TEARFULNESS
FRETFULNESS
HURTFULNESS
LUSTFULNESS
PLAYFULNESS
UNIFORMNESS
DRUNKENNESS
FOREIGNNESS
MARCHIONESS
CHAMPIONESS
SLENDERNESS
ENDLESSNESS
GODLESSNESS
USELESSNESS
AIMLESSNESS
SINLESSNESS
WITLESSNESS
ARTLESSNESS
LAWLESSNESS
JOYLESSNESS
HIDEOUSNESS
PITEOUSNESS
DUBIOUSNESS
VICIOUSNESS
TEDIOUSNESS
BILIOUSNESS
COPIOUSNESS
SERIOUSNESS
FURIOUSNESS
OBVIOUSNESS
DEVIOUSNESS
ANXIOUSNESS
NOXIOUSNESS
ZEALOUSNESS
CALLOUSNESS
HEINOUSNESS
OMINOUSNESS
POMPOUSNESS
AMOROUSNESS
RIOTOUSNESS
ARDUOUSNESS
SINUOUSNESS
COMPACTNESS
PERFECTNESS
CORRECTNESS
DEFIANTNESS
ANCIENTNESS
PRESENTNESS
CORRUPTNESS
EARNESTNESS
SHALLOWNESS
DIVINGDRESS
SUPERIORESS
CHEESEPRESS
COTTONPRESS
SPECTATRESS
PROTECTRESS
CONDUCTRESS

ENCHANTRESS
PRECEPTRESS
ADVENTURESS
VISCOUNTESS
DOUBLECROSS
BLUNDERBUSS
WHEREABOUTS
MICROCOCCUS
SARCOPHAGUS
CUNNILINGUS
SAGITTARIUS
CONVOLVULUS
NOSTRADAMUS
BORBORYGMUS
LAURUSTINUS
NOCTILUCOUS
URTICACEOUS
CYCADACEOUS
OSTREACEOUS
SPATHACEOUS
FERULACEOUS
SOLANACEOUS
SAPONACEOUS
PIPERACEOUS
CYPERACEOUS
PAPYRACEOUS
AMENTACEOUS
CHARTACEOUS
CRUSTACEOUS
SPONTANEOUS
HOMOGENEOUS
STRAMINEOUS
SULPHUREOUS
UNRIGHTEOUS
UNCOURTEOUS
TERRAQUEOUS
CREOPHAGOUS
XYLOPHAGOUS
TAUTOLOGOUS
TRISTICHOUS
ISOMORPHOUS
PROGNATHOUS
EFFICACIOUS
UNVERACIOUS
INJUDICIOUS
UNCONSCIOUS
COMPENDIOUS
UNMELODIOUS
IRRELIGIOUS
ATRABILIOUS
ANTIBILIOUS
PUNCTILIOUS
IGNOMINIOUS
SYMPHONIOUS
CEREMONIOUS
ACRIMONIOUS
IMPECUNIOUS
OMNIFARIOUS
BURGLARIOUS
TEMERARIOUS

CONCOMITANT
PRECIPITANT
UNREPENTANT
UNIMPORTANT
EQUIDISTANT
INOBSERVANT
UNOBSERVANT
BODYSERVANT
CLAIRVOYANT
SUPERJACENT
INTERJACENT
MAGNIFICENT
GLAUCESCENT
LAPIDESCENT
ACQUIESCENT
ALKALESCENT
OBSOLESCENT
INTUMESCENT
JUVENESCENT
ARBORESCENT
FLUORESCENT
DELITESCENT
REMINISCENT
TRANSLUCENT
SELFEVIDENT
RESPLENDENT
INDEPENDENT
INTELLIGENT
RUBEFACIENT
CALEFACIENT
INEFFICIENT
COEFFICIENT
DISOBEDIENT
INEXPEDIENT
CONSENTIENT
DISSENTIENT
SUBSERVIENT
EQUIPOLLENT
PULVERULENT
PREDICAMENT
DISARMAMENT
TEMPERAMENT
ARBITRAMENT
DISBANDMENT
COMMANDMENT
BOMBARDMENT
REPLACEMENT
EMBRACEMENT
ENHANCEMENT
ADVANCEMENT
DEFORCEMENT
ENFORCEMENT
DIVORCEMENT
TRADUCEMENT
PRESAGEMENT
ASSUAGEMENT
DERANGEMENT
ARRANGEMENT
ENLARGEMENT
ENGORGEMENT

DISABLEMENT
BRABBLEMENT
ENNOBLEMENT
BEGUILEMENT
CONDOLEMENT
CONFINEMENT
ACQUIREMENT
REQUIREMENT
PROCUREMENT
OBSCUREMENT
MEASUREMENT
APPEASEMENT
ENDORSEMENT
BEREAVEMENT
ENSLAVEMENT
ACHIEVEMENT
DEPRIVEMENT
DEVOLVEMENT
INVOLVEMENT
IMPROVEMENT
ENFEOFFMENT
PREJUDGMENT
IMPEACHMENT
BEWITCHMENT
DEBAUCHMENT
REFRESHMENT
GARNISHMENT
FURNISHMENT
NOURISHMENT
DISSEPIMENT
CONCEALMENT
ENTHRALMENT
EMBOWELMENT
ENGRAILMENT
CURTAILMENT
EMBROILMENT
INSTALLMENT
CONTROLMENT
ENLIVENMENT
BEDIZENMENT
ARRAIGNMENT
CONSIGNMENT
ENCHAINMENT
CONTAINMENT
ABANDONMENT
ENVIRONMENT
CONCERNMENT
DISCERNMENT
ADJOURNMENT
SOJOURNMENT
DEVELOPMENT
ENVELOPMENT
IMPRESSMENT
ENGROSSMENT
RECRUITMENT
ENCHANTMENT
APPOINTMENT
COMPARTMENT
COMPORTMENT
DISMASTMENT

FOREPAYMENT
IMPERMANENT
INCONTINENT
IMPERTINENT
GRANDPARENT
TRANSPARENT
INDIFFERENT
BELLIGERENT
OMNIPRESENT
INCOMPETENT
PLENIPOTENT
MULTIPOTENT
INADVERTENT
MELLIFLUENT
INTERFLUENT
INCONGRUENT
DEOBSTRUENT
CONSTITUENT
CARBONPOINT
FINGERPRINT
BUTTERPRINT
COUNTERPLOT
WITENAGEMOT
NONDESCRIPT
BOTTLECHART
COUNTERPART
COUNTERFORT
BLADDERWORT
CHURCHCOURT
TENNISCOURT
FLABBERGAST
DISAFFOREST
PANTIEWAIST
ROMANTICIST
ORTHOPEDIST
CHIROPODIST
POLTERGEIST
GENEALOGIST
OSTEOLOGIST
PATHOLOGIST
MYTHOLOGIST
SOCIOLOGIST
HAGIOLOGIST
PHILOLOGIST
COSMOLOGIST
ETYMOLOGIST
ETHNOLOGIST
HYMNOLOGIST
NECROLOGIST
PETROLOGIST
NEUROLOGIST
TAUTOLOGIST
PHYTOLOGIST
LOGOMACHIST
THEOSOPHIST
TELEPATHIST
SYNDICALIST
COLONIALIST
IMPERIALIST
MATERIALIST

TACHYGRAPHY	DISGUISEDLY	CAUSATIVELY
HYPERTROPHY	UNADVISEDLY	IMITATIVELY
PHOTOGLYPHY	DISPERSEDLY	TENTATIVELY
HOMOEOPATHY	CONFESSEDLY	PRIVATIVELY
UNSEAWORTHY	UNDOUBTEDLY	DEFECTIVELY
BLAMEWORTHY	COLLECTEDLY	EFFECTIVELY
TRUSTWORTHY	CONNECTEDLY	OBJECTIVELY
PRACTICABLY	CONCEITEDLY	ADJECTIVELY
IRREVOCABLY	CONTENTEDLY	INVECTIVELY
COMMENDABLY	UNDAUNTEDLY	DEDUCTIVELY
SERVICEABLY	CONTINUEDLY	SEDUCTIVELY
IMPERMEABLY	NORTHWARDLY	INDUCTIVELY
APPRECIABLY	HOUSEWIFELY	PRIMITIVELY
JUSTIFIABLY	VERSATILELY	NUTRITIVELY
UNSPEAKABLY	WHOLESOMELY	SENSITIVELY
INESTIMABLY	LOATHSOMELY	PARTITIVELY
INFLAMMABLY	WEARISOMELY	INTUITIVELY
CONFORMABLY	OPPORTUNELY	RETENTIVELY
INALIENABLY	INSINCERELY	ATTENTIVELY
IMPREGNABLY	PREMATURELY	INVENTIVELY
TREASONABLY	INTRICATELY	PLAINTIVELY
IRREPARABLY	AGGREGATELY	DECEPTIVELY
INSEPARABLY	IMMEDIATELY	ASSERTIVELY
INTOLERABLY	INVIOLATELY	REFLEXIVELY
INNUMERABLY	PROXIMATELY	EXCEEDINGLY
INSUPERABLY	OBSTINATELY	CONFIDINGLY
UNUTTERABLY	ALTERNATELY	ACCORDINGLY
PLEASURABLY	FORTUNATELY	SEARCHINGLY
UNADVISABLY	TEMPERATELY	RAVISHINGLY
CONVERSABLY	DESPERATELY	SHRINKINGLY
INEXCUSABLY	ELABORATELY	PROVOKINGLY
INTRACTABLY	CORPORATELY	QUIBBLINGLY
RESPECTABLY	DECUSSATELY	TREMBLINGLY
INDUBITABLY	EXQUISITELY	UNFEELINGLY
INDOMITABLY	DISSOLUTELY	SHUFFLINGLY
INHERITABLY	GROTESQUELY	UNFAILINGLY
WARRANTABLY	REPULSIVELY	SPARKLINGLY
ACCOUNTABLY	IMPULSIVELY	APPALLINGLY
COMFORTABLY	EXPANSIVELY	THRILLINGLY
SUPPORTABLY	DEFENSIVELY	UNWILLINGLY
IRREFUTABLY	OFFENSIVELY	BESEEMINGLY
INSCRUTABLY	EXPENSIVELY	UNMEANINGLY
RETRIEVABLY	INTENSIVELY	WANDERINGLY
CONCEIVABLY	OSTENSIVELY	WONDERINGLY
PERCEIVABLY	EXTENSIVELY	LINGERINGLY
IRREMOVABLY	EXPLOSIVELY	WITHERINGLY
IRREDUCIBLY	CORROSIVELY	SIMPERINGLY
DISCERNIBLY	EXCURSIVELY	FALTERINGLY
INDIVISIBLY	IMPASSIVELY	TOTTERINGLY
RESPONSIBLY	EXCESSIVELY	SHIVERINGLY
REPRESSIBLY	DIFFUSIVELY	QUIVERINGLY
PERMISSIBLY	INCLUSIVELY	MURMURINGLY
PERCEPTIBLY	EXCLUSIVELY	TORTURINGLY
SUSCEPTIBLY	COLLUSIVELY	UNCEASINGLY
CORRUPTIBLY	OBTRUSIVELY	PROMISINGLY
CONVERTIBLY	INTRUSIVELY	CARESSINGLY
BAREFACEDLY	PURGATIVELY	ANIMATINGLY
PRETENDEDLY	TALKATIVELY	AFFECTINGLY
UNGUARDEDLY	OPERATIVELY	SLIGHTINGLY
UNFEIGNEDLY	NARRATIVELY	REVOLTINGLY

INSULTINGLY	IDENTICALLY	DECEITFULLY
ASSENTINGLY	CHAOTICALLY	RESENTFULLY
DIVERTINGLY	IDIOTICALLY	SORROWFULLY
UNWITTINGLY	ZYMOTICALLY	GENTLEMANLY
BELIEVINGLY	SCEPTICALLY	ORBICULARLY
REPROVINGLY	ELASTICALLY	AURICULARLY
APPROVINGLY	DEISTICALLY	RETICULARLY
DESERVINGLY	CAUSTICALLY	IRREGULARLY
UNKNOWINGLY	EQUIVOCALLY	UNPOPULARLY
AGONIZINGLY	PYRAMIDALLY	POSTERIORLY
SQUEAMISHLY	CORPOREALLY	NEIGHBOURLY
LICKERISHLY	ADVERBIALLY	GRACELESSLY
UNHEALTHILY	CONNUBIALLY	GUILELESSLY
SECONDARILY	FINANCIALLY	SHAMELESSLY
PECUNIARILY	PAROCHIALLY	BLAMELESSLY
EXEMPLARILY	TRIENNIALLY	CEASELESSLY
CUSTOMARILY	PERENNIALLY	NOISELESSLY
MERCENARILY	SEXENNIALLY	SENSELESSLY
TEMPORARILY	PICTORIALLY	CAUSELESSLY
ARBITRARILY	EDITORIALLY	TASTELESSLY
NECESSARILY	MERCURIALLY	MATCHLESSLY
SEDENTARILY	AMBROSIALLY	FAITHLESSLY
MOMENTARILY	ESSENTIALLY	WORTHLESSLY
VOLUNTARILY	POTENTIALLY	MERCILESSLY
TRIBUTARILY	IMPARTIALLY	TRACKLESSLY
ACCESSORILY	CELESTIALLY	THANKLESSLY
DESULTORILY	CONVIVIALLY	DREAMLESSLY
PROSAICALLY	MEDICINALLY	SLEEPLESSLY
JURIDICALLY	DOCTRINALLY	POWERLESSLY
SYNODICALLY	HEXAGONALLY	DOUBTLESSLY
PACIFICALLY	SECTIONALLY	SHIFTLESSLY
ILLOGICALLY	EMOTIONALLY	FRUITLESSLY
GRAPHICALLY	FRATERNALLY	GUILTLESSLY
ANGELICALLY	COETERNALLY	FAULTLESSLY
DYNAMICALLY	NOCTURNALLY	DAUNTLESSLY
ENDEMICALLY	PRINCIPALLY	HEARTLESSLY
POLEMICALLY	EPISCOPALLY	HAZARDOUSLY
ORGANICALLY	ILLIBERALLY	ERRONEOUSLY
SATANICALLY	SINISTRALLY	RIGHTEOUSLY
BOTANICALLY	UNNATURALLY	PLENTEOUSLY
TECHNICALLY	UNIVERSALLY	BOUNTEOUSLY
LACONICALLY	ELEMENTALLY	COURTEOUSLY
CANONICALLY	CONTINUALLY	BEAUTEOUSLY
SPHERICALLY	PERPETUALLY	ANALOGOUSLY
NUMERICALLY	SPIRITUALLY	AUDACIOUSLY
GENERICALLY	UNGENTEELLY	SAGACIOUSLY
EMPIRICALLY	SCOUNDRELLY	CAPACIOUSLY
SATIRICALLY	UNHEEDFULLY	RAPACIOUSLY
CENTRICALLY	UNMINDFULLY	VERACIOUSLY
WHIMSICALLY	REGARDFULLY	VORACIOUSLY
CLASSICALLY	CHANGEFULLY	VIVACIOUSLY
FANATICALLY	HEALTHFULLY	JUDICIOUSLY
PIRATICALLY	PLENTIFULLY	OFFICIOUSLY
ERRATICALLY	BOUNTIFULLY	MALICIOUSLY
PRACTICALLY	BEAUTIFULLY	DELICIOUSLY
DEICTICALLY	UNDUTIFULLY	FEROCIOUSLY
GENETICALLY	WONDERFULLY	ATROCIOUSLY
HERETICALLY	PRAYERFULLY	CONSCIOUSLY
POLITICALLY	REGRETFULLY	INSIDIOUSLY
FRANTICALLY	FRIGHTFULLY	INVIDIOUSLY

DEPREDATORY	CHRONOMETRY	VINCIBILITY
CASTIGATORY	DOUBLEENTRY	CREDIBILITY
OBJURGATORY	DISCOURTESY	VENDIBILITY
EXPURGATORY	NYMPHOLEPSY	ELIGIBILITY
ENUNCIATORY	LITHOTRIPSY	TANGIBILITY
RETALIATORY	CONTROVERSY	FALLIBILITY
EXPATIATORY	CONTRARIETY	GULLIBILITY
OSCILLATORY	IMPROPRIETY	FEASIBILITY
CONDOLATORY	PERTINACITY	SENSIBILITY
CONSOLATORY	PERIODICITY	PASSIBILITY
TRANSLATORY	CATHOLICITY	POSSIBILITY
CIRCULATORY	VOLCANICITY	PARTIBILITY
GRATULATORY	VULCANICITY	FLEXIBILITY
POSTULATORY	ELECTRICITY	VERSATILITY
ACCLAMATORY	ELLIPTICITY	INFERTILITY
DECLAMATORY	DOMESTICITY	INCREDULITY
EXCLAMATORY	PELLUCIDITY	MAGNANIMITY
REFORMATORY	INTREPIDITY	PARVANIMITY
CHRISMATORY	INFECUNDITY	MASCULINITY
LACRYMATORY	SPONTANEITY	TACITURNITY
EXPLANATORY	HOMOGENEITY	IMPORTUNITY
COSIGNATORY	PHYSICALITY	OPPORTUNITY
DECLINATORY	CRITICALITY	SERENDIPITY
COMMINATORY	VERTICALITY	FAMILIARITY
INCULPATORY	ETHEREALITY	PECULIARITY
EXCULPATORY	PRODIGALITY	CAPILLARITY
EXTIRPATORY	CONJUGALITY	GLOBULARITY
NUNCUPATORY	INFORMALITY	CIRCULARITY
DECLARATORY	ABNORMALITY	VASCULARITY
PREPARATORY	ORIGINALITY	MUSCULARITY
RESPIRATORY	CRIMINALITY	SINGULARITY
INSPIRATORY	NATIONALITY	COLUMNARITY
IMPLORATORY	RATIONALITY	INSALUBRITY
EXPLORATORY	PERSONALITY	INSINCERITY
INCANTATORY	INTERNALITY	INDEXTERITY
DEHORTATORY	EXTERNALITY	INFERIORITY
EXHORTATORY	TEMPORALITY	SUPERIORITY
EXTENUATORY	CORPORALITY	ANTERIORITY
OBSERVATORY	HOSPITALITY	INTERIORITY
CALEFACTORY	IMMORTALITY	EXTERIORITY
MANUFACTORY	PUNCTUALITY	PREMATURITY
VALEDICTORY	EVENTUALITY	GRANDIOSITY
PERFUNCTORY	PROBABILITY	TENEBROSITY
PROHIBITORY	PLACABILITY	PONDEROSITY
PREMONITORY	PECCABILITY	MONSTROSITY
DEGLUTITORY	READABILITY	IMPETUOSITY
RETRIBUTORY	SALEABILITY	PERSPICUITY
COFFEEBERRY	SOCIABILITY	PROMISCUITY
CANDLEBERRY	RELIABILITY	SUPERFLUITY
HUCKLEBERRY	VARIABILITY	PROPINQUITY
QUEENSBERRY	SATIABILITY	OBJECTIVITY
BIBLIOLATRY	WORKABILITY	SENSITIVITY
PHYSIOLATRY	PALPABILITY	RECEPTIVITY
ANGELOLATRY	CULPABILITY	SHERIFFALTY
DEMONOLATRY	IMITABILITY	VICEROYALTY
ALKALIMETRY	SUITABILITY	BLOODGUILTY
CALORIMETRY	PORTABILITY	SOVEREIGNTY
STICHOMETRY	INSTABILITY	UNCERTAINTY
CRANIOMETRY	SALVABILITY	OSTEOPLASTY
SEISMOMETRY	SOLVABILITY	THEOPNEUSTY

SHORTSIGHTED
UNCOVENANTED
BATTLEMENTED
DISCONTENTED
UNFREQUENTED
UNACQUAINTED
DISAPPOINTED
CLOVENFOOTED
WHOLEHEARTED
BLACKHEARTED
LIGHTHEARTED
UNINTERESTED
SULPHURETTED
BEETLEBROWED
SELFEMPLOYED
UNPATRONIZED
CORNMARIGOLD
STRANGLEHOLD
MULTIPLICAND
MISAPPREHEND
UNLIKELIHOOD
BACHELORHOOD
DRAGONSBLOOD
DRAWINGBOARD
COUNCILBOARD
BRISTOLBOARD
CHECKERBOARD
DRAUGHTBOARD
HENCEFORWARD
CARDINALBIRD

----------E

CIRCUMSCRIBE
BLASTFURNACE
FRONTISPIECE
CHIMNEYPIECE
CHIEFJUSTICE
SIGNIFICANCE
COUNTRYDANCE
EXTRAVAGANCE
SURVEILLANCE
APPURTENANCE
PREDOMINANCE
REAPPEARANCE
PROTUBERANCE
INTEMPERANCE
PERSEVERANCE
DISSEVERANCE
REMONSTRANCE
COMPLAISANCE
CONCOMITANCE
ACQUAINTANCE
UNIMPORTANCE
CIRCUMSTANCE
READMITTANCE
DISALLOWANCE
RECONVEYANCE
CLAIRVOYANCE

MAGNIFICENCE
FRONDESCENCE
ACQUIESCENCE
ALKALESCENCE
EMOLLESCENCE
OBSOLESCENCE
JUVENESCENCE
CONCRESCENCE
ARBORESCENCE
CALORESCENCE
FLUORESCENCE
DELITESCENCE
REMINISCENCE
IMPROVIDENCE
RESPLENDENCE
INDEPENDENCE
INTELLIGENCE
DISOBEDIENCE
INEXPEDIENCE
INEXPERIENCE
CONSENTIENCE
SUBSERVIENCE
EQUIPOLLENCE
INCONTINENCE
IMPERTINENCE
TRANSPARENCE
INDIFFERENCE
INTERFERENCE
TRANSFERENCE
BELLIGERENCE
OMNIPRESENCE
INCOMPETENCE
PLENIPOTENCE
INADVERTENCE
IRRESISTENCE
NONEXISTENCE
MISPRONOUNCE
COUNTERFORCE
PHOSPHORESCE
RHODOMONTADE
PARASITICIDE
MOUNTAINSIDE
INEXACTITUDE
CORRECTITUDE
CARPENTERBEE
HINDOOSTANEE
CALABASHTREE
SUBCOMMITTEE
DISADVANTAGE
CORNEXCHANGE
CARTEBLANCHE
CAPERCAILZIE
BOARDINGPIKE
MARLINESPIKE
MASTERSTROKE
BREASTSTROKE
INERADICABLE
INAPPLICABLE
INEXPLICABLE
COMMUNICABLE

INEXTRICABLE
UNDEPENDABLE
INEFFACEABLE
DISPLACEABLE
DISAGREEABLE
CARRIAGEABLE
MARRIAGEABLE
UNMANAGEABLE
UNCHANGEABLE
EXCHANGEABLE
IRREFRAGABLE
INVESTIGABLE
REPROACHABLE
APPROACHABLE
UNQUENCHABLE
UNSEARCHABLE
DIMINISHABLE
IMPERISHABLE
VANQUISHABLE
UNBREATHABLE
BEQUEATHABLE
IRREMEDIABLE
SOLIDIFIABLE
SAPONIFIABLE
CLASSIFIABLE
IDENTIFIABLE
MULTIPLIABLE
UNMISTAKABLE
UNSHRINKABLE
UNREMARKABLE
IRREPEALABLE
UNAPPEALABLE
UNASSAILABLE
RECONCILABLE
COUNSELLABLE
CONTROLLABLE
POLYSYLLABLE
INCONSOLABLE
INCALCULABLE
IRREDEEMABLE
UNIMPUGNABLE
RESTRAINABLE
DISTRAINABLE
UNOBTAINABLE
MAINTAINABLE
UNATTAINABLE
UNIMAGINABLE
INDECLINABLE
CONTAMINABLE
DETERMINABLE
INTERMINABLE
EXTERMINABLE
UNPARDONABLE
CONSCIONABLE
QUESTIONABLE
UNREASONABLE
UNGOVERNABLE
INCOMPARABLE
CONSIDERABLE
IMPONDERABLE

INSUFFERABLE	IRREMISSIBLE	MARSEILLAISE
TRANSFERABLE	TRANSFUSIBLE	PROPAGANDISE
DECIPHERABLE	INCOMPATIBLE	DISFRANCHISE
INVULNERABLE	CONTRACTIBLE	COUNTERPOISE
DISCOVERABLE	DESTRUCTIBLE	PARENTHESISE
UNANSWERABLE	CONTEMPTIBLE	CONTRARIWISE
IRREPAIRABLE	MANIFESTIBLE	FRANKINCENSE
IRRESPIRABLE	INDIGESTIBLE	SUFFRUTICOSE
IMPERFORABLE	IRRESISTIBLE	METAMORPHOSE
COMMEMORABLE	INDISSOLUBLE	MULTIPURPOSE
IMPENETRABLE	CORPSECANDLE	CROSSPURPOSE
DEMONSTRABLE	YANKEEDOODLE	CLOTHESHORSE
UNFAVOURABLE	MADEMOISELLE	MITRAILLEUSE
IMMEASURABLE	EQUIMULTIPLE	CHARNELHOUSE
IMMENSURABLE	CUSTARDAPPLE	COUNCILHOUSE
MANOEUVRABLE	PTERODACTYLE	CHAPTERHOUSE
UNAPPEASABLE	NURSERYRHYME	CHARTERHOUSE
RECOGNISABLE	SUPRAMUNDANE	FLITTERMOUSE
DECOMPOSABLE	EXTRAMUNDANE	CENTUPLICATE
TRANSPOSABLE	SUPERMUNDANE	AUTHENTICATE
UNREPEATABLE	INTERMUNDANE	SOPHISTICATE
TRANSLATABLE	POLYURETHANE	DISAGGREGATE
UNMARKETABLE	ULTRAMONTANE	BILLINGSGATE
CONSOLETABLE	CANTHARIDINE	PATRIARCHATE
RESUSCITABLE	DONKEYENGINE	DISASSOCIATE
UNPROFITABLE	TEREBINTHINE	INTERMEDIATE
PRECIPITABLE	CROSSEXAMINE	DIBRANCHIATE
INHOSPITABLE	PREDETERMINE	PROLETARIATE
UNCHARITABLE	TRANSPONTINE	SECRETARIATE
MERCHANTABLE	EQUESTRIENNE	SUBSTANTIATE
UNTENANTABLE	CURLINGSTONE	INTERPELLATE
DISCOUNTABLE	KALEIDOSCOPE	VERTICILLATE
SURMOUNTABLE	LARYNGOSCOPE	DISCONSOLATE
UNACCEPTABLE	OSCILLOSCOPE	ELECTROPLATE
MANIFESTABLE	GALVANOSCOPE	MISTRANSLATE
ATTRIBUTABLE	ELECTROSCOPE	SOMNAMBULATE
TRANSMUTABLE	SPECTROSCOPE	CANALICULATE
DISREPUTABLE	DEVILMAYCARE	INARTICULATE
INDISPUTABLE	THOROUGHFARE	MISCALCULATE
UNBELIEVABLE	CHROMOSPHERE	CONGRATULATE
UNDECEIVABLE	STRATOSPHERE	RECAPITULATE
IRRESOLVABLE	AMPHITHEATRE	ILLEGITIMATE
IRREPROVABLE	DISCOMPOSURE	OVERESTIMATE
DISALLOWABLE	OVEREXPOSURE	IMPOSTHUMATE
UNEMPLOYABLE	NOMENCLATURE	DISCRIMINATE
CRITICIZABLE	VITRIFACTURE	INDOCTRINATE
PULVERIZABLE	ARCHITECTURE	PREDESTINATE
MAGNETIZABLE	SUBSTRUCTURE	CONGLUTINATE
HYPNOTIZABLE	DISCOMFITURE	BREVIPENNATE
INCORRODIBLE	PISCICULTURE	AFFECTIONATE
INTELLIGIBLE	FLORICULTURE	EXTORTIONATE
INCORRIGIBLE	HORTICULTURE	INVERTEBRATE
INDEFEASIBLE	MISADVENTURE	DECONSECRATE
SUBDIVISIBLE	INTERTEXTURE	CARBOHYDRATE
INDEFENSIBLE	INTERMIXTURE	PREPONDERATE
IRREVERSIBLE	PHOTOGRAVURE	CONGLOMERATE
INACCESSIBLE	OUTMANOEUVRE	UNADULTERATE
COMPRESSIBLE	DRESSINGCASE	COELENTERATE
SUPPRESSIBLE	STEEPLECHASE	REDINTEGRATE
INADMISSIBLE	HIREPURCHASE	DISINTEGRATE

179

POLYMORPHISM	AUSTRALASIAN	FLUORIDATION
CORPOREALISM	SCANDINAVIAN	COMMENDATION
PAROCHIALISM	ANTEDILUVIAN	DEFRAUDATION
FACTIONALISM	LONGSHOREMAN	TRANSUDATION
EMOTIONALISM	WAREHOUSEMAN	SUBLINEATION
COMMENSALISM	COUNTRYWOMAN	CONGREGATION
UNIVERSALISM	COUSINGERMAN	PROMULGATION
SPIRITUALISM	WATERBOATMAN	PROLONGATION
SCOUNDRELISM	COSMOPOLITAN	HOMOLOGATION
SOMNAMBULISM	METROPOLITAN	COMPURGATION
EPICUREANISM	CHURCHWARDEN	DEPRECIATION
TRADUCIANISM	BOWLINGGREEN	APPRECIATION
CONFUCIANISM	DELICATESSEN	DENUNCIATION
HIBERNIANISM	KINDERGARTEN	RENUNCIATION
SECTARIANISM	FRANKENSTEIN	ANNUNCIATION
UNITARIANISM	PANTECHNICON	CONSOCIATION
PRECISIANISM	STEREOPTICON	DISSOCIATION
PANHELLENISM	BOOKSCORPION	DEFORCIATION
PHILISTINISM	CIRCUMCISION	CONCILIATION
SECESSIONISM	REPREHENSION	DESPOLIATION
CAUSATIONISM	APPREHENSION	CALUMNIATION
HELIOTROPISM	INTROVERSION	REPATRIATION
INCENDIARISM	EXTROVERSION	EXPATRIATION
DISSENTERISM	RETROCESSION	PROPITIATION
CONSERVATISM	INTERCESSION	ABBREVIATION
DIAMAGNETISM	INTROMISSION	ASPHYXIATION
DILETTANTISM	INTERMISSION	INSUFFLATION
COLLECTIVISM	TRANSMISSION	SLUMPFLATION
EPITHALAMIUM	REPERCUSSION	ANNIHILATION
QUINQUENNIUM	CIRCUMFUSION	ASSIMILATION
HYPOCONDRIUM	CONGLOBATION	INSTALLATION
HIBERNACULUM	EXACERBATION	CANCELLATION
SUPERNACULUM	PERTURBATION	FLAGELLATION
XYLOBALSAMUM	MASTURBATION	CRENELLATION
UNDERSTRATUM	ADJUDICATION	COMPELLATION
	DIJUDICATION	TESSELLATION
	PACIFICATION	DISTILLATION
-----------N	NIDIFICATION	VITRIOLATION
	CODIFICATION	GENICULATION
SUBTERRANEAN	MODIFICATION	RETICULATION
GEOMETRICIAN	VILIFICATION	ARTICULATION
OBSTETRICIAN	RAMIFICATION	EMASCULATION
DIALECTICIAN	VERIFICATION	INOSCULATION
STATISTICIAN	PURIFICATION	STRIDULATION
EPHEMERIDIAN	GASIFICATION	ACCUMULATION
ANTEMERIDIAN	OSSIFICATION	MANIPULATION
CANTABRIGIAN	RATIFICATION	DEPOPULATION
CARLOVINGIAN	NOTIFICATION	CAPITULATION
MONODELPHIAN	TRIPLICATION	AMALGAMATION
BACCHANALIAN	COMPLICATION	CONCLAMATION
EPISCOPALIAN	SUPPLICATION	PROCLAMATION
ARISTOTELIAN	DIVARICATION	DESQUAMATION
TORRICELLIAN	INTOXICATION	CONCREMATION
NONAGENARIAN	DETRUNCATION	LEGITIMATION
OCTOGENARIAN	REALLOCATION	INFLAMMATION
DOCTRINARIAN	EQUIVOCATION	CONSUMMATION
TOTALITARIAN	CONFISCATION	CONFIRMATION
FUTILITARIAN	INVALIDATION	MALFORMATION
HUMANITARIAN	INTIMIDATION	CONFORMATION
PRESBYTERIAN	DILAPIDATION	REJUVENATION

IMPREGNATION	COMPENSATION	SATISFACTION
CONSIGNATION	DISPENSATION	DISAFFECTION
VATICINATION	MALVERSATION	DISINFECTION
COORDINATION	CONVERSATION	IMPERFECTION
EMARGINATION	INSPISSATION	INTERJECTION
DESALINATION	RETRACTATION	PRESELECTION
INSEMINATION	INHABITATION	GENUFLECTION
DENOMINATION	COHABITATION	INTELLECTION
ILLUMINATION	FELICITATION	RECOLLECTION
CHLORINATION	EXERCITATION	REINSPECTION
GELATINATION	EXCOGITATION	MISDIRECTION
CONDEMNATION	HABILITATION	RESURRECTION
CACHINNATION	DEBILITATION	INSURRECTION
ANTICIPATION	DELIMITATION	CROSSSECTION
EMANCIPATION	EXPLOITATION	INTERDICTION
CONSTIPATION	DECAPITATION	JURISDICTION
EXHILARATION	AUSCULTATION	ANTIFRICTION
CONSECRATION	CONSULTATION	CONSTRICTION
DELIBERATION	SEGMENTATION	REPRODUCTION
DILACERATION	PIGMENTATION	INTRODUCTION
EVISCERATION	AUGMENTATION	SUBSTRUCTION
IMMODERATION	ALIMENTATION	CONSTRUCTION
VOCIFERATION	COMMENTATION	INDISCRETION
EXAGGERATION	FERMENTATION	PRECONDITION
ACCELERATION	PRESENTATION	PRECOGNITION
DECELERATION	SUSTENTATION	MALNUTRITION
DEGENERATION	DISSERTATION	PERQUISITION
REGENERATION	CONTESTATION	DISQUISITION
INCINERATION	PROTESTATION	REIMPOSITION
REMUNERATION	DECRUSTATION	SUPERSTITION
EXASPERATION	STERNUTATION	INTERVENTION
RECUPERATION	CONTINUATION	APPERCEPTION
VITUPERATION	MENSTRUATION	SUBSCRIPTION
OBLITERATION	EFFECTUATION	PRESCRIPTION
ALLITERATION	PERPETUATION	CONSCRIPTION
ADULTERATION	ACCENTUATION	PROSCRIPTION
ASSEVERATION	PRESERVATION	REASSUMPTION
DEFLAGRATION	CONSERVATION	INTERRUPTION
PERSPIRATION	REANNEXATION	INCORRUPTION
EDULCORATION	FARADIZATION	CONTRIBUTION
AMELIORATION	LOCALIZATION	DISTRIBUTION
DECOLORATION	VOCALIZATION	IRRESOLUTION
PERPETRATION	VITALIZATION	SUBSTITUTION
INFILTRATION	EQUALIZATION	CONSTITUTION
FENESTRATION	MOBILIZATION	PROSTITUTION
REGISTRATION	CIVILIZATION	EPENCEPHALON
MINISTRATION	ORGANIZATION	PROLEGOMENON
ILLUSTRATION	COLONIZATION	DESSERTSPOON
INAUGURATION	CANONIZATION	SPERMATOZOON
SULPHURATION	ETHERIZATION	DODECAHEDRON
IDEALISATION	ARBORIZATION	RHOMBOHEDRON
LEGALISATION	VAPORIZATION	RHODODENDRON
MINIMISATION	MONETIZATION	POLYSYNDETON
OPTIMISATION	AMORTIZATION	ENDOSKELETON
MAXIMISATION	STUPEFACTION	CHRISTSTHORN
URBANISATION	TORREFACTION	DRESSINGGOWN
IMMUNISATION	PUTREFACTION	CAPPAGHBROWN
POLARISATION	LIQUEFACTION	
MOTORISATION	PETRIFACTION	
CONDENSATION	VITRIFACTION	

-----------O

LILLIBULLERO
MEZZORILIEVO

-----------P

CHIMNEYSWEEP
DISCIPLESHIP
LAUREATESHIP
CORPORALSHIP
MUSICIANSHIP
ONEUPMANSHIP
CHAIRMANSHIP
GAMESMANSHIP
CRAFTMANSHIP
PARTISANSHIP
CHAPLAINSHIP
CHAMPIONSHIP
RELATIONSHIP
RECORDERSHIP
WRANGLERSHIP
BACHELORSHIP
GOVERNORSHIP
MEDIATORSHIP
DICTATORSHIP
DIRECTORSHIP
EXECUTORSHIP
SURVIVORSHIP
SURVEYORSHIP
VISCOUNTSHIP
ATTORNEYSHIP
COUNTERSCARP

-----------R

INFUNDIBULAR
TABERNACULAR
SUPERNACULAR
RECEPTACULAR
APPENDICULAR
PLURILOCULAR
QUADRANGULAR
ANTIMACASSAR
BRIDECHAMBER
COUNTENANCER
REMEMBRANCER
ENCUMBRANCER
DOUBLEHEADER
INTERPLEADER
CANDLEHOLDER
BOTTLEHOLDER
SURREJOINDER
BRASSFOUNDER
TAPERECORDER
ACKNOWLEDGER
CARPETBAGGER
BALLADMONGER

CHEESEMONGER
COSTERMONGER
BODYSNATCHER
CALLIGRAPHER
IAMBOGRAPHER
LITHOGRAPHER
ORTHOGRAPHER
MYTHOGRAPHER
HAGIOGRAPHER
COSMOGRAPHER
STENOGRAPHER
ETHNOGRAPHER
HYMNOGRAPHER
HYDROGRAPHER
CHIROGRAPHER
PETROGRAPHER
PHOTOGRAPHER
CARTOGRAPHER
FATHERLASHER
ACCOMPLISHER
EXTINGUISHER
FOSTERFATHER
FOSTERMOTHER
TROUBLEMAKER
CABINETMAKER
STREETWALKER
SKRIMSHANKER
HEADSHRINKER
DOUBLEDEALER
CONVENTICLER
INTERMEDDLER
SWASHBUCKLER
SLEDGEHAMMER
YELLOWHAMMER
STRENGTHENER
STRAIGHTENER
COMMISSIONER
FOUNDATIONER
CONFECTIONER
EXHIBITIONER
PRACTITIONER
RESOLUTIONER
DRAWINGPAPER
CHERRYPEPPER
SHARECROPPER
EAVESDROPPER
ARMOURBEARER
MANUFACTURER
BREATHALYSER
CONTRADICTER
ARITHMOMETER
ENDOSMOMETER
GALVANOMETER
DECLINOMETER
PSYCHROMETER
ELECTROMETER
SPECTROMETER
GALACTOMETER
STEPDAUGHTER
MANSLAUGHTER

GASTARBEITER
DISENCHANTER
TRANSPLANTER
COMPLIMENTER
EXPERIMENTER
SHARPSHOOTER
COURTPLASTER
SCHOOLMASTER
CASHREGISTER
WHENCESOEVER
ENGINEDRIVER
CAMPFOLLOWER
STAYINGPOWER
PROSELYTIZER
CONQUISTADOR
BRIGADEMAJOR
COUNTERTENOR
TRANSGRESSOR
HYPOTHECATOR
SIGNIFICATOR
SCARIFICATOR
VERSIFICATOR
COMMUNICATOR
AVERRUNCATOR
CONSOLIDATOR
ACCOMMODATOR
INVESTIGATOR
INTERROGATOR
IMPROPRIATOR
APPROPRIATOR
CONTEMPLATOR
CONFABULATOR
PERAMBULATOR
GESTICULATOR
DISSIMULATOR
EXPOSTULATOR
DISSEMINATOR
EXTERMINATOR
PEREGRINATOR
ASSASSINATOR
IMPERSONATOR
PARTICIPATOR
REVERBERATOR
REFRIGERATOR
COMMISERATOR
COLLABORATOR
CORROBORATOR
COMMEMORATOR
SEQUESTRATOR
DEMONSTRATOR
RESUSCITATOR
CHIROPRACTOR
PRIMOGENITOR
ELECTROMOTOR
INTERLOCUTOR
HIPPOCENTAUR
ENTREPRENEUR
RESTAURATEUR
TECHNICOLOUR
MISDEMEANOUR

YOUTHFULNESS	GRIEVOUSNESS	SACRILEGIOUS
TRUTHFULNESS	ABSTRACTNESS	CONTUMELIOUS
FANCIFULNESS	INDIRECTNESS	SUPERCILIOUS
MERCIFULNESS	SUCCINCTNESS	QUERIMONIOUS
THANKFULNESS	DISTINCTNESS	PARSIMONIOUS
SCORNFULNESS	DISCREETNESS	MULTIFARIOUS
MOURNFULNESS	STRAIGHTNESS	MULTIVARIOUS
CHEERFULNESS	EXPLICITNESS	INSALUBRIOUS
POWERFULNESS	DECREPITNESS	VAINGLORIOUS
BLISSFULNESS	FREQUENTNESS	OSTENTATIOUS
DOUBTFULNESS	STALWARTNESS	DISPUTATIOUS
FRUITFULNESS	INEXPERTNESS	RAMBUNCTIOUS
BOASTFULNESS	AMBASSADRESS	COMPUNCTIOUS
UNLAWFULNESS	WEDDINGDRESS	GENTILITIOUS
LUKEWARMNESS	COPYINGPRESS	UNPROPITIOUS
STUBBORNNESS	FORNICATRESS	INNUTRITIOUS
TOGETHERNESS	BENEFACTRESS	ADSCITITIOUS
NEEDLESSNESS	INSTRUCTRESS	CEMENTITIOUS
MINDLESSNESS	HEADMISTRESS	ADVENTITIOUS
LIFELESSNESS	ANOTHERGUESS	GAMOPETALOUS
NAMELESSNESS	STRADIVARIUS	MONOPETALOUS
TAMELESSNESS	HIPPOPOTAMUS	OCTOPETALOUS
TIMELESSNESS	LIGNIPERDOUS	ANEMOPHILOUS
HOMELESSNESS	ACANTHACEOUS	ENDOPHYLLOUS
HOPELESSNESS	CORALLACEOUS	POLYPHYLLOUS
CARELESSNESS	ARGILLACEOUS	UNSCRUPULOUS
SELFLESSNESS	COROLLACEOUS	TRIDACTYLOUS
RUTHLESSNESS	SCHORLACEOUS	PHAENOGAMOUS
PITILESSNESS	DIATOMACEOUS	CRYPTOGAMOUS
RECKLESSNESS	GALLINACEOUS	AMPHISTOMOUS
HARMLESSNESS	PERTINACEOUS	CYCLOSTOMOUS
FORMLESSNESS	CARBONACEOUS	PSEUDONYMOUS
PAINLESSNESS	FURFURACEOUS	QUADRUMANOUS
HELPLESSNESS	ACHLAMYDEOUS	MUCILAGINOUS
FEARLESSNESS	ADVANTAGEOUS	IMPETIGINOUS
TACTLESSNESS	SUCCEDANEOUS	CONTERMINOUS
BOOTLESSNESS	TEMPORANEOUS	EXALBUMINOUS
SPOTLESSNESS	SIMULTANEOUS	EXSANGUINOUS
RESTLESSNESS	SUBCUTANEOUS	COTYLEDONOUS
LISTLESSNESS	PERGAMENEOUS	ANTHOCARPOUS
VITREOUSNESS	DISCOURTEOUS	ANGIOCARPOUS
SPACIOUSNESS	SARCOPHAGOUS	DODECANDROUS
GRACIOUSNESS	LITHOPHAGOUS	LATICIFEROUS
PRECIOUSNESS	OPHIOPHAGOUS	GLANDIFEROUS
STUDIOUSNESS	SAPROPHAGOUS	FRONDIFEROUS
SPURIOUSNESS	COPROPHAGOUS	CONCHIFEROUS
FACTIOUSNESS	PHYTOPHAGOUS	CUPULIFEROUS
CAPTIOUSNESS	RHIZOPHAGOUS	TITANIFEROUS
CAUTIOUSNESS	HETEROLOGOUS	SEMINIFEROUS
SEDULOUSNESS	STEATOPYGOUS	LUMINIFEROUS
POPULOUSNESS	LEIOTRICHOUS	RESINIFEROUS
LUMINOUSNESS	TRIADELPHOUS	STANNIFEROUS
VIGOROUSNESS	MONOMORPHOUS	SUDORIFEROUS
HUMOROUSNESS	PERVICACIOUS	SOPORIFEROUS
SONOROUSNESS	CONTUMACIOUS	SANGUIFEROUS
DEXTROUSNESS	INAUSPICIOUS	SYNANTHEROUS
COVETOUSNESS	UNSUSPICIOUS	CANTANKEROUS
SENSUOUSNESS	MERETRICIOUS	OBSTREPEROUS
UNCTUOUSNESS	SUBCONSCIOUS	UNPROSPEROUS
TORTUOUSNESS	INCOMMODIOUS	SLAUGHTEROUS

TETRAPTEROUS	DISPLACEMENT	INTERMITTENT
COLEOPTEROUS	MISPLACEMENT	CIRCUMFLUENT
MACROPTEROUS	ENTRANCEMENT	INCONSEQUENT
PREPOSTEROUS	COMMENCEMENT	MAGNILOQUENT
AMBIDEXTROUS	DENOUNCEMENT	TURNINGPOINT
ERYTHEMATOUS	RENOUNCEMENT	COUNTERPOINT
GLAUCOMATOUS	ANNOUNCEMENT	INTUSSUSCEPT
ATHEROMATOUS	FOREBODEMENT	GEOPHYSICIST
INFELICITOUS	DISAGREEMENT	VELOCIPEDIST
DISINGENUOUS	ENVISAGEMENT	HIPPOPHAGIST
CONTEMPTUOUS	DISLODGEMENT	MUSICOLOGIST
PRESUMPTUOUS	ESTRANGEMENT	LEXICOLOGIST
BRONTOSAURUS	INFRINGEMENT	TOXICOLOGIST
	DISGORGEMENT	CONCHOLOGIST
	ACCOUCHEMENT	PSYCHOLOGIST
-----------T	ENFEEBLEMENT	MORPHOLOGIST
	INVEIGLEMENT	CRANIOLOGIST
COMMISSARIAT	ENTANGLEMENT	ENTOMOLOGIST
INTERCONNECT	EMBEZZLEMENT	SEISMOLOGIST
BALANCESHEET	POSTPONEMENT	PHRENOLOGIST
LUMBERJACKET	DETHRONEMENT	TECHNOLOGIST
MISINTERPRET	ENTHRONEMENT	DEMONOLOGIST
DRIVINGSHAFT	APPRAISEMENT	CHRONOLOGIST
CHIMNEYSHAFT	CHASTISEMENT	DENDROLOGIST
MIDDLEWEIGHT	DISGUISEMENT	GLOSSOLOGIST
CARPETKNIGHT	DISBURSEMENT	DEONTOLOGIST
PLOUGHWRIGHT	EMPRESSEMENT	EGYPTOLOGIST
AFORETHOUGHT	MISSTATEMENT	METALLURGIST
AFTERTHOUGHT	RETRIEVEMENT	PARAGRAPHIST
SELFPORTRAIT	ENCROACHMENT	TELEGRAPHIST
MICROCIRCUIT	RETRENCHMENT	MONOGRAPHIST
CLINKERBUILT	ENTRENCHMENT	GYMNOSOPHIST
JURISCONSULT	BLANDISHMENT	HYDROPATHIST
CONGRATULANT	ADMONISHMENT	CORPOREALIST
MISDEMEANANT	ASTONISHMENT	CONVIVIALIST
DEATHWARRANT	LANGUISHMENT	UNIVERSALIST
BLACKCURRANT	BEQUEATHMENT	SPIRITUALIST
RECALCITRANT	REINSTALMENT	BIBLIOPOLIST
DISINFECTANT	DISANNULMENT	SOMNAMBULIST
CIRCUMJACENT	IMPRISONMENT	NOCTAMBULIST
CONTABESCENT	EMBLAZONMENT	PHLEBOTOMIST
INCANDESCENT	BEWILDERMENT	PYROTECHNIST
RECRUDESCENT	DECIPHERMENT	TRAMPOLINIST
CONVALESCENT	DISINTERMENT	EXPANSIONIST
EFFLORESCENT	EMBITTERMENT	IMMERSIONIST
DELIQUESCENT	MALTREATMENT	EXCURSIONIST
EFFERVESCENT	MISTREATMENT	SECESSIONIST
CONCUPISCENT	RECOMMITMENT	EXCLUSIONIST
CORESPONDENT	REINVESTMENT	EDUCATIONIST
JURISPRUDENT	READJUSTMENT	ISOLATIONIST
COUNTERAGENT	DISENDOWMENT	CREMATIONIST
INTRANSIGENT	REDEPLOYMENT	SALVATIONIST
CONSTRINGENT	UNEMPLOYMENT	TRADITIONIST
STUPEFACIENT	SUPEREMINENT	COALITIONIST
LIQUEFACIENT	SUBCONTINENT	ABOLITIONIST
FEBRIFACIENT	FOSTERPARENT	RECEPTIONIST
INSUFFICIENT	UNDERCURRENT	ELOCUTIONIST
INCONVENIENT	INTERCURRENT	EVOLUTIONIST
SANGUINOLENT	MISREPRESENT	MICROSCOPIST
MUCOPURULENT	INCONSISTENT	STEREOTYPIST

PSYCHIATRIST
BEHAVIOURIST
CARICATURIST
THEOREMATIST
OBSCURANTIST
ORTHODONTIST
PAEDOBAPTIST
THERAPEUTIST
COLLECTIVIST
NORTHERNMOST
SOUTHERNMOST

-----------W

BROTHERINLAW

-----------X

PNEUMOTHORAX

-----------Y

STRAIGHTAWAY
SUPERHIGHWAY
INTERMEDIACY
ILLEGITIMACY
PANTISOCRACY
GERONTOCRACY
UNREGENERACY
EXTRAVAGANCY
ORNITHOMANCY
PREOCCUPANCY
CONCOMITANCY
TRANSLUCENCY
RESPLENDENCY
INEFFICIENCY
INEXPEDIENCY
SUBSERVIENCY
EQUIPOLLENCY
TRANSPARENCY
INCOMPETENCY
PLENIPOTENCY
INADVERTENCY
CONSTITUENCY
CHERRYBRANDY
CHANCEMEDLEY
BOWLINGALLEY
EARNESTMONEY
OVERSIMPLIFY
PHARMACOLOGY
MICROBIOLOGY
LITURGIOLOGY
DACTYLIOLOGY
EPIDEMIOLOGY
BACTERIOLOGY
ECCLESIOLOGY
EPISTEMOLOGY

ANTHROPOLOGY
PNEUMATOLOGY
DIALECTOLOGY
ZOOPHYTOLOGY
LEXICOGRAPHY
CHALCOGRAPHY
PALAEOGRAPHY
STEREOGRAPHY
CHOREOGRAPHY
GLYPHOGRAPHY
BIBLIOGRAPHY
PHYSIOGRAPHY
OCEANOGRAPHY
ORGANOGRAPHY
SELENOGRAPHY
CHRONOGRAPHY
GLOSSOGRAPHY
CRYPTOGRAPHY
CHARTOGRAPHY
BRACHYGRAPHY
CHRESTOMATHY
PRAISEWORTHY
INERADICABLY
COMMUNICABLY
DISAGREEABLY
UNQUENCHABLY
IMPERISHABLY
IRREMEDIABLY
INCONSOLABLY
IRREDEEMABLY
UNFATHOMABLY
INTERMINABLY
QUESTIONABLY
UNREASONABLY
UNGOVERNABLY
INCOMPARABLY
CONSIDERABLY
INSUFFERABLY
UNANSWERABLY
IMPENETRABLY
DEMONSTRABLY
UNFAVOURABLY
IMMEASURABLY
UNCHARITABLY
TRANSMUTABLY
DISREPUTABLY
IRREVERSIBLY
INCOMPATIBLY
CONTEMPTIBLY
IRRESISTIBLY
SHAMEFACEDLY
CONFOUNDEDLY
DETERMINEDLY
UNPREPAREDLY
DISPLEASEDLY
CONTRACTEDLY
PROTRACTEDLY
ABSTRACTEDLY
DISTRACTEDLY
UNEXPECTEDLY

DISPIRITEDLY
UNOBSERVEDLY
UNDESERVEDLY
UNRESERVEDLY
BLACKGUARDLY
FROLICSOMELY
UNHANDSOMELY
TRANSVERSELY
IMMACULATELY
ARTICULATELY
LEGITIMATELY
CONSUMMATELY
INORDINATELY
COORDINATELY
EFFEMINATELY
PASSIONATELY
DELIBERATELY
IMMODERATELY
DEGENERATELY
INACCURATELY
INADEQUATELY
INCOMPLETELY
INDEFINITELY
INAPPOSITELY
PERSUASIVELY
DISSUASIVELY
INDECISIVELY
COMPULSIVELY
CONVULSIVELY
RESPONSIVELY
DISCURSIVELY
SUCCESSIVELY
DIGRESSIVELY
REPRESSIVELY
IMPRESSIVELY
OPPRESSIVELY
POSSESSIVELY
SUBMISSIVELY
CONCLUSIVELY
INDICATIVELY
NOMINATIVELY
IMPERATIVELY
FIGURATIVELY
MEDITATIVELY
DERIVATIVELY
ATTRACTIVELY
SUBJECTIVELY
REFLECTIVELY
COLLECTIVELY
RESPECTIVELY
VINDICTIVELY
ADJUNCTIVELY
DISCRETIVELY
DEFINITIVELY
INFINITIVELY
TRANSITIVELY
SUGGESTIVELY
DIMINUTIVELY
CONVINCINGLY
FORBIDDINGLY

PROPITIOUSLY
NUTRITIOUSLY
FACTITIOUSLY
FICTITIOUSLY
LICENTIOUSLY
INCAUTIOUSLY
OBSEQUIOUSLY
LASCIVIOUSLY
IMPERVIOUSLY
SCANDALOUSLY
SCURRILOUSLY
MARVELLOUSLY
MIRACULOUSLY
RIDICULOUSLY
SCRUPULOUSLY
EQUANIMOUSLY
SYNONYMOUSLY
DIAPHANOUSLY
VILLAINOUSLY
LIBIDINOUSLY
VOLUMINOUSLY
GLUTTONOUSLY
VIVIPAROUSLY
SLANDEROUSLY
VOCIFEROUSLY
UNGENEROUSLY
PROSPEROUSLY
ADULTEROUSLY
BOISTEROUSLY
CHIVALROUSLY
INDECOROUSLY
TRAITOROUSLY
IDOLATROUSLY
DISASTROUSLY
FELICITOUSLY
CALAMITOUSLY
CIRCUITOUSLY
UBIQUITOUSLY
GRATUITOUSLY
FORTUITOUSLY
PORTENTOUSLY
CONTIGUOUSLY
CONTINUOUSLY
TUMULTUOUSLY
VOLUPTUOUSLY
INDISCREETLY
CONCORDANTLY
DISCORDANTLY
TRIUMPHANTLY
NONCHALANTLY
INTOLERANTLY
UNPLEASANTLY
EXORBITANTLY
INCONSTANTLY
COMPLACENTLY
BENEFICENTLY
EVANESCENTLY
ANTECEDENTLY
COINCIDENTLY
DESPONDENTLY

ASTRINGENTLY
CONTINGENTLY
SUFFICIENTLY
OMNISCIENTLY
CONVENIENTLY
EQUIVALENTLY
MALEVOLENTLY
BENEVOLENTLY
FRAUDULENTLY
IRREVERENTLY
CONCURRENTLY
IMPENITENTLY
OMNIPOTENTLY
CONSISTENTLY
PERSISTENTLY
INFREQUENTLY
SUBSEQUENTLY
CONSEQUENTLY
APPENDECTOMY
PHARYNGOTOMY
ANTHROPOTOMY
PALAEOBOTANY
ANTHROPOGENY
MULLIGATAWNY
ORNITHOSCOPY
DEUTEROSCOPY
SPECTROSCOPY
PHILANTHROPY
INTERLINEARY
INTERMEDIARY
SUPERCILIARY
RESIDENTIARY
PENITENTIARY
SUBMAXILLARY
PREMAXILLARY
CONSTABULARY
SEPTUAGENARY
TERCENTENARY
VALETUDINARY
DISCIPLINARY
COTYLEDONARY
EXPANSIONARY
PROBATIONARY
DEFLATIONARY
REFLATIONARY
INFLATIONARY
EXTORTIONARY
EVOLUTIONARY
ELEEMOSYNARY
CONTEMPORARY
PLEBISCITARY
PARAMILITARY
SACRAMENTARY
PROTHONOTARY
PETTIFOGGERY
HABERDASHERY
ARCHDEACONRY
MODIFICATORY
SUPPLICATORY
EQUIVOCATORY

CONFISCATORY
COMMENDATORY
SUBFEUDATORY
TRANSUDATORY
DEPRECIATORY
APPRECIATORY
DENUNCIATORY
CONCILIATORY
CALUMNIATORY
ABBREVIATORY
DISTILLATORY
DEAMBULATORY
EMASCULATORY
MANIPULATORY
DESQUAMATORY
INFLAMMATORY
CONFIRMATORY
LACHRYMATORY
CONDEMNATORY
ANTICIPATORY
EXAGGERATORY
ACCELERATORY
REGENERATORY
RECUPERATORY
PERSPIRATORY
COMPENSATORY
DISPENSATORY
STERNUTATORY
CONSERVATORY
SATISFACTORY
INTERDICTORY
INTRODUCTORY
DISQUISITORY
CONTRIBUTORY
WHORTLEBERRY
ICHTHYOLATRY
GALVANOMETRY
TRIGONOMETRY
ELECTROMETRY
BIOCHEMISTRY
ZOOCHEMISTRY
IDIOSYNCRASY
PERSPICACITY
MULTIPLICITY
ECCENTRICITY
AUTHENTICITY
INELASTICITY
DISCOMMODITY
SIMULTANEITY
INCORPOREITY
TECHNICALITY
WHIMSICALITY
PRACTICALITY
CORPOREALITY
CONNUBIALITY
CONGENIALITY
ESSENTIALITY
IMPARTIALITY
CONVIVIALITY
SUBNORMALITY

------------A

DYSMENORRHOEA
ENCYCLOPAEDIA
PHARMACOPOEIA
PARAPHERNALIA
XEROPHTHALMIA
MORPHINOMANIA
HYPERMETROPIA
QUINQUAGESIMA
ECHINODERMATA

------------C

HYPOCHONDRIAC
ANAPHRODISIAC
ENCYCLOPAEDIC
ANTISPASMODIC
PRESCIENTIFIC
STRATIGRAPHIC
LEXICOGRAPHIC
PALAEOGRAPHIC
STEREOGRAPHIC
SEISMOGRAPHIC
CRYPTOGRAPHIC
UNPHILOSOPHIC
THERIOMORPHIC
HETEROMORPHIC
PLECTOGNATHIC
PLATYCEPHALIC
HOLOMETABOLIC
ANGLOCATHOLIC
PATHOGNOMONIC
KALEIDOSCOPIC
LARYNGOSCOPIC
SPECTROSCOPIC
PHILANTHROPIC
STRATOSPHERIC
ARCHBISHOPRIC
PHOTOELECTRIC
TRIGONOMETRIC
ELECTROMETRIC
PNEUMOGASTRIC
CATEGOREMATIC
DIAPHRAGMATIC
MONOGRAMMATIC
LIPOGRAMMATIC
MONOCHROMATIC
POLYCHROMATIC
PSYCHOSOMATIC
IDIOSYNCRATIC
UNSYMPATHETIC
POLYSYNTHETIC
ANTINEPHRITIC
TRANSATLANTIC
HETEROPLASTIC
MATERIALISTIC
NATIONALISTIC
RATIONALISTIC

DETERMINISTIC
ANACHRONISTIC
PALAEOCRYSTIC
ANTISCORBUTIC

------------D

INEXPERIENCED
EARTHLYMINDED
DISADVANTAGED
DISTINGUISHED
UNDIVERSIFIED
SELFSATISFIED
UNACCOMPANIED
DRAGGLETAILED
UNENLIGHTENED
COARSEGRAINED
UNDISCIPLINED
UNIMPASSIONED
DISILLUSIONED
UNCONDITIONED
FOREMENTIONED
CROSSGARTERED
VERSICOLOURED
MULTICOLOURED
PARTICOLOURED
UNRECOMPENSED
UNEMBARRASSED
PREFABRICATED
AUTHENTICATED
SOPHISTICATED
UNAPPRECIATED
UNASSIMILATED
SUPERANNUATED
WELLRESPECTED
UNPRECEDENTED
UNREPRESENTED
UNINTERRUPTED
DOUBLEHEARTED
BROKENHEARTED
DISINTERESTED
PHOSPHURETTED
UNINTERMITTED
DOUBLETONGUED
MISUNDERSTAND
NEIGHBOURHOOD
CAMPEACHYWOOD
CENTREFORWARD

------------E

BOOKINGOFFICE
CHURCHSERVICE
OVERABUNDANCE
DISAPPEARANCE
PREPONDERANCE
INTERMITTANCE
CONTABESCENCE

INCANDESCENCE
RECRUDESCENCE
CONVALESCENCE
EFFLORESCENCE
INFLORESCENCE
DELIQUESCENCE
DEFERVESCENCE
EFFERVESCENCE
CONCUPISCENCE
TRANSCENDENCE
JURISPRUDENCE
INTRANSIGENCE
INCONVENIENCE
SUPEREMINENCE
CIRCUMFERENCE
MULTIPRESENCE
MISADVERTENCE
INCONSISTENCE
CIRCUMFLUENCE
INCONSEQUENCE
MAGNILOQUENCE
SOMNILOQUENCE
DISSIMILITUDE
CHRISTMASTREE
CHOPPINGKNIFE
INTERMARRIAGE
FOREKNOWLEDGE
BALLCARTRIDGE
COUNTERCHANGE
COUNTERCHARGE
GENTLEMANLIKE
UNWORKMANLIKE
STATESMANLIKE
COUNTERSTROKE
INDESCRIBABLE
IMPERTURBABLE
MULTIPLICABLE
IMPRACTICABLE
RECOMMENDABLE
IRREPLACEABLE
UNSERVICEABLE
PRONOUNCEABLE
KNOWLEDGEABLE
CHALLENGEABLE
INDEFATIGABLE
UNIMPEACHABLE
INAPPRECIABLE
INDISSOCIABLE
ELECTRIFIABLE
DIVERSIFIABLE
UNJUSTIFIABLE
TETRASYLLABLE
IRRECLAIMABLE
UNCONFORMABLE
CONSTRAINABLE
ASCERTAINABLE
DISCIPLINABLE
UNFASHIONABLE
COMPANIONABLE
OBJECTIONABLE

UNMENTIONABLE
EXCEPTIONABLE
UNCONQUERABLE
IRRECOVERABLE
DISINTEGRABLE
DISHONOURABLE
COMMENSURABLE
CONJECTURABLE
INCONDENSABLE
INDISPENSABLE
UNSURPASSABLE
UNPREDICTABLE
BILLIARDTABLE
INTERPRETABLE
DRESSINGTABLE
UNINHABITABLE
DISCREDITABLE
UNWARRANTABLE
REPRESENTABLE
UNPRESENTABLE
UNACCOUNTABLE
UNCOMFORTABLE
INSUPPORTABLE
TRANSPORTABLE
INCONTESTABLE
UNFORGETTABLE
TRANSMITTABLE
CONTRIBUTABLE
DISTRIBUTABLE
IRRETRIEVABLE
INCONCEIVABLE
UNPERCEIVABLE
INDISSOLVABLE
VOLATILIZABLE
INCONVINCIBLE
EFFERVESCIBLE
INCOGNOSCIBLE
UNDISCERNIBLE
REPREHENSIBLE
APPREHENSIBLE
SUPERSENSIBLE
IRRESPONSIBLE
IRREPRESSIBLE
UNIMPRESSIBLE
INEXPRESSIBLE
TRANSMISSIBLE
IMPERCEPTIBLE
INSUSCEPTIBLE
UNSUSCEPTIBLE
PRESCRIPTIBLE
INCORRUPTIBLE
INCONVERTIBLE
INEXHAUSTIBLE
INCOMBUSTIBLE
BLISTERBEETLE
COTTONTHISTLE
ANTIHISTAMINE
CONVERSAZIONE
CINNAMONSTONE
DAGUERREOTYPE

QUESTIONNAIRE
CONSERVATOIRE
CHROMATOPHORE
PRIMOGENITURE
ARBORICULTURE
COMMERCIALISE
DEPERSONALISE
REVOLUTIONISE
CHEVALDEFRISE
TRANSISTORISE
ANAGRAMMATISE
BOARDINGHOUSE
DWELLINGHOUSE
CLEARINGHOUSE
PSYCHOANALYSE
QUADRUPLICATE
EXCOMMUNICATE
PROGNOSTICATE
BACCALAUREATE
REINTERROGATE
QUADRIFOLIATE
PROFESSORIATE
INAPPROPRIATE
DIFFERENTIATE
CIRCUMVALLATE
INFUNDIBULATE
APPENDICULATE
INTEROSCULATE
SOLIDUNGULATE
UNDERESTIMATE
INSUBORDINATE
DECONTAMINATE
INDETERMINATE
PROCRASTINATE
IMPARIPINNATE
COMPASSIONATE
DISPASSIONATE
PROPORTIONATE
INCONSIDERATE
EQUIPONDERATE
SUPERSATURATE
INTERDIGITATE
UNDERGRADUATE
HERMAPHRODITE
HYPOPHOSPHITE
ORNITHICHNITE
ARCHIMANDRITE
CARTEDEVISITE
QUADRIPARTITE
SCULPTURESQUE
COMPREHENSIVE
CORRESPONSIVE
RETROGRESSIVE
QUALIFICATIVE
SIGNIFICATIVE
JUSTIFICATIVE
COMMUNICATIVE
ACCOMMODATIVE
INVESTIGATIVE
INTERROGATIVE

CONTEMPLATIVE
APPROXIMATIVE
RATIOCINATIVE
SUBORDINATIVE
CONTAMINATIVE
RECRIMINATIVE
DETERMINATIVE
AGGLUTINATIVE
CONFEDERATIVE
REFRIGERATIVE
UNCOOPERATIVE
COMMISERATIVE
CORROBORATIVE
COMMEMORATIVE
EXPECTORATIVE
CONCENTRATIVE
DEMONSTRATIVE
REMONSTRATIVE
AUTHORITATIVE
ARGUMENTATIVE
FREQUENTATIVE
COUNTERACTIVE
RETROSPECTIVE
INTROSPECTIVE
CONTRADICTIVE
INDISTINCTIVE
UNINSTRUCTIVE
UNIMAGINITIVE
TRANSPOSITIVE
CIRCUMVENTIVE
ELECTROMOTIVE
CONTRACEPTIVE
TRANSCRIPTIVE
DENATIONALIZE
DISNATURALIZE
OCCIDENTALIZE
INDIVIDUALIZE
MOHAMMEDANIZE
PARTICULARIZE
EPIGRAMMATIZE
PROTESTANTIZE
VENTRILOQUIZE

------------F

BLINDMANSBUFF

------------G

BREECHLOADING
CARPETBEDDING
CROSSBREEDING
UNDERSTANDING
CONDESCENDING
CORRESPONDING
UNITPACKAGING
CROSSHATCHING
UNDERCLOTHING

CHUCKFARTHING
PENNYFARTHING
HOUSEBREAKING
HEARTBREAKING
DOUBLEDEALING
BLOODCURDLING
SPINECHILLING
NONCONFORMING
STRENGTHENING
UNCOMPLAINING
DEADRECKONING
EAVESDROPPING
DRINKOFFERING
BURNTOFFERING
LONGSUFFERING
MANUFACTURING
PREPOSSESSING
LEVELCROSSING
ACCOMMODATING
SELFDEFEATING
ROLLERSKATING
FLOODLIGHTING
LADYINWAITING
DISAPPOINTING
UNINTERESTING
HAIRSPLITTING

------------H

MARSIPOBRANCH
KAFFEEKLATSCH
CINEMATOGRAPH
PHONAUTOGRAPH
CLOISTERGARTH

------------I

ANTHROPOPHAGI

------------K

COUNTERATTACK
THUNDERSTRUCK
TONGUEINCHEEK

------------L

MINERALOGICAL
TOXICOLOGICAL
PSYCHOLOGICAL
PHYSIOLOGICAL
ENTOMOLOGICAL
PHRENOLOGICAL
TECHNOLOGICAL
CHRONOLOGICAL
GLOSSOLOGICAL

DEONTOLOGICAL
EMBRYOLOGICAL
SYNECDOCHICAL
PARAGRAPHICAL
IDEOGRAPHICAL
XYLOGRAPHICAL
MONOGRAPHICAL
TOPOGRAPHICAL
TYPOGRAPHICAL
PHILOSOPHICAL
PHILOMATHICAL
UNAPOSTOLICAL
IATROCHEMICAL
PETROCHEMICAL
LOGARITHMICAL
PYROTECHNICAL
MICROSCOPICAL
INTRATROPICAL
EXTRATROPICAL
INTERTROPICAL
HEMISPHERICAL
PHYLACTERICAL
PSYCHIATRICAL
UNSYMMETRICAL
MICROMETRICAL
HYDROMETRICAL
LACKADAISICAL
PROBLEMATICAL
UNGRAMMATICAL
SYMPTOMATICAL
STRATEGETICAL
SYMPATHETICAL
PARENTHETICAL
PERIPATETICAL
STALAGMITICAL
HYPERCRITICAL
STALACTITICAL
ENCOMIASTICAL
METHODISTICAL
PANTHEISTICAL
DIALOGISTICAL
SYLLOGISTICAL
CATECHISTICAL
EUCHARISTICAL
HERMENEUTICAL
INTERSIDEREAL
EXTRAJUDICIAL
INTERCOLONIAL
AMBASSADORIAL
GUBERNATORIAL
PROPRIETORIAL
EXTERRITORIAL
INQUISITORIAL
CONTROVERSIAL
UNSUBSTANTIAL
CONSEQUENTIAL
VENTRILOQUIAL
QUADRAGESIMAL
INFINITESIMAL
COUNTERSIGNAL

CEREBROSPINAL
ARCHIDIACONAL
CONGRESSIONAL
PROGRESSIONAL
CONVOCATIONAL
COEDUCATIONAL
CONJUGATIONAL
TERMINATIONAL
MULTINATIONAL
SUPERNATIONAL
INTERNATIONAL
RESPIRATIONAL
INSPIRATIONAL
GRAVITATIONAL
COMPUTATIONAL
OBSERVATIONAL
CONJUNCTIONAL
INSTRUCTIONAL
UNCONDITIONAL
INQUISITIONAL
PREPOSITIONAL
PROPOSITIONAL
SUPPOSITIONAL
UNINTENTIONAL
INSTITUTIONAL
CHOREPISCOPAL
FORAMINIFERAL
QUADRILATERAL
QUADRILITERAL
COROLLIFLORAL
THALAMIFLORAL
PRETERNATURAL
ARCHITECTURAL
PISCICULTURAL
FLORICULTURAL
HORTICULTURAL
INTRAPARIETAL
PREDICAMENTAL
TEMPERAMENTAL
ENVIRONMENTAL
DEVELOPMENTAL
GROUNDCONTROL
TABLESPOONFUL
DISRESPECTFUL

------------M

PARALLELOGRAM
ANTILOGARITHM
BUTCHERSBROOM
UMBRACULIFORM
COCHLEARIFORM
METEMPIRICISM
SCHOLASTICISM
CONTRABANDISM
BLACKGUARDISM
SADOMASOCHISM
CATASTROPHISM
PROVINCIALISM

COMMERCIALISM
IMMATERIALISM
INDUSTRIALISM
COLLOQUIALISM
PHENOMENALISM
UNILATERALISM
SCRIPTURALISM
ACCIDENTALISM
SACERDOTALISM
INDIVIDUALISM
CONCEPTUALISM
INFALLIBILISM
MONOMETALLISM
POLYDACTYLISM
REPUBLICANISM
MOHAMMEDANISM
VEGETARIANISM
PEDESTRIANISM
EQUESTRIANISM
PHILHELLENISM
IMPRESSIONISM
PERFECTIONISM
PROTECTIONISM
EXHIBITIONISM
REVOLUTIONISM
THEANTHROPISM
APOGEOTROPISM
VERNACULARISM
PARTICULARISM
FILIBUSTERISM
PANSPERMATISM
COSMOPOLITISM
POCOCURANTISM
PROTESTANTISM
VENTRILOQUISM
PERICHONDRIUM
PALAEOTHERIUM
CHRYSANTHEMUM
ODONTOGLOSSUM

------------N

MALACOSTRACAN
LATINAMERICAN
ANGLOAMERICAN
MEDITERRANEAN
TERPSICHOREAN
PAEDIATRICIAN
METAPHYSICIAN
MATHEMATICIAN
ARITHMETICIAN
MACHIAVELLIAN
SHAKESPEARIAN
AUTHORITARIAN
NECESSITARIAN
VALEDICTORIAN
ANTICHRISTIAN
LIGHTHOUSEMAN
NIGHTWATCHMAN

PRIVATEERSMAN
PANICSTRICKEN
WEATHERBEATEN
MONOCOTYLEDON
CARRIERPIGEON
CONDESCENSION
COMPREHENSION
INTERSPERSION
ANIMADVERSION
NONAGGRESSION
RETROGRESSION
TRANSGRESSION
DECOMPRESSION
PREPOSSESSION
DISPOSSESSION
PRETERMISSION
HYPOTHECATION
PREJUDICATION
SPECIFICATION
CALCIFICATION
ACIDIFICATION
QUALIFICATION
JOLLIFICATION
MOLLIFICATION
NULLIFICATION
AMPLIFICATION
MUMMIFICATION
CHYMIFICATION
MAGNIFICATION
LIGNIFICATION
SIGNIFICATION
SCARIFICATION
CLARIFICATION
GLORIFICATION
PETRIFICATION
VITRIFICATION
FALSIFICATION
VERSIFICATION
BEATIFICATION
GRATIFICATION
RECTIFICATION
ACETIFICATION
CERTIFICATION
FORTIFICATION
MORTIFICATION
JUSTIFICATION
MYSTIFICATION
REPUBLICATION
REDUPLICATION
COMMUNICATION
PREVARICATION
DECORTICATION
EXCORTICATION
DOMESTICATION
RECIPROCATION
CONSOLIDATION
ACCOMMODATION
BACKWARDATION
SUFFUMIGATION
INVESTIGATION

INTERROGATION
PRONUNCIATION
DOMICILIATION
IMPROPRIATION
APPROPRIATION
EXPROPRIATION
INTERCALATION
BLOODRELATION
INTERRELATION
DISSIMILATION
HORRIPILATION
CONSTELLATION
FLOCCILLATION
SCINTILLATION
MACHICOLATION
EXTRAPOLATION
INTERPOLATION
CONTEMPLATION
CONFABULATION
FUNAMBULATION
PERAMBULATION
PANDICULATION
VERMICULATION
MATRICULATION
GRATICULATION
DENTICULATION
GESTICULATION
TRIANGULATION
STRANGULATION
DISSIMULATION
ENCAPSULATION
EXPOSTULATION
DISESTIMATION
APPROXIMATION
MISCEGENATION
CONCATENATION
RATIOCINATION
HALLUCINATION
SUBORDINATION
PREORDINATION
CONTAMINATION
DISSEMINATION
RECRIMINATION
PREDOMINATION
DETERMINATION
EXTERMINATION
DEFIBRINATION
PEREGRINATION
ASSASSINATION
AGGLUTINATION
IMPERSONATION
REINCARNATION
CONSTERNATION
PARTICIPATION
PREOCCUPATION
EQUILIBRATION
REVERBERATION
PROTUBERATION
INCARCERATION
CONFEDERATION

CONSIDERATION
PROLIFERATION
REFRIGERATION
AGGLOMERATION
COMMISERATION
CONFLAGRATION
TRANSPIRATION
COLLABORATION
CORROBORATION
DETERIORATION
DISCOLORATION
COMMEMORATION
INCORPORATION
EXPECTORATION
CONCENTRATION
ORCHESTRATION
SEQUESTRATION
DEMONSTRATION
REMONSTRATION
PREFIGURATION
CONFIGURATION
DISFIGURATION
EXTRAVASATION
ITALICISATION
VERBALISATION
SOCIALISATION
SERIALISATION
STABILISATION
STERILISATION
SYSTEMISATION
VICTIMISATION
MECHANISATION
MODERNISATION
VULGARISATION
MESMERISATION
AUTHORISATION
GLAMORISATION
TERRORISATION
DRAMATISATION
SENSITISATION
DESERTISATION
IMPROVISATION
ACCLIMATATION
SUPERFETATION
RESUSCITATION
PREMEDITATION
REGURGITATION
SEXPLOITATION
DECREPITATION
PRECIPITATION
SUPPLANTATION
DISPLANTATION
REORIENTATION
ORNAMENTATION
FRAGMENTATION
SEDIMENTATION
REGIMENTATION
DOCUMENTATION
ARGUMENTATION
CONFRONTATION

POLICESTATION
MANIFESTATION
AFFORESTATION
TRANSMUTATION
PERSCRUTATION
INDIVIDUATION
OVERVALUATION
ANIMALIZATION
PLURALIZATION
TANTALIZATION
SYPHILIZATION
FOSSILIZATION
SUBTILIZATION
FERTILIZATION
ECONOMIZATION
VULCANIZATION
GALVANIZATION
SOLEMNIZATION
CARBONIZATION
HARMONIZATION
CAUTERIZATION
PULVERIZATION
DEODORIZATION
TEMPORIZATION
CICATRIZATION
MAGNETIZATION
COUNTERACTION
DISCONNECTION
RETROSPECTION
INTROSPECTION
CONTRADICTION
CIRCUMDUCTION
SUPERADDITION
JUXTAPOSITION
DECOMPOSITION
SUPERPOSITION
INTERPOSITION
INDISPOSITION
TRANSPOSITION
CONTRAVENTION
CIRCUMVENTION
COUNTERMOTION
CONTRACEPTION
PRECONCEPTION
MISCONCEPTION
TRANSCRIPTION
DISPROPORTION
CROSSQUESTION
INTERLOCUTION
ELECTROCUTION
MESENCEPHALON
LEPIDODENDRON
GRAPPLINGIRON
COUNTERPOISON
HEATHROBINSON

------------O

INCOMMUNICADO
GENERALISSIMO

------------P

CONSTABLESHIP
CANDIDATESHIP
ASSOCIATESHIP
SENESCHALSHIP
PROCONSULSHIP
SUFFRAGANSHIP
LIBRARIANSHIP
SWORDSMANSHIP
STATESMANSHIP
CRAFTSMANSHIP
DRAFTSMANSHIP
YACHTSMANSHIP
SPORTSMANSHIP
SUBDEACONSHIP
COMPANIONSHIP
REGISTRARSHIP
COMMANDERSHIP
COPARTNERSHIP
PRESBYTERSHIP
CONFESSORSHIP
MODERATORSHIP
INSPECTORSHIP
PROTECTORSHIP
PRECENTORSHIP
COADJUTORSHIP
PRESIDENTSHIP
SECRETARYSHIP

------------R

THERMONUCLEAR
INTERPETIOLAR
TINTINNABULAR
PERPENDICULAR
QUADRILOCULAR
INTERCELLULAR
SHOCKABSORBER
INTELLIGENCER
VIDEORECORDER
SCANDALMONGER
SCHOOLTEACHER
LEXICOGRAPHER
CHALCOGRAPHER
CHOREOGRAPHER
BIBLIOGRAPHER
OCEANOGRAPHER
CHRONOGRAPHER
GLOSSOGRAPHER
CRYPTOGRAPHER
OWNEROCCUPIER
FORTUNETELLER

PADDLESTEAMER
VACUUMCLEANER
COTTONSPINNER
CHIMNEYCORNER
BLOTTINGPAPER
UNDERSTRAPPER
DOUBLECROSSER
SACCHARIMETER
PYRHELIOMETER
ALCOHOLOMETER
VOLUMENOMETER
SACCHAROMETER
SYMPIESOMETER
PNEUMATOMETER
GRANDDAUGHTER
COUNTERFEITER
HELTERSKELTER
CALICOPRINTER
DANCINGMASTER
DRAWINGMASTER
STATIONMASTER
QUARTERMASTER
HARBOURMASTER
ROLLERCOASTER
TONGUETWISTER
BALLASTHEAVER
WHITHERSOEVER
PHILOSOPHIZER
TRANQUILLIZER
SERGEANTMAJOR
BURNINGMIRROR
MULTIPLICATOR
SOPHISTICATOR
INTERMEDIATOR
SOMNAMBULATOR
CONGRATULATOR
DISCRIMINATOR
PREDESTINATOR
TRANSMIGRATOR
ADMINISTRATOR
TERGIVERSATOR
SUBCONTRACTOR
SEMICONDUCTOR

------------S

MATERFAMILIAS
PATERFAMILIAS
THAUMATURGICS
HYDRODYNAMICS
CALLISTHENICS
HYDROKINETICS
CHREMATISTICS
PHARMACEUTICS
PROBABILITIES
BELLESLETTRES
SCHIZOMYCETES
DADDYLONGLEGS
ELEPHANTIASIS

ORGANOGENESIS
HETEROGENESIS
SYNECPHONESIS
AMNIOCENTESIS
MONONUCLEOSIS
METAMORPHOSIS
BUTTERFINGERS
STRUCTURELESS
BEGINNINGLESS
COMPANIONLESS
CHARACTERLESS
BAREFACEDNESS
UNGUARDEDNESS
COLLECTEDNESS
CONCEITEDNESS
CONTENTEDNESS
PEACEABLENESS
AGREEABLENESS
MALLEABLENESS
TEACHABLENESS
LAUGHABLENESS
AVAILABLENESS
SEPARABLENESS
VENERABLENESS
MISERABLENESS
ADMIRABLENESS
DESIRABLENESS
INCURABLENESS
ENDURABLENESS
ADVISABLENESS
EXCUSABLENESS
PALATABLENESS
EXCITABLENESS
EQUITABLENESS
IMMUTABLENESS
IMMOVABLENESS
ALLOWABLENESS
ILLEGIBLENESS
INVISIBLENESS
PLAUSIBLENESS
WHOLESOMENESS
LOATHSOMENESS
WEARISOMENESS
LIGHTSOMENESS
MASCULINENESS
OPPORTUNENESS
PREMATURENESS
OBSTINATENESS
TEMPERATENESS
ELABORATENESS
EXQUISITENESS
DISSOLUTENESS
GROTESQUENESS
PERVASIVENESS
REPULSIVENESS
EXPANSIVENESS
OFFENSIVENESS
EXPENSIVENESS
INTENSIVENESS
EXTENSIVENESS

CORROSIVENESS
IMPASSIVENESS
DIFFUSIVENESS
EXCLUSIVENESS
OBTRUSIVENESS
INTRUSIVENESS
COMBATIVENESS
TALKATIVENESS
DEFECTIVENESS
EFFECTIVENESS
OBJECTIVENESS
SECRETIVENESS
PRIMITIVENESS
SENSITIVENESS
RETENTIVENESS
ATTENTIVENESS
INVENTIVENESS
PLAINTIVENESS
DECEPTIVENESS
RECEPTIVENESS
ASSERTIVENESS
CONFIDINGNESS
UNWILLINGNESS
SQUEAMISHNESS
LICKERISHNESS
YELLOWISHNESS
FOOLHARDINESS
UNWORLDLINESS
NIGGARDLINESS
DASTARDLINESS
BROTHERLINESS
SPRIGHTLINESS
UNSIGHTLINESS
SECONDARINESS
CUSTOMARINESS
VISIONARINESS
ARBITRARINESS
SEDENTARINESS
MOMENTARINESS
VOLUNTARINESS
DESULTORINESS
UNSAVOURINESS
UNTHRIFTINESS
PRACTICALNESS
EQUIVOCALNESS
UNMINDFULNESS
CHANGEFULNESS
HEALTHFULNESS
PLENTIFULNESS
BOUNTIFULNESS
UNSKILFULNESS
WONDERFULNESS
MASTERFULNESS
PRAYERFULNESS
FORGETFULNESS
FRIGHTFULNESS
DECEITFULNESS
SORROWFULNESS
BOUNDLESSNESS
GRACELESSNESS

SHAMELESSNESS
BLAMELESSNESS
SHAPELESSNESS
NOISELESSNESS
SENSELESSNESS
CAUSELESSNESS
TASTELESSNESS
WORTHLESSNESS
MERCILESSNESS
PENNILESSNESS
TRACKLESSNESS
POWERLESSNESS
SIGHTLESSNESS
GUILTLESSNESS
FAULTLESSNESS
POINTLESSNESS
DAUNTLESSNESS
HEARTLESSNESS
RIGHTEOUSNESS
PLENTEOUSNESS
COURTEOUSNESS
AUDACIOUSNESS
SAGACIOUSNESS
SALACIOUSNESS
TENACIOUSNESS
CAPACIOUSNESS
RAPACIOUSNESS
VORACIOUSNESS
VIVACIOUSNESS
JUDICIOUSNESS
OFFICIOUSNESS
MALICIOUSNESS
DELICIOUSNESS
FEROCIOUSNESS
ATROCIOUSNESS
CONSCIOUSNESS
INSIDIOUSNESS
INVIDIOUSNESS
MELODIOUSNESS
EGREGIOUSNESS
RELIGIOUSNESS
LITIGIOUSNESS
INGENIOUSNESS
IMPERIOUSNESS
DELIRIOUSNESS
LABORIOUSNESS
NOTORIOUSNESS
PENURIOUSNESS
LUXURIOUSNESS
VEXATIOUSNESS
FRACTIOUSNESS
FACETIOUSNESS
SEDITIOUSNESS
BUMPTIOUSNESS
OBLIVIOUSNESS
OBNOXIOUSNESS
FRIVOLOUSNESS
CREDULOUSNESS
PENDULOUSNESS
TREMULOUSNESS

QUERULOUSNESS
POISONOUSNESS
LUDICROUSNESS
PONDEROUSNESS
DANGEROUSNESS
LECHEROUSNESS
DEXTEROUSNESS
CLAMOROUSNESS
MONSTROUSNESS
MOMENTOUSNESS
ASSIDUOUSNESS
IMPETUOUSNESS
IMPERFECTNESS
INCORRECTNESS
TRANSIENTNESS
STEADFASTNESS
MILLIONAIRESS
CONSPIRATRESS
MASSACHUSETTS
GASTROCNEMIUS
HYDROCEPHALUS
GASTEROPODOUS
MEMBRANACEOUS
ARUNDINACEOUS
CINCHONACEOUS
PAPAVERACEOUS
STERCORACEOUS
CAMPHORACEOUS
EQUISETACEOUS
FRUMENTACEOUS
DICHLAMYDEOUS
PORCELLANEOUS
MISCELLANEOUS
INSTANTANEOUS
CONSENTANEOUS
HETEROGENEOUS
EXSANGUINEOUS
PHYLLOPHAGOUS
ENTOMOPHAGOUS
PENTASTICHOUS
PENTADELPHOUS
OPHIOMORPHOUS
ORTHOGNATHOUS
HYSTERANTHOUS
INEFFICACIOUS
PERSPICACIOUS
SANCTIMONIOUS
SURREPTITIOUS
SUPERSTITIOUS
CONSCIENTIOUS
MEGACEPHALOUS
MESOCEPHALOUS
ENTOMOPHILOUS
ZYGODACTYLOUS
PHANEROGAMOUS
CLEISTOGAMOUS
MONOTHALAMOUS
POLYTHALAMOUS
PUSILLANIMOUS
ANGIOSPERMOUS

GYMNOSPERMOUS
DIATHERMANOUS
PLATITUDINOUS
MULTITUDINOUS
CARTILAGINOUS
ACOTYLEDONOUS
AUTOCHTHONOUS
PROTEROGYNOUS
HETEROCARPOUS
OVOVIVIPAROUS
PROTERANDROUS
RHOPALOCEROUS
NICKELIFEROUS
FOSSILIFEROUS
CORALLIFEROUS
METALLIFEROUS
UMBELLIFEROUS
BALSAMIFEROUS
POLLINIFEROUS
STAMINIFEROUS
ALUMINIFEROUS
CARBONIFEROUS
STOLONIFEROUS
ARGENTIFEROUS
APHANIPTEROUS
LEPIDOPTEROUS
HYMENOPTEROUS
HETEROPTEROUS
CHEIROPTEROUS
GRAMINIVOROUS
INSECTIVOROUS
UNADVENTUROUS
ERYSIPELATOUS
EXANTHEMATOUS
MONOTREMATOUS
INCONSPICUOUS
DISCONTINUOUS
VENTRILOQUOUS
ELECTROPHORUS

------------T

PRETERPERFECT
ELECTROMAGNET
HUNDREDWEIGHT
FEATHERWEIGHT
COUNTERWEIGHT
CLINCHERBUILT
INSIGNIFICANT
SUPERABUNDANT
DRILLSERGEANT
SUPERDOMINANT
EQUIPONDERANT
SEARCHWARRANT
REJUVENESCENT
SELFCONFIDENT
OVERCONFIDENT
VICEPRESIDENT
CORRESPONDENT

SELFINDULGENT
CIRCUMAMBIENT
DELIRIFACIENT
INTERLACEMENT
PRONOUNCEMENT
REINFORCEMENT
DISENGAGEMENT
MISMANAGEMENT
DISPARAGEMENT
ENCOURAGEMENT
DISOBLIGEMENT
REARRANGEMENT
RECONCILEMENT
OUTSETTLEMENT
PREFIGUREMENT
DISFIGUREMENT
ADMEASUREMENT
FRANCHISEMENT
ADVERTISEMENT
REIMBURSEMENT
REINSTATEMENT
OVERSTATEMENT
ESTABLISHMENT
EMBELLISHMENT
REPLENISHMENT
ACCOMPANIMENT
DISEMBARKMENT
ENLIGHTENMENT
ASCERTAINMENT
ENTERTAINMENT
APPORTIONMENT
MISGOVERNMENT
REDEVELOPMENT
DISMEMBERMENT
ENCOMPASSMENT
EMBARRASSMENT
REAPPOINTMENT
MALADJUSTMENT
EQUIDIFFERENT
COBELLIGERENT
GRANDILOQUENT
TREASURECHEST
CONTRABANDIST
GYNAECOLOGIST
ARCHAEOLOGIST
PHRASEOLOGIST
ORNITHOLOGIST
ASSYRIOLOGIST
CAMPANOLOGIST
CRIMINOLOGIST
METEOROLOGIST
MARTYROLOGIST
DERMATOLOGIST
HERPETOLOGIST
ICHTHYOLOGIST
THAUMATURGIST
SADOMASOCHIST
STENOGRAPHIST
PHONOGRAPHIST
HIEROGLYPHIST

HOMOEOPATHIST
PROVERBIALIST
IMMATERIALIST
INDUSTRIALIST
COLLOQUIALIST
UNILATERALIST
SCRIPTURALIST
INDIVIDUALIST
CONCEPTUALIST
INFALLIBILIST
MONOMETALLIST
VIOLONCELLIST
DEUTEROGAMIST
PHYSIOGNOMIST
NONCONFORMIST
SUCCESSIONIST
IMPRESSIONIST
EMIGRATIONIST
ANNEXATIONIST
PERFECTIONIST
PROJECTIONIST
PROTECTIONIST
EXHIBITIONIST
OPPOSITIONIST
CONVENTIONIST
CORRUPTIONIST
CONTORTIONIST
REVOLUTIONIST
STETHOSCOPIST
CRANIOSCOPIST
MISANTHROPIST
PARTICULARIST
AGRICULTURIST
MELODRAMATIST
ANAGRAMMATIST
EPIGRAMMATIST
EXPERIMENTIST
CONTRAPUNTIST
CONTROVERTIST
PHARMACEUTIST
VENTRILOQUIST
PSYCHOANALYST
HORSECHESTNUT

------------W

DAUGHTERINLAW

------------X

CEPHALOTHORAX
CONCAVOCONVEX
CONVEXOCONVEX
ARCHAEOPTERYX

------------Y

CIRCUMJACENCY
RECRUDESCENCY
CONVALESCENCY
DEFERVESCENCY
TRANSCENDENCY
INSUFFICIENCY
INCONSISTENCY
ROUGHANDREADY
INTERSTRATIFY
SACROSANCTIFY
ANTHROPOPHAGY
HELMINTHOLOGY
CHRONOBIOLOGY
OPHTHALMOLOGY
PALAEOZOOLOGY
PALAEONTOLOGY
AUTOBIOGRAPHY
STEGANOGRAPHY
CLIMATOGRAPHY
ANTHROPOPATHY
UNTRUSTWORTHY
IMPRACTICABLY
INDEFATIGABLY
UNJUSTIFIABLY
UNCONFORMABLY
UNFASHIONABLY
COMPANIONABLY
OBJECTIONABLY
UNCONQUERABLY
IRRECOVERABLY
DISHONOURABLY
COMMENSURABLY
INDISPENSABLY
DISCREDITABLY
UNWARRANTABLY
UNCOMFORTABLY
INSUPPORTABLY
INCONTESTABLY
IRRETRIEVABLY
INCONCEIVABLY
REPREHENSIBLY
IRRESPONSIBLY
IRREPRESSIBLY
INEXPRESSIBLY
INCORRUPTIBLY
INEXHAUSTIBLY
UNDISTURBEDLY
CONSTRAINEDLY
GOODNATUREDLY
INTERRUPTEDLY
TROUBLESOMELY
CLANDESTINELY
INOPPORTUNELY
APPROPRIATELY
APPROXIMATELY
SUBORDINATELY
DETERMINATELY
UNFORTUNATELY

IMPORTUNATELY	INVOLUNTARILY	MATRIMONIALLY
CONSIDERATELY	PERFUNCTORILY	PATRIMONIALLY
INTEMPERATELY	PHARISAICALLY	PARTICIPIALLY
PRECIPITATELY	COXCOMBICALLY	MAGISTERIALLY
PICTURESQUELY	SPASMODICALLY	MINISTERIALLY
INOFFENSIVELY	RHAPSODICALLY	MEDIATORIALLY
INEXPENSIVELY	STRATEGICALLY	DICTATORIALLY
PROGRESSIVELY	THEOLOGICALLY	TERRITORIALLY
UNOBTRUSIVELY	LETHARGICALLY	INVENTORIALLY
PREDICATIVELY	EVANGELICALLY	TERRESTRIALLY
PROVOCATIVELY	PARABOLICALLY	SUBSTANTIALLY
CORRELATIVELY	EPIDERMICALLY	EXPONENTIALLY
APPELLATIVELY	METONYMICALLY	DEFERENTIALLY
SUPERLATIVELY	PURITANICALLY	INFERENTIALLY
SPECULATIVELY	ALLEGORICALLY	REVERENTIALLY
AFFIRMATIVELY	CATEGORICALLY	PENITENTIALLY
ALTERNATIVELY	PLETHORICALLY	INFLUENTIALLY
PREPARATIVELY	DIAMETRICALLY	PROVISIONALLY
COMPARATIVELY	SYMMETRICALLY	EDUCATIONALLY
QUALITATIVELY	GEOMETRICALLY	SENSATIONALLY
COMMUTATIVELY	ECCENTRICALLY	TRADITIONALLY
INEFFECTIVELY	PANEGYRICALLY	CONDITIONALLY
PROSPECTIVELY	NONSENSICALLY	INTENTIONALLY
PERSPECTIVELY	INTRINSICALLY	EXCEPTIONALLY
RESTRICTIVELY	EXTRINSICALLY	CONJECTURALLY
DISTINCTIVELY	PRAGMATICALLY	TRANSVERSALLY
INSTINCTIVELY	ENIGMATICALLY	FUNDAMENTALLY
CONJUNCTIVELY	ASTHMATICALLY	SACRAMENTALLY
DISJUNCTIVELY	GRAMMATICALLY	SENTIMENTALLY
OBSTRUCTIVELY	IDIOMATICALLY	INEFFECTUALLY
DESTRUCTIVELY	AXIOMATICALLY	DISGRACEFULLY
INSTRUCTIVELY	AUTOMATICALLY	DISTASTEFULLY
INQUISITIVELY	PRISMATICALLY	REPROACHFULLY
SUBSTANTIVELY	PNEUMATICALLY	DISTRESSFULLY
INATTENTIVELY	SYNTACTICALLY	DISTRUSTFULLY
DESCRIPTIVELY	DIALECTICALLY	RECTANGULARLY
PRESUMPTIVELY	ENERGETICALLY	GRANDMOTHERLY
CONSUMPTIVELY	PROPHETICALLY	UNNEIGHBOURLY
ATTRIBUTIVELY	SYNTHETICALLY	DEFENCELESSLY
CONSECUTIVELY	AESTHETICALLY	REMORSELESSLY
DISPARAGINGLY	SPLENETICALLY	THOUGHTLESSLY
ENCOURAGINGLY	THEORETICALLY	SPONTANEOUSLY
DISOBLIGINGLY	PARASITICALLY	SULPHUREOUSLY
ASTONISHINGLY	AUTHENTICALLY	UNRIGHTEOUSLY
LANGUISHINGLY	PATRIOTICALLY	EFFICACIOUSLY
THREATENINGLY	PROLEPTICALLY	INJUDICIOUSLY
COMPLAININGLY	BOMBASTICALLY	COMPENDIOUSLY
PERSEVERINGLY	SARCASTICALLY	IRRELIGIOUSLY
DISTRESSINGLY	GYMNASTICALLY	PUNCTILIOUSLY
DEPRECATINGLY	FANTASTICALLY	IGNOMINIOUSLY
PENETRATINGLY	ATHEISTICALLY	CEREMONIOUSLY
INSINUATINGLY	SOPHISTICALLY	ACRIMONIOUSLY
AGGRAVATINGLY	REALISTICALLY	BURGLARIOUSLY
EVERLASTINGLY	STATISTICALLY	OPPROBRIOUSLY
INTERESTINGLY	EGOTISTICALLY	MERITORIOUSLY
OVERFLOWINGLY	PARADOXICALLY	INDUSTRIOUSLY
PATRONIZINGLY	INCORPOREALLY	ILLUSTRIOUSLY
PRELIMINARILY	DIPHTHONGALLY	EXPEDITIOUSLY
EXTEMPORARILY	PREJUDICIALLY	PRETENTIOUSLY
UNNECESSARILY	SUPERFICIALLY	SENTENTIOUSLY

CONTENTIOUSLY
INCREDULOUSLY
BLASPHEMOUSLY
MAGNANIMOUSLY
DICHOTOMOUSLY
SYNCHRONOUSLY
ODORIFEROUSLY
PESTIFEROUSLY
ADVENTUROUSLY
PRECIPITOUSLY
NECESSITOUSLY
CONSPICUOUSLY
PERSPICUOUSLY
PROMISCUOUSLY
MELLIFLUOUSLY
SUPERFLUOUSLY
INCONGRUOUSLY
TEMPESTUOUSLY
MISCHIEVOUSLY
CIRCUMSPECTLY
SIGNIFICANTLY
EXTRAVAGANTLY
PREDOMINANTLY
COMPLAISANTLY
CONCOMITANTLY
PRECIPITANTLY
EQUIDISTANTLY
MAGNIFICENTLY
TRANSLUCENTLY
IMPROVIDENTLY
RESPLENDENTLY
INDEPENDENTLY
INTELLIGENTLY
INEFFICIENTLY
DISOBEDIENTLY
INEXPEDIENTLY
INCONTINENTLY
IMPERTINENTLY
TRANSPARENTLY
INDIFFERENTLY
INCOMPETENTLY
INADVERTENTLY
MELLIFLUENTLY
PHYSIOTHERAPY
IMMUNOTHERAPY
BIBLIOTHECARY
INTERSTELLARY
QUINCENTENARY
EXTRAORDINARY
CONVULSIONARY
CONCESSIONARY
CONFESSIONARY
POSSESSIONARY
CONFECTIONARY
CONCRETIONARY
DISCRETIONARY
EXPEDITIONARY
TRANSITIONARY
CONVENTIONARY
PRECAUTIONARY

REVOLUTIONARY
PARLIAMENTARY
COMPLEMENTARY
SUPPLEMENTARY
COMPLIMENTARY
INTEGUMENTARY
CONFECTIONERY
SIGNIFICATORY
JUSTIFICATORY
INTERROGATORY
CONFABULATORY
GESTICULATORY
EXPOSTULATORY
RATIOCINATORY
HALLUCINATORY
RECRIMINATORY
EXTERMINATORY
REVERBERATORY
REFRIGERATORY
CORROBORATORY
REMONSTRATORY
IMPROVISATORY
CONTRADICTORY
INTERLOCUTORY
ANTHROPOLATRY
ANTHROPOMETRY
MOTHERCOUNTRY
HETEROGENEITY
THEATRICALITY
ARTIFICIALITY
IRRATIONALITY
IMPERSONALITY
INHOSPITALITY
HORIZONTALITY
INDIVIDUALITY
HOMOSEXUALITY
IMPROBABILITY
ABSORBABILITY
IMPLACABILITY
IMPECCABILITY
PREDICABILITY
APPLICABILITY
MANAGEABILITY
CHANGEABILITY
PERISHABILITY
UNRELIABILITY
INSATIABILITY
NEGOTIABILITY
INVIOLABILITY
ATTAINABILITY
PONDERABILITY
PREFERABILITY
VULNERABILITY
ANSWERABILITY
PENETRABILITY
MENSURABILITY
PROFITABILITY
UNSUITABILITY
ACCEPTABILITY
COMMUTABILITY

RECEIVABILITY
RESOLVABILITY
IMPROVABILITY
SQUEEZABILITY
INVINCIBILITY
INCREDIBILITY
INELIGIBILITY
CORRIGIBILITY
INTANGIBILITY
INFALLIBILITY
EXPANSIBILITY
DEFENSIBILITY
INSENSIBILITY
OSTENSIBILITY
EXTENSIBILITY
REVERSIBILITY
IMPASSIBILITY
ACCESSIBILITY
ADMISSIBILITY
REMISSIBILITY
IMPOSSIBILITY
DIFFUSIBILITY
COMPATIBILITY
IMPARTIBILITY
DIGESTIBILITY
RESISTIBILITY
REFLEXIBILITY
INFLEXIBILITY
DISSOLUBILITY
CONTRACTILITY
PUSILLANIMITY
NONCONFORMITY
CONSANGUINITY
CONFRATERNITY
UNFAMILIARITY
DISSIMILARITY
PARTICULARITY
TRIANGULARITY
AMBIDEXTERITY
IMPECUNIOSITY
DISCONTINUITY
ASSOCIATIVITY
RADIOACTIVITY
GALVANOPLASTY

------------A

CLAUSTROPHOBIA
ORNITHODELPHIA
CZECHOSLOVAKIA
LEUCOCYTHAEMIA
HYPERNATRAEMIA
PHANTASMAGORIA
HYPERAESTHESIA
INTELLIGENTSIA

------------C

ANTAPHRODISIAC
OPISTHOGRAPHIC
AUTOBIOGRAPHIC
ORNITHODELPHIC
BRACHYCEPHALIC
DIAHELIOTROPIC
PHANTASMAGORIC
APOPHTHEGMATIC
HERMAPHRODITIC
ANTIPHLOGISTIC
SOMNAMBULISTIC
CHARACTERISTIC

------------D

UNACKNOWLEDGED
COPPERBOTTOMED
COPPERFASTENED
SCATTERBRAINED
AFOREMENTIONED
PARALLELEPIPED
PARALLELOPIPED
UNPREPOSSESSED
UNAPPROPRIATED
UNINCORPORATED
UMPREMEDITATED
PUBLICSPIRITED
CHICKENHEARTED
DOUBLEBREASTED
BRISTOLDIAMOND

------------E

INSIGNIFICANCE
SUPERABUNDANCE
COUNTERBALANCE
DISCOUNTENANCE
DISENCUMBRANCE
EQUIPONDERANCE
RECONNAISSANCE
DISINHERITANCE
DISCONTINUANCE
REJUVENESCENCE
SELFCONFIDENCE

CORRESPONDENCE
CROSSREFERENCE
GRANDILOQUENCE
VERISIMILITUDE
FIBROCARTILAGE
BLANKCARTRIDGE
INCOMMUNICABLE
EXCOMMUNICABLE
UNDERSTANDABLE
IRREPROACHABLE
INAPPROACHABLE
ACCOMPLISHABLE
EXTINGUISHABLE
IRRECONCILABLE
UNCONTROLLABLE
DODECASYLLABLE
QUADRISYLLABLE
INDETERMINABLE
UNCONSCIONABLE
IMPRESSIONABLE
PROPORTIONABLE
UNQUESTIONABLE
INCONSIDERABLE
INDECIPHERABLE
UNDISCOVERABLE
INDECOMPOSABLE
UNDECOMPOSABLE
UNTRANSLATABLE
DISRESPECTABLE
CONTRADICTABLE
INSURMOUNTABLE
INTRANSMUTABLE
CRYSTALLIZABLE
UNRECOGNIZABLE
IRRECOGNIZABLE
UNINTELLIGIBLE
COMPREHENSIBLE
INCOMPRESSIBLE
INSUPPRESSIBLE
INDESTRUCTIBLE
CONTROVERTIBLE
KNITTINGNEEDLE
WASHINGMACHINE
BATHINGMACHINE
SELFDISCIPLINE
NITROGLYCERINE
RADIOTELEPHONE
PHENOBARBITONE
OPHTHALMOSCOPE
CONCESSIONAIRE
COMMISSIONAIRE
COUNTERMEASURE
FELLOWCREATURE
DISTEMPERATURE
SUPERSTRUCTURE
DISINVESTITURE
BIRDOFPARADISE
DISENFRANCHISE
CONTRAINDICATE
CIRCUMNAVIGATE

SUPERPHOSPHATE
FORISFAMILIATE
DISAPPROPRIATE
MISAPPROPRIATE
CIRCUMAMBULATE
INDISCRIMINATE
PREDETERMINATE
DISINCORPORATE
INTERPENETRATE
INCOMMENSURATE
OVERCOMPENSATE
CONCAVOCONCAVE
CONVEXOCONCAVE
MULTIPLICATIVE
UNAPPRECIATIVE
DISCRIMINATIVE
CONGLUTINATIVE
ADMINISTRATIVE
INTERPRETATIVE
REPRESENTATIVE
SUPERSENSITIVE
HYPERSENSITIVE
SUBSTANTIALIZE
SENTIMENTALIZE
DECHRISTIANIZE
DISILLUSIONIZE

------------G

CASTLEBUILDING
DISTINGUISHING
SPRINGCLEANING
WINDOWSHOPPING
MOUNTAINEERING
ELECTIONEERING
UNCOMPROMISING
TELEPROCESSING
ELECTROPLATING
DISCRIMINATING
UNINTERMITTING

------------H

ENCEPHALOGRAPH
BOROUGHENGLISH

------------K

COMPOSINGSTICK

------------L

POLYSYLLABICAL
AMPHIBOLOGICAL
ARCHAEOLOGICAL
PHRASEOLOGICAL

ORNITHOLOGICAL
TERMINOLOGICAL
METEOROLOGICAL
ICHTHYOLOGICAL
ZINCOGRAPHICAL
ORTHOGRAPHICAL
STENOGRAPHICAL
HYDROGRAPHICAL
CHOROGRAPHICAL
PHOTOGRAPHICAL
HIEROGLYPHICAL
PHYSIOGNOMICAL
MISANTHROPICAL
CATADIOPTRICAL
ANAGRAMMATICAL
EPIGRAMMATICAL
EMPYREUMATICAL
COSMOPOLITICAL
METROPOLITICAL
ECCLESIASTICAL
ENTHUSIASTICAL
PARAPHRASTICAL
PERIPHRASTICAL
POLYTHEISTICAL
PHARMACEUTICAL
PROPAEDEUTICAL
HEMISPHEROIDAL
EXTRAPAROCHIAL
CONSPIRATORIAL
COMMENTATORIAL
EXCREMENTITIAL
CONSUBSTANTIAL
CIRCUMSTANTIAL
REMINISCENTIAL
QUINTESSENTIAL
SUPERCELESTIAL
TRIDIMENSIONAL
INTERCESSIONAL
CONGREGATIONAL
DENOMINATIONAL
ORGANISATIONAL
CONVERSATIONAL
DISSERTATIONAL
INTERJECTIONAL
INSURRECTIONAL
JURISDICTIONAL
CONSTRUCTIONAL
DISQUISITIONAL
UNCONVENTIONAL
CONSCRIPTIONAL
CONSTITUTIONAL
ARCHIEPISCOPAL
CAPTAINGENERAL
CIRCUMLITTORAL
LAMELLIROSTRAL
RECURVIROSTRAL
ARBORICULTURAL
ANTISCRIPTURAL
DRESSREHEARSAL
TRANSCENDENTAL

CATHERINEWHEEL
CHAMBERCOUNSEL
BOARDINGSCHOOL

------------M

PERIPATETICISM
HYPERCRITICISM
EVANGELICALISM
SENSATIONALISM
TRADITIONALISM
SENTIMENTALISM
CONTINENTALISM
ROSICRUCIANISM
SABBATARIANISM
PROLETARIANISM
EGALITARIANISM
UTILITARIANISM
LIBERTARIANISM
ANTIQUARIANISM
ZOROASTRIANISM
ULTRAMONTANISM
APHELIOTROPISM
INDIFFERENTISM

------------N

BROBDINGNAGIAN
SESQUIPEDALIAN
QUADRAGENARIAN
VALETUDINARIAN
LATITUDINARIAN
DISCIPLINARIAN
PREDESTINARIAN
SACRAMENTARIAN
WONDERSTRICKEN
HANDICRAFTSMEN
TATTERDEMALION
INTERCOMMUNION
INAPPREHENSION
SOLIDIFICATION
LAPIDIFICATION
SIMPLIFICATION
CALORIFICATION
CLASSIFICATION
STRATIFICATION
SANCTIFICATION
FRUCTIFICATION
STULTIFICATION
QUANTIFICATION
IDENTIFICATION
BEAUTIFICATION
REVIVIFICATION
MULTIPLICATION
MISAPPLICATION
PREFABRICATION
AUTHENTICATION
SOPHISTICATION

RETROGRADATION
RECOMMENDATION
SUBINFEUDATION
INTERLINEATION
DISAGGREGATION
INTERMEDIATION
RECONCILIATION
SUBSTANTIATION
DISEMBARKATION
INTERPELLATION
SOMNAMBULATION
MISCALCULATION
OVERPOPULATION
CONGRATULATION
RECAPITULATION
MISINFORMATION
TRANSFORMATION
FOREORDINATION
DISINCLINATION
DISCRIMINATION
INDOCTRINATION
PREDESTINATION
CONGLUTINATION
DECONSECRATION
CONGLOMERATION
REDINTEGRATION
DISINTEGRATION
INTERMIGRATION
RECALCITRATION
ADMINISTRATION
COMMENSURATION
CIRCUMGYRATION
BASTARDISATION
TRIVIALISATION
DECIMALISATION
OPTIMALISATION
LIBERALISATION
DEMOBILISATION
IMMOBILISATION
REORGANISATION
HOMOGENISATION
ANTAGONISATION
MILITARISATION
BOWDLERISATION
PASTEURISATION
CASTRAMETATION
INTERPRETATION
INCAPACITATION
REHABILITATION
DISORIENTATION
IMPLEMENTATION
REPRESENTATION
TRANSPORTATION
CIRCUMNUTATION
SUPERANNUATION
SPECIALIZATION
GENERALIZATION
MINERALIZATION
DEMORALIZATION
CENTRALIZATION

NEUTRALIZATION
NATURALIZATION
CAPITALIZATION
EVANGELIZATION
VOLATILIZATION
MACADAMIZATION
ENTHRONIZATION
FRATERNIZATION
DEPOLARIZATION
TABULARIZATION
SECULARIZATION
POPULARIZATION
DECOLORIZATION
STIGMATIZATION
DEMONETIZATION
REMONETIZATION
CIRCUMSPECTION
MASSPRODUCTION
REINTRODUCTION
RECONSTRUCTION
CONTRAPOSITION
SUPERSCRIPTION
AUTOSUGGESTION
REDISTRIBUTION
CIRCUMLOCUTION
RUBBERSOLUTION
CIRCUMVOLUTION
RECONSTITUTION

------------P

APPRENTICESHIP
CONTROLLERSHIP
CHANCELLORSHIP
COUNSELLORSHIP
PROCURATORSHIP
PROPRIETORSHIP
LIEUTENANTSHIP
ACCOUNTANTSHIP
COMMISSARYSHIP

------------R

CLOAKANDDAGGER
AUTOBIOGRAPHER
HERESIOGRAPHER
FAIRYGODMOTHER
PLEASURESEEKER
BILLIARDMARKER
FELLOWCOMMONER
CARTRIDGEPAPER
TELETYPEWRITER
TROUBLESHOOTER
BREADANDBUTTER
CARDINALFLOWER
MICROPROCESSOR
PROGNOSTICATOR
PROCRASTINATOR

BOACONSTRICTOR
SUPERCONDUCTOR
CIRCUMFERENTOR

------------S

THERMODYNAMICS
ELECTROSTATICS
PHELLOPLASTICS
INEXPRESSIBLES
MEPHISTOPHELES
HIPPOPOTAMUSES
METEMPSYCHOSIS
PLEURAPOPHYSIS
PSYCHOANALYSIS
PROSTAGLANDINS
CORNETAPISTONS
KNICKERBOCKERS
EXPRESSIONLESS
DISENGAGEDNESS
INDISPOSEDNESS
CONTRACTEDNESS
ABSTRACTEDNESS
DISTRACTEDNESS
DISJOINTEDNESS
IMPLACABLENESS
DESPICABLENESS
FORMIDABLENESS
CHANGEABLENESS
CHARGEABLENESS
PERISHABLENESS
UNSOCIABLENESS
UNRELIABLENESS
INVARIABLENESS
INSATIABLENESS
INVIOLABLENESS
ATTAINABLENESS
ABOMINABLENESS
REASONABLENESS
SEASONABLENESS
SUFFERABLENESS
VULNERABLENESS
DEPLORABLENESS
HONOURABLENESS
FAVOURABLENESS
CENSURABLENESS
IMPASSABLENESS
CREDITABLENESS
CHARITABLENESS
UNSUITABLENESS
ACCEPTABLENESS
DETESTABLENESS
DECEIVABLENESS
RECEIVABLENESS
IMPROVABLENESS
INVINCIBLENESS
INTANGIBLENESS
INFLEXIBLENESS
FROLICSOMENESS

BLITHESOMENESS
METTLESOMENESS
INORDINATENESS
COORDINATENESS
EFFEMINATENESS
PASSIONATENESS
DELIBERATENESS
DEGENERATENESS
INDEFINITENESS
IRRESOLUTENESS
PERSUASIVENESS
RESPONSIVENESS
DISCURSIVENESS
AGGRESSIVENESS
IMPRESSIVENESS
OPPRESSIVENESS
EXPRESSIVENESS
POSSESSIVENESS
SUBMISSIVENESS
PERMISSIVENESS
CONCLUSIVENESS
DECORATIVENESS
FIGURATIVENESS
ATTRACTIVENESS
REFLECTIVENESS
VINDICTIVENESS
PRODUCTIVENESS
DEFINITIVENESS
REPETITIVENESS
DIMINUTIVENESS
UNFRIENDLINESS
SLATTERNLINESS
DISORDERLINESS
STATIONARINESS
OBLIGATORINESS
DEROGATORINESS
REFRACTORINESS
TRANSITORINESS
UNGRACEFULNESS
REVENGEFULNESS
REMORSEFULNESS
UNGRATEFULNESS
DESPITEFULNESS
UNFAITHFULNESS
UNTRUTHFULNESS
UNMERCIFULNESS
DISDAINFULNESS
DELIGHTFULNESS
THOUGHTFULNESS
UNFRUITFULNESS
DISGUSTFULNESS
FREESPOKENNESS
FRIENDLESSNESS
GROUNDLESSNESS
REGARDLESSNESS
SPEECHLESSNESS
BREATHLESSNESS
THRIFTLESSNESS
WEIGHTLESSNESS
RELENTLESSNESS

STUPENDOUSNESS
OUTRAGEOUSNESS
COURAGEOUSNESS
FALLACIOUSNESS
LOQUACIOUSNESS
PERNICIOUSNESS
AUSPICIOUSNESS
SUSPICIOUSNESS
CAPRICIOUSNESS
PRECOCIOUSNESS
PERFIDIOUSNESS
FASTIDIOUSNESS
COMMODIOUSNESS
CONTAGIOUSNESS
ABSTEMIOUSNESS
HARMONIOUSNESS
PRECARIOUSNESS
GREGARIOUSNESS
MYSTERIOUSNESS
CENSORIOUSNESS
INFECTIOUSNESS
FLAGITIOUSNESS
PROPITIOUSNESS
LICENTIOUSNESS
INCAUTIOUSNESS
OBSEQUIOUSNESS
IMPERVIOUSNESS
SCANDALOUSNESS
SCURRILOUSNESS
MIRACULOUSNESS
SCRUPULOUSNESS
LIBIDINOUSNESS
VIVIPAROUSNESS
PROSPEROUSNESS
BOISTEROUSNESS
INDECOROUSNESS
CIRCUITOUSNESS
FORTUITOUSNESS
CONTIGUOUSNESS
CONTINUOUSNESS
TUMULTUOUSNESS
INCESTUOUSNESS
INDISTINCTNESS
INDISCREETNESS
UNPLEASANTNESS
DISENCHANTRESS
SCHOOLMISTRESS
FRINGILLACEOUS
RANUNCULACEOUS
PAPILIONACEOUS
ZINGIBERACEOUS
ZINZIBERACEOUS
CUCURBITACEOUS
COTEMPORANEOUS
EXTEMPORANEOUS
CONSANGUINEOUS
ICHTHYOPHAGOUS
HETEROMORPHOUS
PLECTOGNATHOUS
UNOSTENTATIOUS

CONTRADICTIOUS
SUPPOSITITIOUS
MACROCEPHALOUS
MICROCEPHALOUS
OPISTHOCOELOUS
HETEROPHYLLOUS
TETRADACTYLOUS
PENTADACTYLOUS
QUADRIGEMINOUS
DICOTYLEDONOUS
FORAMINIFEROUS
SACCHARIFEROUS
COROLLIFLOROUS
SANGUINIVOROUS
PACHYDERMATOUS
PARENCHYMATOUS
UNPRESUMPTUOUS

-------------T

COLOURSERGEANT
SUPERINCUMBENT
SUBARBORESCENT
INTERDEPENDENT
SUPERINTENDENT
SELFSUFFICIENT
DISCOURAGEMENT
DISARRANGEMENT
MISMEASUREMENT
BOULEVERSEMENT
DIVERTISSEMENT
UNDERSTATEMENT
DISEMBOGUEMENT
AGGRANDIZEMENT
ACKNOWLEDGMENT
ACCOMPLISHMENT
IMPOVERISHMENT
EXTINGUISHMENT
RELINQUISHMENT
DISENTHRALMENT
DISEMBOWELMENT
SELFGOVERNMENT
DISENCHANTMENT
DISCONTENTMENT
DISAPPOINTMENT
ENCYCLOPAEDIST
ICHTHYOPHAGIST
PHARMACOLOGIST
BACTERIOLOGIST
ECCLESIOLOGIST
ANTHROPOLOGIST
PNEUMATOLOGIST
CHALCOGRAPHIST
PALAEOGRAPHIST
MINISTERIALIST
EXISTENTIALIST
EDUCATIONALIST
SENSATIONALIST
UNIPERSONALIST

TRIPERSONALIST
SENTIMENTALIST
CONTINENTALIST
PHARMACOPOLIST
ELECTROCHEMIST
ULTRAMONTANIST
VIVISECTIONIST
OBSTRUCTIONIST
DESTRUCTIONIST
PROHIBITIONIST
REQUISITIONIST
SPECTROSCOPIST
PHILANTHROPIST
PISCICULTURIST
FLORICULTURIST
HORTICULTURIST
PARAGRAMMATIST

-------------W

CHIMNEYSWALLOW

-------------Y

INSIGNIFICANCY
CRYSTALLOMANCY
CORRESPONDENCY
CIRCUMAMBIENCY
NEUROPATHOLOGY
PHYTOPATHOLOGY
ELECTROBIOLOGY
TEROTECHNOLOGY
NEUROHYPNOLOGY
HOOTCHYKOOTCHY
PHYTOGEOGRAPHY
ANTHROPOGRAPHY
CINEMATOGRAPHY
CHROMATOGRAPHY
DACTYLIOGLYPHY
IRREPROACHABLY
IRRECONCILABLY
UNCONTROLLABLY
UNCONSCIONABLY
PROPORTIONABLY
UNQUESTIONABLY
INCONSIDERABLY
UNINTELLIGIBLY
COMPREHENSIBLY
INDESTRUCTIBLY
CONTROVERTIBLY
UNRESTRAINEDLY
GOODHUMOUREDLY
DISCONTENTEDLY
FAINTHEARTEDLY
PRECONCERTEDLY
INTERMEDIATELY
DISCONSOLATELY
INARTICULATELY

ILLEGITIMATELY
DISCRIMINATELY
AFFECTIONATELY
COMMENSURATELY
REPREHENSIVELY
INCONCLUSIVELY
DENOMINATIVELY
OPINIONATIVELY
VITUPERATIVELY
ILLUSTRATIVELY
QUANTITATIVELY
IRRESPECTIVELY
CONSTRUCTIVELY
INTRANSITIVELY
DISTRIBUTIVELY
DISCOURAGINGLY
OVERWHELMINGLY
OVERPOWERINGLY
ENTERPRISINGLY
EXCRUCIATINGLY
DISAPPROVINGLY
PROPITIATORILY
SATISFACTORILY
SCIENTIFICALLY
GENEALOGICALLY
TELEOLOGICALLY
PATHOLOGICALLY
MYTHOLOGICALLY
ETYMOLOGICALLY
ASTROLOGICALLY
TAUTOLOGICALLY
GEOGRAPHICALLY
BIOGRAPHICALLY
IDIOPATHICALLY
HYPERBOLICALLY
ASTRONOMICALLY
HISTRIONICALLY
ENHARMONICALLY
SYNCHRONICALLY
TELESCOPICALLY
METAPHORICALLY
BAROMETRICALLY
CONCENTRICALLY
GEOCENTRICALLY
METAPHYSICALLY
MATHEMATICALLY
EMBLEMATICALLY
SYSTEMATICALLY
DIPLOMATICALLY
DEMOCRATICALLY
HYPOSTATICALLY
ALPHABETICALLY
APOLOGETICALLY
CATECHETICALLY
ANTITHETICALLY
HYPOTHETICALLY
ARITHMETICALLY
HYPOCRITICALLY
SCHOLASTICALLY
PLEONASTICALLY

EULOGISTICALLY
OPTIMISTICALLY
APHORISTICALLY
INARTIFICIALLY
CONFIDENTIALLY
PROVIDENTIALLY
PESTILENTIALLY
PREFERENTIALLY
LONGITUDINALLY
PROFESSIONALLY
DISCRETIONALLY
CONVENTIONALLY
PROPORTIONALLY
SUPERNATURALLY
UNSCRIPTURALLY
EXPERIMENTALLY
INSTRUMENTALLY
INTELLECTUALLY
UNSUCCESSFULLY
ADVANTAGEOUSLY
SIMULTANEOUSLY
DISCOURTEOUSLY
CONTUMACIOUSLY
PERTINACIOUSLY
INAUSPICIOUSLY
MERETRICIOUSLY
SUBCONSCIOUSLY
SACRILEGIOUSLY
CONTUMELIOUSLY
SUPERCILIOUSLY
QUERIMONIOUSLY
PARSIMONIOUSLY
INHARMONIOUSLY
MULTIFARIOUSLY
OSTENTATIOUSLY
ADVENTITIOUSLY
UNSCRUPULOUSLY
OBSTREPEROUSLY
UNPROSPEROUSLY
PREPOSTEROUSLY
DISINGENUOUSLY
CONTEMPTUOUSLY
PRESUMPTUOUSLY
INSUFFICIENTLY
INCONVENIENTLY
SUPEREMINENTLY
INCONSISTENTLY
INTERMITTENTLY
MAGNILOQUENTLY
SHOVEHALFPENNY
OPHTHALMOSCOPY
INTERMAXILLARY
TINTINNABULARY
CONSUETUDINARY
INSTITUTIONARY
INTERPLANETARY
UNDERSECRETARY
RECOMMENDATORY
SUPEREROGATORY
CONGRATULATORY

RECAPITULATORY
DISCRIMINATORY
TRANSMIGRATORY
UNSATISFACTORY
CIRCUMLOCUTORY
EXTRINSICALITY
INCORPOREALITY
SUPERFICIALITY
SUBSTANTIALITY
COESSENTIALITY
CONDITIONALITY
SENTIMENTALITY
PRACTICABILITY
INFLAMMABILITY
INALIENABILITY
IRREPARABILITY
INSEPARABILITY
REMUNERABILITY
INSUPERABILITY
CONDENSABILITY
INTRACTABILITY
RESPECTABILITY
PREDICTABILITY
ACCOUNTABILITY
CONCEIVABILITY
IRREMOVABILITY
INDIVISIBILITY
DISTENSIBILITY
RESPONSIBILITY
IMPRESSIBILITY
PERMISSIBILITY
IMPLAUSIBILITY
PERFECTIBILITY
PERCEPTIBILITY
SUSCEPTIBILITY
CORRUPTIBILITY
CONVERTIBILITY
COMBUSTIBILITY
INTERCOMMUNITY
RECTILINEARITY

--------------A

OPHTHALMOPLEGIA
PLEUROPNEUMONIA

--------------C

HISTORIOGRAPHIC
ANTHROPOMORPHIC
DOLICHOCEPHALIC
PARTHENOGENETIC
ELECTROMAGNETIC
INDIVIDUALISTIC
IMPRESSIONISTIC

--------------D

DOUBLEBARRELLED
CROOKSHOULDERED
UNAUTHENTICATED
UNSOPHISTICATED
STRAIGHTFORWARD

--------------E

CHAMBERPRACTICE
PHOSPHORESCENCE
COUNTEREVIDENCE
INTERDEPENDENCE
SUPERINTENDENCE
SUPEREXCELLENCE
WOODYNIGHTSHADE
UNGENTLEMANLIKE
UNSTATESMANLIKE
UNSPORTSMANLIKE
CIRCUMSCRIBABLE
UNPRONOUNCEABLE
INTERCHANGEABLE
CIRCUMNAVIGABLE
DISTINGUISHABLE
HENDECASYLLABLE
PREDETERMINABLE
UNEXCEPTIONABLE
INCOMMENSURABLE
IRREPREHENSIBLE
INTRANSMISSIBLE
IMPRESCRIPTIBLE
WHEELANIMALCULE
TRINITROTOLUENE
FOUNDATIONSTONE
PHENAKISTOSCOPE
COUNTERPRESSURE
ADDISONSDISEASE
PROFESSIONALISE
DEPARTMENTALISE
DEPHLOGISTICATE
INTERCOLLEGIATE

PULMOBRANCHIATE
CONSUBSTANTIATE
CIRCUMSTANTIATE
ANTEPENULTIMATE
METROPOLITANATE
INCOMPREHENSIVE
MISAPPREHENSIVE
MANICDEPRESSIVE
INCOMMUNICATIVE
UNCOMMUNICATIVE
ELECTRONEGATIVE
UNDEMONSTRATIVE
SUPERCONDUCTIVE
SELFDESTRUCTIVE
ELECTROPOSITIVE
CIRCUMSCRIPTIVE
CONVENTIONALIZE
EXPERIMENTALIZE
INTELLECTUALIZE

--------------G

NOTWITHSTANDING
SABBATHBREAKING
UNPREPOSSESSING

--------------H

COUNTERAPPROACH
SCHOOLMASTERISH

--------------L

HYPOCHONDRIACAL
TETRASYLLABICAL
ANTHROPOLOGICAL
ANTIMONARCHICAL
STRATIGRAPHICAL
LEXICOGRAPHICAL
PALAEOGRAPHICAL
BIBLIOGRAPHICAL
PHYSIOGRAPHICAL
UNPHILOSOPHICAL
AMPHITHEATRICAL
ISOPERIMETRICAL
TRIGONOMETRICAL
PHANTASMAGORIAL
ENTREPRENEURIAL
JURISPRUDENTIAL
INCONSEQUENTIAL
OMNIDIRECTIONAL
TRANSPOSITIONAL
DISPROPORTIONAL
GOVERNORGENERAL

--------------M

INFUNDIBULIFORM
EXPERIENTIALISM
PROFESSIONALISM
CONVENTIONALISM
SUPERNATURALISM
INTELLECTUALISM
EPISCOPALIANISM
TOTALITARIANISM
HUMANITARIANISM
PRESBYTERIANISM
COSMOPOLITANISM
CONSERVATIONISM
DIAHELIOTROPISM

--------------N

CHRISTADELPHIAN
ANTITRINITARIAN
PARLIAMENTARIAN
INCOMPREHENSION
MISAPPREHENSION
DECALCIFICATION
EXEMPLIFICATION
INDEMNIFICATION
PERSONIFICATION
ELECTRIFICATION
DEVITRIFICATION
INTENSIFICATION
DIVERSIFICATION
EXCOMMUNICATION
PROGNOSTICATION
DIFFERENTIATION
CONTRAVALLATION
CIRCUMVALLATION
INSUBORDINATION
DECONTAMINATION
SELFEXAMINATION
INDETERMINATION
PROCRASTINATION
RECONSIDERATION
TRANSLITERATION
TRANSFIGURATION
ROMANTICISATION
STANDARDISATION
MATERIALISATION
RATIONALISATION
HOSPITALISATION
IMMORTALISATION
SYNCHRONISATION
CANISTERISATION
COMPUTERISATION
EXTEMPORISATION
MINIATURISATION
INTERDIGITATION
TRANSPLANTATION
SUPPLEMENTATION
EXPERIMENTATION

INSTRUMENTATION
DISCONTINUATION
ETHEREALIZATION
NATIONALIZATION
EXTERNALIZATION
CRYSTALLIZATION
DISORGANIZATION
DECARBONIZATION
FORMULARIZATION
DECARBURIZATION
ACCLIMATIZATION
DEMAGNETIZATION
DISSATISFACTION
INTERCONNECTION
MISCONSTRUCTION
INTROSUSCEPTION
CIRCUMSCRIPTION

-------------P

DRAUGHTSMANSHIP
CHAMBERLAINSHIP
CONNOISSEURSHIP

-------------R

HISTORIOGRAPHER
CIRCUMNAVIGATOR
PRESTIDIGITATOR

-------------S

ELECTRODYNAMICS
ELECTROKINETICS
PARTHENOGENESIS
GASTROENTERITIS
DIAPHRAGMATITIS
PRACTICABLENESS
INFLAMMABLENESS
TREASONABLENESS
INSEPARABLENESS
INTOLERABLENESS
INEXCUSABLENESS
INTRACTABLENESS
ACCOUNTABLENESS
INSCRUTABLENESS
CONCEIVABLENESS
CORRUPTIBLENESS
COMBUSTIBLENESS
TROUBLESOMENESS
APPROPRIATENESS
CONSIDERATENESS
INTEMPERATENESS
PICTURESQUENESS
INOFFENSIVENESS
CORRELATIVENESS
DISTINCTIVENESS

DESTRUCTIVENESS
IMAGINITIVENESS
ACQUISITIVENESS
INQUISITIVENESS
INATTENTIVENESS
DESCRIPTIVENESS
TRUSTWORTHINESS
GENTLEMANLINESS
FRAGMENTARINESS
BLOODGUILTINESS
FANTASTICALNESS
SUPERFICIALNESS
DISGRACEFULNESS
RESOURCEFULNESS
DISTASTEFULNESS
REPROACHFULNESS
DISTRUSTFULNESS
DEFENCELESSNESS
REMORSELESSNESS
THOUGHTLESSNESS
HOMOGENEOUSNESS
UNRIGHTEOUSNESS
EFFICACIOUSNESS
INJUDICIOUSNESS
UNCONSCIOUSNESS
IRRELIGIOUSNESS
CEREMONIOUSNESS
ILLUSTRIOUSNESS
PRETENTIOUSNESS
SENTENTIOUSNESS
CONTENTIOUSNESS
TREACHEROUSNESS
ADVENTUROUSNESS
CONSPICUOUSNESS
PERSPICUOUSNESS
MISCHIEVOUSNESS
CIRCUMSPECTNESS
TRANSPARENTNESS
ORNITHORHYNCHUS
PERGAMENTACEOUS
MONOCHLAMYDEOUS
DISADVANTAGEOUS
CIRCUMFORANEOUS
CONTEMPORANEOUS
ANTHROPOPHAGOUS
UNSELFCONSCIOUS
EXCREMENTITIOUS
BRACHYCEPHALOUS
HETERODACTYLOUS
PULCHRITUDINOUS
VICISSITUDINOUS
ECHINODERMATOUS

-------------T

STRAITWAISTCOAT
SPEAKINGTRUMPET
COUNTERIRRITANT
ACKNOWLEDGEMENT

DISENTANGLEMENT
AFFRANCHISEMENT
ENFRANCHISEMENT
ECLAIRCISSEMENT
COUNTERMOVEMENT
REESTABLISHMENT
DISILLUSIONMENT
OVERDEVELOPMENT
OPHTHALMOLOGIST
PALAEONTOLOGIST
EXPERIENTIALIST
CONFESSIONALIST
CONVENTIONALIST
SUPERNATURALIST
AGRICULTURALIST
EXPERIMENTALIST
INSTRUMENTALIST
INTELLECTUALIST
EMANCIPATIONIST
CONVERSATIONIST
PRESERVATIONIST
CONSERVATIONIST
INSURRECTIONIST
CONSTRUCTIONIST
INTERVENTIONIST
PSYCHOTHERAPIST
PHYSIOTHERAPIST
ARBORICULTURIST

-------------Y

ARCHIEPISCOPACY
SELFSUFFICIENCY
PALAEOPHYTOLOGY
CRYSTALLOGRAPHY
TELEPHOTOGRAPHY
INTERCHANGEABLY
DISTINGUISHABLY
UNCONSTRAINEDLY
DISINTERESTEDLY
INAPPROPRIATELY
INDETERMINATELY
COMPASSIONATELY
DISPASSIONATELY
PROPORTIONATELY
INCONSIDERATELY
COMPREHENSIVELY
RETROGRESSIVELY
COMMUNICATIVELY
INTERROGATIVELY
CONTEMPLATIVELY
DEMONSTRATIVELY
AUTHORITATIVELY
ARGUMENTATIVELY
UNDERSTANDINGLY
CONDESCENDINGLY
CORRESPONDINGLY
EXTRAORDINARILY
DISCRETIONARILY

CONTRADICTORILY
PHYSIOLOGICALLY
ENTOMOLOGICALLY
PHRENOLOGICALLY
TECHNOLOGICALLY
CHRONOLOGICALLY
IDEOGRAPHICALLY
TOPOGRAPHICALLY
PHILOSOPHICALLY
LOGARITHMICALLY
MICROSCOPICALLY
UNGRAMMATICALLY
SYMPTOMATICALLY
HYDROSTATICALLY
STRATEGETICALLY
SYMPATHETICALLY
PARENTHETICALLY
HYPERCRITICALLY
ENCOMIASTICALLY
EUPHEMISTICALLY
HERMENEUTICALLY
THERAPEUTICALLY
EXTRAJUDICIALLY
INTERCOLONIALLY
INQUISITORIALLY
CONTROVERSIALLY
CONSEQUENTIALLY
INTERNATIONALLY
CONJUNCTIONALLY
UNCONDITIONALLY
PREPOSITIONALLY
UNINTENTIONALLY
PRETERNATURALLY
TEMPERAMENTALLY
DISRESPECTFULLY
PERPENDICULARLY
INSTANTANEOUSLY
CONSENTANEOUSLY
INEFFICACIOUSLY
PERSPICACIOUSLY
UNCEREMONIOUSLY
SANCTIMONIOUSLY
SURREPTITIOUSLY
CONSCIENTIOUSLY
INCONSPICUOUSLY
INSIGNIFICANTLY
CORRESPONDENTLY
QUATERCENTENARY
INTERJECTIONARY
INSURRECTIONARY
UNPARLIAMENTARY
UNCOMPLIMENTARY
SHOOTINGGALLERY
SELFEXPLANATORY
DISSATISFACTORY
CONTEMPORANEITY
CONVENTIONALITY
PROPORTIONALITY
INSTRUMENTALITY
INTELLECTUALITY

HETEROSEXUALITY
INAPPLICABILITY
INEXPLICABILITY
COMMUNICABILITY
DISAGREEABILITY
EXCHANGEABILITY
APPROACHABILITY
DETERMINABILITY
INVULNERABILITY
IMPENETRABILITY
DEMONSTRABILITY
MANOEUVRABILITY
TRANSMUTABILITY
INTELLIGIBILITY
INCORRIGIBILITY
INACCESSIBILITY
COMPRESSIBILITY
INCOMPATIBILITY
CONTRACTIBILITY
DESTRUCTIBILITY
CONTEMPTIBILITY
IRRESISTIBILITY